# vSphere 6 Foundations Exam Official Cert Guide (Exam #2V0-620)

VMware Press is the official publisher of VMware books and training materials, which provide guidance on the critical topics facing today's IT professionals and students. VMware virtualization and cloud infrastructure technologies simplify IT complexity and streamline operations, helping organizations of all kinds and sizes to become more agile, efficient, and profitable.

VMware Press provides proven, technically accurate information that will help you achieve your goals for customizing, building, and maintaining a virtual environment—from the data center to mobile devices to the public, private, and hybrid cloud.

With books, certification and study guides, video training, and learning tools produced by world-class architects and IT experts, VMware Press helps you master a diverse range of topics on virtualization and cloud computing and is the official source of reference materials for preparing for the VMware Certified Professional certifications.

VMware Press is also pleased to have localization partners that can publish its products into more than 42 languages, including, but not limited to, Chinese (Simplified), Chinese (Traditional), French, German, Greek, Hindi, Japanese, Korean, Polish, Russian, and Spanish.

For more information about VMware Press, please visit **vmwarepress.com**.

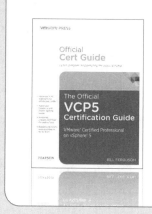

# vSphere 6 Foundations Exam Official Cert Guide (Exam #2V0-620)

## VMware® Certified Professional 6

Bill Ferguson

**vm**ware® PRESS

Hoboken, NJ • Boston • Indianapolis • San Francisco
New York • Toronto • Montreal • London • Munich • Paris • Madrid
Capetown • Sydney • Tokyo • Singapore • Mexico City

# vSphere 6 Foundations Exam Official Cert Guide (Exam #2V0-620)

Copyright © 2017 VMware, Inc.

Published by Pearson Education, Inc.

Publishing as VMware Press

ISBN-10: 0-7897-5649-8

ISBN-13: 978-0-7897-5649-7

Library of Congress Control Number: 2016939401

2    16

## Warning and Disclaimer

## Special Sales

For information about buying this title in bulk quantities, or for special sales opportunities (which may include electronic versions; custom cover designs; and content particular to your business, training goals, marketing focus, or branding interests), please contact our corporate sales department at corpsales@pearsoned.com or (800) 382-3419.

For government sales inquiries, please contact governmentsales@pearsoned.com.

For questions about sales outside the U.S., please contact intlcs@pearson.com.

**EDITOR-IN-CHIEF**
Mark Taub

**PRODUCT LINE MANAGER**
Brett Bartow

**EXECUTIVE EDITOR**
Mary Beth Ray

**VMWARE PRESS PROGRAM MANAGER**
Karl Childs

**DEVELOPMENT EDITOR**
Christopher Cleveland

**MANAGING EDITOR**
Sandra Schroeder

**SENIOR PROJECT EDITOR**
Tonya Simpson

**TECHNICAL EDITORS**
Dave Davis
John Davidson

**COPY EDITOR**
Barbara Hacha

**PROOFREADER**
Gill Editorial Services

**INDEXER**
Publishing Works, Inc

**EDITORIAL ASSISTANT**
Vanessa Evans

**COVER DESIGNER**
Chuti Prasertsith

**COMPOSITOR**
Bumpy Design

# Contents at a Glance

# Table of Contents

## About the Author

**Bill Ferguson**, VCI 3, 4, 5, 6; VCP6-DCV, VCP6-NV; CCSI; and MCT Alumni has been in the computer industry for more than 20 years. Originally in technical sales and IT consulting with Sprint, he made his transition to Certified Technical Trainer in 1997 with ExecuTrain. He now runs his own company, Parallel Connections, as an independent contractor and consultant based in Birmingham, Alabama, working worldwide for most of the national training companies and some regional training companies. In addition, he has written and produced many technical training videos and books. Bill's aspiration is as follows: "My job is to understand the material so well that I can make it easier for others to learn than it was for me to learn. Toward that end, I strive to provide an effective learning environment whether in person, in print, or online."

# Dedications

*I am dedicating this book to my father, who told me when I was still in high school to learn as much about computers as I could. He convinced me to take a Lotus 1-2-3 class and later an A+ class! Thanks, Dad!*

*I am also dedicating this to my mother, who has always given me the encouragement and guidance to accomplish difficult tasks. She continues to be an inspiration to me, even at my age! Thanks, Mom!*

*Finally, I am dedicating this book to my wife, who supports me through the "busy writing weekends" and the late nights that come with taking on a project of this size! Thanks, Wilma, I love you!*

# Acknowledgments

First, I want to thank Mary Beth Ray for giving me the opportunity to write this important book. It's fun and rewarding to be able to continue the "legacy" that we started with the first two books: *The Official VCP5 Certification Guide*, which was the very first Pearson/VMware Press book, and the follow-up book, *Official Cert Guide for VCP5-DCV*, which provided updates for vSphere 5.5.

I also want to thank John Davidson and Dave Davis for their spot-on technical editing of the book. Because of them, I learned a few things myself while writing this book. In addition, the flow and consistency of the book are the result of efforts by Chris Cleveland, who kept me on target with his skilled developmental editing. I would also like to give another special thanks to Dave Davis at VMware, whose firsthand knowledge of the latest products and features in vSphere provided me with the most up-to-date information possible. His review of this book makes it a true VMware/Pearson collaboration. It takes a lot of people to create a book, and I am sure that I do not know all the names of the people who were involved in this one, but thank you.

Finally, I want to acknowledge the encouragement and prayers of my family and friends and the students in my technical classes and Sunday school classes. In Him, all things are possible!

# We Want to Hear from You!

As the reader of this book, *you* are our most important critic and commentator. We value your opinion and want to know what we're doing right, what we could do better, what areas you'd like to see us publish in, and any other words of wisdom you're willing to pass our way.

We welcome your comments. You can email or write us directly to let us know what you did or didn't like about this book—as well as what we can do to make our books better.

*Please note that we cannot help you with technical problems related to the topic of this book.*

When you write, please be sure to include this book's title and author as well as your name, email address, and phone number. We will carefully review your comments and share them with the author and editors who worked on the book.

Email:    VMwarePress@vmware.com

Mail:     VMware Press
          ATTN: Reader Feedback
          800 East 96th Street
          Indianapolis, IN 46240 USA

# Reader Services

Visit our website at www.pearsonitcertification.com/title/9780789756497 and register this book for convenient access to any updates, downloads, or errata that might be available for this book.

# About This Book

Welcome to my *vSphere 6 Foundations Exam Official Cert Guide*. I'm excited about sharing this information with you to help you prepare to take and pass the vSphere 6 Foundations (2V0-620) exam. My original *VCP5-DCV Official Certification Guide*, for the VCP510 test, and the follow-up book, *Official Cert Guide for VCP5-DCV*, for the VCP550 test, have helped many people pass those tests. However, because there have been many changes to the vSphere product over the past four years, I decided to update the book to reflect the new information that you need to know for real life as well as for the new vSphere 6 Foundations test.

I've been a technical trainer/consultant for more than 20 years, and I've taught thousands of students. Because I teach many of my VMware classes online now, I sometimes tell people that "I teach people I can't see to use computers that don't exist in a physical sense." This book is just an extension of that theme.

Because the test blueprint on VMware's website, vmware.com/certification, is your best guide for success on the test, I decided, as before, to write this book as directly to the blueprint as possible. This means that we will jump into topics that might seem to be out of place if this is your first look at virtualization. This leads me to my first assumption, which is that this is not your first look at virtualization. The reason I assume this is that you are preparing to take a test that is of a highly technical nature, so it should seem reasonable to assume that you have had prior knowledge and experience with VMware products, either in the workplace or in technical classes like the ones that I teach. It is with this assumption that I can follow the blueprint as it is written, but I will take into account areas where I think there is a need to backfill information so that you can fully understand the topic that I am discussing.

My second assumption is that you have access to a vSphere 6.0 environment or can build yourself a system on which you can practice what we will discuss so that you will retain it better. We all learn in different ways, but I've found that many in the IT world learn by doing even more than by hearing. Because this is the case, and because it fits well with the blueprint, there will be many times throughout this book when I walk you through the steps. Therefore, it would be best for you to have a system with at least vCenter 6.0 and a couple of ESXi 6.0 hosts installed that you can use to follow along. You could even do this using Workstation 11 and all virtual machines.

As to what you need to learn and remember, my third assumption is that you don't want to know everything there is to know about "all things VMware"—just what is important in your situation and what might be on the test. Based on that assumption, I will try my best not to throw in a lot of additional material that makes you wonder whether you need to know it as well. I will not repeat "this would be good to know for the test" throughout this book because that would get monotonous; however, if it is in this book, you can assume that it is fair game for the vSphere 6 Foundations test.

Finally, my last assumption is that you don't really care how much I know, but what you really care about is whether I can help you learn what you need to know. Toward that end, I will use examples, stories, and analogies to help you understand highly technical topics in a more comfortable manner than you might have experienced before in a technical book. The way I see it, my job is to know this material so well that I can make it easier for you to learn than it was for me to learn. So, if we are all in agreement, let's get started!

## Who Should Read This Book

The VCP certification was recently listed on http://www.techrepublic.com/ as one of the top 10 certifications to hold. If you are currently working with VMware vSphere virtual data centers, it could be a valuable certification for you. If you are considering your options in the IT world, you will not go wrong if you learn about virtualization now. In either case, this book will help you obtain the knowledge and the skills toward becoming a VCP6-DCV, VCP6-NV, VCP6-DTM, or VCP6-CMA.

## Goals and Methods

My number-one goal of this book is a simple one: to help you pass the vSphere 6 Foundations test as part of obtaining the status of VMware Certified Professional 6 for Data Center Virtualization, Network Virtualization, Cloud Management and Automation, or Desktop Mobility.

To aid you in gaining the knowledge and understanding of key vSphere topics, I use the following methods:

- **Opening topics list:** This list defines the topics to be covered in the chapter. Each chapter is a part of the exam blueprint, and the chapters and topics are written in blueprint order.

- **"Do I Know This Already?" quizzes:** At the beginning of each chapter is a quiz. The quizzes and answers/explanations (found in Appendix A) are meant to gauge your knowledge of the subjects. If the answers to the questions do not come readily to you, be sure to read the entire chapter.

- **Key topics:** The key topics indicate important figures, tables, and lists of information that you should know for the exam. They are interspersed throughout the chapter and are listed in table format at the end of the chapter.

- **Review questions:** All chapters conclude with a set of review questions to help you assess whether you have learned the key material in the chapter.

- **Exam-type questions:** Exam questions are included with the printed and digital editions of this book. They are written to be as close as possible to the types of questions that appear on the vSphere 6 Foundations exam.

## How to Use This Book

Although you could read this book cover to cover, I designed it to be flexible enough to allow you to easily move between chapters and sections of chapters to work on the areas that you feel are the most important for you. If you intend to read all the chapters, the order in the book is an excellent sequence to follow.

The core chapters, Chapters 1 through 23, cover the following topics:

- **Chapter 1, "Identifying vSphere Architecture and Solutions":** This chapter focuses on various vSphere editions and the features they provide. I also discuss data center solutions that interact with vSphere, architectures for ESXi and vCenter, and new solutions for the vSphere 6.0 environment.

- **Chapter 2, "Installing and Configuring vCenter Server":** This chapter focuses on the requirements for the vCenter server and its accompanying database. I also discuss sizing the database, licensing the vCenter server, and creating database connections to the vCenter server database.

- **Chapter 3, "Installing and Configuring ESXi":** This chapter focuses on the requirements for installing ESXi and the methods that you can use. I also cover the configuration of NTP, and DNS. Then I cover licensing an ESXi host.

- **Chapter 4, "Configuring vSphere Standard Switches":** This chapter focuses on creating and deleting vSphere Standard Switches. I also cover adding, configuring, and removing vmnics and port groups. In addition, I cover configuring vmkernel ports. Finally, I discuss the use case for a vSphere Standard Switch.

- **Chapter 5, "Configuring vSphere Distributed Switches":** This chapter focuses on vSphere Distributed Switch capabilities and how to make the most of them. I cover creating and deleting a vSphere Distributed Switch, adding, configuring, and removing dvPort groups as well as dvUplink groups, configuring dvPort group settings, and configuring LACP. In addition, I cover migrating virtual adapters to and from a vSphere Standard Switch.

- **Chapter 6, "Configuring vSS and vDS Features":** This chapter focuses on features that are available on vSSs and those that are available on vDSs. I discuss policies such as dvPort blocking, load balancing, and failover. In addition, I discuss configuring VLAN and PVLAN settings and traffic shaping policies. Finally, I discuss enabling TCP Segmentation Offload, jumbo frames. You will be able to determine the appropriate VLAN configuration for a vSphere implementation.

- **Chapter 7, "Connecting Shared Storage Devices to vSphere":** This chapter focuses on the various types of storage from which you can choose for your vSphere and environment and on connecting it to your hosts and VMs. I cover storage adapters and devices, storage naming conventions, hardware and software initiators, zoning/masking LUNs, and configuring iSCSI Port Binding. You will be able to successfully choose and connect the appropriate storage options to your vSphere environment.

- **Chapter 8, "Configuring Software-Defined Storage":** This chapter focuses on the very latest techniques of configuring software-defined storage. I discuss your new options in regard to NFS, VSAN, and VVOLs. You learn about the latest methods of creating shared storage volumes for your vSphere environment.

- **Chapter 9, "Creating and Configuring VMFS and NFS Datastores":** This chapter focuses on the creation and configuration of VMFS and NFS datastores. I discuss supported NFS versions, storage multipathing, VMFS requirements, and configuring and managing VMFS extents. You learn the appropriate methods of creating and configuring datastores for your vSphere environment.

- **Chapter 10, "Creating and Deploying Virtual Machines":** This chapter focuses on creating and deploying virtual machines and the methods that you can use. I also discuss the capabilities of virtual machine hardware and DirectPath I/O Passthrough. In addition, I discuss deploying a Guest OS to a VM and configuring CPU and memory resources. You will be able to make informed decisions regarding the deployment of VMs in your environment.

- **Chapter 11, "Creating and Deploying vApps":** This chapter focuses on creating and deploying vApps. I discuss vApp requirements, cloning and exporting a vApp, and configuring vApp settings. You also learn how to use vApps in your environment.

- **Chapter 12, "Managing Virtual Machine Clones and Templates":** This chapter focuses on creating, configuring, and managing virtual machine clones and templates. I also discuss configuring virtual machine options and configuring CPU and memory reservations and shares. You will know how to manage VMs, clones, and templates in your environment.

- **Chapter 13, "Administering Virtual Machines and vApps":** This chapter focuses on administering VMs and vApps. I discuss the files used by VMs and the location options of configuration files and virtual disks. In addition, I cover common practices for securing VMs, configuring IP pools, and managing a content library.

- **Chapter 14, "Creating and Configuring VMware Clusters":** This chapter focuses on creating and configuring VMware clusters. I discuss issues that relate to DRS and HA. In addition, I discuss adding and removing hosts and VMs on a cluster. You will be able to determine the appropriate failover methodology for your clusters and the required resources for your hosts.

- **Chapter 15, "Planning and Implementing VMware Fault Tolerance":** This chapter focuses on the configuration of fault tolerance for your VMs. I discuss fault tolerance requirements, new capabilities, and network configuration as it relates to fault tolerance.

- **Chapter 16, "Creating and Administering Resource Pools":** This chapter focuses on creating and administering resource pools. I discuss the configuration of resource pool attributes, including vFlash architecture. You also learn how to determine resource pool requirements.

- **Chapter 17, "Migrating Virtual Machines":** This chapter focuses on migrating virtual machines. I discuss the requirements for vMotion and Storage vMotion in regard to your hosts and VMs. In addition, I discuss the very latest options in regard to vMotion, including Enhanced vMotion and Long Distance vMotion. I also discuss snapshots in regard to vMotion and Storage vMotion. You learn best practices in regard to configuring and performing virtual machine migrations.

- **Chapter 18, "Backing Up and Restoring Virtual Machines":** This chapter focuses on backing up and restoring virtual machines. I discuss VMware Data Protection and the latest changes to it. I also discuss creating, deleting, and consolidating virtual machine snapshots. In addition, I discuss vSphere replication. You also learn methods of keeping your VMs and their data safe.

- **Chapter 19, "Updating ESXi and Virtual Machines":** This chapter focuses on updating and patching virtual machines. I also discuss managing host profiles. In addition, you learn how to keep your hosts up to date.

- **Chapter 20, "Performing Basic Troubleshooting of ESXi and vCenter Server":** This chapter focuses on troubleshooting ESXi and vCenter. I discuss troubleshooting guidelines and how to monitor ESXi system health.

- **Chapter 21, "Performing Basic Troubleshooting of ESXi and vCenter Server Operations":** This chapter focuses on troubleshooting ESXi and vCenter Server Operations. I discuss how to verify the network configuration and resources and troubleshoot common storage and VM issues. In addition, I discuss troubleshooting physical network adapter configuration issues, including checking the knowledge base on the Web.

- **Chapter 22, "Performing Basic Troubleshooting of Virtual Machine Operations":** This chapter focuses on troubleshooting options caused by improper VM configuration. I discuss resource contention issues, VMware tools issues, and storage issues. You also learn how to identify the root cause of a problem.

- **Chapter 23, "Monitoring ESXi, vCenter Server, and Virtual Machines":** This chapter focuses on monitoring your hosts, vCenter server, and VMs. I discuss the most common metrics in regard to performance, memory, CPU, networking, and storage. I also discuss monitoring overview and advanced charts. In addition, I cover creating, editing, and deleting a scheduled task.

- **Chapter 24, "Creating and Administering vCenter Server Alarms":** This chapter focuses on creating and administering vCenter Server alarms. I discuss utilizations alarms as well as connectivity alarms. In addition, you learn about configuring alarm triggers and actions.

- **Chapter 25, "Installing and Administering vRealize Operations Manager":** This chapter focuses on installing and managing vRealize Operations Manager. I discuss major and minor badges, architecture, and deploying the appliance. You also learn how to determine the effective resource for a given issue.

- **Chapter 26, "Final Preparation":** This chapter identifies tools for final exam preparation and helps you develop an effective study plan. It contains tips on how to best use the web-based material to study.

## Certification Exam and This Preparation Guide

I wrote this book directly to the vSphere 6 Foundations Exam Blueprint. Each chapter of this book is a section of the blueprint, with all its objectives in the same order as the blueprint. This way, you can easily identify your strengths and work on your weaknesses. Table I-1 lists the vSphere 6 Foundations Exam Blueprint objectives and the chapter of this book that covers them.

**Table I-1**   vSphere 6 Foundations Exam Topics and Chapter References

| Exam Section/Objective | Chapter Where Covered |
| --- | --- |
| **Section 1—Install and Configure vCenter Server and ESXi** | |
| Objective 1.1—Identify vSphere Architecture and Solutions for a given use case. | Chapter 1 |
| Objective 1.2—Install and Configure vCenter Server | Chapter 2 |
| Objective 1.3—Install and configure ESXi | Chapter 3 |
| **Section 2: Configure vSphere Networking** | |
| Objective 2.1—Configure vSphere Standard Switches (vSS) | Chapter 4 |
| Objective 2.2—Configure vSphere Distributed Switches (vDS) | Chapter 5 |
| Objective 2.3—Configure vSS and vDS Policies | Chapter 6 |
| **Section 3—Configure vSphere Storage** | |
| Objective 3.1—Connect Shared Storage Devices to vSphere | Chapter 7 |
| Objective 3.2—Configure Software Defined Storage | Chapter 8 |
| Objective 3.3—Create and Configure VMFS and NFS Datastores | Chapter 9 |
| **Section 4—Deploy and Administer Virtual Machines and vApps** | |
| Objective 4.1—Create and Deploy Virtual Machines | Chapter 10 |
| Objective 4.2—Create and Deploy vApps | Chapter 11 |
| Objective 4.3—Manage Virtual Machine Clones and Templates | Chapter 12 |
| Objective 4.4—Administer Virtual Machines and vApps | Chapter 13 |
| **Section 5—Establish and Maintain Availability and Resource Management** | |
| Objective 5.1—Create and Configure VMware Clusters | Chapter 14 |
| Objective 5.2—Plan and Implement VMware Fault Tolerance | Chapter 15 |
| Objective 5.3—Create and Administer Resource Pools | Chapter 16 |
| Objective 5.4—Migrate Virtual Machines | Chapter 17 |
| Objective 5.5—Backup and Restore Virtual Machines | Chapter 18 |
| Objective 5.6—Update ESXi and Virtual Machines | Chapter 19 |
| **Section 6—Perform Basic Troubleshooting** | |
| Objective 6.1—Perform Basic Troubleshooting of ESXi and vCenter Server | Chapter 20 |
| Objective 6.2—Perform Basic Troubleshooting of ESXi and vCenter Operations | Chapter 21 |
| Objective 6.3—Perform Basic Troubleshooting of Virtual Machine Operations | Chapter 22 |
| Objective 6.4—Identify and Troubleshoot Basic Misconfigurations | Chapter 22 |

| Exam Section/Objective | Chapter Where Covered |
|---|---|
| **Section 7—Monitor a vSphere Implementation** | |
| Objective 7.1—Monitor ESXi, vCenter Server and Virtual Machines | Chapter 23 |
| Objective 7.2—Create and Administer vCenter Server Alarms | Chapter 24 |
| Objective 7.3—Install, Configure and Administer vRealize Operations Manager | Chapter 25 |

## Book Content Updates

Because VMware occasionally updates exam topics without notice, VMware Press might post additional preparatory content on the web page associated with this book at http://www.pearsonitcertification.com/title/9780789756497. It is a good idea to check the website a couple of weeks before taking your exam, to review any updated content that might be posted online. We also recommend that you periodically check back to this page on the Pearson IT Certification website to view any errata or supporting book files that may be available.

## Companion Website

Register this book to get access to the Pearson IT Certification test engine and other study materials plus additional bonus content. Check this site regularly for new and updated postings written by the author that provide further insight into the more troublesome topics on the exam. Be sure to check the box that you would like to hear from us to receive updates and exclusive discounts on future editions of this product or related products.

To access this companion website, follow these steps:

1. Go to www.pearsonITcertification.com/register and log in or create a new account.
2. Enter the ISBN: 9780789756497.
3. Answer the challenge question as proof of purchase.
4. Click the Access Bonus Content link in the Registered Products section of your account page to be taken to the page where your downloadable content is available.

Please note that many of our companion content files can be very large, especially image and video files.

If you are unable to locate the files for this title by following the preceding steps, please visit www.pearsonITcertification.com/contact and select the Site Problems/Comments option. Our customer service representatives will assist you.

# Pearson IT Certification Practice Test Engine and Questions

The companion website includes the Pearson IT Certification Practice Test engine—software that displays and grades a set of exam-realistic multiple-choice questions. Using the Pearson IT Certification Practice Test engine, you can either study by going through the questions in Study Mode or take a simulated exam that mimics real exam conditions. You can also serve up questions in a Flash Card Mode, which displays only the question and no answers, challenging you to state the answer in your own words before checking the actual answers to verify your work.

The installation process requires two major steps: installing the software and then activating the exam. The website has a recent copy of the Pearson IT Certification Practice Test engine. The practice exam (the database of exam questions) is not on this site.

> **NOTE**   The cardboard sleeve in the back of this book includes a piece of paper. The paper lists the activation code for the practice exam associated with this book. Do not lose the activation code. On the opposite side of the paper from the activation code is a unique, one-time-use coupon code for the purchase of the Premium Edition eBook and Practice Test.

### Install the Software

The Pearson IT Certification Practice Test is a Windows-only desktop application. You can run it on a Mac using a Windows virtual machine, but it was built specifically for the PC platform. The minimum system requirements are as follows:

- Windows 10, Windows 8.1, or Windows 7
- Microsoft .NET Framework 4.5 client
- Pentium-class 1 GHz processor (or equivalent)
- 512 MB RAM
- 650 MB disk space plus 50 MB for each downloaded practice exam
- Access to the Internet to register and download exam databases

The software installation process is routine compared with other software installation processes. If you have already installed the Pearson IT Certification Practice Test software from another Pearson product, there is no need for you to reinstall the software. Simply launch the software on your desktop and proceed to activate the practice exam from this book by using the activation code included in the access code card sleeve in the back of the book.

The following steps outline the installation process:

1. Download the exam practice test engine from the companion site.

2. Respond to windows prompts as with any typical software installation process.

The installation process gives you the option to activate your exam with the activation code supplied on the paper in the cardboard sleeve. This process requires you to establish a Pearson website login. You need this login to activate the exam, so do register when prompted. If you already have a Pearson website login, there is no need to register again. Just use your existing login.

## Activate and Download the Practice Exam

After the exam engine is installed, you should activate the exam associated with this book (if you did not do so during the installation process) as follows:

1. Start the Pearson IT Certification Practice Test software from the Windows Start menu or from your desktop shortcut icon.

2. To activate and download the exam associated with this book, from the My Products or Tools tab, click the **Activate Exam** button.

3. At the next screen, enter the activation key from the paper inside the cardboard sleeve in the back of the book. Then click the **Activate** button.

4. The activation process will download the practice exam. Click **Next**, and then click **Finish**.

When the activation process completes, the My Products tab should list your new exam. If you do not see the exam, make sure that you have selected the **My Products** tab on the menu. At this point, the software and practice exam are ready to use. Simply select the exam and click the **Open Exam** button.

To update a particular exam you have already activated and downloaded, display the **Tools** tab and click the **Update Products** button. Updating your exams will ensure that you have the latest changes and updates to the exam data.

If you want to check for updates to the Pearson Cert Practice Test exam engine software, display the **Tools** tab and click the **Update Application** button. You can then ensure that you are running the latest version of the software engine.

### Activating Other Exams

The exam software installation process and the registration process have to happen only once. Then, for each new exam, only a few steps are required. For instance, if you buy another Pearson IT Certification Cert Guide, extract the activation code from the cardboard sleeve in the back of that book; you do not even need the exam engine at this point. From there, all you have to do is start the exam engine (if it's not still up and running) and perform Steps 2 through 4 from the previous list.

### Assessing Exam Readiness

Exam candidates never really know whether they are adequately prepared for the exam until they have completed about 30 percent of the questions. At that point, if you are not prepared, it is too late. The best way to determine your readiness is to work through the "Do I Know This Already?" quizzes at the beginning of each chapter and review the foundation and key topics presented in each chapter. It is best to work your way through the entire book unless you can complete each subject without having to do any research or look up any answers.

### Premium Edition eBook and Practice Tests

This book also includes an exclusive offer for 70% off the Premium Edition eBook and Practice Tests edition of this title. Please see the coupon code included with the cardboard sleeve for information on how to purchase the Premium Edition.

**This chapter covers the following subjects:**

- vSphere Editions and Features

- Data Center Solutions That Interact with vSphere

- ESXi and vCenter Architectures and New Solutions

This section introduces the major components of vSphere and their features. In addition, you learn how vSphere is built and what other solutions it can provide. Finally, the chapter covers data center solutions that interact with vSphere.

## CHAPTER 1

# Identifying vSphere Architecture and Solutions

## "Do I Know This Already?" Quiz

The "Do I Know This Already?" quiz allows you to assess whether you should read this entire chapter or simply jump to the "Exam Preparation Tasks" section for review. If you are in doubt, read the entire chapter. Table 1-1 outlines the major headings in this chapter and the corresponding "Do I Know This Already?" quiz questions. You can find the answers in Appendix A, "Answers to the 'Do I Know This Already?' Quizzes and Chapter Review Questions."

**Table 1-1**  "Do I Know This Already?" Foundation Topics Section-to-Question Mapping

| Foundation Topics Section | Questions Covered in This Section |
|---|---|
| vSphere Editions and Features | 1–3 |
| Data Center Solutions That Interact with vSphere | 4, 8 |
| ESXi and vCenter Architectures and New Solutions | 5–7, 9, 10 |

1. Which of following features is supported on Enterprise Plus but not on Standard? (Choose two.)

   a. vMotion

   b. Storage I/O Control

   c. Distributed switch

   d. SSO

2. Which of the following are supported on Standard, Enterprise Plus, and Enterprise Plus with Operations Management? (Choose two.)

   a. Hot Add

   b. Content Library

   c. DRS and DPM

   d. Flash Read Cache

3. How many vCPUs are supported on vSphere 6 FT with Enterprise Plus?

   a. 1

   b. 2

   c. 4

   d. 8

4. Which of the following is a network virtualization platform that delivers the operational model of a VM, but for network devices?

   a. Auto Deploy

   b. NSX

   c. vCloud Suite

   d. vRealize Operations

5. Which of the following are the two *main* components of a vSphere 6 installation? (Choose two.)

   a. PSC

   b. SSO

   c. vCenter

   d. Certificate Services

6. Which of the following are *not* included in the PSC installation? (Choose two.)

   a. vCenter

   b. Syslog

   c. License Services

   d. Lookup Service

7. Which of the following is *not* a recommended vSphere architecture?

   a. Embedded system linked to embedded system

   b. Embedded system only

   c. Linked system with no high availability

   d. Linked system with high availability

8. Which of the following is a new license edition that enables an organization to rapidly provision servers while minimizing host configuration drift?

    a. vRealize Insight

    b. ROBO

    c. Linked Mode

    d. PSC

9. Which technology provides for the deployment of multiple ESXi servers in minutes by streaming them directly into RAM?

    a. Auto Deploy

    b. App HA

    c. Host Profiles

    d. Reliable Memory

10. Which of the following is a hypervisor-based virtual machine solution that synchronizes virtual disk files using a changed block tracking mechanism?

    a. Auto Deploy

    b. vMotion

    c. Virtual Volumes

    d. vSphere Replication

## Foundation Topics

# Identifying and Explaining vSphere Editions and Features

This section focuses on introducing the various vSphere editions and their features. It discusses your options with regard to ESXi, vCenter, and other related solutions.

### Identifying Available vSphere and vCenter Server Editions

Because the needs of organizations vary widely, VMware provides multiple options of vSphere, which are called *editions*. Each edition offers a defined variety of options that you can use to manage your virtual machines (VMs) and your hosts (the physical computers on which the VMs reside). When you finish reading this book, you will have a much better idea of which features would be most valuable to your organization, and you will understand all the features as they relate to the questions on the test.

For now, this section provides a brief explanation of each feature available in vSphere. Table 1-2 lists the most common editions and the features it makes available. If you understand all this already, you might be more ready for the exam than you think! If not, keep reading, and I will keep filling in the details.

**Table 1-2**   vSphere 6.0 Editions

| vSphere 6.0 Editions (Without Operations Manager) | Standard | Enterprise Plus | Enterprise Plus with Operations Management |
|---|---|---|---|
| **Product Components** | | | |
| License entitlement | Per 1 CPU | Per 1 CPU | Per 1 CPU |
| vMotion * | X (+ Cross vSwitch) | X (+ Cross vSwitch/ Cross vCenter/ Long Distance) | X (+ Cross vSwitch / Cross vCenter / Long Distance) |
| Storage vMotion | X | X | X |
| High Availability | X | X | X |
| Data Protection | X | X | X |
| Fault Tolerance | 2vCPU | 4vCPU | 4vCPU |
| vShield Endpoint | X | X | X |
| vSphere Replication | X | X | X |

| vSphere 6.0 Editions (Without Operations Manager) | Standard | Enterprise Plus | Enterprise Plus with Operations Management |
|---|---|---|---|
| Hot Add | X | X | X |
| Virtual Volumes | X | X | X |
| Storage Policy–Based Management | X | X | X |
| Content Library | X | X | X |
| Storage APIs for Array Integration | X | X | X |
| Reliable Memory | | X | X |
| Big Data Extensions | | X | X |
| Virtual Serial Port Concentrator | | X | X |
| DRS and DPM | | X | X |
| Storage DRS | | X | X |
| Storage I/O Control | | X | X |
| Network I/O Control | | X | X |
| Single Root I/O Virtualization | | X | X |
| Flash Read Cache | | X | X |
| NVIDIA GRID vGPU | | X | X |
| Distributed Switch | | X | X |
| Host Profiles | | X | X |
| Auto Deploy | | X | X |
| App HA | | X | X |
| Consistent Management | | | X |
| Intelligent Operations | | | X |
| Operations Automation | | | X |
| Workload Balancing | | | X |

A brief description of each product feature follows:

- **License Entitlement:** The number of physical processors for which each license is required.

- **vMotion:** Allows the migration of a VM from one physical host to another without disrupting the user. This eliminates the need to have server downtime due to planned hardware downtime.

- **Storage vMotion:** Avoids application downtime for planned storage maintenance by allowing the migration of the VM files across storage arrays while the VMs are running.

- **High Availability:** Provides for the automatic restart of VMs if they are on a host that fails; minimizes server downtime.

- **Data Protection:** An agentless disk-based backup system that provides de-duplication at the destination and is designed for small to medium-size organizations.

- **Fault Tolerance:** Provides continuous availability for VMs with zero downtime and data loss in the event of server failures.

- **vShield Endpoint:** Allows for the offloading of antivirus and antimalware functions to a virtual appliance that acts as a "bastion host" between the VMs and the data. The virtual appliance is the only component that receives antivirus and antimalware updates, thereby eliminating "antivirus storms" associated with all VMs updating at once.

- **vSphere Replication:** A hypervisor-based virtual machine replication solution that synchronizes virtual disk files using a changed block tracking mechanism. vSphere Replication is included on all license levels from Essentials Plus and up.

- **Hot Add:** Allows the addition of CPUs and memory when planned for and needed without disruption or downtime.

- **Virtual Volumes:** A new integration and management framework that virtualizes SAN/NAS arrays and provides for a more efficient storage model that is optimized for virtual environments. New shared data storage can be automatically created when needed, eliminating the "guessing game" typically associated with traditional logical unit numbers (LUNs).

- **Storage Policy–Based Management:** Allows for the prioritization of storage options, reduces the steps in the selection of VM storage, and ensures that VMs are placed on the right type of storage for each VM.

- **Content Library:** A method of storing VM templates and apps so they can be easily published and shared with other parts of your virtual environment. Content can even be shared across vCenter server boundaries. Provides a new level of centralized control and standardization.

- **Storage APIs for Array Integration:** Improves performance and scalability by leveraging efficient array-based operations.

- **Reliable Memory:** An automated system that protects hosts from uncorrectable memory errors by placing the hypervisor and other critical components into memory regions that are identified as "reliable" by the supported hardware.

- **Big Data Extensions:** vSphere Big Data Extensions support multiple Hadoop distributions that make it seamless for IT to deploy, run, and manage Hadoop workloads on one common platform.

- **Virtual Serial Port Concentrator:** Redirects serial ports of VMs so that management traffic is only on the management network, providing a more secure way to manage VMs remotely.

- **DRS and DPM:** Automatically balances VM loads across hosts, optimizing efficiency and power management.

- **Storage DRS:** Provides for more effective balancing of VMs using automated load balancing across datastores in datastore clusters.

- **Storage I/O Control:** Continuously monitors I/O load of storage volumes and dynamically allocates available I/O resources based on administrator settings for specific business needs.

- **Network I/O Control:** Prioritizes network access by continuously monitoring I/O load over the network and dynamically allocating available I/O resources to administrator specified flows to support business needs.

- **Single Root I/O Virtualization:** Allows one PCI Express (PCIe) adapter to be presented as multiple separate logical devices to the virtual machines. Provides users with the capability to offload I/O processing and reduce network latency.

- **Flash Read Cache:** A high-performance read cache layer that dramatically lowers application latency.

- **NVIDIA GRID vGPU:** Combines the virtual machine expertise of VMware with the graphical expertise of NVIDIA to deliver immersive 3D graphics from the cloud that are equivalent to those running on physical PCs.

- **Distributed Switch:** Centralizes provisioning, administration, and monitoring of your virtual network using cluster-level aggregation of resources.

- **Host Profiles:** Simplifies host deployment and compliance using baselines to automate the configuration of multiple hosts.

- **Auto Deploy:** Allows for deployment of multiple vSphere hosts in minutes by streaming the installation directly into RAM.

- **App HA:** A virtual appliance introduced with vSphere 5.5 that works with vSphere HA to provide for

  - The restart of an application service if it detects a failure

  - The restart and the reset of a VM if the application fails to start

**NOTE**   In addition to all the aforementioned features, the vSphere Operations Suite provides for consistent management, intelligent operations, automation, and workload balancing of your vSphere environment.

## Data Center Solutions That Interact with vSphere

VMware offers many other products that integrate with vSphere to provide for a fully operational virtual data center and a Software-Defined Data Center (SDDC). I will not go into detail about each one of these because you don't have to know the details about them for the exam. Besides, each one has its own book. However, it would be wise to know the basics of these for the exam. The products that I identify in this section include NSX, vCloud Suite, vRealize Operations Insight, vSphere Data Protection, and Remote Office Branch Office (ROBO).

- **NSX:** A network virtualization platform that delivers the operational model of a VM, but for network devices and, in fact, entire networks. Virtual networks are programmatically provisioned and managed independent of the underlying hardware. Both simple and complex networks can be created in minutes instead of days or weeks. These virtual networks can include routers, switches, load balancers, firewalls, and even access lists. NSX has the power to transform networking as we know it.

- **vCloud Suite:** A cloud management suite that provides for intelligent management of cloud resources with the goals of control, efficiency, and agility.

- **vRealize Operations Insight:** An integrated offering that delivers performance management, capacity optimization, and real-time log analytics as add-on solutions to vSphere with Operations Management.

- **VMware vSphere Data Protection Advanced:** Provides a customizable backup solution that allows a backup of each VM without the need for agents or additional backup software.

- **vSphere Remote Office Branch Office (ROBO):** A new solution that enables organizations with multiple sites to rapidly provision servers, minimize host configuration drift, and enhance visibility to assist in regulatory compliance.

## ESXi and vCenter Server Architectures and New Solutions

*Architecture* is defined as a style of construction. I think that is a good way to look at ESXi and vCenter architectures as well, because styles are individual and change over time. In other words, the most powerful thing about your architecture is that it can be customized to meet your needs and can be changed over time, as needed.

However, every ESXi and vCenter architecture has some common elements. Using vCenter allows you to aggregate (pull together) the resources from multiple ESXi hosts and then distribute them to the VMs of your choice. You are the "puppeteer" behind the scenes who controls all the CPU, RAM, disk, and network resources that the VMs "see." With full virtualization, the operating systems of the VMs are not even aware of what is actually going on. You present the resources to them in a way that they can understand and work with them, and you can prioritize between specific VMs or groups of VMs.

**NOTE**   You should remember that even though your environment can run multiple hosts, each VM can obtain compute (CPU and memory) resources only from the host on which it is running.

In addition, you use many fewer physical computers because each physical host can run multiple VMs. Of course, if you are going to put "all of your eggs in one basket," you had better have some services and features to provide for availability, security, and scalability. To address this concern, VMware provides features discussed later, such as vMotion, Storage vMotion, HA, DRS, FT, and so on, and continues to add features as needs arise. Again, it's a little early to discuss what might be best for you, but each one of these features will be discussed in detail.

New architecture of vSphere 6.0 is simple in comparison to previous versions of vSphere. It consists of two components: a Platform Services Controller (PSC) and a Virtual Center Server. Each of these components contains many services that are installed as a unit when the main component is installed.

The PSC includes Single Sign-On, License Services, the Lookup Service, the VMware Directory Service, and the VMware Certificate Authority. All these services are installed on one "box," physical or virtual. In fact, you can't "pick and choose" even if you want to, so the installation is very straightforward. For details regarding the platform services controller, you can consult the VMware knowledge base article KB2113115.

The vCenter Services server provides for the vCenter Server, as well as the vSphere Web Client, vCenter Inventory Service, vSphere Auto Deploy, vSphere ESXi Dump Collector, and vSphere Syslog Collector. The vCenter Server, with all these services, *can* be installed on the same "box," physical or virtual, as the PSC. This type of installation is referred to as *embedded*, and is probably the best choice for a very small organization. Figure 1-1 shows an embedded installation of a PSC and a Virtual Center Server.

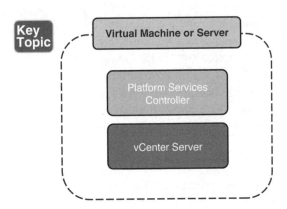

**Figure 1-1**   An "Embedded" Installation of PSC and vCenter Server

Another option is to install the vCenter Server on a separate "box" than the PSC.
This can provide for better performance in a larger organization. You may notice
that I've been a little "fuzzy" in identifying what I mean by "large" or "small."
That's because decisions regarding architecture rarely come down to exact numbers.
There are too many other considerations involving the way that the system will be
managed and the organization's needs—some of which are discussed in the next
chapter, "Installing and Configuring vCenter Server." Figure 1-2 shows a linked
installation of a PSC and a vCenter Server.

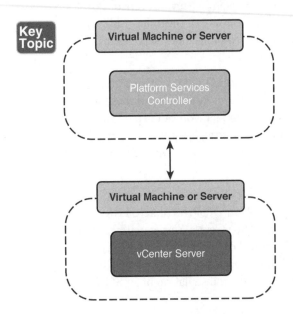

**Figure 1-2**   A Linked Installation of a PSC and a Virtual Center Server

In addition, if your organization has more than one vCenter Server, you can link multiple vCenter Servers to one platform console. When you arrange your environment this way, Enhanced Linked Mode is also included so you can manage multiple vCenter Servers and the hosts connected to them with one single tool, one set of credentials, and one single "pane of glass." Figure 1-3 shows an Enhanced Linked Mode configuration with two vCenter Servers.

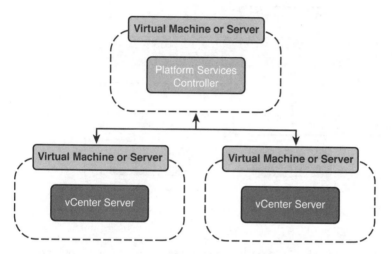

**Figure 1-3**   An Enhanced Linked Mode Installation of a PSC and Two vCenter Servers

You might be thinking, Isn't that like putting too many vCenter "eggs" into the same PSC "basket"? What if the PSC fails? Then wouldn't all the vCenters linked to it have connection issues as well? In a word, yes, unless you also have more than one PSC. You can build your vSphere with two PSCs that balance loads and provide fault tolerance for each other. The recommended architecture in this case is use two separate PSCs connected through a load balancer to all your vCenter Servers. Figure 1-4 shows the recommended architecture that provides Enhanced Linked Mode and High Availability.

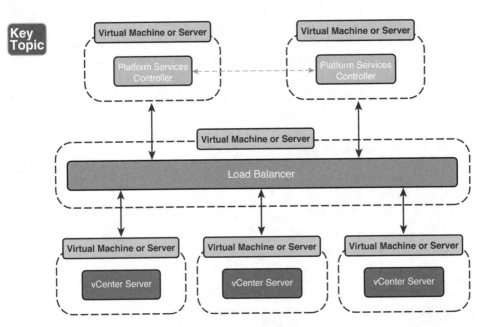

**Figure 1-4**    An Enhanced Linked Mode Installation with Load Balancing and High Availability

Before you start thinking that you can build the architecture in any way you choose without any repercussions, know that three possible configurations are *not* recommended, for real life or for the exam! For example, it's not advisable to link two embedded installations to each other through their PSCs, as shown in Figure 1-5.

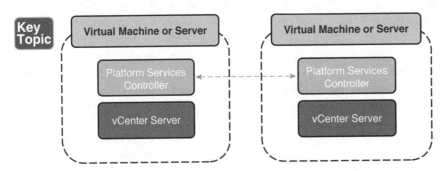

**Figure 1-5**    A Nonrecommended Method of Linking PSCs with Two Embedded Installations

In addition, it's not advisable to link an embedded installation to a linked one, as shown in Figure 1-6.

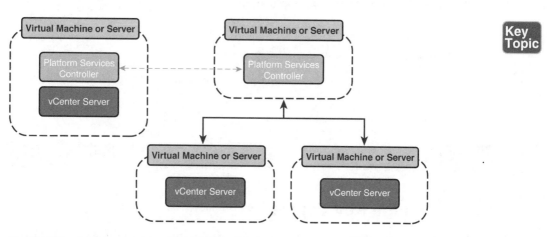

**Figure 1-6**   A Nonrecommended Method of Linking PSCs with One Embedded Solution and One Linked

Finally, it's not recommended to link an embedded installation to a single vCenter Server, as shown in Figure 1-7.

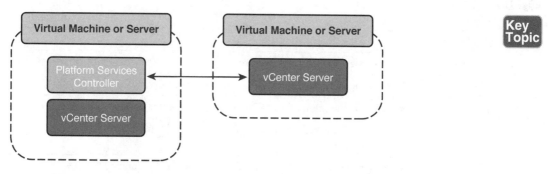

**Figure 1-7**   A Nonrecommended Method of Linking PSCs with One Embedded VC and One Separate

In the next chapter, I discuss installing vCenter server and dig much deeper into some of these options.

## Summary

This chapter covered the following main topics:

- The various editions of vSphere and the features supported by each one.

- Some data center solutions that interact with vSphere.

- Your options in regard to vSphere 6.0 architecture and the recommendations for each one.

## Exam Preparation Tasks

## Review All the Key Topics

Review the most important topics from the chapter, noted with the Key Topic icon in the outer margin of the page. Table 1-3 lists these key topics and the page numbers where each is found.

**Table 1-3**   Key Topics for Chapter 1

| Key Topic Element | Description | Page Number |
|---|---|---|
| Table 1-2 | vSphere 6.0 Editions | 6 |
| Bullet List | A brief description of each feature | 7 |
| Figure 1-1 | An Embedded Installation of PSC and vCenter Server | 12 |
| Figure 1-2 | A Linked Installation of a PSC and a Virtual Center Server | 12 |
| Figure 1-3 | An Enhanced Linked Mode Installation of a PSC and Two vCenter Servers | 13 |
| Figure 1-4 | An Enhanced Linked Mode Installation with Load Balancing and High Availability | 14 |
| Figure 1-5 | A Nonrecommended Method of Linking PSCs with Two Embedded Installations | 14 |
| Figure 1-6 | A Nonrecommended Method of Linking PSCs with One Embedded Solution and One Linked | 15 |
| Figure 1-7 | A Nonrecommended Method of Linking PSCs with One Embedded VC and One Separate | 15 |

## Review Questions

The answers to these review questions are in Appendix A.

1. Which of following features is not supported with only a vSphere Standard license?

   a. vMotion

   b. DRS and DPM

   c. Distributed switch

   d. SSO

2. Which of the following are supported on Standard, Enterprise Plus, and Enterprise Plus with Operations Management? (Choose two.)

   a. vMotion

   b. Storage vMotion

   c. DRS and DPM

   d. Storage DRS

3. Which of the following is the lowest vSphere license level that by itself supports a distributed switch?

   a. Essentials

   b. Standard

   c. Enterprise

   d. Enterprise Plus

4. Which of the following is a network virtualization platform that does for switches and routers what ESXi does for computers?

   a. Auto Deploy

   b. NSX

   c. vCloud Suite

   d. vRealize Operations

5. Which of the following are *not* two of the *main* components of a vSphere 6 installation? (Choose two.)

   a. PSC

   b. SSO

   c. vCenter

   d. Certificate Services

6. Which of the following are included in the PSC installation?

   a. vCenter

   b. Syslog

   c. License Services

   d. Lookup Service

7. Which of the following is *not* a recommended vSphere architecture?

   a. Embedded system linked to linked system

   b. Embedded system only

   c. Linked system with no high availability

   d. Linked system with high availability

8. Which of the following are included with a linked installation of vSphere 6? (Choose two.)

   a. vRealize Insight

   b. ROBO

   c. Linked Mode

   d. PSC

9. Which technology simplifies host deployment and compliance using baselines to automate the configuration of multiple hosts?

   a. Auto Deploy

   b. App HA

   c. Host Profiles

   d. Reliable Memory

**10.** Which of the following is a method of storing VM templates and apps so they can be easily published to other parts of the organization, even across vCenter boundaries?

   **a.** Auto Deploy

   **b.** vMotion

   **c.** Virtual Volumes

   **d.** Content Library

**This chapter covers the following subjects:**

- vCenter Server Database Requirements
- Sizing the vCenter Server Database
- vCenter Server Software Requirements
- Licensing vCenter Server
- Creating a Database Connection to the vCenter Server Database
- Determining Availability Requirements for a vCenter Server

Your vCenter Server and ESXi hosts offer a tremendous number of features and utilities, but to get the most from them, you need to install them properly. This chapter focuses on the proper installation of these important components. You will also learn how to size the vCenter server database and how to provide a license for the vCenter Server.

## CHAPTER 2

# Installing and Configuring vCenter Server

## "Do I Know This Already?" Quiz

The "Do I Know This Already?" quiz allows you to assess whether you should read this entire chapter or simply jump to the "Exam Preparation Tasks" section for review. If you are in doubt, read the entire chapter. Table 2-1 outlines the major headings in this chapter and the corresponding "Do I Know This Already?" quiz questions. You can find the answers in Appendix A, "Answers to the 'Do I Know This Already?' Quizzes and Chapter Review Questions."

**Table 2-1** "Do I Know This Already?" Foundation Topics Section-to-Question Mapping

| Foundation Topics Section | Questions Covered in This Section |
|---|---|
| vCenter Server and vCenter Server Database Requirements | 1, 2 |
| Sizing the vCenter Database | 6, 7, 9, 10 |
| vCenter Server Software Requirements | 3, 4 |
| Licensing vCenter Server | 5 |
| Creating a Database Connection to the vCenter Server Database | 8 |

1. What is the minimum number of CPUs required for vCenter?

   a. 1

   b. 2

   c. 4

   d. 0

**2.** What is the minimum amount of memory required for vCenter?

    **a.** 1 GB

    **b.** 2 GB

    **c.** 4 GB

    **d.** 8 GB

**3.** What is the maximum number of hosts that the vCenter Appliance will support?

    **a.** 50

    **b.** 100

    **c.** 500

    **d.** 1000

**4.** How many more powered on VMs will the Windows-based vCenter support than the vCenter Appliance?

    **a.** 0 (they are the same)

    **b.** 1000

    **c.** 100

    **d.** 500

**5.** After installing a vCenter license, what can you click to verify the features that the license provides?

    **a.** Examine

    **b.** View Features in Use

    **c.** Prepare

    **d.** Type

**6.** Which database is embedded in the vCenter Appliance for vSphere 6?

    **a.** IBM DB2

    **b.** SQL Express

    **c.** Oracle

    **d.** vPostgres database

**7.** How many hosts and VMs will the Windows-based vCenter's embedded vPostgresSQL database support?

    **a.** 20 hosts and 200 VMs

    **b.** 1000 hosts and 10,000 VMs

    **c.** 500 hosts and 5,000 VMs

    **d.** 5 hosts and 50 VMs

**8.** Which of the following is *not* true regarding the OS for a Windows based installation of vCenter?

    **a.** Options for supported servers can be found on the System Compatibility List.

    **b.** 32-bit and 64-bit options are available.

    **c.** A SQL Express database will be embedded, regardless of choice.

    **d.** The SQL Express database will be installed as part of the vCenter installation, and a SQL database can be connected with an ODBC and a DSN.

**9.** How many hosts/clusters are supported with the vCenter Appliance?

    **a.** 64

    **b.** 32

    **c.** 128

    **d.** 16

**10.** What is the maximum number of hosts that the vCenter Appliance can support without an external database?

    **a.** 1000

    **b.** 5

    **c.** 100

    **d.** 500

## Foundation Topics

# vCenter Server and vCenter Database Requirements

This section focuses on the "hardware" requirements for your vCenter Server and its database. Hardware is in quotations because it could mean either physical hardware or virtual hardware, which is actually software. Later in this chapter, you learn about the other software requirements; for now we'll just look at the "hardware."

When I teach VMware vSphere classes in person, I always ask the students whether they use a VM or a physical machine for their vCenter Server, and why? If they use a VM, I ask whether it's Windows-based or the Linux-based vCenter Appliance, and why?

Many people assume that the vCenter Server is such an important component to the virtual environment that it should be a physical machine. In other words, they do not want to have a situation in which they need to have a vCenter machine to fix the virtual environment that is down, but the machine that they need is also a VM and therefore is also down—a "catch 22" type of situation. In reality, because of vSphere features that are discussed later (such as High Availability [HA]), it is acceptable to install the vCenter Server as a VM. In addition, you now have the option of installing a vCenter Appliance that has all the same capabilities and capacity of a Windows-based machine.

You can find the vCenter Server installation software on the vSphere Installation Manager, which also allows you to install the Platform Services Controller (PSC). Before you begin a vCenter installation, make sure that the machine that you are using meets the basic hardware and software requirements. You should also install the Platform Services Controller first, which is discussed later.

The basic "hardware" requirements for any vCenter Server are as follows:

- **Number of CPUs:** 2

- **Processor:** 2.0 GHz or higher Intel or AMD processor

- **Memory:** 4 GB minimum

- **Disk Storage:** 4 GB minimum

- **Operating System:** 64-bit (See the vSphere Compatibility Matrixes in the vSphere Installation and Setup Guide as noted.)

When you know that your system meets all the requirements, you are ready to begin the installation. After you have installed the Platform Services Controller, the vCenter installation is very straightforward. Activity 2-1 walks you through an embedded installation of the PSC and the vCenter Server on a VM.

**Activity 2-1    Installing the PSC and vCenter Server**

1. Obtain the vSphere installation software package (VMware VIMSetup-All 6.0.0) from vmware.com/downloads.

2. On the very simplified installation screen, as shown in Figure 2-1, click **Install** to begin the installation process for vCenter Server.

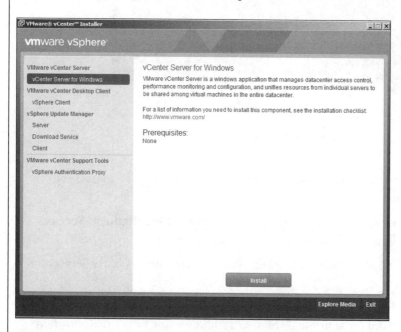

**Figure 2-1**    The Simplified Installation Screen for vCenter

3. Click **Next** when the "Welcome to the VMware vCenter Server 6.0.0 Installer screen appears, as shown in Figure 2-2.

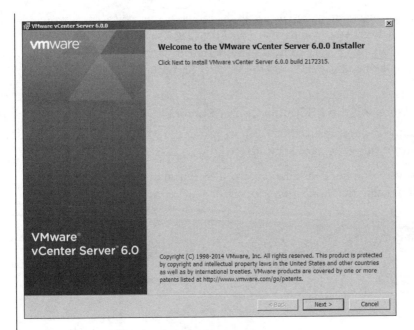

**Figure 2-2**   VIMSetup 6.0.0 Welcome Screen

4. Accept the license agreement (after reading thoroughly, of course) and click **Next**.

5. On the Deployment Type screen, choose **Embedded Platform Services Controller**, and click **Next**, as shown in Figure 2-3.

6. Enter the Fully Qualified Domain Name for your new vCenter Server, and click **Next**.

7. In the Single Sign-On Configuration screen, enter a domain name and the password for your Single Sign-On administrator account, as shown in Figure 2-4. You can accept the default of vsphere.local. It is also not necessary to change the site.

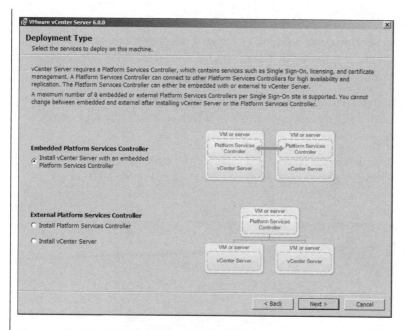

**Figure 2-3**   The New Deployment Type Screen

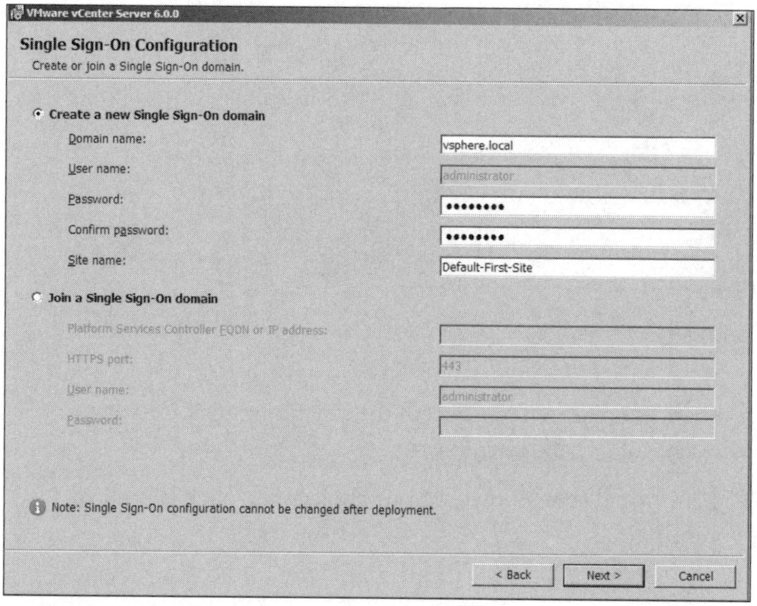

**Figure 2-4**   The Single Sign-On Configuration Screen

8.  Specify whether vCenter Server will use the Windows Local System account or another administrative account. (A separate account is considered more secure and may be required by your organizational guidelines. We use the Windows Local System Account for this example.)

9.  In the Database Settings screen, choose to use the embedded vPostgres database, or specify a DSN and credentials by which to connect to an external database, and click **Next**.

10. On the Configure Ports screen, you can accept the defaults for all ports, unless you have reason to change them, as shown in Figure 2-5, and click **Next**.

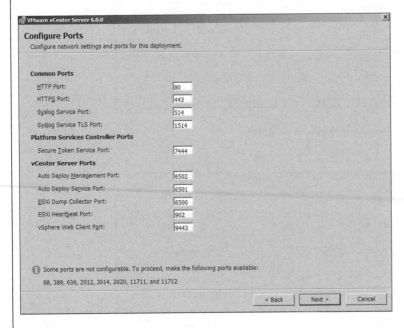

**Figure 2-5**    The Configure Ports Screen

11. On the Destination Folder screen, accept the default or click **Change** to specify a different folder, and click **Next**.

12. On the Ready to Install screen, review your choices and click **Install**, as shown in Figure 2-6.

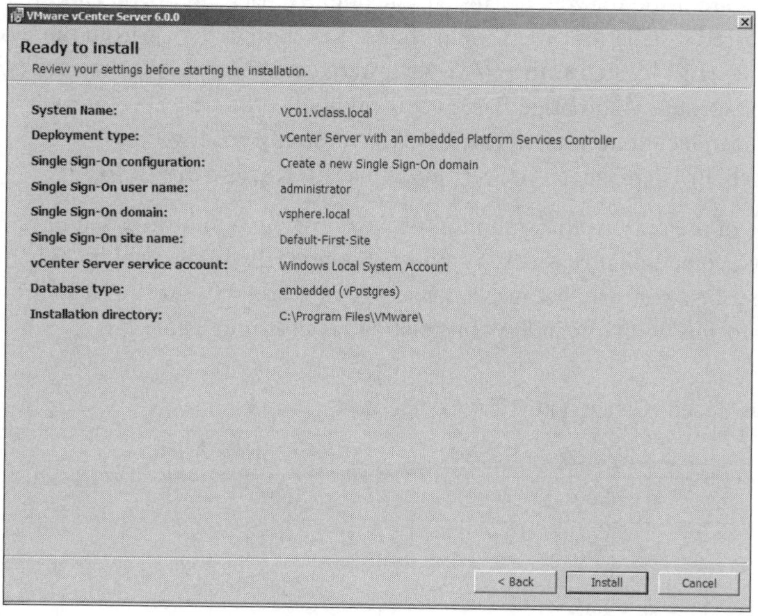

**Figure 2-6**   The Ready to Install Screen

## Sizing the vCenter Server Database

Before installing your vCenter, you need to know the specific database that you will use. This means that you need to have created the database ahead of time, which in turn means that you must know the size of the database that you will need. The vCenter Server has a tool that you can use to calculate the size of the database; however, you cannot use that tool unless you already have a vCenter installed. This might be the case if you installed one with a SQL Express database for demo, but if you do not have an installation, what do you use? There are database-sizing spreadsheets you can use for Microsoft SQL and Oracle database sizing, which are available at http://www.vmware.com/support/pubs. This might be a guess on your part as to how many hosts, VMs, clusters, and so on, but it's better than a complete "shot in the dark."

## vCenter Server Software Requirements

As I'm sure you can imagine, the software requirements for your vCenter Server will depend completely on whether you choose a Windows-based installation or the vCenter Appliance. In fact, if you choose the vCenter Appliance, most of the software choices are made for you, because it's a complete package. If you choose the Windows-based installation, you should choose a Windows Server from the System Compatibility List located at http://www.vmware.com/resources/compatibility/search.php. An excellent Knowledge Base article highlights the best OSs for each version of vCenter, including version 6: http://kb.vmware.com/selfservice/microsites/search.do?language=en_US&cmd=displayKC&externalId=2091273.

In the past, one of the reasons that you might have chosen a Windows-based installation over a vCenter Appliance is that Windows provided greater scalability. That should no longer be a concern, because a properly configured vCenter Appliance can "stand toe-to-toe" with a Windows installation, as shown in Table 2-2.

**Table 2-2**   Windows-Based vCenter and VCSA Comparison

| Metric | Windows Based | vCenter Appliance |
| --- | --- | --- |
| Hosts/vCenter | 1,000 | 1,000 |
| Powered on VMs | 10,000 | 10,000 |
| Hosts/Cluster | 64 | 64 |
| VMs/Cluster | 8,000 | 8,000 |
| Database | Must be external Oracle or SQL for full scalability | Embedded vPostgres database or external Oracle |
| Linked Mode Support | Yes | Yes |

### Licensing vCenter Server

When you first install your vCenter, you have a 60-day eval license that gives you all the features and capabilities of the vCenter Server with a standard license. When you have determined the features that you need, you should license your vCenter Server accordingly. Activity 2-2 walks you through the simple process of applying a license to a vCenter Server.

### Activity 2-2   Applying a License to vCenter

1. Log on to vCenter Server with the vSphere Web Client.

2. Click **Home**, and then select **Licensing** within the icons under Administration.

3. If you are managing multiple vCenter Servers with the same Web Client, select the appropriate vCenter Server from the drop-down box at the top of the screen, right-click your vCenter Server, and click **Assign License**, as shown in Figure 2-7.

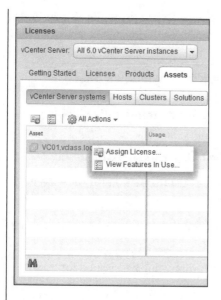

**Figure 2-7**   Licensing a vCenter Server

4. Choose from an existing key or click the green + sign to add a new key, and click **OK**.

5. Optionally, you can enter a label, such as **Production Licenses**.

6. Click **OK** to close the box and store the key.

**NOTE**   You can examine the features that a license provides an asset by right-clicking the asset in the Licenses view and clicking **View Features in Use**.

### Creating a Database Connection to the vCenter Server Database

You can use your vCenter Server's embedded vPostgres database for as long as you need; however, it will severely limit your growth capability because it is supported for only 20 hosts and 200 VMs. In contrast, the vPostgres database embedded in the vCenter Appliance, as noted earlier, will support 1,000 hosts and 10,000 VMs!

In either case, you may want to connect your vCenter Server to an external database that you have prepared or that has been prepared by your database administrator. In that case, you need the data source name (DSN) and the object database connector address (ODBC). After you have both of these, you are ready, but the actual steps will be different, depending on whether you are connecting to a Windows-based vCenter or to the vCenter Appliance. Activity 2-3 walks you through the steps for a Windows system.

> **Activity 2-3   Creating a Database Connection for a Windows Based vCenter Server**
>
> 1. On a Windows 2003 or later server, click **Start, Administrative Tools, Data Sources (ODBC)**.
>
> 2. Select the **System DSN** tab, click **Add**, and then choose **SQL Server**.
>
> 3. Enter the name, description, and specific server information for the server that you want to connect, and click **Next**.
>
> 4. Choose to authenticate with SQL Server using Login ID and password, and enter the credentials required by the server.
>
> 5. After this is done, you can choose the DSN that you have created for your database connection.

## Determining Availability Requirements for vCenter Server

As mentioned previously, your vCenter is the centralized command, control, and communication center for your vSphere environment. So, what happens if it fails and is not available? At first, you might think that it would be a great catastrophic event that would cause all the VMs to stop functioning and break all the network connections at once.

This is not the case. In fact, a loss of the vCenter has an effect only on your ability as an administrator to control the system from the vCenter. You can still log on to individual ESXi hosts with the Windows-based vSphere Client and configure them. In addition, all the networking remains intact, and the VMs function almost normally. However, Distributed Resource Scheduler (DRS), which provides the capability to automatically migrate VMs to balance the load, will be disabled because the vCenter does those calculations and controls those moves. (Chapter 14, "Creating and Configuring VMware Clusters," covers DRS in more detail.) The capability to restart the VMs on a host that fails (HA) will, however, be intact and will restart your VM-based vCenter just as well as any other VM. Chapter 14 also covers HA in greater detail.

So, the main question is, "How long can you continue operations without your vCenter?" If your answer is "at least a few minutes," you might only need to make sure that HA is installed and functional in your host clusters. However, if you do not think that you ever want to lose vCenter, you might even consider using the new fault tolerance (FT) that supports up to four vCPUs with the Enterprise Plus version of vSphere. I discuss FT in detail in Chapter 15, "Planning and Implementing VMware Fault Tolerance."

## Summary

This chapter covered the following main topics:

- vCenter Server and vCenter Database requirements
- Sizing the vCenter Database
- vCenter Server software requirements
- Licensing vCenter Server
- Creating a database connection to the vCenter Server Database
- Determining availability requirements for a vCenter Server

## Exam Preparation Tasks

## Review All the Key Topics

Review the most important topics from the chapter, noted with the Key Topic icon in the outer margin of the page. Table 2-3 lists these key topics and the page numbers where each is found.

**Table 2-3**   Key Topics for Chapter 2

| Key Topic Element | Description | Page Number |
|---|---|---|
| Bullet List | Basic Hardware Requirements for the vCenter Server | 24 |
| Activity 2-1 | Installing PSC and vCenter Server | 25 |
| Table 2-2 | Windows-Based vCenter and VCSA Comparison | 30 |
| Activity 2-2 | Applying a License to vCenter | 30 |
| Activity 2-3 | Creating a Database Connection for a Windows-Based vCenter Server | 32 |

## Review Questions

The answers to these review questions are in Appendix A.

1. What is the maximum number of VMs/clusters on a vCenter Appliance?

   a. 1,000

   b. 2,000

   c. 8,000

   d. 10,000

2. What is the minimum amount of memory required for a vCenter Appliance?

   a. 1 GB

   b. 2 GB

   c. 4 GB

   d. 8 GB

3. What is the maximum number of VMs that the vCenter Appliance will support?

   a. 50

   b. 100

   c. 500

   d. 10,000

4. How many fewer powered-on VMs will the Windows-based vCenter with only an embedded database support than the vCenter Appliance?

   a. 0 (they are the same)

   b. 9,800

   c. 100

   d. 500

5. When assigning a vCenter license, what can you click to determine the details of what it provides?

   a. Assign License

   b. View Features in Use

   c. License Details

   d. Decode

6. Which database is embedded in the Windows-based vCenter for vSphere 6?

    a. IBM DB2

    b. SQL Express

    c. Oracle

    d. vPostgres database

7. How many hosts and VMs will the Windows-based vCenter's embedded database support?

    a. 20 hosts and 200 VMs

    b. 1,000 hosts and 10,000 VMs

    c. 500 hosts and 5,000 VMs

    d. There is no SQL Express database on the Windows version of vCenter.

8. Which of the following is *not* true regarding the vCenter Appliance?

    a. It can support up to 1,000 hosts and 10,000 VMs with its embedded database.

    b. It requires a Windows license for full operability.

    c. It can be connected to an external Oracle database.

    d. It cannot be connected to an external SQL database.

9. How many more hosts/clusters are supported with the Windows-based vCenter than with the vCenter Appliance?

    a. 32

    b. 0 (they are the same)

    c. 16

    d. 4

10. How many more hosts can a vCenter Appliance support with its embedded database than a Windows-based vCenter can support with its embedded database?

    a. 1,000

    b. 100

    c. 980

    d. 500

**This chapter covers the following subjects:**

- ESXi Host Requirements
- Performing an Interactive Installation of ESXi
- Configuring NTP on an ESXi Host
- Configuring DNS and Routing on an ESXi Host
- Licensing an ESXi Host

## CHAPTER 3

# Installing and Configuring ESXi

I can still remember the many configuration steps involved with the installation of earlier versions of ESX. There were so many things to consider and so many places that you could make a mistake that VMware made a video for you to watch to make it easier to know when to make each decision and how.

Well, ESX is not offered after vSphere 4.1, only ESXi. One of the benefits of using ESXi rather than ESX is that the installation is much more straightforward. I tell my students that it is more like installing a new switch than it is like installing a new router or server (much less configuration). Now there is even a way to stream the installation directly into memory and not onto a disk at all. Configuration is also simplified, and there are fewer configuration aspects to consider.

## "Do I Know This Already?" Quiz

The "Do I Know This Already?" quiz allows you to assess whether you should read this entire chapter or simply jump to the "Exam Preparation Tasks" section for review. If you are in doubt, read the entire chapter. Table 3-1 outlines the major headings in this chapter and the corresponding "Do I Know This Already?" quiz questions. You can find the answers in Appendix A, "Answers to the 'Do I Know This Already?' Quizzes and Chapter Review Questions."

**Table 3-1** "Do I Know This Already?" Foundation Topics Section-to-Question Mapping

| Foundation Topics Section | Questions Covered in This Section |
|---|---|
| ESXi Host Requirements | 1, 2 |
| Performing an Interactive Installation of ESXi | 3 |
| Configuring NTP on an ESXi Host | 4, 5, 7 |
| Configuring DNS and Routing on an ESXi Host | 6 |
| Licensing an ESXi Host | 8, 9 |

1. Which of following is *not* a requirement for installing an ESXi host?

   a. 2 CPU cores (minimum)

   b. 8 GB RAM

   c. One or more Gigabit or faster NICs

   d. NX/XD bit enabled for the CPU in host BIOS

2. Which of the following are true with regard to installing an ESXi host. (Choose two.)

   a. Hardware virtualization is required.

   b. Hardware virtualization is required only to support 64-bit VMs.

   c. You can use any physical server.

   d. You can use servers that are listed in the VMware Compatibility Guide.

3. Which of the following is *not* recommended media to use when installing ESXi interactively?

   a. CD/DVD

   b. USB flash drive

   c. PXE

   d. Floppy disk

4. In the vSphere Web Client, which tab under Manage contains the setting for Time Configuration?

   a. Time

   b. Configuration

   c. Settings

   d. NTP

5. Which of the following can be specified to add a time server for a host? (Choose two.)

   a. IP address

   b. Server domain

   c. Hostname

   d. Cluster name

6. In the vSphere Web Client, which tab under Manage contains the setting for DNS configuration?

   a. Networking

   b. TCP/IP

   c. DNS and Routing

   d. Settings

7. Which time zone does ESXi use by default?

   a. EST

   b. CST

   c. UTC (no time zone configuration)

   d. It's dependent on where the ESXi is first installed.

8. In the vSphere Web Client, which section under Home contains the configuration for licensing your ESXi host?

   a. Administration

   b. Configuration

   c. Management

   d. Licensing

9. When licensing the ESXi 6 host, which of the following is true about the Decode option?

   a. The license must be decoded before it can be used.

   b. You can verify that it's the right license and check its expiration date.

   c. It decompresses the compressed license for first use.

   d. The Decode link is *not* presented when adding a license with the vSphere 6 client or vSphere 6 Web Client.

10. Which of the following is the minimum amount of RAM for an ESXi 6.0 host?

   a. 4 MB

   b. 4 TB

   c. 4 GB

   d. 2 GB

## Foundation Topics

This chapter discusses the requirements for ESXi and how to install a host interactively using media or PXE. You also learn how to configure Network Time Protocol (NTP), Domain Name System (DNS) routing, and licensing on your ESXi hosts.

## ESXi Host Requirements

In most cases, the ESXi hosts are one of the only components in the vSphere that is still physical. However, it's even possible to "nest" an ESXi host as a VM on a physical server. This would typically be done in a lab or test environment and is not supported in a production environment. In either case, bare minimum requirements must be met on the server to be used for ESXi before ESXi can be installed. You should make sure that you meet the bare minimums, but in reality most production environments will far exceed them! The following are the bare minimum requirements to install an ESXi host:

- A supported server platform as defined on the VMware Compatibility Guide at http://www.vmware.com/compatibility

- Two CPU cores

- NX/XD bit enabled for the CPU in host BIOS

- 4 GB physical RAM

- Hardware virtualization Intel VT-x or AMD RVI to support 64-bit VMs

- One or more gigabits of faster Ethernet controllers

- SCSI disk or a local, nonnetwork RAID LUN with unpartitioned space

- Hardware virtualization Intel VT-x or AMD RVI to support 64-bit VMs

### Performing an Interactive Installation of ESXi

To install ESXi for vSphere 6.0, access the installer software. There is no GUI installer for ESXi, so the text-based installer is used for new installations and for upgrades. You can obtain the text-based installer from the CD/DVD installation software for ESXi, or you can download the software ISO and burn a CD or DVD. To access the ISO file, connect to http://www.vmware.com/download. You can also load the installation software to a USB flash drive.

After you obtain the software, proceed with the preinstallation checks. You should consider the following:

- Verify that the server hardware clock is set to UTC (BIOS setting).

- Verify that a keyboard and monitor are attached to the machine on which you are installing ESXi, or use a remote management application.

- Consider disconnecting network storage, such as fiber-optic cables and network cables to iSCSI arrays. This will save time on the installation because there will be fewer drives for the installation software to examine as potential candidates for installation.

With the preinstallation checks done, you are ready to proceed with the installation of the ESXi software, as outlined in Activity 3-1.

---

**Activity 3-1    Performing an Interactive Installation of ESXi**

1.  Set the BIOS on the machine to boot from a CD-ROM or USB device, depending on your earlier choice.

2.  Insert the ESXi installer into the CD/DVD drive or connect the USB flash drive.

3.  On the Select a Disk page, select the drive on which to install ESXi and press **Enter**. Caution: If you choose a disk that contains data, a Confirm Disk Selection page appears. You get one chance, so make sure that you do not perform an RGE (resume generating event).

4.  Select the keyboard type for the host.

5.  Enter the root password for the host. (You can leave this blank and fill it in on the first boot. If you do not choose a root password on the first boot, you will see a warning associated with the hosts on the vSphere Client.)

6.  Press **F11** to start the installation.

7.  After the installation is complete, remove the CD/DVD or USB flash drive.

8.  Press **Enter** to reboot the host. You should see a screen with the IP address of the system, as shown in Figure 3-1.

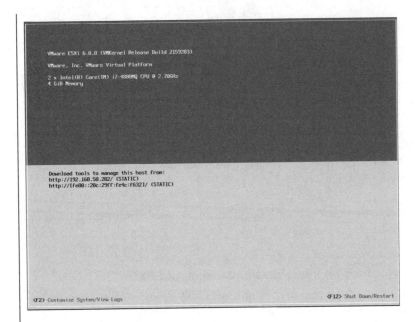

**Figure 3-1**   An ESXi Installation

9. Reset the boot device to be the drive on which you installed ESXi.

### Configuring NTP on an ESXi Host

As you might know, it's important for computers on a network to agree on what time it is, and ESXi is no exception. In addition, it's important to have the correct time set on a system so that logs and reports reflect the correct time; otherwise, you won't know whether it was taken during your peak time or off-peak time. Because your ESXi host is a server in your network, it should agree on the time with the other servers in your network. You should therefore configure the Network Time Protocol (NTP) settings on the host to obtain their time from a trusted time source. What you use as a trusted time source will vary based on your organization's decision. Also, keep in mind that ESXi uses coordinated universal time (UTC) and, therefore, does not have the need or capability for time zone configuration.

Activity 3-2 walks you through configuring NTP on your ESXi host in your vCenter using the vSphere Web Client.

### Activity 3-2    Configuring NTP on a Host in vCenter

1. Log on to your vSphere Web Client.

2. Select **Home, Hosts and Clusters,** and then click your host.

3. Select the **Manage** tab; then select **Settings**.

4. In the blue column, select **Time Configuration,** as shown in Figure 3-2.

**Figure 3-2**   NTP Configuration

5. On the far right side of the screen, click **Edit**.

6. In **NTP Servers**, enter the IP addresses or hostnames of the time server(s).

7. Ensure that the Startup Policy is set to **Start and Stop Manually**, for best security (or select one of the other options), and click **Start**.

8. Click **OK**, and then examine NTP Service Status to confirm that the service is now running.

## Configuring DNS and Routing on an ESXi Host

As with other servers, your ESXi host needs to know how to contact the other components of your network. You should configure the address of a DNS server that your ESXi host can use when needed. Likewise, configure a default gateway to be used by the VMkernel management port. (Networking options are discussed in greater detail in Chapter 4, "Configuring vSphere Standard Switches," and in Chapter 5, "Configuring vSphere Distributed Switches.")

Activity 3-3 walks you through configuring DNS and routing options on your host.

**Activity 3-3   Configuring DNS and Routing Options**

1. Log on to your vSphere Web Client.

2. Select **Home, Hosts and Clusters**, and then click your host.

3. Click the **Manage** tab and then the **Networking** tab.

4. In the blue column, choose **TCP/IP Configuration**.

5. Select the system stack that you want to configure; in this case, configure the **Default** stack.

6. Click the pencil icon above the **System Stack** column.

7. Configure the appropriate DNS information on **DNS Configuration**, and then change to **Routing** to configure the default gateway of the stack, as shown in Figure 3-3.

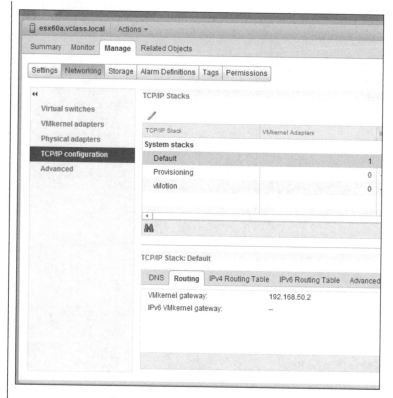

**Figure 3-3**  Configuring DNS and Routing

## Licensing an ESXi Host

As with vCenter, you have 60 days to use your host without a license, and then you must license the host. You should obtain a key and then add the key by logging on to the ESXi host or the vCenter to which you have added the ESXi host.

To add a key and license the host, follow the steps outlined in Activity 3-4.

**Activity 3-4   Adding a License Key to a Host**

1. Log on to your vCenter Server with the vSphere Web Client.

2. Click **Home**, and then select **Licensing** within the icons under Administration.

3. If you are managing more than one vCenter Server, select the appropriate vCenter Server, and then select the **Hosts** tab.

**4.** Right-click the host that you want to license, and then click **Assign License**, as shown in Figure 3-4.

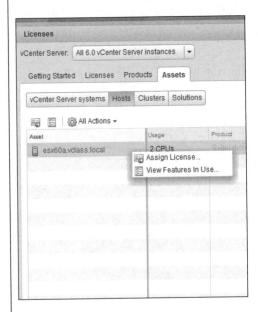

**Figure 3-4** Assign a New License Key

**5.** Choose from an existing key or choose the green + sign and enter the key; then click **Next**, as shown in Figure 3-5. You can also enter an optional label, such as **Production Licenses**.

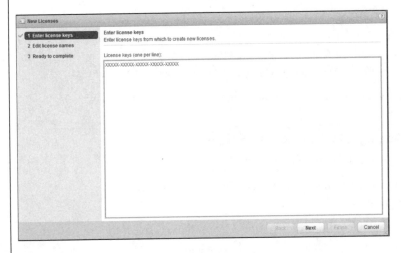

**Figure 3-5** Entering the License Key

> **NOTE**   The Decode option that was included with previous clients is no longer presented with the vSphere 6 client and vSphere 6 Web Client; instead, the View Features in Use is available.
>
> **6.** Click **OK** to save the settings and close the dialog box.

## Summary

This chapter covered the following main topics:

- The ESXi host requirements.

- How to perform an interactive installation of ESXi using media or PXE.

- How to license an ESXi Host through your vSphere Web Client.

## Exam Preparation Tasks

## Review All the Key Topics

Review the most important topics from the chapter, noted with the Key Topic icon in the outer margin of the page. Table 3-2 lists these key topics and the page numbers where each is found.

**Table 3-2**   Key Topics for Chapter 3

| Key Topic Element | Description | Page Number |
|---|---|---|
| Bullet List | ESXi Host Requirements | 40 |
| Activity 3-1 | Performing an Interactive Installation of ESXi | 41 |
| Activity 3-2 | Configuring NTP on a Host in vCenter | 43 |
| Activity 3-3 | Configuring DNS and Routing Options | 44 |
| Activity 3-4 | Adding a License Key to a Host | 45 |

## Review Questions

The answers to these review questions are in Appendix A.

1. Which of the following is *not* a requirement for installing an ESXi host?

   a. 4 CPU cores (minimum)

   b. 4 GB RAM

   c. One or more gigabit or faster NICs

   d. NX/XD bit enabled for the CPU in host BIOS

2. Which of the following are *not* true with regard to installing an ESXi host?

   a. Hardware virtualization is required.

   b. Hardware virtualization is required only to support 64-bit VMs.

   c. You can use any physical server.

   d. You can use servers that are listed in the VMware Compatibility Guide.

3. Which of the following is *not* true in regard to installing ESXi interactively?

   a. You can use a CD/DVD-based ISO file.

   b. You can use a USB flash drive.

   c. You should never use a PXE boot.

   d. You can use a physical CD/DVD.

4. In the vSphere Web Client, which tab under Manage contains the setting for Time Configuration?

   a. Time

   b. Configuration

   c. Settings

   d. NTP

5. Which of the following can be specified to add a time server for a host? (Choose two.)

   a. IP address

   b. Server domain

   c. Hostname

   d. Cluster name

6. In the vSphere Web Client, which tab under Manage contains the setting for DNS configuration?

    a. Networking

    b. TCP/IP

    c. DNS and Routing

    d. Settings

7. Which time zone does ESXi use by default?

    a. EST

    b. CST

    c. UTC (no time zone configuration)

    d. It's dependent on where the ESXi is first installed.

8. In the vSphere Web Client, which section under Home contains the configuration for licensing your ESXi host?

    a. Administration

    b. Configuration

    c. Management

    d. Licensing

9. When licensing the ESXi host with a vSphere 6 Web Client, which of the following is true regarding the Decode option?

    a. The license must be decoded before it can be used.

    b. You can verify that it's the right license and check its expiration date.

    c. It decompresses the compressed license for first use.

    d. Clicking Decode is *not* available when adding a license.

10. Which of the following is the minimum amount of RAM for an ESXi 6.0 host?

    a. 4 MB

    b. 4 TB

    c. 4 GB

    d. 2 GB

**This chapter covers the following subjects:**

- vSphere Standard Switch (vSS) Capabilities
- Creating/Deleting a vSphere Standard Switch
- Adding/Editing/Removing vmics on a vSphere Standard Switch
- Adding/Editing/Removing Port Groups on a vSphere Standard Switch
- Configuring VMkernel Ports for Network Services
- Determining Use Cases for a vSphere Standard Switch

In our discussion on vSphere networking, I address many topics, such as vSphere standard switches (vSS) capabilities, creating and configuring vSphere standard switches, and adding, configuring, and removing vmnics and port groups on vSphere standard switches. In addition, you walk through the steps to configure each of these settings.

## CHAPTER 4

# Configuring vSphere Standard Switches

To keep from becoming overwhelmed with the technology, you should focus on two primary questions. The first question is, "What types of connections can I create, and what do they do?" The second is, "Where does the 'virtual world' meet the 'physical world,' and how is that point of reference defined?" If you focus on these two questions, the rest of the picture will come to your mind.

## "Do I Know This Already?" Quiz

The "Do I Know This Already?" quiz allows you to assess whether you should read this entire chapter or simply jump to the "Exam Preparation Tasks" section for review. If you are in doubt, read the entire chapter. Table 4-1 outlines the major headings in this chapter and the corresponding "Do I Know This Already?" quiz questions. You can find the answers in Appendix A, "Answers to the 'Do I Know This Already?' Quizzes and Chapter Review Questions."

**Table 4-1** "Do I Know This Already?" Section-to-Question Mapping

| Foundation Topics Section | Questions Covered in This Section |
| --- | --- |
| VSphere Standard Switch (vSS) Capabilities | 1, 3 |
| Creating/Deleting a vSphere Standard Switch | 4 |
| Adding/Editing/Removing vmnics on a vSphere Standard Switch | 5, 6 |
| Configuring VMkernel Ports for Network Services | 2, 7, 8 |
| Adding/Configuring/Removing Port Groups on a vSphere Standard Switch | 9 |
| Determining Use Cases for a vSphere Standard Switch | 10 |

1. Which of the following are *not* true about port groups on a vSS? (Choose two.)

    a. You can add a new VMkernel port to an existing switch.

    b. You can add a new VM port to an existing switch.

    c. You can have only one port group on each switch.

    d. You always need to assign a vmnic to a port group.

2. Which of the following is *not* a common use or configuration of a VMkernel port?

    a. IP storage

    b. Storage vMotion

    c. vMotion

    d. Management

3. Which of the following is true about switch and port group policies on a vSS?

    a. Switch settings override port group settings.

    b. You cannot configure port group settings different from switch settings.

    c. There are no switch settings on a vSS.

    d. Port group settings override switch settings for the VMs on the port group.

4. Which of the following are true regarding the creation of a new vSS?

    a. You should use the Add Host Networking link within Virtual Switches on the menu.

    b. You cannot create more than one vSS on a host.

    c. You should create a new vSS for each VM port group.

    d. You might be able to use a new VM port group instead of a new vSS.

5. Which of the following is another name for a vmnic?

    a. vnic

    b. Adapter

    c. Port group

    d. Switch

**6.** Which of the following are physical aspects of a vmnic that you can configure? (Choose two.)

    **a.** Speed

    **b.** VLAN

    **c.** Duplex

    **d.** Port group

**7.** Which of the following is *not* a reason to use a VMkernel port?

    **a.** vMotion

    **b.** Storage vMotion

    **c.** VSAN

    **d.** IP Storage

**8.** Which of the following are reasons to use a VMkernel port? (Choose two.)

    **a.** Fault-tolerant logging

    **b.** VSAN

    **c.** Storage vMotion

    **d.** HA

**9.** Which of the following are *not* true regarding port groups on a vSphere standard switch? (Choose two.)

    **a.** Switch configuration supersedes port group configuration.

    **b.** You can have only one port group on each switch.

    **c.** You cannot create a port group within a port group.

    **d.** Port group configuration supersedes switch configuration.

**10.** What is the minimum license requirement for creating a vDS?

    **a.** Enterprise Plus

    **b.** Enterprise

    **c.** Standard

    **d.** Essentials Plus

## Foundation Topics

# vSphere Standard Switch (vSS) Capabilities

A vSphere standard switch (vSS) is a logical construct within one ESXi host that connects virtual machines (VMs) to other VMs on the same switch. In addition, using connections called uplinks, it can connect VMs to other virtual or physical machines on other ESX/ESXi hosts, other vSSs in the same host, or anywhere in the physical environment.

A vSS models a simple Layer 2 switch that provides networking for the VMs connected to it. It can direct traffic between VMs on the switch as well as link them to external networks. Figure 4-1 shows a diagram of a vSS. (I would take a picture of one for you, but they exist only in a software state!) Note that there are actually two VMkernel ports on the vSS in this ESXi host. One is for management (management network), and the other is for other purposes described later in this section.

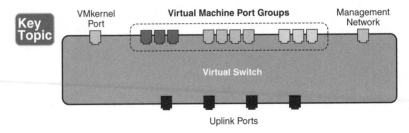

**Figure 4-1**   A Diagram of a vSphere Standard Switch

As mentioned earlier, a vSS models an Ethernet Layer 2 switch on which a virtual machine network interface card (vNIC) can connect to its port and thereby be connected to other machines on the same switch, or off the switch by way of an uplink to the physical world. Each uplink adapter also uses a port on a vSS. As suggested earlier, one of the main questions to ask yourself is, "What types of connections can I create?" The next section discusses connections on vSSs.

You can create two main types of connections on vSSs: VMkernel ports and VM port groups. The difference between these two types of connections is dramatic. It is important to understand how each type of connection is used.

VMkernel ports are used to connect the VMkernel to external services that it controls. They should not be confused with VMkernel itself, which is the embedded hypervisor that is part of the ESXi software on the host. There is only one VMkernel on an ESXi host, but there can be many VMkernel ports. In fact, it is best practice to use a separate VMkernel port for each type of external communication that the VMkernel requires. The six main types of VMkernel communication from a vSS that require the use of a VMkernel port are as follows:

- **IP storage:** iSCSI or networked-attached storage (NAS). (Chapter 7, "Connecting Shared Storage Devices to vSphere," covers these in more detail.)

- **vMotion:** A VMkernel port is required and a separate network is highly recommended. (Chapter 17, "Migrating Virtual Machines," covers vMotion in more detail.)

- **Management:** Because ESXi does not have a service console or service console ports, management is performed through a specially configured VMkernel port. This includes provisioning traffic settings as well.

- **Fault-tolerant logging:** A feature in vSphere that allows a high degree of hardware fault tolerance for the VMs involved, but also requires a separate and distinct VMkernel port. (Chapter 15, "Planning and Implementing VMware Fault Tolerance," covers fault-tolerant logging in greater detail.)

- **VSAN:** Virtual storage-area network (VSAN) is a new type of storage that is available only on vSphere 5.5 and later. It leverages the capacity of the local drives to create a flexible storage area. VSAN is discussed in more detail in Chapter 8, "Configuring Software-Defined Storage," but for now you should understand that it uses a VMkernel port.

- **vSphere Replication:** vSphere Replication is a service that is included with most license levels of vSphere (Essentials Plus and higher) that provides a second copy of a VM at an alternate location for the purpose of disaster recovery. See Chapter 18, "Backing Up and Restoring Virtual Machines," for more information.

The second type of port, the VM port group, is used ly to connect VMs to the virtual switches. These ports are primarily a Layer 2 connection that does not require any configuration other than a label to identify a port group, such as Production. A VLAN can be configured on a port group, but that is optional. You can have multiple VM port groups on a single switch and use them to establish different policies, such as security, outbound traffic shaping, and NIC teaming for various types of VMs.

## Creating/Deleting a vSphere Standard Switch

The first question you might want to ask yourself is, "Do I really need a new vSS?" The answer to this question might not be as straightforward as you think. You do not necessarily need a new vSS for every new port or group of ports, because you can also add components to the vSS that you already have. In fact, you might make better use of your resources by adding to a vSS that you already have instead of creating a new one. The section "Adding/Configuring/Removing Port Groups on a vSphere Standard Switch," discusses the power of using port groups and policies. In this section, you learn how to create a new vSS and how to delete a vSS that you no longer require.

For example, if you want to use the Web Client to create a new vSS for a VMkernel port used for vMotion, follow the steps outlined in Activity 4-1.

### Activity 4-1   Creating a New vSphere Standard Switch

1. Log on to your Web Client.

2. Select **Home** and then **Hosts and Clusters**.

3. Select the ESX host on which you want to create the new vSS, and then click **Manage** and then **Networking**.

4. Select the first option in the blue area, **Virtual Switches**.

5. In the upper-left area, click the **Add Host Networking** link, as shown in Figure 4-2.

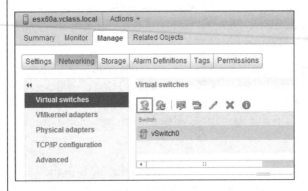

**Figure 4-2**   The Add Host Networking Link on a vSS

**6.** Choose the connection type. In this case, choose to create a VMkernel Network Adapter, as shown in Figure 4-3, and click **Next**.

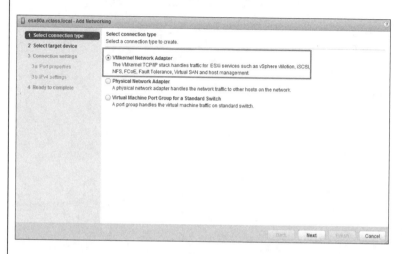

**Figure 4-3** Selecting the VMkernel Connection Type

**7.** Choose **New Standard Switch** and click **Next**, as shown in Figure 4-4.

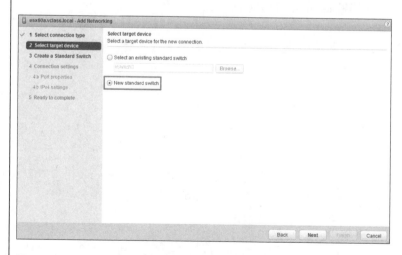

**Figure 4-4** Selecting to Create a New Switch

8. Click the Add Adapters link **+** under Assigned adapters, as shown in Figure 4-5, and click **Next**.

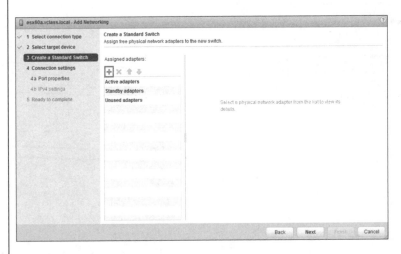

**Figure 4-5** The Add Adapters Link

9. Choose the network adapter (vmnic) that you will assign to this VMkernel port, and click **OK**, as shown in Figure 4-6.

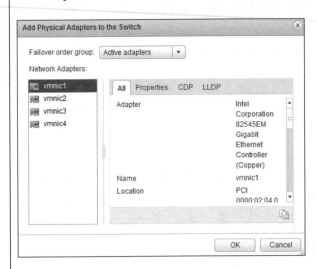

**Figure 4-6** Selecting an Adapter

**10.** Review the properties of the adapter that you have assigned, and then click **Next**, as shown in Figure 4-7.

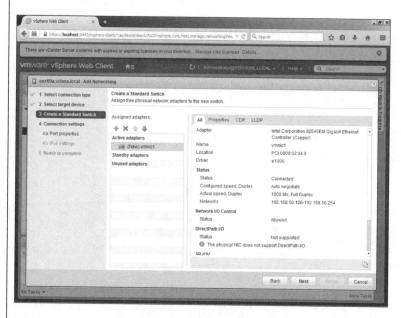

**Figure 4-7**    Reviewing the Network Properties of the Link

**11.** Type a Network label for the VMkernel port; in this case, use vMotion. Then assign a VLAN ID(optional), TCP/IP stack, and Available services; in this case, select to use this for **vMotion traffic**, as shown in Figure 4-8.

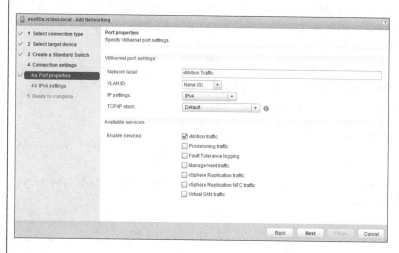

**Figure 4-8**    Assigning a Network Label and Available Services

12. Assign an IP address to the port, or use DHCP to assign, as shown in Figure 4-9.

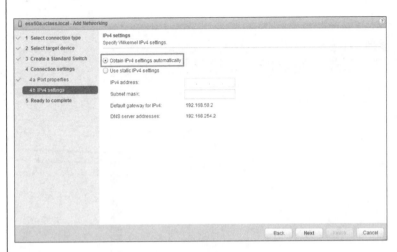

**Figure 4-9**   Assigning an IP Address

13. Review your settings, and select **Finish**.

### Deleting a vSphere Standard Switch

There might come a time when you no longer require a vSS that you have in your inventory. For example, you might have chosen to upgrade to a vSphere distributed switch (vDS), or you are changing the networking on each of the hosts to provide consistency across the hosts, which is a very good idea. In this case, follow the steps outlined in Activity 4-2.

**Activity 4-2   Deleting a vSphere Standard Switch**

1. Log on to your vSphere Web Client.

2. Select **Home** and then **Hosts and Clusters**.

3. Select the ESX host on which you want to delete the vSS.

4. Click **Manage** and then **Networking**, and then in the blue area below, select **Virtual Switches**.

5. Click the switch that you want to remove (in this case, remove vSwitch4), and then on the **Remove Selected Standard Switch** link, as shown in Figure 4-10.

**Figure 4-10**   Deleting a vSphere Standard Switch

6. Click **Yes** to confirm the removal of the switch.

## Adding/Editing/Removing vmnics on a vSphere Standard Switch

As mentioned earlier, you might not want to create a new vSwitch every time you need a new connection. In fact, you will make better use of your resources by adding to a current switch, thereby leveraging port groups and NIC teaming. In this section, you learn how to add new vmnics (also called adapters) to a switch that you already have. You also learn how to remove a vmnic from a switch if you no longer require it.

To add a new vmnic to an existing switch, you should follow the steps in Activity 4-3.

**Activity 4-3   Adding a vmnic to a Switch**

1. Log on to your vSphere Web Client.

2. Select **Home** and then **Hosts and Clusters**.

3. Select the ESX host on which you would like to edit the vSS.

4. Click **Manage** and then **Networking**, and then in the blue area below, select **Virtual Switches**.

5. Click the **Add Host Networking** link, select **Physical Network Adapter**, and click **Next.**

6. On the Select Target Device dialog box, choose **Select an Existing Switch,** and if necessary, select **Browse** to locate the switch, as shown in Figure 4-11.

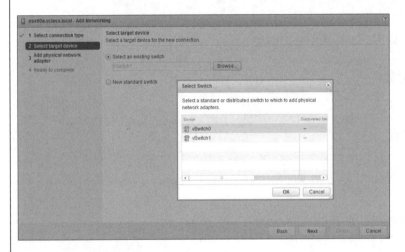

**Figure 4-11**    Selecting the Target Device

7. Click the Add Adapters link **+** and select the vmnic that you want to add, as shown in Figure 4-12.

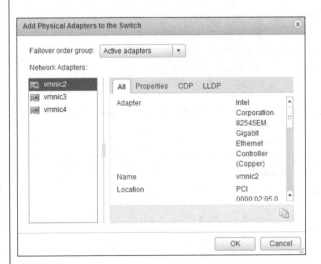

**Figure 4-12**    The Add Adapters Link

**8.** Review your settings and properties and then select **Next**, as shown in Figure 4-13. Click **OK**.

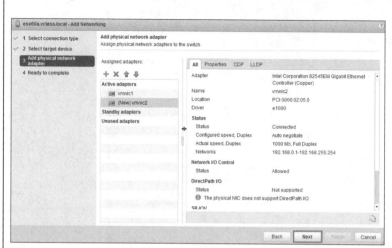

**Figure 4-13**   Reviewing vmnic Settings

**9.** Select **Finish** to complete the addition of the new vmnic on the switch.

Sometimes you will need to change the settings of a vmnic that you have already configured for a vSS. For example, you might want to edit the physical configuration, such as the speed and duplex settings, to match those of a physical switch to which your ESXi host is connected. To edit the physical configuration of the vmnic, follow the steps outlined in Activity 4-4.

**Activity 4-4   Configuring the Physical Aspects of a vmnic**

**1.** Log on to your vSphere Web Client.

**2.** Select **Home** and then **Hosts and Clusters**, as shown in Figure 4-14.

**Figure 4-14**    Hosts and Clusters in the Web Client

   **3.** Select the ESXi host on which you want to edit the vSS.

   **4.** Click **Manage** and then **Networking**, and then in the blue area below, select **Virtual Switches**.

   **5.** Click the virtual switch that contains the vmnic that you want to configure, and click the vmnic that you want to configure, as shown in Figure 4-15.

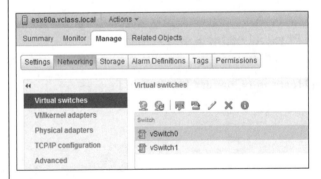

**Figure 4-15**    Choosing the vmnic

6. Click the **Edit Adapter Settings** link that looks like a pencil, as shown in Figure 4-16. Choose the speed and duplex setting for the vmnic and click **OK**.

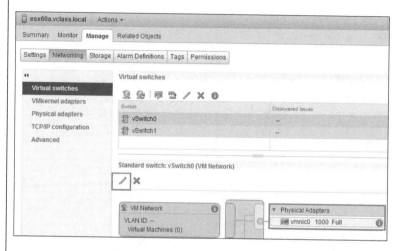

**Figure 4-16**   The Edit Adapter Settings Link

There might come a time when you need to remove a vmnic from a switch. This might happen if you are changing network settings to provide consistency or if you intend to use the vmnic on a new switch. If you need to remove a vmnic from a vSS, follow the steps outlined in Activity 4-5.

**Activity 4-5   Removing a vmnic from a vSphere Standard Switch**

1. Log on to your vSphere Web Client.

2. Select **Home** and then **Hosts and Clusters**.

3. Select the ESX host on which you want to remove the vmnic.

4. Click **Manage** and then **Networking**, and then in the blue area below, click **Virtual Switches**.

5. Select the virtual switch on which it is connected, and click the **Manage the Physical Adapters Connected to the Selected Switch** link, as shown in Figure 4-17. Then select the vmnic that you want to remove and click the **Remove Selected** link, as shown in Figure 4-18.

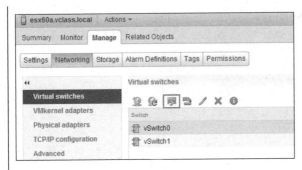

**Figure 4-17**   The Manage the Physical Adapters Connected to the Selected Switch Link

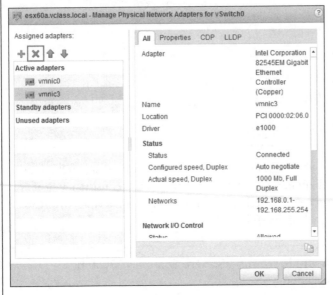

**Figure 4-18**   Removing the vmnic from the vSwitch

# Configuring VMkernel Ports for Network Services

As mentioned earlier, you would create a VMkernel port for six main reasons:

- Management
- IP storage
- Fault-tolerant logging
- VSAN
- vMotion
- vSphere Replication

Each of these is discussed in greater detail in later chapters, but for now, you should understand that they all share the same configuration requirements for network services (namely, an IP address and subnet mask). In addition, you should know that all VMkernel ports share the same default gateway of their IP stack in 5.5 and earlier, but vSphere 6 contains a separate IP stack for vMotion, as discussed in Chapter 17, "Migrating Virtual Machines." You might also want to configure a VLAN, and you will want to enable the port with the services for which it was created (such as vMotion, management, or fault-tolerant logging).

To configure a VMkernel port with network services, you should configure the IP settings of the port group to which it is assigned. Port group configuration is covered in greater detail later in this chapter. For now, if you want to configure the IP settings of a VMkernel port, follow the steps outlined in Activity 4-6.

---

**Activity 4-6    Configuring a VMkernel Port for Network Services**

1. Log on to your vSphere Web Client.

2. Select **Home** and then **Hosts and Clusters**.

3. Select the ESX host on which you want to configure the VMkernel port.

4. Click **Manage** and then **Networking**, and then in the blue area below, select **Virtual switches**.

5. Select the switch that contains the VMkernel port that you want to configure, and then select the VMkernel port, as shown in Figure 4-19.

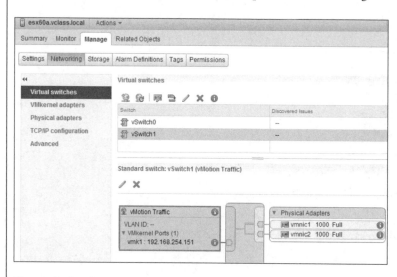

**Figure 4-19**    Selecting the VMkernel Port

6. Click the **Edit Settings** icon that looks like a pencil, and then configure the network settings such as Properties, Security, Traffic Shaping, and Teaming and Failover, as shown in Figure 4-20. You can also configure a VLAN, as shown in Figure 4-21.

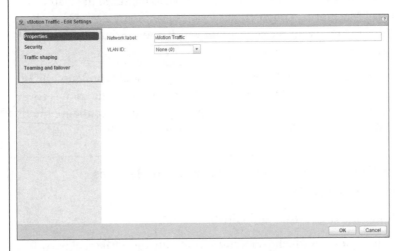

**Figure 4-20** Editing Network Settings on VMkernel Port

**Figure 4-21** Editing VLAN Settings on VMkernel Port

7. Click **OK** to save your settings.

# Adding/Configuring/Removing Port Groups on a vSphere Standard Switch

The main reason to use port groups is to get more than one function out of each switch. This is possible because port group configuration supersedes switch configuration. Because of this, you can have policies for security, traffic shaping, NIC teaming, and so on that apply to the switch, but you can also have a separate policy for each that applies to any port group on which the settings differ from those of the switch. This tremendously improves your flexibility and gives you additional security options. In this section, you learn about adding, editing, and removing port groups on a vSS.

Suppose you decide to add a new group of VMs on which you will test software and monitor performance. Furthermore, suppose you decide that you will not create a new switch, but that you will instead add the VMs to a switch that you already have in your inventory. However, suppose the VMs that are already on the switch are not for testing and development, but are actually in production. Chances are good that you do not want to "mix them in" with the new testing VMs, but how can you keep them separate without creating a new vSS?

If you create a new port group and assign a different vmnic to it, you can manage the new testing VMs separately from the production VMs, even though they are both on the same vSS. In this case, you might want to label your existing port group Production and label your new port group Test-Dev. It does not matter what label you use, but it is a best practice to relate it to the function of the port group, which is generally related to the function of the VMs that will be on it. Also, you should strive for consistency across all your ESXi hosts in a small organization or at least across all the hosts in the same cluster in a medium-sized or large organization. (Chapter 5, "Configuring vSphere Distributed Switches," covers clusters in greater detail.)

So, what was the purpose of all of that labeling? Well, after you have done that, you have settings for each port group that apply only to that port group. You can make important changes to port group policies, such as security, traffic shaping, and NIC teaming, that will override any settings on the vSS properties tabs. Details of these port group policies are covered later in Chapter 6, "Configuring vSS and vDS Features." For now, if you want to add a new VM port group to an existing vSS, follow the steps outlined in Activity 4-7.

**Activity 4-7   Adding a Port Group to a vSphere Standard Switch**

1. Log on to your vSphere Web Client.

2. Select **Home** and then **Hosts and Clusters**.

3. Select the ESX host on which you want to add the port group.

4. Click **Manage** and then **Networking**, and in the blue area below, select the vSwitch on which you want to add the port group.

5. Click the **Add Host Networking** link and then **Virtual Machine Port Group for a Standard Switch**, and click **Next**, as shown in Figure 4-22.

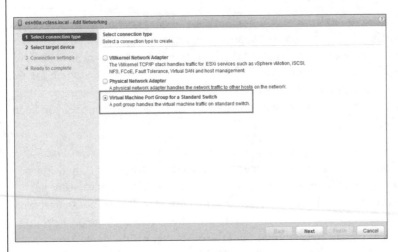

**Figure 4-22**   Adding a New Port Group to a vSS

6. Leave the selection on the vSwitch that you have chosen and click **Next**.

7. Enter the label that you want to use (such as Test-Dev) and the VLAN if you are using a VLAN, as shown in Figure 4-23. Click **Next**.

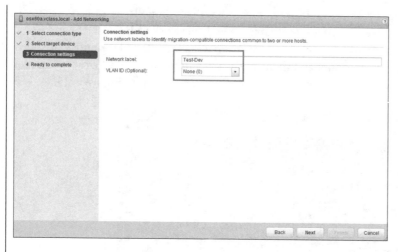

**Figure 4-23**    Entering a Network Label

8. On the Ready to Complete page, review your configuration settings and click **Finish**.

Your new port group should appear on your vSwitch. This new port group is now completely configurable. Just click the **Edit Settings** icon that looks like a pencil and configure the security, traffic shaping, and NIC teaming as you need, as shown in Figure 4-24. The configuration of port group policies is covered in detail in Chapter 6.

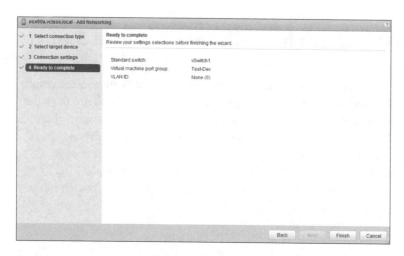

**Figure 4-24**    Port Group Configuration

Finally, you might want to remove a port group that you no longer need. This might happen because you are reorganizing your network or because you are no longer using the VMs to which the port group was associated. To remove the port group, click the port group, and then click the **Remove Selected Port Group** icon (the red X), and confirm your selection to remove, as shown in Figure 4-25.

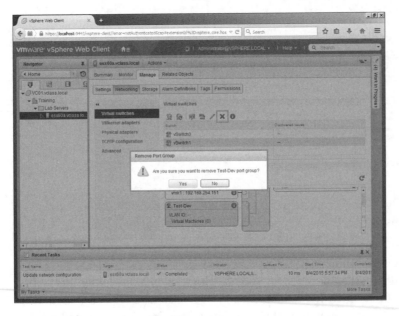

**Figure 4-25**   Removing a Port Group

# Determining Use Cases for a vSphere Standard Switch

Now that you have seen how you would create and manage a vSS, let's talk about why you would want one in the first place. In other words, what would cause you to use a vSS instead of a vDS? One practical reason might be that you do not have the appropriate license to use a vDS. As discussed in Chapter 1, "Identifying vSphere Architecture and Solutions," creating a vDS typically requires an Enterprise Plus license. Another reason might be that you have a small- to medium-size organization, and therefore, the settings on a vSS are sufficient for your needs. Your organization can have many hosts, and those hosts can communicate to each other using vSSs.

The main point to consider is how you can keep the networking that is inside of each ESXi host consistent with the networking that is inside the other hosts, or at least all the hosts in the same cluster. If possible, you should have the same number of vSSs in each of your hosts and the same port groups on each of them (at least the ones that are in the same clusters). In fact, even the consistent spelling of the port group names is important. In addition, to leverage the power of port groups, you should have as few vSSs on each host as possible while still maintaining consistency across the hosts. If you balance these two factors in your organization as much as possible, you will be on the right track.

## Exam Preparation Tasks

## Review All the Key Topics

Review the most important topics from the chapter, noted with the Key Topic icon in the outer margin of the page. Table 4-2 lists these key topics and the page numbers where each is found. Know the capabilities of a vSS and how to configure it's port groups. Understand how to create, configure, edit, and delete these components and policies.

**Table 4-2**  Key Topics for Chapter 4

| Key Topic Element | Description | Page Number |
|---|---|---|
| Figure 4-1 | A Diagram of a vSphere Standard Switch | 54 |
| Bullet List | Uses of VMkernel Ports | 55 |
| Activity 4-1 | Creating a New vSphere Standard Switch | 56 |
| Activity 4-2 | Deleting a vSphere Standard Switch | 60 |
| Activity 4-3 | Adding a vmnic to a Switch | 61 |
| Activity 4-4 | Configuring the Physical Aspects of a vmnic | 63 |
| Activity 4-5 | Removing a vmnic from a vSphere Standard Switch | 65 |
| Activity 4-6 | Configuring a VMkernel Port for Network Services | 67 |
| Activity 4-7 | Adding a Port Group to a vSphere Standard Switch | 70 |

## Review Questions

The answers to these review questions are in Appendix A.

1. Which of the following is *not* a valid use for a VMkernel port?

   a. IP storage

   b. vMotion

   c. FT logging

   d. Storage vMotion

2. Which of the following are types of connections on a vSS on an ESXi host? (Choose two.)

   a. Service console

   b. VM port groups

   c. Host bus adapter

   d. VMkernel ports

3. Which of the following is true about switch and port group policies on a vSS?

   a. Switch settings override port group settings.

   b. You cannot configure port group settings different from switch settings.

   c. There are no switch settings on a vSS.

   d. Port group settings override switch settings for the VMs on the port group.

4. Which of the following are true regarding the creation of a new vSS?

   a. You should use the Add Host Networking link within Virtual Switches on the menu.

   b. You cannot create more than one vSS on a host.

   c. You should create a new vSS for each VM port group.

   d. You might be able to use a new VM port group instead of a new vSS.

5. Which of the following is another name for a vmnic?

   a. vnic

   b. Physical nic

   c. Port group

   d. Switch

**6.** Which of the following are *not* physical aspects of a vmnic? (Choose two.)

    **a.** Speed

    **b.** VLAN

    **c.** Duplex

    **d.** Port group

**7.** Which of the following is a reason to use a VMkernel port?

    **a.** vMotion

    **b.** Storage vMotion

    **c.** HA

    **d.** Fibre channel storage

**8.** Which of the following are reasons to use a VMkernel port? (Choose two.)

    **a.** Fault-tolerant logging

    **b.** VSAN

    **c.** Storage vMotion

    **d.** HA

**9.** Which of the following are true regarding port groups on a vSphere standard switch? (Choose two.)

    **a.** Switch configuration supersedes port group configuration.

    **b.** You can have only one port group on each switch.

    **c.** You cannot create a port group within a port group.

    **d.** Port group configuration supersedes switch configuration.

**10.** What is the minimum license requirement for creating a vSS?

    **a.** Enterprise Plus

    **b.** Enterprise

    **c.** Standard

    **d.** Essentials

**This chapter covers the following subjects:**

- vSphere Distributed Switch Capabilities
- Creating/Deleting a vSphere Distributed Switch
- Adding/Removing ESXi Hosts from a vSphere Distributed Switch
- Adding/Configuring/Removing dvPort Groups
- Adding/Removing Uplink Adapters to dvUplink Groups
- Configuring vSphere Distributed Switch General and dvPort Group Settings
- Creating/Configuring/Removing Virtual Adapters
- Migrating Virtual Adapters to/from a vSphere Standard Switch
- Migrating Virtual Machines to/from a vSphere Standard Switch
- Configuring LACP on Uplink Port Groups
- Determining Use Cases for a vSphere Distributed Switch

Now that you understand what a virtual switch does and that consistency of configuration is a key component, what if I were to tell you that there is a way to guarantee consistency by associating a virtual switch to more than one host at the same time? That's what a vDS does.

## CHAPTER 5

# Configuring vSphere Distributed Switches

A vDS is the same as a vSS in many ways, except that it can be connected to more than one host at the same time, which makes a radical difference. I know what you're thinking: "Is it similar to a vSS or radically different?" Well, in a word, "Yes." It's similar in that it uses the same types of connections (namely, VMkernel ports and VM port groups). It's also similar in that the point at which the virtual world meets the physical world is an important thing to know and understand. However, it's radically different because it is managed centrally in the vCenter and can be connected to multiple hosts at the same time. In fact, a single vSphere 6.0 vDS can be connected to as many as 1,000 hosts. Because of this difference, vDSs come with a whole new set of terms to understand.

In this section, I discuss the capabilities of a vDS, along with creating and deleting a vDS and adding and removing ESXi hosts. In addition, this section covers adding, configuring, and removing dvPort groups and dvUplinks (new terms in vDSs). A vDS also has virtual adapters just like a vSS, except that they can be connected to more than one host. You learn about creating, configuring, migrating, and removing virtual adapters, as well as migrating VMs to and from a vDS. In addition, you learn how to determine a use case for a vSphere distributed switch.

## "Do I Know This Already?" Quiz

The "Do I Know This Already?" quiz allows you to assess whether you should read this entire chapter or simply jump to the "Exam Preparation Tasks" section for review. If you are in doubt, read the entire chapter. Table 5-1 outlines the major headings in this chapter and the corresponding "Do I Know This Already?" quiz questions. You can find the answers in Appendix A, "Answers to the 'Do I Know This Already?' Quizzes and Chapter Review Questions."

**Table 5-1**  "Do I Know This Already?" Section-to-Question Mapping

| Foundation Topics Section | Questions Covered in This Section |
|---|---|
| vSphere Distributed Switch Capabilities | 2 |
| Creating/Deleting a vSphere Distributed Switch | 1 |
| Adding/Removing ESXi Hosts from a vSphere Distributed Switch | 3 |
| Adding/Configuring/Removing dvPort Groups | 4 |
| Adding/Removing Uplink Adapters to dvUplink Groups | 5 |
| Configuring vSphere Distributed Switch General and dvPort Group Settings | 10 |
| Creating/Configuring/Removing Virtual Adapters | 7 |
| Migrating Virtual Adapters to/from a vSphere Standard Switch | 8 |
| Migrating Virtual Machines to/from a vSphere Standard Switch | 9 |
| Configuring LACP on Uplink Port Groups | 5 |
| Determining Use Cases for a vSphere Distributed Switch | 6 |

1. Which view should you be in to create a new vDS?

    a. Hosts and Clusters

    b. Networking

    c. VMs and Templates

    d. You can create a vDS in any view.

2. What is the minimum number of hosts that you can connect to a vSphere 6.0 vDS?

    a. 500

    b. 10

    c. 1,000

    d. 1

3. Which is the maximum number of hosts that can be added to a single vDS?

    a. 1,000

    b. 50

    c. 10,000

    d. There is no limit.

**4.** Which of the following is a capability of a vDS but not of a vSS?

    **a.** Outbound traffic shaping

    **b.** Ingress traffic shaping

    **c.** VLAN segmentation

    **d.** NIC teaming

**5.** What is the maximum number of uplinks that you can configure for each LAG on a vDS?

    **a.** 10

    **b.** 100

    **c.** 24

    **d.** 32

**6.** What is the minimum level of licensing required to support a vDS?

    **a.** Enterprise

    **b.** Enterprise Plus

    **c.** Standard

    **d.** Essentials Plus

**7.** Which of the following is *not* a part of the configuration of a VMkernel port?

    **a.** IP address

    **b.** Subnet mask

    **c.** Default gateway

    **d.** DNS address

**8.** What is the minimum number of ports that you can have on a LAG on a vSphere 6.0 vDS?

    **a.** 1

    **b.** 2

    **c.** 32

    **d.** 10

9. Which of the following are valid methods to migrate multiple VMs from a vSS onto a vDS? (Choose two.)

   a. Change the vnic setting for each VM.

   b. Use the Migrate Virtual Machine Wizard.

   c. Storage vMotion

   d. DRS

10. Which of the following can be configured on vDS, but not on a vSS? (Choose two.)

    a. Inbound traffic shaping

    b. Outbound traffic shaping

    c. Private VLANs

    d. NIC teaming

## Foundation Topics

# vSphere Distributed Switch Capabilities

It's likely that you want to know what vDSs can do that vSSs cannot do. In other words, "Why should I consider using one instead of the other?" In fact, a large list of features are specific to a vDS, but to really understand them, you need to see what they both can do and then what only the vDS can do. Table 5-2 illustrates the features that are common between vSSs and vDSs and then those that are unique to vDSs.

**Table 5-2**   vSS Capabilities Versus vDS Capabilities

|  | vSS | vDS |
|---|---|---|
| Layer 2 switch | X | X |
| VLAN segmentation | X | X |
| 802.1Q tagging | X | X |
| NIC teaming | X | X |
| Outbound traffic shaping | X | X |
| Inbound traffic shaping |  | X |
| VM network port block |  | X |
| Private VLANs |  | X |
| Load-based teaming |  | X |
| Data-center-level management |  | X |
| Network vMotion |  | X |
| vSphere switch APIs |  | X |
| Per-port policy settings |  | X |
| Port state monitoring |  | X |
| Link Layer Discovery Protocol (LLDP) |  | X |
| User-defined network I/O control |  | X |
| NetFlow |  | X |
| Port mirroring |  | X |
| Backup, Restore, Export, Import Configuration |  | X |
| LACP |  | X |

The following briefly describes each of the features available on a vDS that are not available on a vSS:

- **Inbound traffic shaping:** A port group setting that can throttle the aggregate bandwidth inbound to the switch. This might be useful for a port group containing VMs that are being used as web servers.

- **VM network port block:** Specific ports can be configured as "blocked" for a specified VM's use. This might be helpful for troubleshooting or for advanced configurations.

- **Private VLANs:** This is a vSphere implementation of a VLAN standard that is available on the latest physical switches. With regard to vSphere, private virtual local-area networks (PVLANs) can be created in the vSphere that are used only in the vSphere and not on your external network. In essence, a PVLAN is a VLAN within a VLAN. In addition, the PVLANs in your vSphere can be kept from seeing each other. Chapter 6, "Configuring vSS and vDS Features," covers PVLANs in greater depth.

- **Load-based teaming:** You can configure network load balancing in a much more intelligent fashion than with vSSs by enabling the system to recognize the current load on each link before making frame forwarding decisions. This could be useful if the loads that are on each link vary considerably over time.

- **Data-center-level management:** A vDS is managed from the vCenter as a single switch from the control plane, even though many hosts are connected to each other at the I/O plane. This provides a centralized control mechanism and guarantees consistency of configuration.

- **Network vMotion:** Because a port group that is on a vDS is connected to multiple hosts, a VM can migrate from one host to another without changing port groups. The positive effect of this is that the attributes assigned to the port group (such as security, traffic shaping, and NIC teaming) migrate as well.

- **vSphere switch APIs:** Third-party switches have been and are being created that can be installed in the control plane. On switches such as the Cisco Nexus 1000v, the true essence of the switch is installed into the vCenter as a virtual appliance (VA).

- **Per-port policy settings:** Most of the configuration on a vDS is at the port group level, but it can be overridden at the individual port level. This allows you tremendous flexibility with regard to port settings such as security, traffic shaping, and so on.

- **Port state monitoring:** Each port on vDS can be managed and monitored independently of all other ports. This means that you can quickly identify an issue that relates to a specific port.

- **Link Layer Discovery Protocol:** Similar to Cisco Discovery Protocol (CDP), Link Layer Discovery Protocol (LLDP) enables vDSs to discover other devices, such as switches and routers, that are directly connected to them. The advantage of LLDP is that it is an open protocol that is not proprietary to Cisco.

- **User-defined network I/O control:** You can set up a quality of service (QoS) (of a sort), but instead of defining traffic paths by protocols, you can define the traffic paths by types of VMware traffic. In earlier versions of vDSs, you could define traffic as vMotion, Management, and others, but now you can define your own categories. This adds to flexibility in network control and design.

- **NetFlow:** You can use the standard for traffic monitoring, NetFlow, to monitor, analyze, and log traffic flows in your vSphere. This enables you to easily monitor virtual network flows with the same tools that you use to monitor traffic flows in the physical network. Your vDS can forward NetFlow information to a monitoring machine in your external network.

- **Port mirroring:** Most commonly used with intrusion detection systems (IDSs) and intrusion prevention systems (IPSs), port mirroring provides for a copy of a packet to be sent to a monitoring station so that traffic flows can be monitored without the IPS/IDS skewing the data. Port mirroring is new to vSphere 5.x and later vDSs.

- **Backup, Restore, Import, Export Configuration:** You can back up a configuration of a vDS so that it can easily be restored later or even exported from one vDS and imported onto another one. This saves time and increases network flexibility.

- **LACP:** Link Aggregation Control Protocol (LACP) allows for the combining of multiple physical links into one logical link for the purposes of fault tolerance and load balancing.

## Creating/Deleting a vSphere Distributed Switch

The first thing to consider if you want to create a vDS is your license level, because, for the most part, they can be created only with an Enterprise Plus license. You probably could create them with the 60-day evaluation license, but you would then need to purchase an Enterprise Plus license before the evaluation period expires; otherwise, your switch would cease to function. You also must consider the level of hosts that you have in the data center onto which you are adding the switch, because this will impact the version of the switch that you create. So, to begin to create a new vDS, follow the steps outlined in Activity 5-1.

**NOTE**  In the first quarter of 2016, VMware allowed that a vSphere Distributed Switch could be created and used with a Standard license and an accompanying NSX license. (See Knowledge Base Article 2135310.) This is an exception to the rule; assume for test purposes that an Enterprise Plus license is required to support a vSphere Distributed Switch, unless you are specifically given information regarding NSX.

## Activity 5-1   Creating a New vSphere Distributed Switch

1. Log on to your vSphere Web Client.

2. Select **Home** and then **Networking**.

3. Right-click your data center and select **Distributed Switch**, and then **New Distributed Switch** as shown in Figure 5-1.

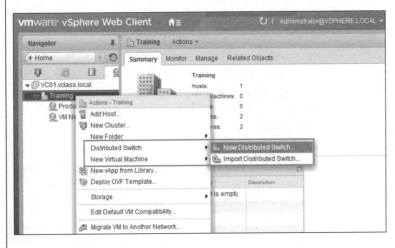

**Figure 5-1**   Creating a New vDS

4. Type the name for your new vDS, as shown in Figure 5-2. Click **Next**.

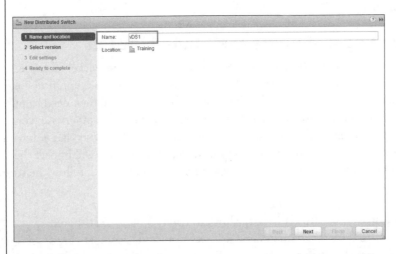

**Figure 5-2**   Naming Your vDS

**5.** Select the version for your new vDS, as shown in Figure 5-3. You should select a version that is compatible with the hosts that will be connected to this switch. Click **Next**.

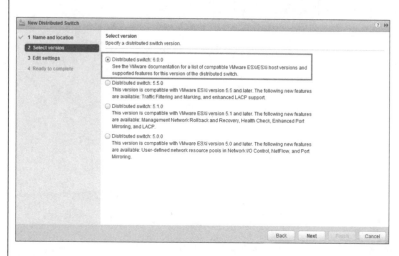

**Figure 5-3**   Selecting the Version for the vDS

**6.** From Edit settings, choose the number of uplinks that you will allow on this switch. (The default is four, but this number can be changed later if needed.) Then choose whether to create a default port group and, if so, what to name it. Finally, choose whether to enable Network I/O control on this switch, as shown in Figure 5-4. Click **Next**.

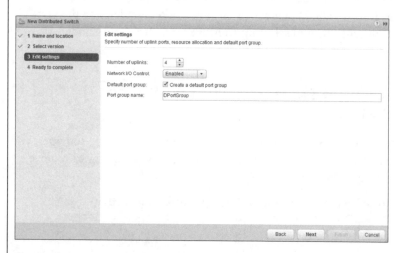

**Figure 5-4**   Settings for the vDS

7.  On the Ready to Complete page, review your configuration settings, as shown in Figure 5-5, and click **Finish**.

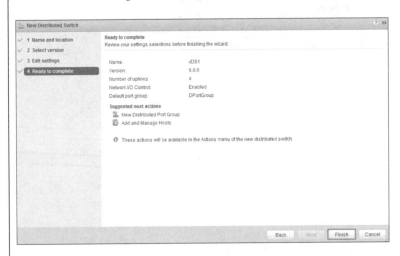

**Figure 5-5**   Reviewing Configuration Settings of a New vDS

### Deleting a vDS

You might assume that deleting a vDS would just be a matter of right-clicking it and selecting to remove it. This is almost true. However, you first need to remove the hosts and the port groups from the vDS. Then you can right-click it and select to remove it. The next two sections cover (among other topics) removing hosts and port groups from a vDS. When you know how to do that, deleting the vDS is as simple as right-clicking and selecting **Remove from Inventory** under All vCenter Actions.

## Adding/Removing ESXi Hosts from a vSphere Distributed Switch

You can add hosts to a vDS after you have created it. In the following activities, you first see how to add a host to an existing vDS, and then you learn how to remove a host from an existing vDS.

To add a host to an existing vDS, follow the steps outlined in Activity 5-2.

### Activity 5-2    Adding a Host to a vSphere Distributed Switch

1. Log on to your vSphere Web Client.

2. Select **Home** and then **Networking**.

3. Right-click the vDS on which you want to add a host, and click **Add and Manage Hosts**, as shown in Figure 5-6.

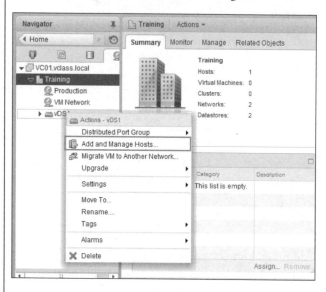

**Figure 5-6**   Adding and Managing Hosts After Creating a vDS

4. Select **Add Hosts**, as shown in Figure 5-7. Click **Next**.

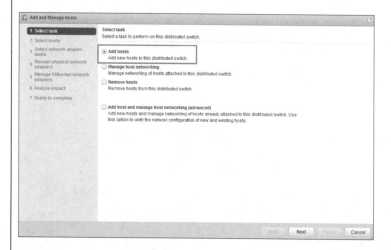

**Figure 5-7**   Selecting Add Hosts

5. Click the New Hosts link **+** and choose from the list of hosts that are compatible with the vDS, as shown in Figure 5-8. Click **OK**, and then click **Next**. Click **Next** again.

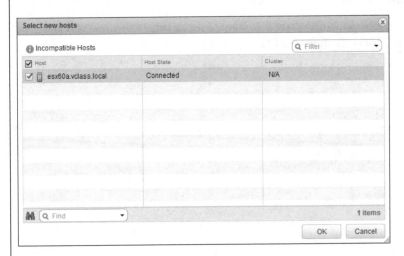

**Figure 5-8**   The New Hosts Link and Selecting Hosts

6. Select to perform any additional network adapter tasks, such as managing physical adapters, managing virtual adapters, migrating virtual machine networking, or even managing advanced legacy host settings, as shown in Figure 5-9. Click **Next**.

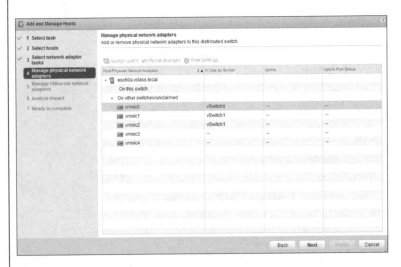

**Figure 5-9**   Additional Network Adapter Tasks

7. If you have chosen to manage physical adapters, select an unclaimed adapter for your switch or take one from a switch that you are not using, click a vmnic, and then the **Assign Uplink** link to assign the adapter, as shown in Figure 5-10. You should be very careful here, but the system will alert you to any negative impact before completing the task. Click **Next**.

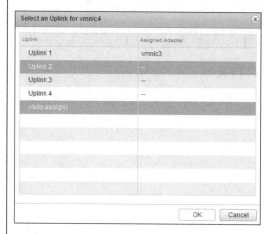

**Figure 5-10**  Assigning an Uplink to a vDS

8. The Analyze impact screen shown in Figure 5-11 will show you any potential issues caused by your configuration changes. (Note that I only added one host for now, but I will create a vDS with more hosts later.) Click **Next**.

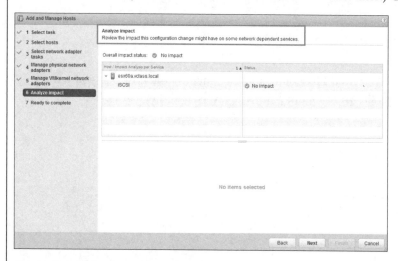

**Figure 5-11**  The Analyze Impact Screen

9. On the Ready to Complete page, review your configuration and click **Finish**.

To remove a host from an existing vDS, follow the steps outlined in Activity 5-3.

**Activity 5-3  Removing a Host from a vSphere Distributed Switch**

1. Log on to your vSphere Web Client.

2. Select **Home** and then **Networking**.

3. Right-click the vDS on which you want to remove a host, and then click **Add and Manage Hosts**.

4. Click **Remove Hosts** and then click **Next**, as shown in Figure 5-12.

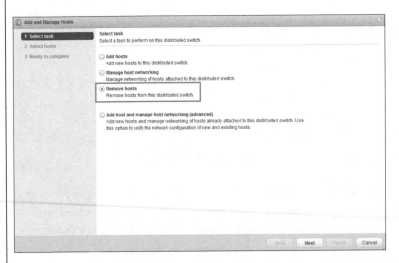

**Figure 5-12**  Removing a Host from a VDS

5. Click the **Attached Hosts** link and then identify the host that you want to remove, as shown in Figure 5-13. Click **OK**, and then click **Next**.

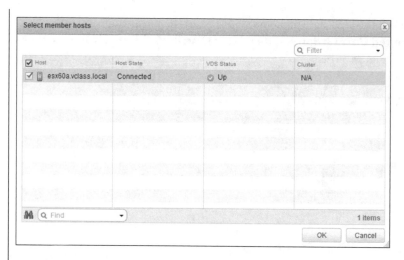

**Figure 5-13**   Removing a Host

6. On the Ready to Complete page, confirm that the number of hosts that you are removing is correct and click **Finish**. (I will leave this host in place, because I'm not done yet.)

## Adding/Configuring/Removing dvPort Groups

As you might remember, port groups allow you to get more than one set of attributes out of the same switch. This is especially true with vDS port groups. The port groups that you create on a vDS are connected to all the hosts to which the vDS is connected; hence, they are called distributed virtual port groups (*dvPort groups*). Because a vSphere 6.0 vDS can be connected to up to 1,000 hosts, the dvPort groups can become very large and powerful. After you create port groups on a vDS, you can migrate your VMs to the dvPort groups. In the following activities, you learn how to add, configure, and remove dvPort groups on vDSs.

To add a port group to a vDS, follow the steps outlined in Activity 5-4.

**Activity 5-4   Adding a Port Group to a vSphere Distributed Switch**

1. Log on to your vSphere Web Client.

2. Select **Home** and then **Networking**.

3. Right-click the vDS on which you want to add the port group and select **Distributed Port Group** and then **New Distributed Port Group**, as shown in Figure 5-14.

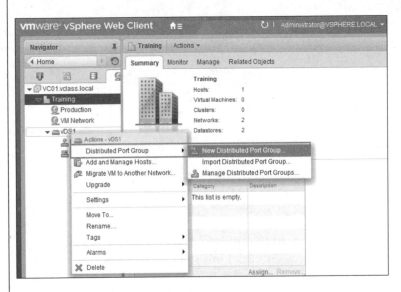

**Figure 5-14**   Adding a Port Group to a vDS

4. Type a name for your new port group that will help you identify the types of VMs that you place on that port group, as shown in Figure 5-15. Click **Next**.

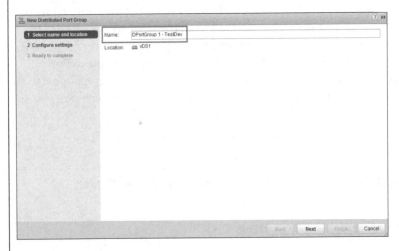

**Figure 5-15**   Naming a dvPort Group

5. Configure the settings for your port group, such as port binding, port allocation, VLAN type, and number of ports (these are discussed in detail later in this chapter), as shown in Figure 5-16. Click **Next**.

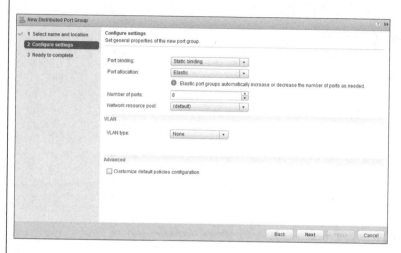

**Figure 5-16**   Configuring Port Group Settings

6. On the Ready to Complete page, confirm your selections by clicking **Finish**.

The next major section discusses configuring port groups in great detail and covers configuring vSS and vDS policies. For now, I will just point out the steps involved in accessing the area in which you can configure the policies of port groups on vDSs. To begin to configure a port group on a vDS, follow the steps outlined in Activity 5-5.

**Activity 5-5   Configuring Port Groups on a vSphere Distributed Switch**

1. Log on to your vSphere Web Client.

2. Select **Home** and then **Networking**.

3. Expand on the vDS on which you want to configure the port group, right-click the port group that you want to configure, and select **Edit Settings**, as shown in Figure 5-17.

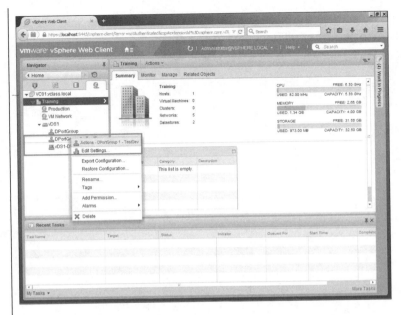

**Figure 5-17** Configuring a dvPort Group

Over time, your networking needs will change, and you might decide to reorganize by removing some port groups. Take care not to "orphan" the VMs by removing the port group while they are still assigned to it. Instead, carefully consider your options and simply migrate the VMs to another port group as part of your plan. Your options with regard to vSS and vDS policies are covered in Chapter 6. For now, I'll just point out how you would go about removing a port group that you no longer need.

To remove a port group that you no longer are using, follow the steps outlined in Activity 5-6.

**Activity 5-6   Removing a Port Group from a vSphere Distributed Switch**

1. Log on to your vSphere Web Client.

2. Select **Home** and then **Networking**.

3. Click the vDS on which you want to remove the port group and expand it so that you can see the dvPort groups. Migrate any vnics of VMs off of the port group.

4. Right-click the port group that you want to remove and select **Delete**, as shown in Figure 5-18.

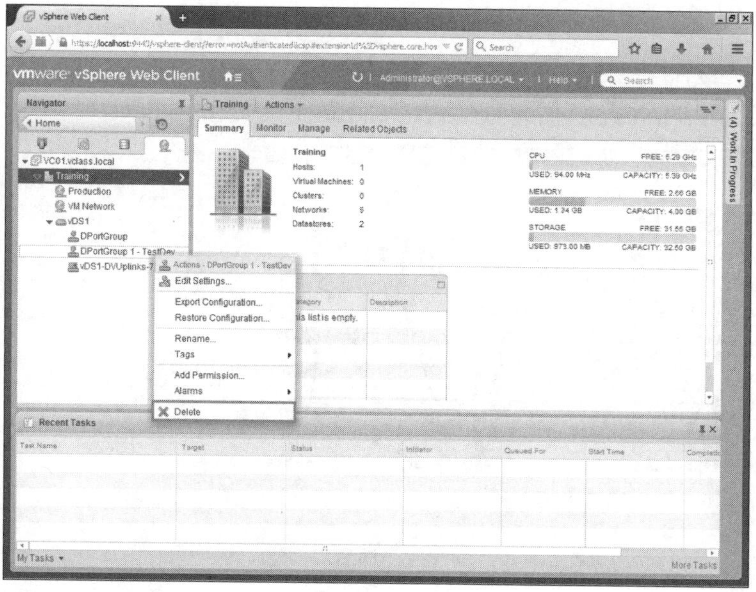

**Figure 5-18**    Removing a dvPort Group

5. Confirm your selection by clicking **Yes**.

## Adding/Removing Uplink Adapters to dvUplink Groups

As shown in Figure 5-19, dvUplink groups connect your vDS to the hidden switches that are contained in your hosts and then from there to the physical world. This allows you to control networking at the control plane on the vDS while the actual input/output (I/O) is still passing from host to host at the I/O plane. Each host keeps its own network configuration in its hidden switch that is created when you add a host to a vDS. This ensures that the network will continue to function, even if your vCenter fails or is not available.

That's a lot of terminology all at once, but as you might remember, I said that one of the main things to understand was where the virtual meets the physical. You should know that the dvUplink groups are virtual, but the uplink adapters lead to physical adapters. Connecting multiple uplink adapters to a dvUplink group opens

up the possibilities of load balancing and fault tolerance, which are discussed in
Chapter 6. For now, I will show you how to add and remove uplink adapters.

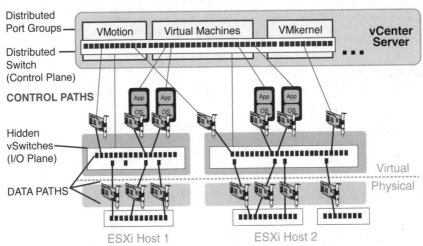

Figure 5-19  Distributed Switch Architecture

To add uplink adapters to a dvUplink group, follow the steps outlined in
Activity 5-7.

**Activity 5-7   Adding an Uplink Adapter to a dvUplink Group**

1. Log on to your vSphere Web Client.

2. Select **Home** and then **Hosts and Clusters**.

3. Select the host on which you want to configure an uplink and then select the
   **Add Host Networking** link.

4. On the Select Connection Type screen, select **Physical Network Adapter**,
   as shown in Figure 5-20.

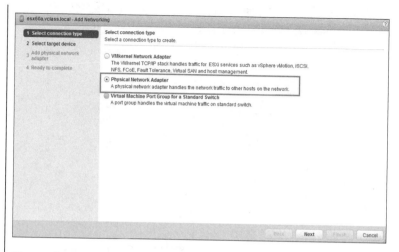

**Figure 5-20**   Selecting a Physical Adapter

5. Click **Browse**, select the vDS to which you want to configure the host uplink, and click **OK**, as shown in Figure 5-21. Click **Next**.

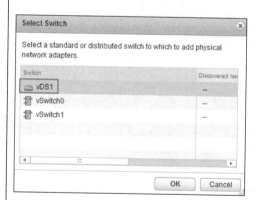

**Figure 5-21**   Selecting the vDS

6. Click the uplink and then on the Add Adapter **+** link and choose the adapter to add, as shown in Figure 5-22. Click **Next**.

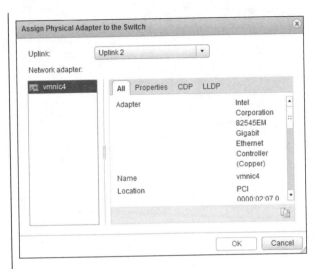

**Figure 5-22**   Adding an Adapter to a vDS

7. Choose an available vmnic and the uplink to which you will assign it, as shown in Figure 5-23. Click **Next**.

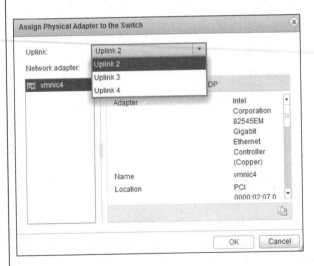

**Figure 5-23**   Choosing the Uplink

8. On the Ready to Complete page, verify your settings, and click **Finish**.

When you reorganize, you might want to remove an uplink from a dvUplink group. Activity 5-8 outlines the process to remove the uplink.

### Activity 5-8 Removing an Uplink Adapter from a dvUplink Group

1. Log on to your vSphere Web Client.

2. Select **Home** and then **Hosts and Clusters**.

3. Select the host on which you want to configure, click **Manage** and then **Networking**, and in the blue area below, click **Virtual Switches.**

4. Select the vDS from which you want to remove the adapter, and click the **Manage the Physical Network Adapters Connected to the Selected Switch** link, as shown in Figure 5-24.

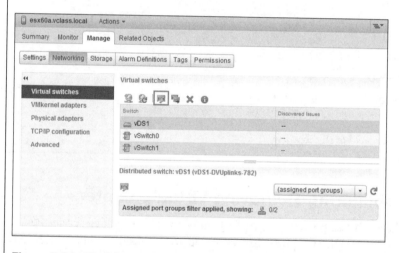

**Figure 5-24** The Manage Physical Network Adapters Link

5. Choose the vmnic that you want to remove, and then click the **Remove Selected Adapters** link (the red X), as shown in Figure 5-25.

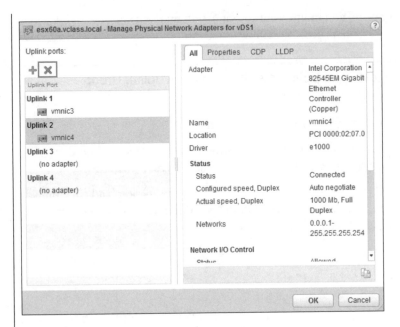

**Figure 5-25**   Removing an Uplink from a vDS

6.  Click **OK** to close the window.

## Creating/Configuring/Removing Virtual Adapters

Prior to vSphere 5.0 and ESXi 5.0, virtual adapters on vDSs included service console ports as well as VMkernel ports. In fact, if you are still using legacy ESX hosts in your virtual data center, you must take into account that they will require a service console port on either a vSS or a vDS, for the purpose of connecting to and managing the switch from the physical world. Because ESXi 5.0 and later hosts do not have service consoles, they also do not have service console ports, so with regard to this topic, I will limit the discussion of virtual adapters to VMkernel ports. This section covers creating, configuring, and removing virtual adapters.

As you might remember, you create VMkernel ports for one of six main reasons: IP storage, management, vMotion, VSAN, vSphere Replication, or FT logging. There is only one VMkernel on the ESXi host, which is the hypervisor, but there can be many VMkernel ports. To create a new VMkernel port on a vDS, you create and configure a VMkernel virtual adapter.

To create a virtual adapter, follow the steps outlined in Activity 5-9.

**Activity 5-9   Creating a Virtual Adapter**

1. Log on to your vSphere Web Client.

2. Select **Home** and then **Hosts and Clusters**.

3. Select the host on which you want to configure a virtual adapter and click **Manage** and then **Networking**.

4. Click the **Add Host Networking** link, and then click **VMkernel Network Adapter**, as shown in Figure 5-26. Click **Next**.

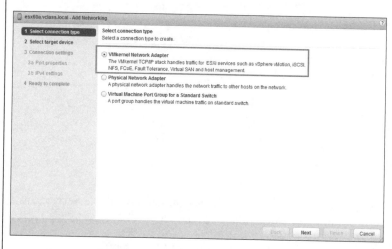

**Figure 5-26**   Adding a VMkernel Adapter

5. On the Add Networking screen, select **Select an Existing Network**, click **Browse**, and then select the vDS and port group on which you want to add the VMkernel port, as shown in Figure 5-27. Click **OK**, and then click **Next**.

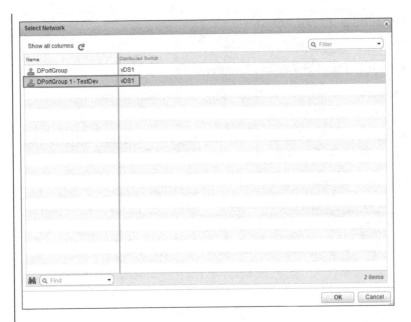

**Figure 5-27**    Selecting an Existing dvPort Group

6. Configure the port properties, such as IP Settings and Available Services, as desired, as shown in Figure 5-28. Click **Next**.

**Figure 5-28**    Configuring Port Properties

7. Configure the IP address or allow one to be configured by DHCP, as shown in Figure 5-29. Click **Next**.

**Figure 5-29**    Configuring the IP Address

8. On the Ready to Complete page, review your settings and click **Finish**.

After you finish configuring it, you can check the setting of your virtual adapter by coming back to **VMkernel Adapters** for the host, as shown in Figure 5-30. To make changes to those configuration settings, you can select the **Edit Settings** link that looks like a pencil and edit the properties of the virtual adapter.

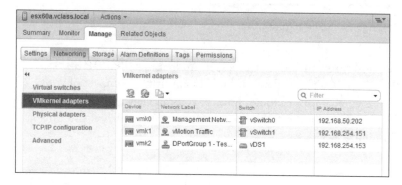

**Figure 5-30**    Viewing Adapter Settings

To configure a virtual adapter, follow the steps outlined in Activity 5-10.

**Activity 5-10    Configuring a Virtual Adapter**

1. Log on to your vSphere Web Client.

2. Select **Home** and then **Hosts and Clusters**.

3. Select the host on which you want to configure a virtual adapter and then select **Manage** and then **Networking**.

4. In the blue area below, select **VMkernel Adapters**.

5. Click the adapter on which you want to edit settings, and click the **Edit Settings** link that looks like a pencil, as shown in Figure 5-31.

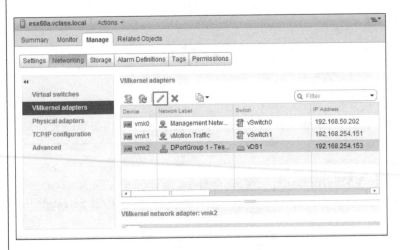

**Figure 5-31**    Configuring VMkernel Adapters

6. Edit settings as desired, including vmnics, IP Addressing, TCP/IP Stacks, and Available Services. You will also be able to confirm the impact of your changes before you commit to them. Finally, you can view and confirm the results of your changes in the **VMkernel Adapters** section when you finish; as shown in Figure 5-32.

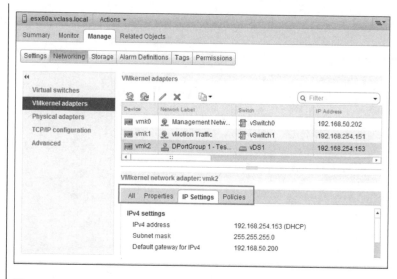

**Figure 5-32**   Confirming Changes to VMkernel Adapters

7. Click **OK** to confirm and save all your changes.

When things change and you no longer need the service that the VMkernel port was providing, you can free up the vmnic by removing it from the virtual adapter.

To remove a vmnic from a VMkernel adapter, follow the steps outlined in Activity 5-11.

---

### Activity 5-11    Removing a VMkernel Adapter

1. Log on to your vSphere Web Client.

2. Select **Home** and then **Hosts and Clusters**.

3. Select the host on which you want to remove a virtual adapter and then select **VMkernel Adapters**.

4. Select the VMkernel adapter that you want to remove, and then click the **Remove Selected Network Adapter** link (the red X), as shown in Figure 5-33.

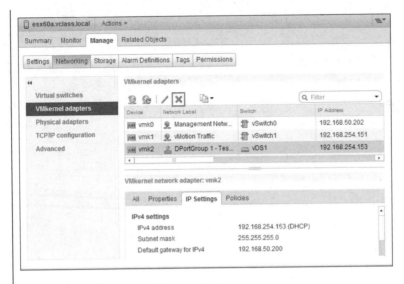

**Figure 5-33**   Removing a Virtual Adapter

5.  Click **Analyze Impact** to be sure that you are not disconnecting a currently used adapter, or click **OK** when you are sure that you want to remove the adapter, as shown in Figure 5-34.

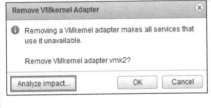

**Figure 5-34**   Analyzing the Impact

## Migrating Virtual Adapters to/from a vSphere Standard Switch

You do not necessarily have to migrate virtual adapters from your vSSs to your vDSs, but you might want to, especially if your ultimate goal is to do away with the vSS altogether. In that case, make sure that all the VMkernel ports that you have been using on your vSSs are successfully migrated to your vDSs. This section shows how you can use the tools provided by the vCenter to easily migrate VMkernel ports from vSSs to vDSs.

To migrate virtual adapters from a vSS to a vDS, follow the steps outlined in
Activity 5-12.

**Activity 5-12    Migrating Virtual Adapters from a vSS to a vDS**

1. Log on to your vSphere Web Client.

2. Select **Home** and then **Hosts and Clusters**.

3. Select the host on which you want to migrate a virtual adapter and click
   **Manage** and then **Networking**.

4. In the blue area below, select **Virtual Switches,** and then select the switch to
   which you want to migrate the virtual adapter.

5. Click the **Migrate Physical or Virtual Adapters to This Distributed
   Switch** link and then choose **Manage VMkernel Adapters**, as shown in
   Figure 5-35. Click **Next**.

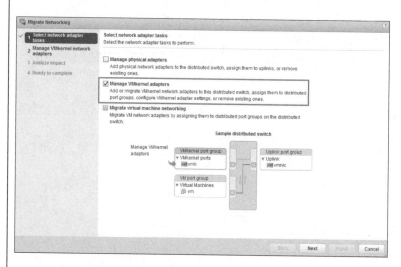

**Figure 5-35**    Migrating Networking

6. Click the VMkernel port that you want to migrate, and then click **Assign
   Port Group**, as shown in Figure 5-36. Click **Next**.

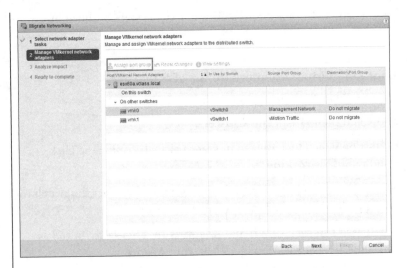

**Figure 5-36**   Choosing the VMkernel Port to Migrate

7.  Select the destination dvPort group on the vDS to which you want to
    migrate the VMkernel port, as shown in Figure 5-37. Click **OK**, and then
    click **Next**.

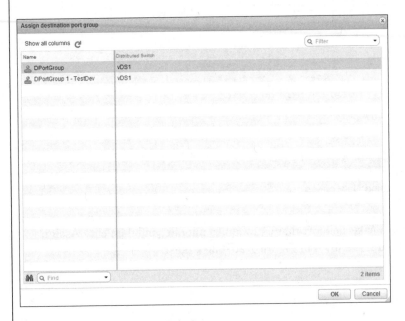

**Figure 5-37**   Choosing a dvPort Group

8. Verify that there is no negative impact. Click **Next**.

9. On the Ready to Complete page, review your settings and then confirm by clicking **Finish**.

## Migrating Virtual Machines to/from a vSphere Standard Switch

As you learned earlier, the purpose of port groups is to get more than one function from a switch. In other words, port groups give you options on which to connect your VMs. You can configure different policies on port groups that are specific to the VMs that you will connect to them. In this regard, port groups on vDSs are no different from those on vSSs; they both give you more options for your VMs.

To help you understand the concept of migrating the VMs from a vSS to a vDS, suppose for a moment that the switches are physical. You walk into your network closet and you have some switches that have been there for years. They are old and noisy, and they have a limited set of features compared to new switches available today. As luck would have it, you received some money in the budget to buy a shiny new switch that has lots of features that the old noisy switches do not have. You have racked the switch and powered it up for testing, and you are now ready to start moving the cables that the computers are using from the old switch to the new switch.

In essence, this is the opportunity that you have when you create a new vDS. You can take advantage of all the new features of vDS, but only after you have moved the VMs over to the vDS. You could do this one at time, much like you would be forced to do in the physical world, but there are tools in vSphere that make it much faster and easier to move multiple VMs at the same time. In this section, you learn how you would move an individual VM from a vSS to a vDS, or vice versa, and then you learn how to use the tools provided by vSphere to move multiple VMs at the same time. In both cases, the focus will be on the VM port group, which you might remember is one of the connection types that are very important.

To migrate a single VM to/from a vDS, follow the steps outlined in Activity 5-13.

### Activity 5-13   Migrating a Single VM to/from a vDS

1. Log on to your vSphere Web Client.

2. Select **Home** and then **Hosts and Clusters**.

3. Right-click the VM that you want to migrate and select **Edit Settings**, as shown in Figure 5-38.

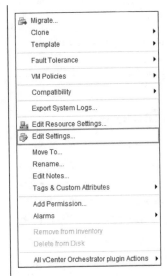

**Figure 5-38**   Migrating a VM to/from a vDS

4. Choose the network adapter that you want to migrate and the Network label (port group) to which you want to migrate it and ensure the **Connected** box is checked, as shown in Figure 5-39.

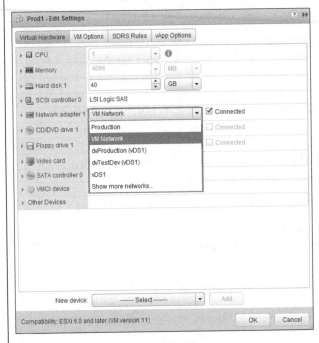

**Figure 5-39**   Choosing the Port Group

5. Click **OK** to confirm and save your settings.

6. If the port group is on a different IP subnet, you might need to release and renew the IP address of the VM or restart the OS.

If you have only a few VMs to move, this might be an attractive option for you and your organization. However, if you have many VMs to move, you might want a better way that will allow you to move many VMs at once.

To migrate multiple VMs from one port group to another simultaneously, follow the steps outlined in Activity 5-14.

**Activity 5-14   Migrating Multiple VMs Using vSphere**

1. Log on to your vSphere Web Client.

2. Select **Home** and then **Networking**.

3. Right-click the vDS to which you want to migrate VMs, and choose **Migrate VM to Another Network**, as shown in Figure 5-40.

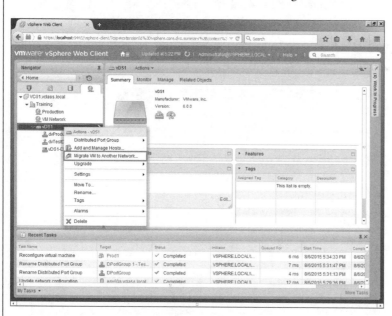

**Figure 5-40**   Migrating Multiple VMs

4. Browse to select the source and destination networks, as shown in Figure 5-41. You can also select **No Network** to pick up the VMs that are not connected to any network. Click **Next**.

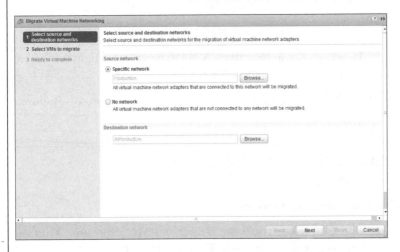

**Figure 5-41** Choosing the Source and Destination

5. Choose the VMs that you want to migrate from the results of the search, as shown in Figure 5-42. Click **Next**.

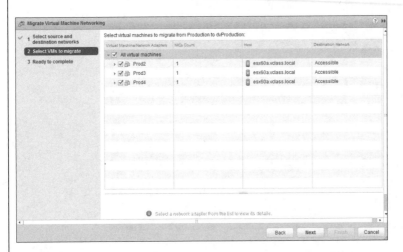

**Figure 5-42** Selecting the VMs to Migrate

**6.** On the Ready to Complete page, review your choices and then confirm by clicking **Finish**, as shown in Figure 5-43.

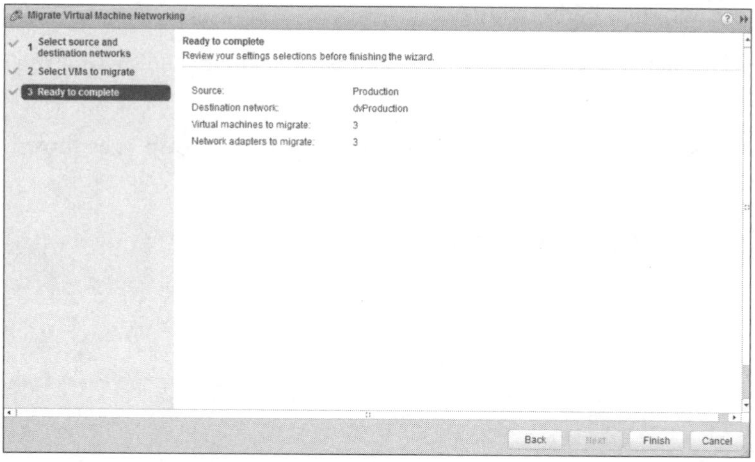

**Figure 5-43**   The Ready to Complete Page

# Configuring LACP on Uplink Port Groups

As previously discussed, you can have more than one vmnic configured for a port group to provide for load balancing and fault tolerance. The options discussed thus far treat each physical link as a separate logical link. For fault tolerance, one link can take the place of another; whereas for load balancing, you use software methods to determine which link is used by each VM for each session.

As an alternative, what if you could combine the bandwidth of several physical links into one logical link for the purposes of providing additional throughput and fault tolerance? The difference is that even if one of the physical links has an issue, the logical link still stays up, albeit with a little less throughput than before. Of course, if you are going to make this work, you have to configure it on both vSphere and on the connecting switches.

With vSphere 5.5 and later, you can set up *link aggregation groups* (LAGs) that connect to switches that support dynamic link aggregation. vSphere 5.1 allowed only one LAG per vDS, but vSphere 5.5 and later allow up to 64 LAGs per vDS, with up to 24 physical ports on each LAG. This gives you a tremendous flexibility, especially if you already have physical switches that support dynamic link aggregation.

To configure LACP on uplink port groups, you should follow the steps outlined in Activity 5-15.

**Activity 5-15   Configuring LACP on Uplink Port Groups**

1. Log on to your vCenter Server through your vSphere Web Client.

2. Click **Home** and then **Networking**.

3. Click the vDS that you want to configure and click **Manage** and then **Settings**.

4. Click **LACP** and then click the **New Link Aggregation Group +**, as shown in Figure 5-44.

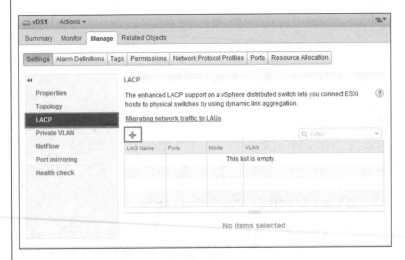

**Figure 5-44**   Creating a New Link Aggregation Group

5. Give your new LAG a name and set the number of ports, mode, and load balancing mode based on the capabilities and settings of the physical switches to which it is connecting, as shown in Figure 5-45. Click **OK.**

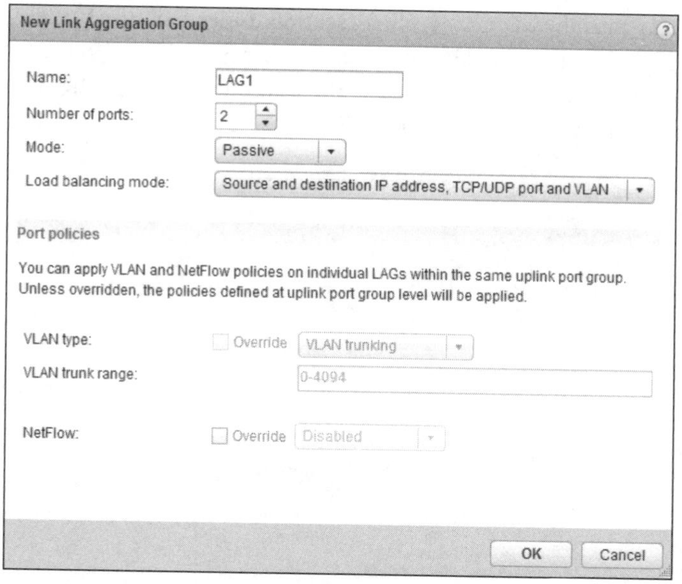

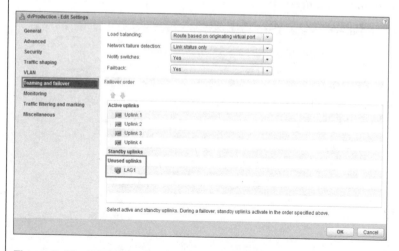

**Figure 5-45** Naming and Configuring a New Link Aggregation Group

**6.** Right-click the dvPort group to which you will assign the LAG, click **Edit Settings**, and then click **Teaming and Failover**, as shown in Figure 5-46.

**Figure 5-46** Editing the Settings of the dvPortGroup

**7.** Move the new LAG into the Standby Uplinks section under Failover Order, as shown in Figure 5-47, and click **OK**. Move any other Standby links to Unused. (You can ignore the warning because this is intermediate configuration and you know exactly what you are doing!)

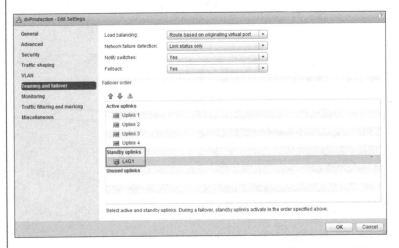

**Figure 5-47** Configuring a Link Aggregated Group in Teaming and Failover

**8.** Right-click the vDS in the left pane (Navigator), and then **Add and Manage Hosts**, as shown in Figure 5-48.

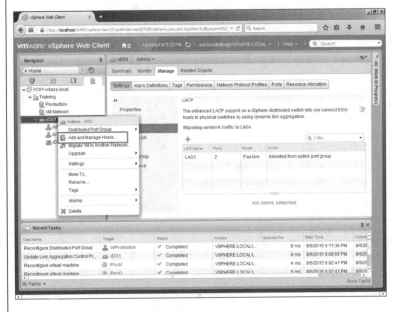

**Figure 5-48** Add and Manage Hosts

9. Click **Manage Host Networking**, and then click **Next**, as shown in Figure 5-49.

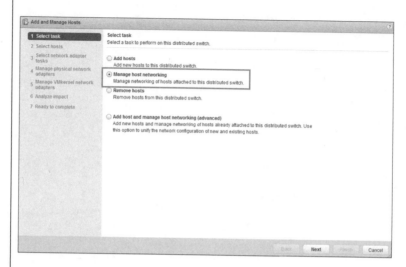

**Figure 5-49** Selecting to Manage Host Networking

10. Click **Attach Hosts**, and then attach the hosts that you want to include, as shown in Figure 5-50.

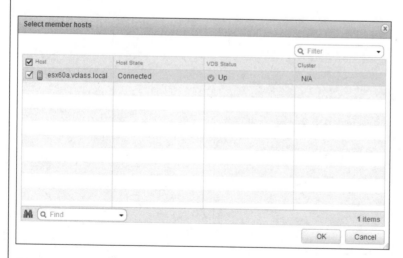

**Figure 5-50** Selecting Member Hosts

**11.** Click **Manage Physical Adapters** and clear the other options, as shown in Figure 5-51.

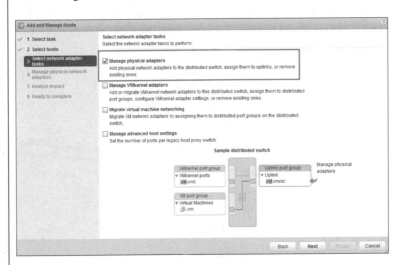

**Figure 5-51**   Managing Physical Adapters for Hosts

**12.** Assign the uplinks that you chose to the new LAG ports for each host, as shown in Figure 5-52. Click **Next**.

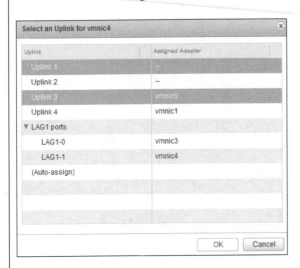

**Figure 5-52**   Assigning Uplinks to the LAG Ports

13. Review the Analyze impact screen to make sure that you are not affecting VM status, as shown in Figure 5-53. Click **Next.** Click **Finish**.

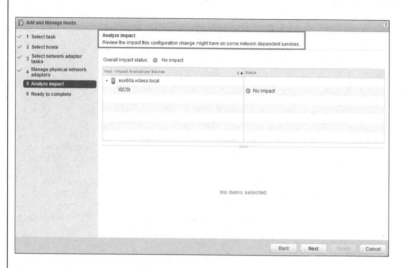

**Figure 5-53** The Analyze Impact Screen

14. Right-click the dvPort group to which you will assign the new LAG, and then select **Edit Settings** and then **Teaming and Failover**.

15. Move the LAG into Active Uplinks and then move any other uplinks to Unused, as shown in Figure 5-54. Click **OK** to save all settings and close the window.

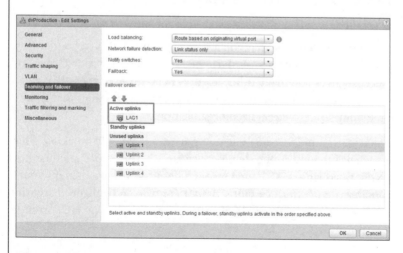

**Figure 5-54** Moving LAG to Active Uplinks

16. The dvPort group (in this case, dvProduction) will now use the LAG for its connection, as shown in Figure 5-55.

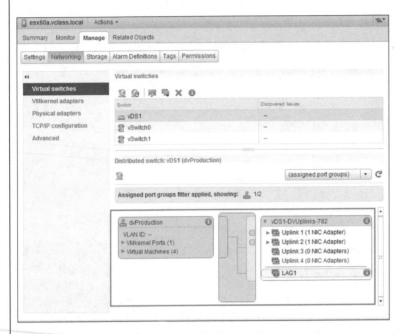

**Figure 5-55** vDS Topology with LAG

# Determining Use Cases for a vSphere Distributed Switch

As I mentioned earlier, if you decide that you are going to use a vDS in your vSphere, you typically need to obtain an Enterprise Plus license. Of course, the Enterprise Plus license gives you many other features in addition to those that relate to networking, but this section focuses on networking features and ways that they might benefit a medium-sized to large-sized organization.

As outlined previously in Table 5-2, many features are available only on vDSs. They include features such as inbound traffic shaping, private VLANs, more granular port control for blocking, mirroring, LACP, and so on. These features can benefit your organization by giving you greater flexibility, tighter control, and enhanced security in your network. How you use them will likely vary based on what you are currently using in the physical world.

One of the nice things about this decision is that it does not have to be an "all or nothing" one. In other words, you can continue to use vSSs and begin to incorporate vDSs. You can leave your VMkernel ports or even service console ports (on ESX hosts) on the vSSs and use only VM port groups on the vDSs if you so desire. It's up to you to decide what will be best for your virtual networking now and into the future and how to best use the features that VMware provides. The flexibility is there, and it's your decision as to its implementation in your virtual network and its connection to your physical network.

## Summary

This chapter covered the following main topics:

- Identifying the capabilities of vSSs and the creation, configuration, editing, and removal of vSSs and the port groups they contain.

- The creation, configuration, management, and removal of vDSs and the port groups that they contain, including comparing and contrasting their features with those of vSSs.

- The configuration of LACP and the process of creating LAGs and assigning them to uplinks.

## Exam Preparation Tasks

## Review All the Key Topics

Review the most important topics from the chapter, noted with the Key Topic icon in the outer margin of the page. Table 5-3 lists these key topics and the page numbers where each is found.

**Table 5-3**  Key Topics for Chapter 5

| Key Topic Element | Description | Page Number |
|---|---|---|
| Bullet List | vDS Capabilities | 82 |
| Activity 5-1 | Creating a New vSphere Distributed Switch | 84 |
| Activity 5-2 | Adding a Host to a vSphere Distributed Switch | 87 |
| Activity 5-3 | Removing a Host from a vSphere Distributed Switch | 90 |

## Review Questions

The answers to these review questions are in Appendix A.

1. Which of the following is *not* a valid use for a VMkernel port?

    a. IP storage

    b. vMotion

    c. FT logging

    d. VM Port Group

2. What is the maximum number of hosts that you can connect to a vSphere 6.0 vDS?

    a. 500

    b. 10

    c. 1,000

    d. 32

**3.** Which of the following is configurable on a vDS but not on a vSS?

   **a.** Private VLANs

   **b.** NIC teaming

   **c.** Outbound traffic shaping

   **d.** 802.1Q tagging

**4.** Which of the following is a capability of a vDS but not of a vSS?

   **a.** Outbound traffic shaping

   **b.** Network Migration of Policies

   **c.** VLAN segmentation

   **d.** NIC teaming

**5.** What is the maximum number for LAGs that you can have on a vSphere 6.0 vDS?

   **a.** 1,000

   **b.** 50

   **c.** 64

   **d.** 10,000

**6.** Which discovery protocol is configurable on a vDS, but not on a vSS?

   **a.** CDP

   **b.** SNMP

   **c.** LLDP

   **d.** SMTP

**7.** Which of the following is *not* a part of the configuration of a VMkernel port?

   **a.** IP address

   **b.** Subnet mask

   **c.** Default gateway

   **d.** MAC address

8. Which of the following are not possible with a vSS but are possible with a vSphere 6.0 vDS?

    a. Per-port policy settings

    b. vMotion

    c. User-defined network I/O Control

    d. Load balancing

9. Which of the following tools allows you to migrate multiple VMs from a vSS onto a vDS?

    a. vMotion

    b. The Migrate Virtual Machine Wizard

    c. Storage vMotion

    d. DRS

10. Which tool should you use to remove a vmnic from a vDS?

    a. The Manage the Physical Network Adapters Connected to the Selected Switch link

    b. The Teaming and Failover tool

    c. The Add and Remove Host Networking tool

    d. The Manage Networks tab

**This chapter covers the following subjects:**

- Common vSS and vDS Policies
- Configuring dvPort Group Blocking Policies
- Configuring Load Balancing and Failover Policies
- Configuring VLAN and PVLAN Settings
- Configuring Traffic Shaping Policies
- Enabling TCP Segmentation Offload Support for a Virtual Machine
- Enabling Jumbo Frames Support on Appropriate Components
- Determining Appropriate VLAN Configuration for a vSphere Implementation

In this section, I identify common vSS and vDS policies and discuss how you can configure them on your port groups. In addition, you learn about TCP Segmentation Offload support for VMs, jumbo frames support, and VLAN configuration. Although this section most specifically addresses vDSs, some vSS configuration is included so you can easily see the differences and determine which type of switch will best suit your needs. This method of explanation will also help you understand the differences between the two types of switches for the test.

# Configuring vSS and vDS Features

## "Do I Know This Already?" Quiz

The "Do I Know This Already?" quiz allows you to assess whether you should read this entire chapter or simply jump to the "Exam Preparation Tasks" section for review. If you are in doubt, read the entire chapter. Table 6-1 outlines the major headings in this chapter and the corresponding "Do I Know This Already?" quiz questions. You can find the answers in Appendix A, "Answers to the 'Do I Know This Already?' Quizzes and Chapter Review Questions."

**Table 6-1** "Do I Know This Already?" Section-to-Question Mapping

| Foundation Topics Section | Questions Covered in This Section |
|---|---|
| Common vSS and vDS Policies | 1, 2 |
| Configuring dvPort Group Blocking Policies | 3 |
| Configuring Load Balancing and Failover Policies | 4 |
| Configuring VLAN and PVLAN Settings | 5, 6 |
| Configuring Traffic Shaping Policies | 7 |
| Enabling TCP Segmentation Offload Support for a Virtual Machine | 8 |
| Enabling Jumbo Frames Support on Appropriate Components | 9 |
| Determining Appropriate VLAN Configuration for a vSphere Implementation | 10 |

1. Which of the following is not configurable as a port group policy?

   a. Security

   b. Traffic Shaping

   c. MTU

   d. Teaming and Failover

2. Which of the following is a default setting for vSS security policies in regard to promiscuous mode, mac address changes, and forged transmits?

   a. accept, reject, reject

   b. reject, accept, accept

   c. accept, reject, accept

   d. reject, reject, reject

3. Which of the following is true about dvPort Group blocking policies?

   a. The default for the setting is Yes.

   b. You should never configure the setting to No.

   c. Configuring this setting has no effect on traffic.

   d. This setting should be used as a "one-off" when you want to isolate all the VMs on a port group for a short period of time.

4. Which of the following is the correct definition of a NIC team?

   a. A NIC team is a group of vnics on a VM.

   b. A NIC team is a group of vmnics on a VM.

   c. A NIC team is a group of vmnics that are on the same vswitch or port group.

   d. A NIC team is a group of vnics that are on the same vswitch or port group.

5. Which type of Private VLAN is the remaining piece that is not separated from the primary VLAN?

   a. Community

   b. Enterprise

   c. Promiscuous

   d. Isolated

6. Which type of Private VLAN is used to create a separate network that is used only by a defined group of VMs within your vSphere environment?

   a. Isolated

   b. Primary

   c. Promiscuous

   d. Community

7. Which of the following are true regarding traffic shaping for vSphere Standard switches on vSphere 6.0? (Choose two.)

   a. Only outbound traffic shaping is supported.

   b. Inbound and outbound traffic shaping is supported.

   c. Burst size should always be set to a defined Kbps.

   d. Average bandwidth should be set to a defined Kbps.

8. Which of the following is true regarding TSO?

   a. The MTU on all switches must be configured to support TSO.

   b. An enhanced vmxnet adapter must be configured on the VM.

   c. TSO requires an MTU of at least 64 KB.

   d. VMware Tools is not required on the VM that is using TSO.

9. Which of the following is the correct setting to enable Jumbo Frames on a vSwitch?

   a. 9000 Kbps

   b. 1500 KB

   c. 9000 KB

   d. 1500 Kbps

10. Which of the following are best practices in regard to VLAN support on a vSwitch? (Choose two.)

   a. Always combine all essential services, such as Management, vMotion, and IP Storage, on the same physical NIC for easier management.

   b. Whenever possible, separate all essential services to separate VLANs and separate physical NICs.

   c. Keep all essential services on the same physical NIC to avoid a VLAN hopping attack.

   d. If separate physical NICs are not possible, then at least use a separate VLAN.

**Foundation Topics**

## Common vSS and vDS Policies

Policies are configuration settings that enable you to customize your switches and port groups with regard to traffic control, security, and so on. In general, you can set a policy that applies to a larger network object and then "tweak" the policy to establish new settings for a smaller network object within the larger network object. The biggest difference between how this applies to vSSs versus vDSs is the network objects that are used for the larger and smaller configurations.

With regard to vSSs, policies can be set at the switch level or at the port group level. Policies that are set at the switch level apply to all the ports on the switch, unless overridden by policies set at the port group level. In other words, policies that are set at the port group level override any policies that are set at the switch level. This allows you to get the "best of both worlds." For example, you could set strong security policies for the switch but then allow a "weakening" of the security policies on one port group that is to be used for testing and development.

There are three main policies for vSSs:

- Security

- Traffic shaping

- Teaming and Failover

Each policy can be set at the switch level and be overridden at the port group level if necessary. You can set these policies in the properties of the switch and/or port group.

To identify and configure switch and port group settings, follow the steps outlined in Activity 6-1.

## Activity 6-1    Identifying Common vSS Policies

1. Log on to your vSphere Web Client.

2. Select **Home** and then **Hosts and Clusters**.

3. Click the host that contains the vSS that you want to configure, click **Manage** and then **Networking**, and in the blue area, select **Virtual Switches**, as shown in Figure 6-1.

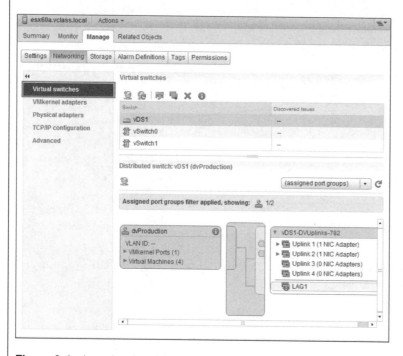

**Figure 6-1**   Locating the vSSs

4. Click the vSS that you want to configure, and then click the **Edit Settings** link that looks like a pencil, as shown in Figure 6-2.

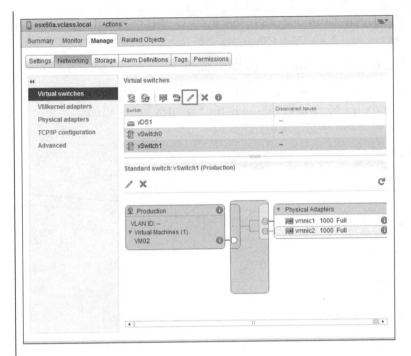

**Figure 6-2** Editing vSS Policies

5. Note the settings for Properties, Security, Traffic Shaping, and Teaming and Failover, as shown in Figure 6-3.

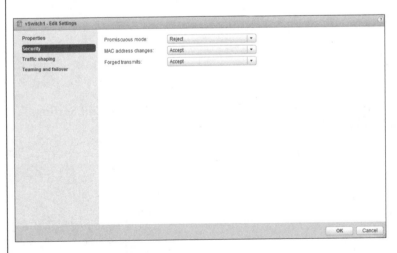

**Figure 6-3** Policies for vSS Switches

6. Later in this section, many of these settings are discussed in more detail. For now, just browse the settings, and then click **OK** or **Cancel** when you finish.

7. Click a port group within the switch and click the **Edit Settings** icon for it, as shown in Figure 6-4.

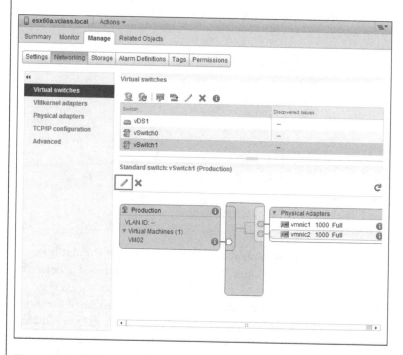

**Figure 6-4**    Editing Port Group Policies

8. Note the selections for Properties, Security, Traffic Shaping, and Teaming and Failover.

9. Open the Security, Traffic Shaping, and Teaming and Failover settings and note the difference, especially the white "override box." This setting will cause the port group to override the switch. Figure 6-5 shows an example for Security.

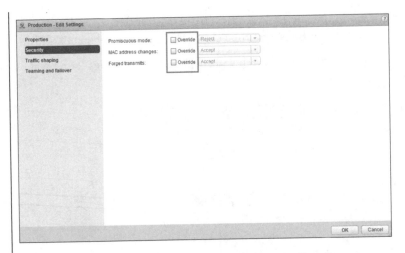

**Figure 6-5**   Default Security Settings for a vSS and Its Port Groups

**10.** Click **OK** or **Cancel** when you have finished.

So, now that you've seen the policies available for vSSs, you might wonder how the policies differ for vDSs. As I mentioned earlier, the main difference is between "what overrides what." As you have now seen in vSSs, most settings are on the switch level, with the port group settings occasionally overriding those of the switch. If you think about it, this cannot really apply in a vDS, because the vDS could span multiple hosts (up to 1,000) and be connected to a huge virtual network that would have different settings in each of its individual segments or locations. For this reason, only a few settings apply to a vDS on the switch level. Instead, most policies are applied at the port group level. Now, before you start thinking that this will give you less flexibility, you should know that these policies can be overridden at the individual port level. In other words, there is even more flexibility in vDSs than there is in vSSs.

Policies that can be set at the port group level on a vDS and be overridden at the port level include Security, Traffic Shaping, VLAN, Teaming and Failover, Resource Allocation, Monitoring, Miscellaneous (port blocking), and Advanced (override settings).

To identify these policy settings for a particular port group, follow the steps outlined in Activity 6-2.

**Activity 6-2   Identifying Common vDS Port Group Policies**

1. Log on to your vSphere Web Client.

2. Select **Home** and then **Networking**.

3. Right-click the dvport group that you want to examine and select **Edit Settings**.

4. Note the list of settings that are available, as shown in Figure 6-6.

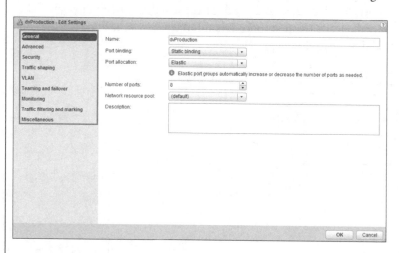

**Figure 6-6**   Port Group Policies on a vDS

5. View each of the settings, noting their features versus those of vSSs and those settings that exist here that are not on vSSs, such as inbound (ingress) traffic shaping.

6. When you have finished, click **OK** or **Cancel** to close.

You might be wondering how you can override these settings at each port. It's a two-step process. First, you configure the port group to allow changes to a particular setting at port level, and then you locate the port that you want to configure. For example, suppose that you wanted to configure a setting for security on a specific port that will override your security settings for the port group. In that case, follow the steps outlined in Activity 6-3.

**Activity 6-3    Overriding vDS Port Group Policies at the Port Level**

1. Log on to your vSphere Web Client.

2. Select **Home** and then **Networking**.

3. Right-click the port group that you want to configure and click **Edit Settings**.

4. Select **Advanced** from the list of policies, and then in the column labeled Override Port Policies, select **Allowed** for those policies that you want to be able to override; leave the rest set to **Disabled**, as shown in Figure 6-7. Note that I allowed Security Policy.

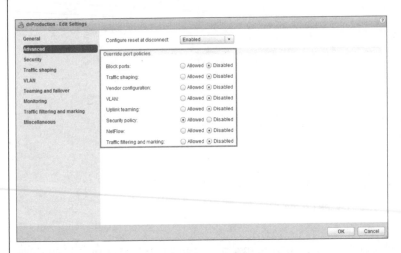

**Figure 6-7**    Editing Override Settings on a vDS Port Group

5. You can also enable or disable the **Configure Reset at Disconnect** for the options that you have allowed. Click **OK** to save all your settings and close the window.

## Configuring dvPort Group Blocking Policies

You might have noticed that I included Miscellaneous in the list of port group policies and specified that it involves port group blocking. The reason is that's what it says on the dialog box. Interestingly enough, as shown in Figure 6-8, it also says "Selecting Yes will shut down all ports in a port group. This might disrupt the normal network operations of the hosts or VMs using the ports." Gee, ya think?

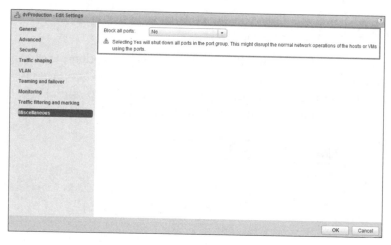

**Figure 6-8**   Configuring dvPort Group Blocking

Based on this, why would anyone want to select Yes? Well, this isn't your every-day setting. It's more of a "one-off" scenario setting that can come in handy if you know how to use it. Suppose that you want to isolate all machines on a port group from the network for a period of time while you make a software change. After the change, you want to connect them all again.

You could remove the vmnics from the port group, but what about any internal links? Also, you could disconnect each of the vNICs on the individual VMs, but what if there are many VMs, and what if you miss one or two of them? With the option of dvPort group blocking, you can throw a "master switch" that disables networking for all VMs on that port group, no matter where they are connected. Before you throw that switch, however, make sure that you are on the right port group and that the VMs on the port group are the ones that you want to isolate.

## Configuring Load Balancing and Failover Policies

If you assign more than one vmnic (physical NIC) to a switch or port group, you can configure load balancing and failover policies using the vmnics that you assign. This is the concept of *NIC teaming*, which you should clearly understand is not using more than one vNIC on a VM, but instead using more than one vmnic on a switch or port group. This section discusses configuring load balancing and failover poli-cies, first on vSSs and then on vDSs.

On a vSS, as you might remember, NIC teaming is one of the three policies that you can configure at the switch level or at the port group level. As discussed, any policy setting that you configure at the port group level will override the settings at the switch level. So, now I will discuss the policies that you can configure at the switch level and override at the port group level.

On a port group of a vSS or a vDS, you will find a list of policy exceptions, as shown on a vSS for Teaming and Failover in Figure 6-9. They are called *exceptions* because they each have a default setting, but that setting can be changed if necessary. Each of these settings and the options that you have are discussed next.

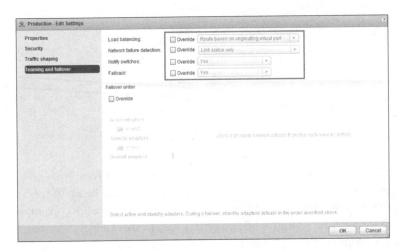

**Figure 6-9**   Policy Exceptions on Port Groups

## Load Balancing

There are five load balancing options from which you can choose:

- **Route based on the originating virtual port ID:** The physical NIC is determined by the ID of the virtual port to which the VM is connected. This option has the lowest overhead and is the default option for vSSs and port groups on vSSs.

- **Route based on source MAC hash:** All of VM's outbound traffic is mapped to a specific physical NIC that is based on the MAC address associated with the VM's virtual network interface card (vNIC). This method has relatively low overhead and is compatible with all switches[md]even those that do not support the 802.3ad protocol.

- **Route based on IP hash:** The physical NIC for each outbound packet is chosen based on a hash of the source and destination addresses contained in the packet. This method has the disadvantage of using more CPU resources;

however, it can provide better distribution of traffic across the physical NICs. This method also requires the 802.3ad link aggregation support or Ether-Channel on the switch.

- **Route based on physical NIC load:** The virtual switch checks the actual load of the physical uplinks and takes steps to reduce overloaded uplinks by redirecting traffic to the other available uplinks. Only available on the vDS.

- **Use explicit failover order:** The switch will always choose from its list of active adapters the highest order uplink that is not currently in use.

Make these choices based on your virtual networking needs and on how your virtual network connects to your physical network.

### Network Failover Detection

As discussed earlier, one of the reasons that you might want to assign more than one vmnic to a switch or port group is that you will have redundancy, so if one physical NIC fails, another one can take over. But how will you know whether your redundancy is still intact? The following are your two options with regard to network failure detection:

- **Link Status Only:** This option relies solely on the link status that the network adapter provides. In other words, "Do I feel electricity?" or with fiber, "Do I see a light?" This option detects cable pulls and physical switch failures, but it does not detect configuration errors that are beyond the directly connected switch. This method has no overhead and is the default.

- **Beacon Probing:** This option listens for link status but also sends out beacon packets from each physical NIC that it expects to be received on the other physical NIC. In this way, physical issues can be detected as well as configuration errors, such as improper settings on Spanning Tree Protocol (STP) or VLANs. Also, you should not use Beacon Probing with IP-hash load balancing because the way the beacon traffic is handled does not work well with this option and can cause a "network flapping" error.

### Notify Switches

The main job of a physical switch is to learn the MAC addresses of the computers and other devices on the network to which it is connected. If these change, its job is to make the change in its MAC address table. In most cases, you want to notify the physical switch of any changes in your virtual network that affect the MAC address table of the physical switch, but not always. The following are your two simple options with regard to notifying switches:

- **Yes:** If you select this option, the switch is notified whenever a VM's traffic will be routed over a different physical NIC because of a failover event. In most cases, this is the setting that you want to configure because it offers the lowest latency for failover occurrence and for vMotion migrations.

- **No:** If you select this option, the switch will not be notified and will not make the changes to its MAC address table. You should select this option only if you are using Microsoft Network Load Balancing (NLB) in unicast mode because selecting **Yes** prevents the proper function of Microsoft Network Load Balancing in unicast mode.

### Failback

On each switch and/or port group, you can assign vmnics (physical NICs) as Active, Standby, or Unused, as shown in Figure 6-10.

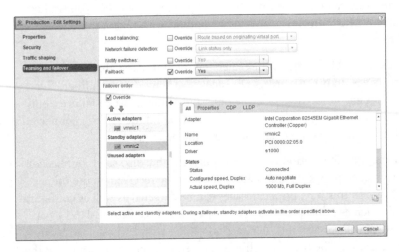

**Figure 6-10**   Active and Standby NICs and Failback

If a vmnic is listed as Active, it will be used unless it fails. If a vmnic fails, the first vmnic in the Standby list is used. Now, what if the first vmnic should come back? Then should you go back to it immediately, or should you stay with the vmnic that is currently working fine? The following are your two simple options for Failback settings:

- **Yes:** If you select this option, a failed adapter that has recovered will be returned to Active status immediately after its recovery, thereby replacing the vmnic that is working fine. This might be an advantage if the primary adapter is somehow superior to the secondary one, such as a faster speed or other features. The disadvantage of this option is that a "flapping" connection could cause the system to play "ping pong" with itself, continually changing between adapters.

- **No:** If you select this option and an adapter fails and then recovers, the adapter that took its place when it failed will continue to be used. This "if it ain't broke, don't fix it" approach avoids the "ping pong" of the other option but might leave the traffic on a slower or less desirable adapter.

On a vDS, many of the settings are reasoned in the same way, but the dialog boxes are a little different. In addition, as previously mentioned, the settings are typically configured at the port group level and can be overridden at the port level. As you might recall, Teaming and Failover is one of the policy settings that you can edit for port groups.

When you are on the right dialog box, you will notice that the settings are the same, except that they can be overridden at the individual port level, as shown on Figure 6-11.

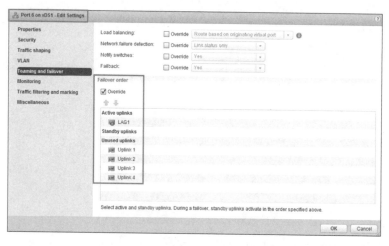

**Figure 6-11**   Override Settings for Failover Order at Port Level on a vDS

# Configuring VLAN and PVLAN Settings

Virtual local-area networks (VLANs) are commonly used in today's networks to create and manage subnets in networks that contain many switches. They offer a high degree of flexibility and security and are useful for carrying many subnets on one or a few cables using a packet marking method called tagging. vSphere fully supports IEEE 802.1Q tagging.

Because this is not a Cisco discussion, or a Cisco test, you don't need to know all the details of VLAN configuration, but you should know how to configure your port group properties or individual port properties to work with the VLANs that you already have in your organization. The bottom line is that if you want to bring more subnets in and out of your virtual network than you want to use physical NICs to carry, you need to use VLANs and 802.1Q tagging. VLANs also give you the flexibility to use the load balancing and fault-tolerance options, described previously, in more creative ways.

I will first discuss the configuration of VLANs on a vSS and then on a vDS. For each type of switch, I cover your options and the impact of your decisions. In addition, you learn the advantages of using a vDS versus a vSS with regard to VLANs.

On vSS port groups, you can configure the VLAN setting on the General tab of the properties for the port group, as shown in Figure 6-12. You can do so by typing the VLAN number from your network in the box labeled VLAN ID (Optional). If you have VMs that need to receive packets from more than one subnet and provide their own tagging for more than one subnet, you should select **All (4095)**.

**Figure 6-12**   VLAN Configuration on a vSS Port Group

On vDS port groups, you can configure the VLAN in a much more granular fashion. You might have noticed that the VLAN setting is one of the options under Policies. On this setting, you have three options from which to choose: VLAN, VLAN Trunking, and Private VLAN. This section discusses each option briefly and illustrates how you would configure them.

## Configuring VLAN Policy Settings on a vDS

If you select VLAN, the screen changes, and you are presented with a simple box in which you can input a number, as shown in Figure 6-13. This number should be an actual VLAN number that you are using on your physical network and that you want to incorporate into your virtual network as well, on this port group. Your range of choices is from 1 to 4094.

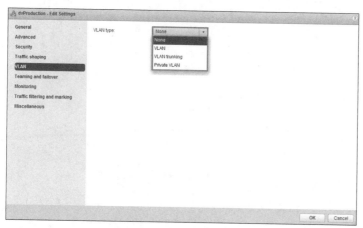

**Figure 6-13**    VLAN Configuration on a vDS

## Configuring VLAN Trunking Policies on a VDS

This option establishes the port group as a trunk that can carry multiple VLANs to VMs that are connected to it. However, rather than having to carry all 4094 VLANs just to have more than one, on vDSs, this setting can be pruned to carry only the VLANs or range of VLANs that you specify, as shown in Figure 6-14.

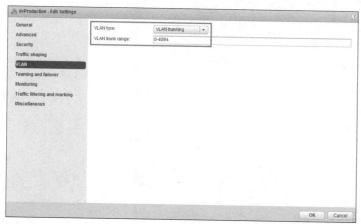

**Figure 6-14**    VLAN Trunking Configuration on a vDS

## Configuring Private VLAN Policy Settings on a vDS

This setting, shown in Figure 6-15, allows you to use a VLAN that you have created on the vDS that can be used only by your vSphere environment and not by your external network.

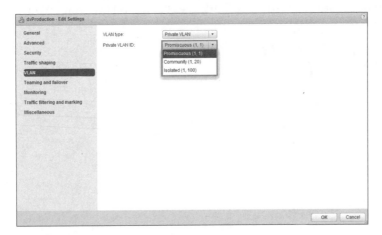

**Figure 6-15**   Configuring a Private VLAN

To create a private VLAN, in essence, you further segment a VLAN that you are already receiving into the switch. You must first create these on the vDS. To do this, right-click the vDS and select **Settings** and then **Edit Private VLAN**, as shown in Figure 6-16.

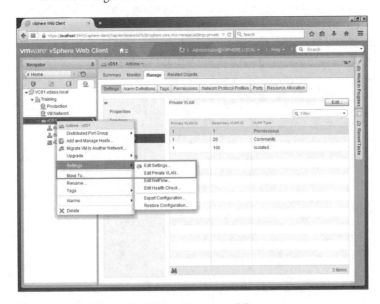

**Figure 6-16**   Private VLAN Creation on a vDS

You can create and use three types of private VLANs in your vSphere as highlighted previously in Figure 6-15:

- **Promiscuous:** This is named (numbered) by the primary VLAN that you chose from your physical network. It is the remaining piece that is not separated from the primary VLAN. VMs on this VLAN can be reached by any VM in the same primary VLAN.

- **Isolated:** This is a private VLAN used to create a separate network for one VM in your virtual network that is not used at all in the physical world. It can be used to isolate a highly sensitive VM, for example. If a VM is in an isolated VLAN, it will not communicate with any other VMs in other isolated VLANs or in other community VLANs. It can communicate with promiscuous VLANs.

- **Community:** This is a private VLAN used to create a separate network to be shared by more than one VM. This VLAN is also used only in your virtual network and not in your physical network. VMs on community VLANs can communicate only to other VMs on the same community or to VMs on a promiscuous VLAN.

## Configuring Traffic Shaping Policies

By default, all the VMs on a port group have an unlimited share of the bandwidth assigned to that port group, and all the port groups have an unlimited share of the bandwidth that is provided by the uplinks on the virtual switch. This is true on vSSs and vDSs. In other words, by default, it is an "all you can eat buffet" for all the VMs on the switch, regardless of which port group.

When you decide to use traffic shaping, your goal should be to free up available bandwidth by limiting the bandwidth usage on port groups that contain VMs that can function with less bandwidth. This might not be as straightforward as it first seems. You might be thinking that there are some "bandwidth hogs" on your network that you want to traffic shape right away. If those have anything to do with Voice over Internet Protocol (VoIP) or video, you might want to reconsider your options. In fact, you might want to traffic shape port groups that hold VMs that are file and print servers first, because they can take the bandwidth reduction hit, and thereby give the VoIP and video VMs more available bandwidth. However, traffic shaping should never be done without first studying your virtual network to determine what you want to accomplish and to find out if you have the resources to accomplish it.

Your options for traffic shaping are very different on vSSs versus vDSs. In addition, the tools that you use to configure them are different. This section first discusses your traffic shaping options on vSSs and then examines your additional options on vDSs.

### Traffic Shaping Policies for vSphere Standard Switches

On vSSs, all traffic shaping is for outbound traffic only. This is the case regardless of which version vSS you are using. You might have heard that inbound traffic shaping is available in vSphere. This is true, but only with vDS port groups (which are discussed next). As with other policies, you can configure traffic shaping on a vSS at the switch level, and then you can override it at the port group level. After you enable traffic shaping, you can configure three main settings for outbound traffic on vSS switches and port groups, as shown with their default settings (not configured yet) in Figure 6-17.

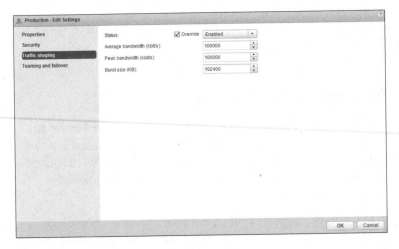

**Figure 6-17** Traffic Shaping on vSS

The following is a brief description of each of these settings:

- **Average bandwidth (kbit/s):** This establishes the number of kilobits per second to allow across a port, averaged over time. It should be an amount based on that which you have observed or monitored in the past.

- **Peak bandwidth (kbit/s):** This is the maximum aggregate traffic measured in kilobits per second that will be allowed for a port group or switch. It should be an amount that will not hamper the effective use of the VMs connected to the port group or switch.

- **Burst size (KB):** This is the maximum number of bytes to be allowed in a burst. A burst is defined as exceeding the average bandwidth. This setting determines how long the bandwidth can exceed the average as a factor of how far it has exceeded the average. The higher it goes, the less time it can spend there. In other words, this setting is a factor of "bandwidth X time."

### Traffic Shaping Policies for vSphere Distributed Switches

On vDSs, traffic shaping can be configured for the port group and be overridden if necessary at the individual port level, just as with other policies. The biggest difference from that of vSSs is that it can be configured for both inbound (ingress) and outbound (egress) traffic. You might have noticed that traffic shaping is listed under the policies of a vDS port group and/or individual port, as shown in Figure 6-18.

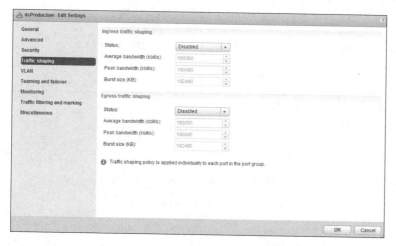

**Figure 6-18**    Traffic Shaping on vDS Port Groups

You can choose to enable ingress (inbound), egress (outbound), neither, or both. The other settings are much the same as those for vSSs. You can use ingress traffic to control the amount of bandwidth that hits a port group in a given period of time. This might be useful for web servers as an additional throttling mechanism.

## Enabling TCP Segmentation Offload Support for a Virtual Machine

TCP Segmentation Offload (TSO) enhances the networking performance of VMs by allowing the TCP stack to emit very large frames (up to 64 KB), even though the maximum transmission unit (MTU) of the interface is much smaller. The network adapter then separates the large frames into MTU-sized frames and prepends an adjusted copy of the original TCP/IP headers. In other words, you can send more data through the network in a given time, and the vNIC on the VM can "take sips from the fire hose." This is especially useful for VMkernel ports that are being used for iSCSI. TSO is enabled by default for the VMkernel port but must be enabled on the VM.

As you can imagine, not just any vNIC can handle TSO. In fact, not just any OS can handle it, either. If you want to use TSO, you must install an enhanced vmxnet adapter. You can enable TSO support on the VMs that run the following guest OSs:

- Microsoft Windows Server 2003 Enterprise Edition with Service Pack 2 or later (32 bit and 64 bit)

- Red Hat Enterprise Linux 4 (64 bit) or later

- SUSE Linux Enterprise Server 10 or later (32 bit and 64 bit)

To replace the existing adapter and enable TSO, follow the steps outlined in Activity 6-4.

**Activity 6-4   Enabling TSO on a VM**

1. Log on to your vCenter Server through your vSphere Web Client.

2. Locate the VM that you want to configure.

3. Right-click the VM and click **Edit Settings**.

4. Select the network adapter from the Virtual Hardware list.

5. Record the network settings and the MAC address that the network adapter is using, as shown in Figure 6-19.

**Figure 6-19**  Enabling TSO on a VM

6. Click **Remove** to remove the network adapter from the VM.

7. Click **Add**, select **Ethernet Adapter**, and click **Next**.

8. In the Adapter Type group, select **Enhanced vmxnet**.

9. Select the network setting and MAC address that the old network adapter was using and click **Next**.

10. Click **Finish**, and then click **OK**.

11. If the VM is not set to upgrade the VMware tools when powered on, upgrade the VMware tools now; otherwise, just restart the VM to upgrade the tools.

## Enabling Jumbo Frames Support on Appropriate Components

Another way to enhance network performance and reduce CPU load is through the use of jumbo frames. Enabling jumbo frame support on your ESXi host and VMs allows them to send out much larger frames than normal into the network (9,000 bytes versus 1,518 bytes). If you are going to send the larger frames, the physical network to which you are sending them must be enabled for jumbo frames as well. Before you enable jumbo frames on your ESXi host and VMs, check your vendor documentation to ensure that your physical adapter supports them.

You can then enable jumbo frames for the VMkernel interfaces and for the VMs. Of course, the actual steps to enable jumbo frame support for vSSs are different from those for vDSs. This section first covers enabling jumbo frames on vSSs, then on vDSs, and finally on VMs.

## Enabling Jumbo Frames for VMkernel Interface on a vSS

To enable jumbo frames on a VMkernel interface, you only need to change the MTU for the interface. On a vSS, you can make this change in the properties of the switch, as outlined in the steps in Activity 6-5.

**Activity 6-5   Enabling Jumbo Frames for a VMkernel Interface on a vSS**

1. Log on to your vCenter Server through your vSphere Web Client.

2. Click **Home** and then **Hosts and Clusters**.

3. Select the ESXi host that contains the VMkernel port that you want to configure, then select **Manage** and then **Networking,** and in the blue area below, select **Virtual Switches**.

4. Select the vSwitch that contains the VMkernel port that you want to configure, and then click the **Edit Settings** icon that looks like a pencil, as shown in Figure 6-20.

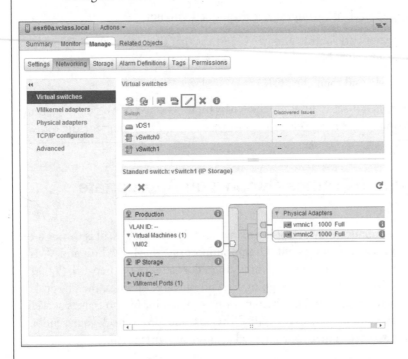

**Figure 6-20**   Editing Settings on a vSS

5. Set the MTU to **9000**, as shown in Figure 6-21, and click **OK** to confirm and save.

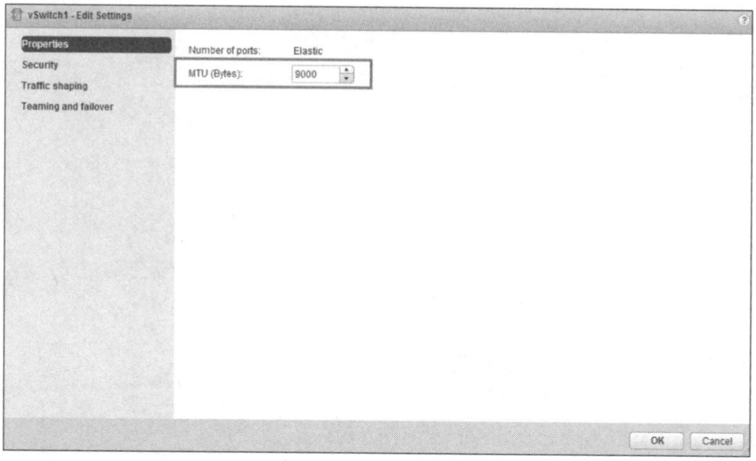

| vSwitch1 - Edit Settings | | |
|---|---|---|
| **Properties** | Number of ports: | Elastic |
| Security | MTU (Bytes): | 9000 |
| Traffic shaping | | |
| Teaming and failover | | |

| | OK | Cancel |

**Figure 6-21**    Enabling Jumbo Frames on a vSS

## Enabling Jumbo Frames on a vDS

You can enable jumbo frames for an entire vDS. Just as with the VMkernel port on the vSS, you must increase the MTU. Activity 6-6 outlines the steps that you should take.

**Activity 6-6    Enabling Jumbo Frames on a vDS**

1. Log on to your vCenter Server through your vSphere Web Client.

2. Click **Home** and then **Networking**.

3. Right-click the vDS that you want to configure and click **Settings** and then **Edit Settings**.

4. Click **Advanced**, and then set Maximum MTU to **9000**, as shown in Figure 6-22.

**Figure 6-22**   Enabling Jumbo Frames on a vDS

    **5.** Click **OK** to confirm your change and save.

### Enabling Jumbo Frame Support on Virtual Machines

After you have enabled jumbo frames on your physical network and your virtual switches, configuring the VMs to work with them is a matter of installing the proper vNIC on the VM and configuring the guest OS to use it. You might think that the best vNIC to use would be the vmxnet3. However, there is a known issue with the vmxnet3, so you should choose either the vmxnet2 (enhanced vmxnet) or the e1000 vnic, whichever is best for the OS on the VM. (The precise configuration of the guest OS to use jumbo frames will vary by guest OS and is beyond the scope of this text.)

## Determining Appropriate VLAN Configuration for a vSphere Implementation

VLANs can be a powerful tool if used correctly in your network. You can create and control multiple subnets using the same vmnic, or a group of subnets with a small group of vmnics, and provide for load balancing and fault tolerance as well. Using multiple subnets enhances the flexibility and the security of your network because the subnets can indicate a defined purpose for that part of the network, such as iSCSI storage, vMotion, management, NFS datastores, and so on (all of which are covered in Chapters 7 and 8). VLANs provide some security if configured properly, but they can also be susceptible to a VLAN hopping attack whereby a person who has access to one VLAN can gain access to the others on the same cable. This is not a good scenario, especially if one of the other networks is the management network. You can typically prevent this situation by properly configuring your physical switches and keeping them up to date with firmware and patches.

Still, an even more defined way to separate the components of your network is by using a new vmnic for each one. This is referred to as *physical separation*. It is considered even more secure than VLANs because it avoids the VLAN hopping attack. It is a best practice to use a separate vmnic for each type of network that you create. For example, you should use a separate vmnic for VM port groups than you do for management VMkernel ports. Also, you should separate vmnics for each type of VMkernel port whenever possible. For example, it would be best to have a different vmnic for each of your VMkernel ports for vMotion, FT logging, iSCSI storage, NFS datastores, and management.

To recap, you are supposed to make use of the VLANs while at the same time using a separate vmnic for just about everything. How can these two best practices possibly coexist? Figure 6-23 illustrates an example whereby a different vmnic is used as the active adapter for each important service, but at the same time, VLANs are used to allow those adapters to be a standby adapter for another service. (In the table, *A* stands for active, *S* for standby, and *U* for unused.)

This is just one scenario on one ESXi host's vSS, but it shows the power of what can be done when you begin to use all your options. I hope you can take the principles learned from this scenario and apply them to your own virtual network. Examine Figure 6-23 to determine what you like about it and what you want to change. For example, adding another physical switch would definitely be a good practice. What else do you see? Again, this is just one scenario of many. So, see whether you can take what I have discussed and build your own scenarios.

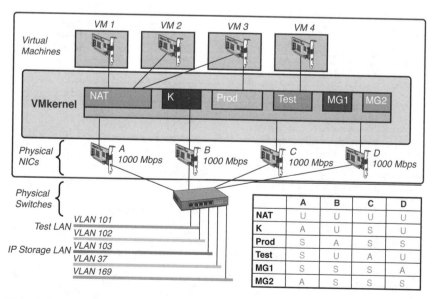

**Figure 6-23**   An Example of VLAN Configuration on a vSS

# Summary

This chapter covers the following main topics:

- Common vSS and vDS policies, including policies such as Security, Traffic Shaping, and Teaming and Failover

- The creation and use of VLANs and PVLANs on vSSs and vDSs

- The configuration of TSO and Jumbo frames to scale your network

- Appropriate configuration for VLAN in a vSphere implementation

# Exam Preparation Tasks

## Review All the Key Topics

Review the most important topics from the chapter, noted with the Key Topic icon in the outer margin of the page. Table 6-2 lists these key topics and the page numbers where each is found. Know the main differences between vSSs and vDSs, and the port groups on each. Understand how to create, configure, edit, and delete these components and policies.

**Table 6-2**  Key Topics for Chapter 6

| Key Topic Element | Description | Page Number |
|---|---|---|
| List | Three Main Policies for vSSs | 130 |
| Activity 6-1 | Identifying Common vSS Policies | 131 |
| Activity 6-2 | Identifying Common vDS Port Group Policies | 135 |
| Activity 6-3 | Overriding vDS Port Group Policies at the Port Level | 136 |
| Bullet List | Settings for Traffic Shaping | 146 |
| Activity 6-4 | Enabling TSO on a VM | 148 |
| Activity 6-5 | Enabling Jumbo Frames for a VMkernel Interface on a vSS | 150 |
| Activity 6-6 | Enabling Jumbo Frames on a vDS | 151 |

## Review Questions

The answers to these review questions are in Appendix A.

1. Which of the following is the default load balancing policy for vSSs?

    a. Route based on the originating port ID

    b. Route based on source MAC hash

    c. Route based on IP hash

    d. Use explicit failover order

2. Which protocol must be supported by the physical switches in your environment in order to use route based on IP hash as your Load Balancing algorithm?

    a. 802.11

    b. 802.1Q

    c. 802.5

    d. 802.3ad

3. If you configure policies on a specific port group that conflict with policies on the vSS, which of the following will result?

    a. The port group policies on the switch always override those on a port group.

    b. The port group policies override the switch policies for the VMs on that port group.

    c. The port group policies will override those on the switch and will be applied to all VMs on all port groups.

    d. You cannot create this configuration.

**4.** Which of the following are true regarding Network Failure detection? (Choose two.)

    **a.** Link Status Only can detect configuration errors that are on the far side of your physical switch.

    **b.** Beacon Probing can detect configuration errors that are on the closest physical switch to the ESXi host.

    **c.** Link Status Only relies only on the link status that the network adapter provides, such as an Ethernet cable being removed or physical switch power failures.

    **d.** Link Status Only can only detect configuration errors that are on the far side of your physical switch.

**5.** Which of the following is the traffic shaping metric for average bandwidth, peak bandwidth, and burst size, respectively?

    **a.** Kbps, Kbps, KB

    **b.** KB, KB, KB

    **c.** Kbps, Kbps, Kbps

    **d.** KB, KB, Kbps

**6.** What should you change to enable TSO on a VMkernel interface on ESXi 5.x?

    **a.** You must place a check mark in the correct configuration parameter.

    **b.** TSO is enabled by default on all VMkernel interfaces on ESXi 5.x and later.

    **c.** You need more than one vmnic assigned to the port.

    **d.** You must enable the interface for IP storage as well.

**7.** Which of the following are true in regard to traffic shaping on a vSwitch? (Choose two.)

    **a.** You should always set up traffic shaping as soon as you create a vSwitch.

    **b.** All traffic shaping for all vSSs is outbound only.

    **c.** Without traffic shaping, the vnics will not be able to get bandwidth.

    **d.** Traffic shaping can be configured for an individual port on vDSs.

8. If you have a vDS network policy configured for a port group and a conflicting network policy configured for a specific port within the port group, which of the following will result?

   a. The port group policy overrides the specific port policy.

   b. A configuration error will be indicated.

   c. The specific port setting overrides the port group setting for the VM on that port.

   d. The specific port setting is applied to all VMs connected to the port group.

9. Which of the following are load balancing policies that do not require 802.3ad or EtherChannel on the switch? (Choose two.)

   a. Route based on IP hash

   b. Route based on Source MAC hash

   c. Route based on originating virtual port ID

   d. Link State Only

10. To which of the following can VMs in a community VLAN communicate? (Choose two.)

   a. The promiscuous VLAN from which it was created

   b. Other community VLANs

   c. Other VMs on the same community VLAN

   d. VMs on isolated VLANs

**This chapter covers the following subjects:**

- Storage Adapters and Devices
- Storage Naming Conventions
- Hardware/Dependent Hardware/Software iSCSI Initiators
- Zoning and LUN Masking
- Creating an NFS Share for Use with vSphere
- Configuring and Editing Hardware and Independent Hardware Initiators
- Configuring and Editing Software Initiator Settings

Suppose that you are happy with the host on which some of your virtual machines (VMs) reside, and you do not plan to move them. In other words, for some of your VMs, features such as vMotion, high availability (HA), Distributed Resource Scheduler (DRS), and Distributed Power Management (DPM) have no value for you. In that case, the best place to keep all the files that those VMs will need might be only on the local (direct attached) drives of the host.

## CHAPTER 7

# Connecting Shared Storage Devices to vSphere

Of course, this does not apply to all of your VMs, and chances are good that you want to use the aforementioned features for most of your VMs. This means that you will have to create and maintain some type of shared storage. This shared storage will in turn provide the redundancy and centralized management that you require. You could provide this in some form of centralized shared storage, such as a storage-area network (SAN) or network-attached storage (NAS); or you could use a virtual SAN (*VSAN*) that works through vSphere and leverages the capacity of your local storage and the speed of your local SSDs to create a flexible shared storage environment. VSANs are discussed in Chapter 8, "Configuring Software-Defined Storage."

This chapter covers connecting shared storage devices to vSphere, along with storage naming conventions. It also covers the configuration of hardware and software initiators used for iSCSI, zoning and LUN masking, and iSCSI port binding.

## "Do I Know This Already?" Quiz

The "Do I Know This Already?" quiz allows you to assess whether you should read this entire chapter or simply jump to the "Exam Preparation Tasks" section for review. If you are in doubt, read the entire chapter. Table 7-1 outlines the major headings in this chapter and the corresponding "Do I Know This Already?" quiz questions. You can find the answers in Appendix A, "Answers to the 'Do I Know This Already?' Quizzes and Chapter Review Questions."

**Table 7-1**  Headings and Questions

| Foundation Topics Section | Questions Covered in This Section |
|---|---|
| Storage Adapters and Devices | 1 |
| Storage Naming Conventions | 2 |
| Hardware/Independent Hardware/Software iSCSI Initiators | 4 |
| Zoning and LUN Masking | 3 |
| Creating an NFS Share for Use with vSphere | 5, 6 |
| Configuring and Editing Hardware and Dependent Hardware Initiators | 7, 10 |
| Configuring and Editing Software Initiator Settings | 8, 9 |

1. Which of the following is *not* a type of storage adapter?

    a. Fibre Channel

    b. Network-attached storage

    c. VMFS

    d. Fibre Channel over Ethernet

2. In the runtime name of VMFS datastore vmhba1:0:2:4, to which storage processor is the datastore connected?

    a. 1

    b. 4

    c. 0

    d. 2

3. Which of the following can prevent a host from seeing LUNs that are on a storage processor to which it is connected?

    a. Zoning

    b. Shares

    c. Permissions

    d. Masking

**4.** What type of iSCSI initiator can allow a host to boot from a SAN LUN with no additional software?

   **a.** Software

   **b.** Dependent Hardware

   **c.** Hardware (independent hardware)

   **d.** All iSCSI initiators can allow a host to boot from a SAN LUN.

**5.** Which of the following is not a requirement for configuring an NFS share for use with vSphere?

   **a.** Sync

   **b.** Case-sensitive shared folder

   **c.** Root squash

   **d.** IP address or hostname

**6.** Which of the following is not true when creating an NFS share for use with vSphere?

   **a.** To run VMs, you should always configure the permissions to read-only.

   **b.** The default permissions of the share are read and write.

   **c.** Your share will always be treated as case sensitive.

   **d.** You should use sync rather than async for the type of communication.

**7.** Which of the following are *true* regarding dependent hardware initiators? (Choose two.)

   **a.** The card contains a network adapter and an iSCSI engine.

   **b.** No VMkernel port is required

   **c.** You must associate the card with a VMkernel port and then configure it.

   **d.** You must enable the iSCSI engine on the card after you install it.

**8.** Which of the following is the default port used for iSCSI?

   **a.** 902

   **b.** 123

   **c.** 8472

   **d.** 3260

9. Which of the following are required to use the iSCSI software initiator? (Choose two.)

   a. A network card that supports TOE.

   b. A network card that is compatible with vSphere.

   c. Use the default Software Storage Adapter, already added during initial installation.

   d. Add a new storage adapter for software iSCSI.

10. Which of the following is true about iSCSI port binding?

   a. It binds a VMkernel port to a vnic on a specific VM.

   b. It binds two virtual ports to each other for redundancy.

   c. It binds a VMkernel port to a specific iSCSI adapter.

   d. It cannot be used with third parties.

## Foundation Topics

# Storage Adapters and Devices

As mentioned earlier, there are many reasons that shared storage is often superior to local storage. This is true even outside of a virtual data center. Some of the reasons that shared storage is preferable to local storage in vSphere are the following:

- Central repository that is accessible from multiple hosts
- Scalable and recoverable implementations
- Clustering of VMs across physical hosts
- Data replication
- Using VMware vMotion, HA, DRS, and DPM

Because we are all in agreement that shared storage is important to have, let's look at how to configure and manage shared storage in vSphere.

## Identifying Storage Adapters and Devices

At its essence, a storage adapter is like a glorified NIC that is used for storage. In fact, with the help of the VMkernel, a normal supported NIC can be used for some types of storage. This section focuses on four main types of storage adapters:

- Fibre Channel
- Fibre Channel over Ethernet (FCoE)
- iSCSI
- Network-attached storage (NAS)

For each, I will briefly describe the technology and identify its advantages and disadvantages. Figure 7-1 shows an overview of these storage technologies.

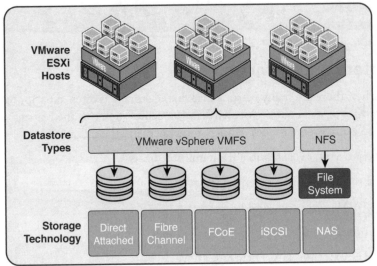

**Figure 7-1**   Storage Overview

## DAS (Direct Attached Storage)

This type of storage is directly connected to the host machine and is accessible without any additional software. It is not considered shared storage that can be used by more than one host.

## Fibre Channel

You might have noticed that Fibre Channel is generally spelled with an "re" at the end rather than an "er." The "re" refers to the technology that began in the 1980s by a European group and has evolved substantially since then. Generally speaking, Fibre Channel is a technology used primarily for storage-area networking (SAN). In spite of its name, it can use fiber-optic cable or copper cable. Fibre Channel has a lower overhead than TCP/IP and is offered with speeds of 1, 2, 4, 8, 10, and 20 Gbps. The main advantages of Fibre Channel are its flexibility and the fact that it does not put a load on the Ethernet network. Its chief disadvantage is cost; Fibre Channel implementations often cost considerably more than other options.

## FCoE

Fibre Channel over Ethernet (FCoE) is an encapsulation of Fibre Channel frames so they can be sent over Ethernet networks. FCoE allows the Fibre Channel protocol to be used on Ethernet networks of 10 Gbps or higher speeds. You can use a specialized type of adapter called a converged network adapter (CNA) or, beginning with vSphere 5, you can connect any supported network adapter to a VMkernel port to be used for Fibre Channel. The main advantage is that you do not have to support both a Fibre Channel fabric and an Ethernet network, but instead can consolidate all networking and storage to the Ethernet network. The chief disadvantages are the higher cost of cards suitable for FCoE and the additional traffic on the Ethernet.

## iSCSI

Internet Small Computer System Interface (iSCSI) is one of those terms that does not define what it does at all! iSCSI is a common networking standard for linking data storage facilities that is based on the Internet Protocol (IP). iSCSI facilitates data transfers by carrying SCSI commands over an IP network, generally the intranets of organizations. It is mostly used on local-area networks (LANs), but it can also be used on wide-area networks (WANs), or even through the Internet with the use of tunneling protocols. vSphere supports up to 10 Gbps iSCSI.

## NAS

Network-attached storage (NAS) is file-level data storage provided by a computer that is specialized to provide not only the data but also the file system for the data. In some ways, NAS is like a glorified mapped drive. The similarity is that the data to which you are connecting is seen as a share on the NAS device. The difference is that the device that is storing the data and providing the file system is specially designed for just this purpose and is generally extremely efficient at sharing the files. Protocols that can be used on an NAS include Common Internet File Systems (CIFS) and Network File Systems (NFS). The only one of these that is supported in vSphere is NFS. As discussed in Chapter 8, vSphere 6 supports both NFS version 3 and NFS version 4.1.

## VSAN

Virtual storage-area network (VSAN) is a new type of shared storage that is very different from all of the others previously discussed. It leverages the local drives of hosts to create a virtual storage area made up of multiple physical drives that are dispersed among the hosts in a vSphere cluster. Each VMs disk (vmdk file) is treated as a separate object that can be assigned attributes, such as how many times it should be replicated and over how many disks in the VSAN. In addition, VSAN leverages the power of any additional solid state drives (SSDs) on the hosts in the cluster for read caching and write buffering to improve performance. VSAN is simple to use after you have a vSphere 5.5 or later cluster, and you have created the VMkernel ports for it (at least one for each host) and enabled it in the cluster. VSAN is covered in greater depth in Chapter 8.

# Storage Naming Conventions

As you can see, you have a great number of technologies from which to choose to build your datastores for your vSphere. In Chapter 9, "Creating and Configuring VMFS and NFS Datastores," I will discuss much more specifically how you build your datastores and exactly how you use them. For now, this section focuses on how you identify the physical storage locations with which you will create your datastores.

Your naming convention will depend on the technology that you have chosen. If you are using local drives or a SAN technology, such as iSCSI or Fibre Channel, you will use a naming convention associated with a vmhba. If you are using NAS, your naming convention will be associated with the share name of the data source. In this section, each of these naming conventions is discussed as it relates to vSphere.

## Storage Naming Conventions for Local and SAN

The naming convention that vSphere uses to identify a physical storage location that resides on a local disk or on a SAN consists of several components. In fact, you can refer to the location a few different ways depending on the question that you are asking and how specific you really need to get. The following are the three most common naming conventions for local and SAN and a brief description of each:

- **Runtime name:** Uses the convention *vmhbaN:C:T:L*, where

    - *vm* stands for VMkernel.

    - *hba* is host bus adapter.

    - *N* is a number corresponding to the host bus adapter location (starting with 0).

    - *C* is channel, and the first connection is always 0 in relation to vSphere. (An adapter that supports multiple connections will have different channel numbers for each connection.)

    - *T* is target, which is a storage adapter on the SAN or local device.

    - *L* is logical unit number (LUN), which is described in more detail in Chapter 9.

A runtime name is created by the host and is relative only to the installed adapters at the time of creation; it might be changed if adapters are added or replaced and the host is restarted.

- **Canonical name:** The Network Address Authority (NAA) ID that is a unique identifier for the LUN. This name is guaranteed to be persistent even if adapters are added or changed and the system is rebooted.

- **SCSI ID:** The unique SCSI identifier that signifies the exact disk or disks that are associated with a LUN.

You can access the runtime name of a storage location by examining the Adapter Details, as illustrated in Activity 7-1.

---

### Activity 7-1    Accessing the Runtime Name for a Datastore

1. Log on to your vSphere Web Client.

2. Select **Hosts and Clusters** view, click the host that contains the datastore, then click **Manage** and then **Storage**.

3. In the blue area below, click **Storage Adapters**.

4. Choose the storage adapter, and then under Adapter Details, choose **Paths**, as shown in Figure 7-2. You can view the runtime name, target, and LUN information for the adapter.

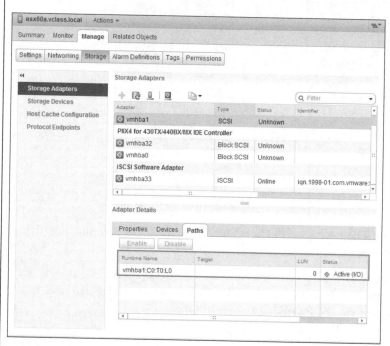

**Figure 7-2**   Viewing the Runtime Name

The naming convention for an NFS datastore is simply the name of the target that you create on the NFS Server. This can be an IP address or a hostname. Also, you can use a folder hierarchy for the share and give it a name on your host. Chapter 8 covers NFS shares in much more detail.

## Hardware/Dependent Hardware/Software iSCSI Initiators

Suppose that you decide to go with iSCSI as your storage technology of choice. Now you have yet another decision to make. This decision centers on how much work you want the VMkernel to do with regard to iSCSI versus how much you want to pay for your NICs that will be used for iSCSI. Figure 7-3 illustrates your choices.

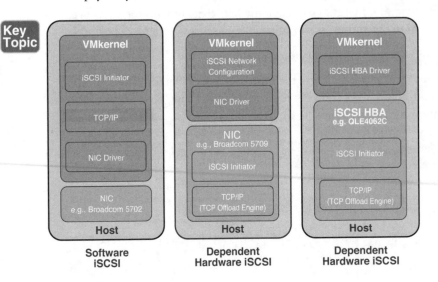

**Figure 7-3**   iSCSI Initiators

Two processes have to take place to create effective iSCSI storage:

- **Discovery:** The process of the host finding the iSCSI storage and identifying the LUNs that are presented.

- **TCP offload:** The process of deferring some of the management aspects of the TCP connection from the host's CPU. The device or service that does this is referred to as the TCP Offload Engine (TOE).

The real question then is whether you want the VMkernel to be associated with discovery and/or with TOE. You have three choices, as follows:

- **Hardware (independent hardware) iSCSI initiator:** In this case, a smarter and more expensive adapter is used that provides for discovery of the LUN as well as TOE. This completely removes the responsibility from the VMkernel and from the processors on the host. VMkernel ports are not required for this type of card. The host has only to supply the card with the drivers, and the card does the rest. If you have determined that your VMkernel is overloaded, this is an option that can improve performance.

- **Dependent hardware iSCSI initiator:** In this case, the card provides for the TOE, but the VMkernel must first provide the discovery of the LUN. This takes some of the work off the VMkernel and the processors on the host, but not all of it. In addition, VMkernel ports are required for this type of card. If possible, they should be on the same subnet as the iSCSI array that contains the data. In addition, if possible, the cards should be dedicated to this service.

- **Software iSCSI initiator:** In this case, the VMkernel provides for the discovery of the LUNs as well as for the TOE. The disadvantage of this type of initiator is that the VMkernel is doing all the work. This fact does not necessarily mean that performance will suffer. If the VMkernel is not otherwise overloaded, benchmark tests show this type of initiator to be every bit as fast as the others. In addition, software initiators allow for options such as bidirectional Challenge Handshake Authentication Protocol (CHAP) and per-target CHAP, which are discussed later in Chapter 9.

## Zoning and LUN Masking

One of your goals as a virtual data center administrator is to configure a method whereby your hosts can see a physical storage array on the SAN and, in essence, ask it, "What LUNs do you have for me today?" Meanwhile, the storage administrator's goal is to make sure that all LUNs are accessed appropriately and that the data on them is protected. These two goals should not be at odds with each other; instead, you and your storage administrator should be working as a team to protect each other. If you were able to access a LUN that you should not actually use, and you accidentally deleted important data, I would call that an RGE (resumé-generating event), and I hope to help you avoid those.

A couple of practices used with Fibre Channel SANs can be employed by the storage administrator to keep you from seeing LUNs that you have no need to see. These are referred to as *zoning* and *masking*. Zoning and masking are two different methods of accomplishing a similar result.

## Zoning

As you can see in Figure 7-4, each component (also called a node) of a Fibre Channel fabric is identified uniquely by a 64-bit address that is expressed in hexadecimal, called a World Wide Name (WWN). I focus on two types of nodes: the storage processor and the Fibre Channel host bus adapter (HBA). The storage administrator can configure zoning on the Fibre Channel switches to control which WWNs can see which other WWNs through the switch fabric, also referred to as *soft zoning*. In addition, the Fibre Channel switch might employ *hard zoning*, which determines which ports of the switch will be connected to storage processors. The purpose of using both of these methods is to keep you from accidentally accessing storage processors that do not apply to you, and thereby accessing volumes that do not apply to you either.

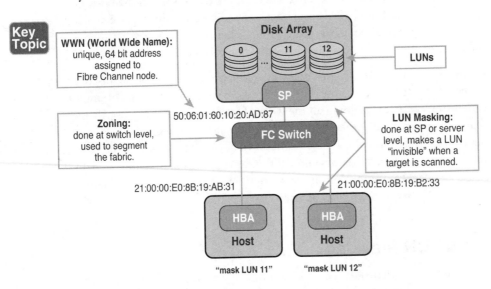

**Figure 7-4**    Zoning and Masking

## Masking

Whereas *zoning* is controlling which HBAs can see which SPs through the switch fabric, *masking* is controlling what the SPs tell the host with regard to the LUNs that they can provide. In other words, you or the storage administrator can configure the SP to "lie" to you about the LUNs to which it is connected. You might configure masking on your host if you notice that you can see a LUN that you know should not be used, but a much better practice is to contact the storage administrator to have the change made on the SP. In fact, masking cannot be done in the GUI of an ESXi 5.x or later host, but only on the command line. So, what does that tell you? It should tell you that VMware recommends that the masking be done on the SP through communication with the storage administrator. That way, everyone knows about it, and it does not cause "troubleshooting opportunities" later.

### Scanning/Rescanning Storage

As previously discussed, the datastores that you create will be connected to physical storage capacity on a local disk, SAN, or NAS. vSphere offers many alternatives to suit your needs and to allow you to make changes when needed. When you add a new host, that host automatically scans up to 256 Fibre Channel SAN LUNs (0–255). If you are installing the host locally, you might want to keep the Fibre Channel disconnected until you have the host installed, and then connect the Fibre Channel and perform the scan. However, iSCSI storage is automatically scanned whenever you create and configure a new iSCSI storage adapter.

In the interim, if you make a change to the physical storage, you should rescan to make sure that your hosts see the latest physical storage options. This is not done automatically because it takes resources to perform the scan, so VMware leaves it to your control as to when the scan should be done. To rescan the storage of your host, follow the steps in Activity 7-2.

---

**Activity 7-2    Rescanning the Storage of an ESXi Host**

1. Log on to your vSphere Web Client.

2. Select **Hosts and Clusters** view, click the host that contains the datastore, and then click **Manage** and then **Storage**.

3. Select the **Rescan Storage** link, as shown in Figure 7-5.

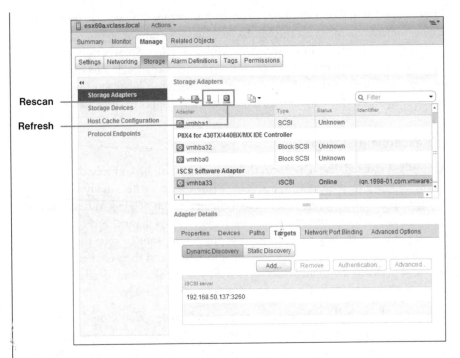

**Rescan**

**Refresh**

**Figure 7-5**   The Refresh and Rescan Links for ESXi Host Storage

4. Choose whether to scan for new storage devices, scan for new VFMS volumes, or both, as shown in Figure 7-6. Click **OK**.

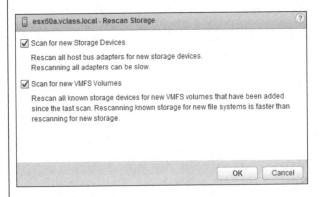

**Figure 7-6**   Scanning for New Storage Devices and Volumes

# Creating an NFS Share for Use with vSphere

As mentioned earlier, you can use a different method to accomplish the same result (storage options for VMs) by configuring an NFS share. An NFS share is generally located on a computer that is specialized for creating and sharing files using the NFS protocol. This type of computer is referred to as an NAS device. The overall system and practice of using an NAS device to provide shared files is generally referred to as using an NFS server. An NFS server contains one or more directories that can be shared with your ESXi hosts over a TCP/IP network. Your ESXi host will use one of its VMkernel ports to access the share.

To create an NFS server, start with an NAS device that you have built on a Windows, Linux, or UNIX box or that you have acquired through a third party. You must configure the share with the appropriate permissions and other attributes (also known as flags) so that your ESXi host can use its VMkernel ports to gain access to the share. The main aspects of your configuration should be as follows:

- A hostname or IP address that will be used as the target of the share. Take great care to always use the same IP address when connecting multiple hosts to the datastore. If the NAS device has two IP addresses, even for redundancy, it will be seen as two different datastores and not as one shared datastore.

- The shared folder or hierarchy of folders. This is case sensitive.

- Read-Write permissions for the share, so that you can configure your side for normal permissions or for Read-Only, as needed. You should not use Read-Only if you will be running VMs from this datastore.

- Sync (synchronous) rather than asynchronous for the type of communication. If you are going to run VMs, you need the system to communicate that a task is done when it is actually done, not when it is listed to be done or when it has begun.

- No root_squash. As a security measure, most administrators configure NFS shares with root_squash so that an attack presenting itself as root will not be given privileges. (In fact, it is the default setting.) Because this might keep you from accessing the VM files, you should configure the NFS share with no root_squash.

## Connecting to an NAS Device

After the NFS server is created, connecting to the NAS device is rather simple. You add a new storage location, but instead of it being another LUN, it is the share that you have created on the NAS. You can then configure the new storage to be normal (Read and Write) or Read-Only. As mentioned before, use Read-Only only if you are configuring the share for ISO files and not to store VM files. Also, for better performance and security, you should use a different VMkernel port on a separate vmnic.

To connect to an NAS device that is being used as an NFS server, follow the steps in Activity 7-3.

**Activity 7-3   Connecting to an NAS Device Used as an NFS Server**

1. Log on to your vSphere Web Client.

2. Select **Home** and then **Datastores**.

3. Right-click the data center in which you want to create the new NFS Data-store and select **Storage** and then **New Datastore**, as shown in Figure 7-7.

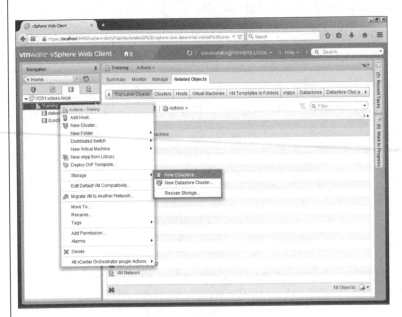

**Figure 7-7**   Creating a New NFS Datastore

4. Confirm your choice of data center by clicking **Next**, and then choose **NFS** under **Type**, as shown in Figure 7-8.

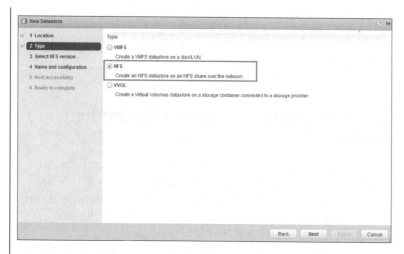

**Figure 7-8**   Choosing the NFS Type of Datastore

5.  Choose the version of NFS that you need. (Version 4.1 is covered in Chapter 8; for now, choose NFS 3). Click **Next**. Enter the datastore name, the IP address or hostname of the target NAS device, and the folder (case sensitive). Also, choose whether to mount NFS Read-Only, as shown in Figure 7-9. (You should not mount Read-Only if you intend to use this datastore for VMs.) Click **Next**.

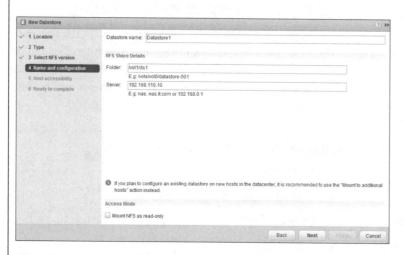

**Figure 7-9**   Configuring the NFS Datastore

> **6.** Monitor the progress of the datastore creation in the Recent Tasks pane. When this process is complete, you should see your new datastore in the Datastores view under your data center.

## Configuring and Editing Hardware and Dependent Hardware Initiators

As mentioned earlier, an independent hardware adapter (sometimes referred to as just a hardware adapter) is specifically manufactured to handle both TOE and discovery, and therefore requires no VMkernel port. You should follow the instructions that come with the card to install the software and then install the card so it can be recognized by your host. Specifics may vary by manufacturer.

A dependent hardware iSCSI adapter is a specialized third-party adapter that you have purchased to install into your ESXi host (for example, a Broadcom 5709 NIC). When you install the adapter, it presents two components to the same port: a simple network adapter and an iSCSI engine. After installation, the iSCSI engine appears on your list of storage adapters. It is enabled by default, but to use it, you must associate it with a VMkernel port and then configure it. You should also follow any third-party documentation associated with the card.

## Configuring and Editing Software Initiator Settings

Instead of purchasing expensive cards that perform the discovery or TOE, you can rely on the VMkernel to do both. To configure a software iSCSI initiator, you must add an iSCSI software initiator and associate it to a VMkernel port. It is a best practice to use a separate vmnic for each type of IP storage that you use. To enable software iSCSI initiator settings, follow the steps outlined in Activity 7-4.

**Activity 7-4   Enabling Software iSCSI Initiator Settings**

1. Log on to your vSphere Web Client.

2. Click your host and then on **Manage** and on **Storage**.

3. Click the **Add New Storage Adapter +** link, as shown in Figure 7-10, and choose **iSCSI Software Adapter**.

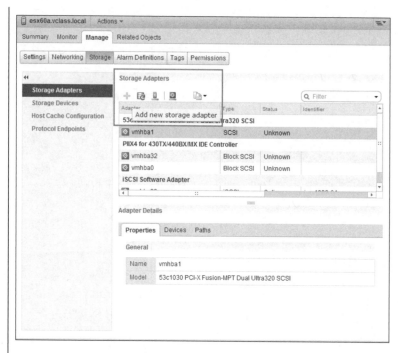

**Figure 7-10**   Adding Storage Adapters

**4.** In the iSCSI Software Adapter warning box, click **OK**.

**5.** Monitor Recent Tasks and Storage Adapters until the new adapter is created, and then select the new adapter and click the **Properties** link under Details.

**6.** From the new adapter's Properties dialog box, open the Dynamic Discovery tab and click **Add**.

**7.** Click the new adapter and then the **Targets** tab in Adapter Details at the bottom of the screen. Then click **Dynamic Discovery**, and finally click **Add**. Type the IP address or hostname of the storage process on the iSCSI array, as shown in Figure 7-11. You can leave the port at 3260. Rescan storage adapters as recommended.

**Figure 7-11**   Addressing an iSCSI Target

8. If CHAP will be configured, first uncheck the **Inherit settings from parent** option; then click **CHAP**, and enter the secret and mutual CHAP secret (if you are configuring for both). You can also elect to inherit the CHAP from the parent settings, which is discussed later in this chapter.

### Configuring iSCSI Port Binding

When you configure iSCSI port binding, you associate specific VMkernel ports to specific iSCSI adapters. You can associate more than one so that if one should fail, the other can take its place. In this way, you can create a multipath configuration with storage that presents only a single storage portal, such as DELL EqualLogic or HP/Lefthand.

You should configure iSCSI port binding using the steps in Activity 7-5.

## Activity 7-5   Configuring iSCSI Port Binding

1. Log on to your vSphere Web Client.

2. Click your host and then on **Manage,** and then **Storage**.

3. In the blue area, click **Storage Adapters** and then click the storage adapter that you want to configure, as shown in Figure 7-12.

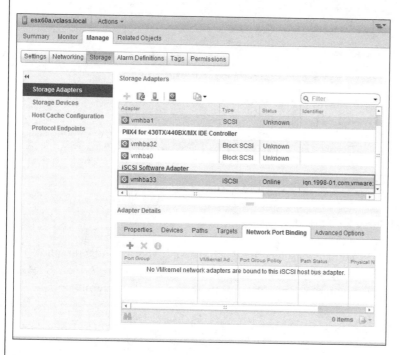

**Figure 7-12**   Selecting a Storage Adapter

4. In Adapter Details, click the **Network Port Binding** tab, as shown in Figure 7-13.

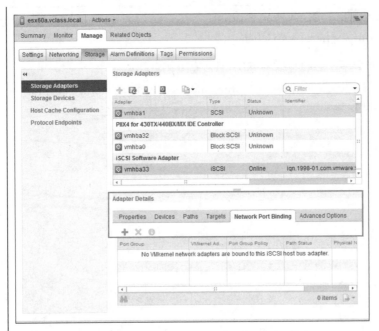

**Figure 7-13**  The Network Port Binding Configuration Tab

5. Click the **Add +** link, and select the Port Group, VMkernel Adapter, and Physical (Network) Adapter that you want to bind (see Figure 7-14). All iSCSI targets should be on the same subnet as their associated VMkernel ports.

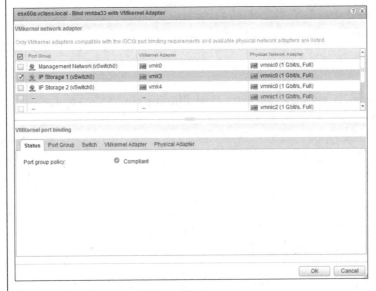

**Figure 7-14**  Binding a VMkernel Port

# Summary

This chapter covered the following main topics:

- The different types of storage adapters that you can use to create shared storage in your vSphere environment. Also covered were the naming conventions used to identify storage locations.

- Hardware, dependent hardware, and software initiators used for iSCSI. Also covered were zoning and masking to ensure that you can get to what you need but are protected from accidentally deleting data or having your data accidentally deleted by someone else.

- Creating and configuring NFS shares, iSCSI resources, and iSCSI port binding.

## Exam Preparation Tasks

## Review All the Key Topics

Review the most important topics from the chapter, noted with the Key Topic icon in the outer margin of the page. Table 7-2 lists these key topics and the page numbers where each is found. Know the main differences between storage types, such as VMFS and NFS. Understand the differences between storage technologies, such as Fibre Channel, iSCSI, NAS, and vSAN. Know how to create, configure, expand, and delete datastores.

**Table 7-2**  Key Topics for Chapter 7

| Key Topic Element | Description | Page Number |
|---|---|---|
| Bullet List | Advantages of Shared Storage | 163 |
| Figure 7-1 | Storage Overview | 164 |
| Bullet List | Storage Naming Conventions | 166 |
| Activity 7-1 | Accessing the Runtime Name for a Datastore | 167 |
| Figure 7-3 | iSCSI Initiators | 168 |
| Figure 7-4 | Zoning and Masking | 170 |
| Activity 7-2 | Rescanning the Storage of an ESXi Host | 171 |
| Bullet List | Configuring an NFS Server | 173 |
| Activity 7-3 | Connecting to an NAS Device Used as an NFS Server | 174 |
| Activity 7-4 | Enabling Software iSCSI Initiator Settings | 176 |
| Activity 7-5 | Configuring iSCSI Port Binding | 179 |

## Review Questions

The answers to these review questions are in Appendix A.

1.  Which storage adapter type is similar to a mapped drive?

    a. SAN

    b. Fibre Channel

    c. FCoE

    d. NAS

2.  Which two types of iSCSI initiator provide for TOE without the use of the VMkernel? (Choose two.)

    a. Software

    b. Independent hardware

    c. Thin provisioned

    d. Dependent hardware

3.  Which type of Fibre Channel network segmentation method controls whether one WWN can see another WWN?

    a. LUN masking

    b. Zoning

    c. VLAN

    d. VPN

4.  Which permissions should be set on an NAS datastore that will be used to store VM files?

    a. Read

    b. Root

    c. Read-Write

    d. Full Access

5.  In the runtime name vmhba1:0:2:3, what is the number of the storage processor?

    a. 0

    b. 1

    c. 2

    d. 3

6. Which of the following is a Network Address Authority unique identifier for a LUN?

   a. Canonical name

   b. SCSI ID

   c. Runtime name

   d. hba

7. Which of the following is the correct definition for zoning?

   a. Segmentation that defines which LUNs are visible on a WWN.

   b. Segmentation that defines which WWNs are visible to which WWNs through the switch fabric.

   c. The creation of network zones through VMkernel ports.

   d. A pointer file that is used to direct traffic to specific storage areas.

8. Which of the following is the correct definition for masking?

   a. Controlling what the storage processors tell the host with regard to the LUNs they can provide.

   b. Segmentation that defines which WWNs are visible to which WWNs through the switch fabric.

   c. The creation of network zones through VMkernel ports.

   d. A pointer file that is used to direct traffic to specific storage areas.

9. Which of the following is not true in regard to configuration of an NFS to support VMs?

   a. You should always set the permission for the share to Read-Only.

   b. You should set the communication type to sync.

   c. The share name is case sensitive.

   d. "No root squash" should be used on the share.

10. Which type of iSCSI initiator does not require a VMkernel port?

    a. Independent Hardware

    b. Dependent Hardware

    c. Software

    d. All iSCSI initiators require a VMkernel port.

**This chapter covers the following subjects:**

- Benefits of NFS 4.1

- Virtual SAN Hardware Requirements

- Virtual SAN Network Requirements

- Use Cases for VSAN Configurations

- Configuring and Managing Virtual Volumes

Whereas the previous chapter covered the "tried and true" storage methods that have been around for many years, this one addresses the very latest storage techniques that change the way we look at storage. It covers your latest options in regard to NFS datastores and benefits that you might gain by using NFS 4.1 instead of 3.0. It also covers the hardware and network requirements for new types of storage, such as VSAN and VVOLs.

## CHAPTER 8

# Configuring Software-Defined Storage

## "Do I Know This Already?" Quiz

The "Do I Know This Already?" quiz allows you to assess whether you should read this entire chapter or simply jump to the "Exam Preparation Tasks" section for review. If you are in doubt, read the entire chapter. Table 8-1 outlines the major headings in this chapter and the corresponding "Do I Know This Already?" quiz questions. You can find the answers in Appendix A, "Answers to the 'Do I Know This Already?' Quizzes and Chapter Review Questions."

**Table 8-1**  Headings and Questions

| Foundation Topics Section | Questions Covered in This Section |
| --- | --- |
| Benefits of NFS 4.1 | 1, 2 |
| Virtual SAN Hardware Requirements | 3, 4 |
| Virtual SAN Network Requirements | 5, 6 |
| Use Cases for VSAN Configurations | 7 |
| Configuring and Managing Virtual Volumes (VVOLS) | 8, 9, 10 |

**1.** Which of following is *not* true regarding NFS 4.1?

    **a.** You can use the traditional authentication mechanism that uses the root account.

    **b.** You can use an Active Directory account and Kerberos authentication.

    **c.** You can attach NFS 4.1 to the same array at the same time as NFS 3.

    **d.** NFS 4.1 can provide multipathing that NFS 3 cannot provide.

2. Which of the following are true regarding NFS 4.1 authentication? (Choose two.)

   a. The default form of authentication still requires no_root_squash.

   b. The default form of authentication does not require no_root_squash.

   c. You can use only Active Directory accounts, not the root account.

   d. You can use the root account or change the configuration to use an Active Directory account.

3. What is the maximum number of hosts in a vSphere 6 cluster that supports Virtual SAN?

   a. 2

   b. 4

   c. 64

   d. 8

4. How many magnetic disks are used at a minimum for capacity in a hybrid disk group?

   a. 1

   b. 2

   c. 0

   d. 3

5. Which of the following is *not* true regarding Virtual SAN?

   a. Hybrid configurations must have a minimum of 1 Gbps connections between hosts.

   b. All-flash configurations must have a minimum of 10 Gbps connections between hosts.

   c. All hosts must have at least one disk in the VSAN to use the VSAN for their VMs.

   d. IPv6 is not supported for VSAN at this time.

6. Which of the following is true regarding VSAN configuration?

   a. All hosts must be connected to the same Layer 2 network.

   b. Multipathing support is not required between switches or routers.

   c. Minimum host bandwidth is the same for hybrid and all-flash configurations.

   d. VSAN fully supports both IPv4 and IPv6.

7. Which of the following are true regarding VSAN use cases? (Choose two.)

   a. VSAN allows for software-based control of storage on hosts.

   b. VSAN requires that more LUNs are created, just for VSAN.

   c. With VSAN, companies can add storage capacity every time they add a host.

   d. VSAN cannot be used for VDI environments.

8. Which of the following are required to use VVOLs? (Choose two.)

   a. At least one magnetic disk and one SSD per host

   b. At least two SSDs per host

   c. Create a Virtual Datastore

   d. Register Service Providers

9. What is the purpose of the virtual datastore in VVOLs?

   a. The virtual datastore provides the actual storage for the VM files.

   b. The virtual datastore represents the logical connection to the physical volumes that will store the VM files.

   c. The virtual datastore in VVOLs is equivalent to a storage processor in iSCSI volumes.

   d. A virtual datastore is not required for VVOLs.

10. Which of the following is the name for the connection from the host to its underlying VVOL storage?

    a. Storage processor

    b. Virtual volume

    c. Protocol endpoint

    d. Storage container

## Foundation Topics

# Benefits of NFS 4.1

vSphere 6.0 is the first version of vSphere to support NFS 4.1. This means that you can take advantage of the additional features provided by this protocol as long as your system fully supports it and you are willing to change methods for all hosts connected to a specific NFS array. This is because NFS 4.1 uses server-side locking, whereas NFS 3 uses a proprietary client-side locking. This makes the two protocols incompatible with each other. As a result, it is a best practice to use only one type of protocol access on each NFS array, either NFS 4.1 or NFS 3. This is clearly called out on the configuration wizard with a "yellow bang," as shown in Figure 8.1, because only vSphere 6 and later hosts will support NFS 4.1, which means that all your hosts will have to be upgraded along with your NFS array.

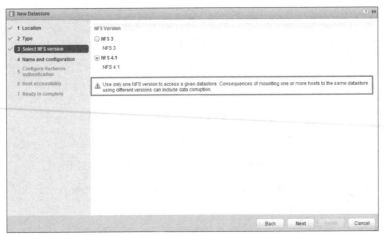

**Figure 8-1**   Configuration Wizard Warning

So, with that out of the way, let's discuss the benefits that you will gain if you decide to make the change. These benefits are in the form of better performance and availability through multipathing load balancing and in the form of security.

### NFS v4.1 Multipathing and Load Balancing

In NFS 3, there is no provision for load balancing or multipathing because there is no way to configure more than one server address. As shown in Figure 8-2, the NFS 4.1 configuration wizard makes it easy to configure multiple addresses, which you can then use to configure multipathing. You simply add addresses with a comma between them and click the "+" sign. The wizard then indicates clearly the addresses that are being added, as shown in Figure 8-3.

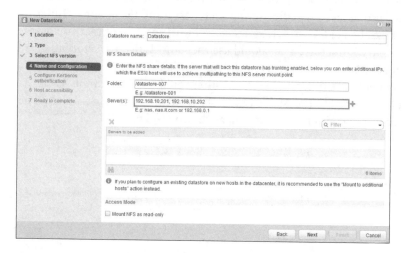

**Figure 8-2**  Configuring Multiple Addresses for Multipathing

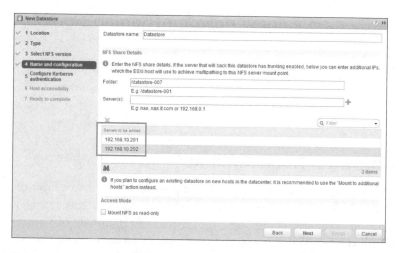

**Figure 8-3**  Confirming Multiple Addresses for Multipathing

## Additional Security in NFS 4.1 Provided by Kerberos Authentication

In NFS 3, authentication at the NFS server is provided by giving the root account access to the share. As you may remember from Chapter 7, "Connecting Shared Storage Devices to vSphere," you even had to turn off the inherent "root squash" protection for that share. This is an effective method, but it certainly is not the most secure way to handle the connection.

In NFS 4.1, you can still use root account and the traditional no_root_squash setting, but can also define a specific user on each host using the command-line configuration of **esxsfg-nas -U -v 4.1**, as associated with an account that you have created in your Active Directory. You should use the same Active Directory user for all hosts that are going to be associated with each other. If two ESXi hosts in the same environment have different users, vMotion could fail. In addition, each ESXi host should be joined to the Active Directory domain, and Kerberos should be enabled in the datastore configuration wizard, as shown in Figure 8-4.

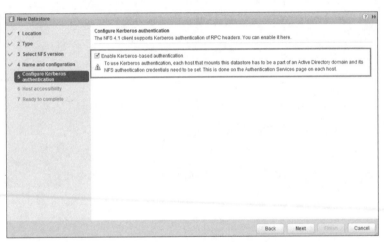

**Figure 8-4**    Enabling Kerberos Authentication for NFS v4.1

## Virtual SAN Hardware Requirements

Virtual SAN (VSAN) is a vSphere cluster setting that provides a distributed layer of software that runs natively on all the hosts in the cluster and creates a shared storage area that all the hosts can use. It requires a host cluster of a minimum of 3 hosts and can be used with clusters containing up to the current maximum of 64 hosts. VSAN is relatively easy to configure and provides many benefits with regard to your vSphere storage options.

VSAN is a software-defined approach that turns otherwise wasted local storage volumes on hosts into an aggregated shared storage location that supports HA, DRS, and so on. However, to participate in a VSAN cluster, your hosts must have the correct hardware configuration. This section discusses the hardware requirements for a host to participate in a VSAN.

There are many hardware requirements in regard to VSAN. They generally fall into the categories of storage, memory, and CPU. As you can imagine, the storage-related requirements are by far the most stringent and detailed, as shown in Table 8-2.

**Table 8-2**  Hardware Requirements for VSAN

| Storage Component | Requirements |
|---|---|
| Cache | One SAS or SATA solid state disk (SSD) or PCIe flash device. |
| | Cache devices must not be formatted with VMFS or any other file system. |
| Virtual Machine Data Storage | Either one magnetic disk (for hybrid configuration) or one SAS or SATA solid state disk (SSD) or PCIe flash device. |
| Storage Controllers | SAS, SATA, or RAID in passthrough or RAID 0 mode. |

In general, you need two disks; both can be SSD, or one can be magnetic and the other SSD. One disk will be used for storage capacity while the other will be used only for read caching and write buffering to improve performance.

In addition, each host should contain a minimum of 32 GB of memory. This will accommodate the maximum configuration of five disk groups (capacity and caching) and seven devices per group, per host.

Finally, you should consider that VSAN will place a load on the CPU of the host. The actual load will vary depending on your configuration and use of the VSAN. The additional load should not be more than 10 percent of current CPU load on the host. It should also be mentioned that hosts in the cluster that do not participate in the VSAN can still benefit from storing associated VM files in the VSAN.

## Virtual SAN Network Requirements

In addition to general hardware requirements, there are many network requirements and considerations with regard to VSAN. Many of these may already be met, just by the fact that you have a vSphere cluster in place, but you will need to meet all of them to support VSAN. Table 8-3 shows the networking requirements for VSAN in vSphere 6.0.

**Table 8-3** Network Requirements for VSAN

| Networking Component | Requirement |
| --- | --- |
| Host bandwidth | Dedicated 1 Gbps for hybrid configurations. |
| | Dedicated or shared 10 Gbps for all-flash configurations. |
| Connection between hosts | Each host must be part of the VSAN cluster to use the resources provided by the VSAN. |
| Host network | All hosts must be connected to the same Layer 2 network. |
| Multicast | Multicast must be enabled on all switches and routers that will handle VSAN traffic. |
| IPv4 and IPv6 support | VSAN is currently supported for only IPv4. IPv6 is not supported at this time. |

## Use Cases for VSAN Configurations

In essence, VSAN provides the same opportunity for storage management that the vSphere provides for compute resource management—software-based control with a "single pane of glass." For a business that is experiencing tremendous growth, VSAN can add storage capacity every time the business purchases a new host. In addition, VSAN removes a layer of complexity associated with creating partitions and logical unit numbers (LUNs) that may or may not be used, depending on what transpires for the business in the future. Instead, each vmdk and snapshot can be individually controlled for redundancy and performance within the same aggregated datastore. It's truly a new and different way of looking at storage that will begin to transform both server and virtual desktop interface (VDI) environments in the years to come.

## Configuring and Managing Virtual Volumes (VVOLs)

Much like VSAN, VVOLs provide a software-based policy management solution. The difference is that this storage solution can extend well beyond the local disk capacity of your hosts. VVOLs allow you to do away with Gold, Silver, and Bronze storage type "guessing games" that might cause you to overprovision some levels of storage while underprovisioning others. With VVOLs, the right level of storage can be provisioned automatically when each VM is created. In the long run, this also saves time because you (or your storage admin) will not have to create the partitions and the LUNs that go with the traditional storage guessing games.

However, configuring VVOLs for the first time requires that you follow a series of steps to provide for the resources and the connections for acquiring and managing them. It's important that you understand each of these steps and perform them in the right order. This section covers the steps necessary to configure and manage VVOLs. I start with the general steps and then cover each one in more detail.

The general steps required to configure VVOLs are as follows:

**Step 1.**     Register storage providers for virtual volumes.

**Step 2.**     Create a virtual datastore.

**Step 3.**     Review and manage protocol endpoints.

**Step 4.**     Optionally, modify multipathing policies.

## Registering Storage Providers for Virtual Volumes

Third-party storage vendors provide software that works through VMware APIs for Storage Awareness (VASA). This software is referred to as Storage Provider (not the vendor). Your VVOLs will use this software to provide communication between the vSphere and the storage. The storage characteristics appear in the VM Storage Policies interface so you can use them to create storage policies for the VMs. These policies can then be enforced to provide for the redundancy of the VM files and their performance characteristics. To use VVOLs, you must first register these storage providers. You can register a new Storage Provider on the Manage/ Storage Providers tab of the vCenter Server in your vSphere Web Client, as shown in Figure 8-5. The credentials that you will use to authenticate to a specific provider URL can be obtained from your storage vendor or your storage administrator.

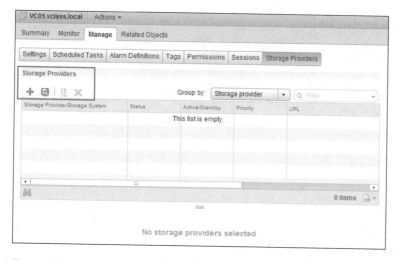

**Figure 8-5**    Registering a New Storage Provider

## Create a Virtual Datastore

After you have registered the Storage Providers to be used with your VVOLs, you then need to create a datastore that will represent the logical connection to the physical volumes that provide the storage. You begin to create a new VVOL in much the same way that you create any other datastore, by right-clicking your data center in Datastores view, then clicking **Storage** and then **New Datastore**, as shown in Figure 8-6. You should then select **Next** and then **VVOL**, as shown in Figure 8-7. Then it's just a matter of associating the backing storage container to your new datastore, as shown in Figure 8-8.

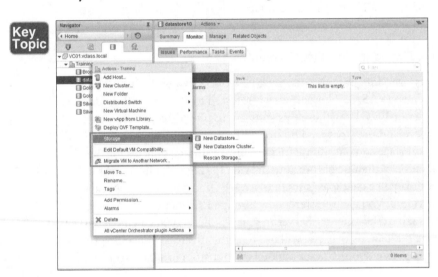

**Figure 8-6**   Creating a New Datastore

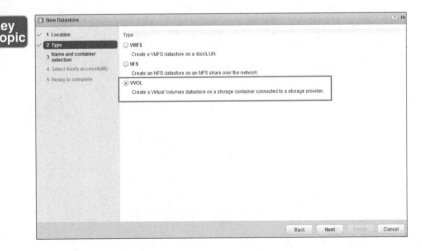

**Figure 8-7**   Choosing VVOL for New Datastore Type

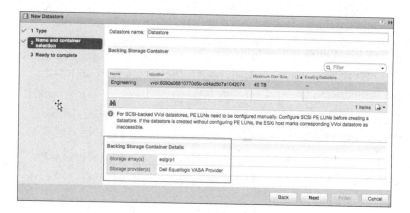

**Figure 8-8**    Associating Backing Storage to New Virtual Datastore

### Review and Manage Protocol Endpoints

Much like iSCSI uses targets or storage processors to provide a connection of the host to the underlying storage, the VVOL system uses an entity called a protocol endpoint (PE). Protocol endpoints are exported, along with their associated storage containers, by the storage system through the storage provider software. They become visible in the vSphere Web Client after you map a storage container to a virtual datastore. You can view and modify the protocol endpoints as needed by clicking the **Manage** and then **Storage** tabs of the host, as shown in Figure 8-9.

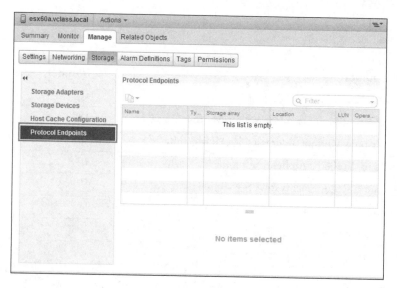

**Figure 8-9**    The Protocol Endpoints Link

## Summary

This chapter covered the following main topics:

- The benefits of NFS v4.1—in particular, its capabilities in regard to multi-pathing and authentication.

- An overall discussion of VSAN, including VSAN hardware requirements, VSAN networking requirements, and general use cases for VSAN.

- Creating and managing VVOLs in vSphere. This included a brief discussion on the purpose of VVOLs as well as the overall steps included in creating them.

## Exam Preparation Tasks

## Review All the Key Topics

Review the most important topics from the chapter, noted with the Key Topic icon in the outer margin of the page. Table 8-4 lists these key topics and the page numbers where each is found. Know the main differences between storage types, such as VMFS and NFS. Understand the differences between storage technologies, such as Fibre Channel, iSCSI, NAS, and vSAN. Know how to create, configure, expand, and delete datastores.

**Table 8-4** Key Topics for Chapter 8

| Key Topic Element | Description | Page Number |
|---|---|---|
| Figure 8-1 | Configuration Wizard Warning | 188 |
| Figure 8-2 | Configuring Multiple Addresses for Multipathing | 189 |
| Figure 8-3 | Confirming Multiple Addresses for Multipathing | 189 |
| Figure 8-4 | Enabling Kerberos Authentication for NFS 4.1 | 190 |
| Table 8-2 | Hardware Requirements for VSAN | 191 |
| Table 8-3 | Network Requirements for VSAN | 192 |
| Step list | Steps required for configuring VVOLs | 193 |
| Figure 8-5 | Registering a New Storage Provider | 193 |

| Key Topic Element | Description | Page Number |
|---|---|---|
| Figure 8-6 | Creating a New Datastore | 194 |
| Figure 8-7 | Choosing VVOL for New Datastore Type | 194 |
| Figure 8-8 | Associating Backing Storage to New Virtual Datastore | 195 |
| Figure 8-9 | The Protocol Endpoints Link | 195 |

## Review Questions

The answers to these review questions are in Appendix A.

1. Which of the following are true regarding NSX 4.1? (Choose two.)

    a. You can use the traditional authentication mechanism that uses the root account.

    b. You can use an Active Directory account and Kerberos authentication.

    c. You can attach NFS 4.1 to the same array at the same time as NFS 3.

    d. NFS 4.1 can provide the same type of multipathing that NFS 3 can provide.

2. Which of the following are *not* true regarding NFS 4.1 authentication? (Choose two.)

    a. The default form of authentication still requires no_root_squash.

    b. The default form of authentication does not require no_root_squash.

    c. You can only use Active Directory accounts, not the root account.

    d. You can use the root account or change the configuration to use an Active Directory account.

3. What is the minimum number of hosts in a cluster that supports VSAN?

    a. 2

    b. 4

    c. 3

    d. 8

4. How many magnetic disks are used at a minimum for capacity in an all-flash disk group?

   a. 1

   b. 2

   c. 0

   d. 3

5. Which of the following are true regarding VSAN?

   a. Hybrid configurations must have a minimum of 1 Gbps connections between hosts.

   b. All-flash configurations must have a minimum of 1 Gbps connections between hosts.

   c. All hosts must have at least one disk in the VSAN to use the VSAN for their VMs.

   d. IPv6 is not supported for VSAN at this time.

6. Which of the following are *not* true regarding VSAN configuration?

   a. All hosts must be connected to the same Layer 2 network.

   b. Multipathing support is not required between switches or routers.

   c. Minimum host bandwidth is the same for hybrid configurations; which is 1/10 that for all-flash configurations.

   d. VSAN fully supports both IPv4 and IPv6.

7. Which of the following are *not true* regarding VSAN use cases? (Choose two.)

   a. VSAN allows for software-based control of storage on hosts.

   b. VSAN requires that more LUNs are created, just for VSAN.

   c. With VSAN, companies can add storage capacity every time they add a host.

   d. VSAN cannot be used for VDI environments.

8. Which of the following are *not* required to use VVOLs? (Choose two.)

   a. At least one magnetic disk and one SSD per host

   b. At least two SSDs per host

   c. Create a virtual datastore.

   d. Register service providers.

9. What is the purpose of the protocol endpoint in VVOLs?

   a. The protocol endpoint provides the actual storage for the VM files.

   b. The virtual datastore represents the logical connection to the physical volumes that will store the VM files.

   c. The protocol endpoint in VVOLs is equivalent to a storage processor in iSCSI volumes.

   d. A protocol endpoint is not required for VVOLs.

10. Which of the following is the name for the connection from the host to its underlying VVOL storage?

   a. Storage processor

   b. Virtual volume

   c. Protocol endpoint

   d. Storage container

**This chapter covers the following subjects:**

- Supported NFS Versions
- Configuring NFS Storage for vmdk Formatting
- Configuring Storage Multipathing (SAN)
- Determining VMFS Requirements
- Configuring and Managing VMFS Extents

The previous chapter covered methods of connecting storage to hosts. In this chapter I discuss utilizing the storage that is provided by the host. This includes utilizing both NFS datastores as well as VMFS datastores to create reliable storage environments for VMs. In addition, I discuss improving reliability and performance through storage multipathing.

## CHAPTER 9

# Creating and Configuring VMFS and NFS Datastores

## "Do I Know This Already?" Quiz

The "Do I Know This Already?" quiz allows you to assess whether you should read this entire chapter or simply jump to the "Exam Preparation Tasks" section for review. If you are in doubt, read the entire chapter. Table 9-1 outlines the major headings in this chapter and the corresponding "Do I Know This Already?" quiz questions. You can find the answers in Appendix A, "Answers to the 'Do I Know This Already?' Quizzes and Chapter Review Questions."

**Table 9-1** Foundation Topics

| Foundation Topics Section | Questions Covered in This Section |
|---|---|
| Supported NFS Versions | 1 |
| Configuring NFS Storage for vmdk Formatting | 2, 3 |
| Configuring Storage Multipathing (SAN) | 4, 5 |
| Determining VMFS Requirements | 6 |
| Configuring and Managing VMFS Extents | 7, 8, 9, 10 |

1. Which of the following is *not* true with regard to NFS 4.1?

   a. vSphere 6 supports both NFS 3 and NFS 4.1.

   b. You can mount both NFS 3 and NFS 4.1 on the same array at the same time.

   c. NFS 3 is not compatible with NFS 4.1.

   d. You will have to upgrade any legacy hosts to support NFS 4.1.

**2.** When you are creating an NFS share for storing VM files, which of the following are true? (Choose two.)

   **a.** You should leave the default setting in regard to Mount NFS as Read-Only.

   **b.** You will need read and write permission to the share.

   **c.** You should check the box to Mount NFS as Read-Only.

   **d.** You should only need read permission to the share.

**3.** Which of the following is true regarding configuring NFS for vmdk files in vSphere 6?

   **a.** NFS 4.1 offers Kerberos Authentication.

   **b.** NFS 4.1 defaults to root authentication.

   **c.** NFS 3 is no longer supported.

   **d.** Configuring Kerberos Authentication requires only one check box and no other configuration on the host.

**4.** Which of the following multipathing options will be automatically configured by your host if it is connected to a SAN that is configured as Active/Active?

   **a.** Fixed

   **b.** MRU

   **c.** Round-robin

   **d.** There is no autoconfiguration of multipathing.

**5.** Which of the following multipathing policies uses more than one path during a data transfer session?

   **a.** Only MRU

   **b.** Only round-robin

   **c.** Only fixed

   **d.** All multipathing policies use more than one path during a data transfer session.

**6.** Which of the following are true regarding VMFS-3 in vSphere 6? (Choose two.)

  **a.** vSphere 6 supports upgrading VMFS-3 to VMFS-5.

  **b.** You can create both VMFS-3 and VMFS-5 datastores in vSphere 6.

  **c.** VMFS-5 datastores can contain 64 TB extents.

  **d.** VMFS-5 can support only 2 TB virtual disks.

**7.** Which of the following are true regarding VMFS extents? (Choose two.)

  **a.** A datastore with only one LUN will have one extent.

  **b.** A datastore with only one LUN can have no extents.

  **c.** Adding a new extent to a datastore requires another LUN.

  **d.** You can add an extent to a datastore on the same LUN.

**8.** Which of the following are true regarding expanding a datastore in vSphere 6? (Choose two.)

  **a.** You always expand a datastore by adding to one of its current extents.

  **b.** You can expand a datastore by adding an extent.

  **c.** Datastores can be both expanded and extended.

  **d.** Datastores cannot be both expanded and extended.

**9.** Which of the following are true regarding expanding an extent for a VMFS datastore? (Choose two.)

  **a.** All extents can be expanded, regardless of how they were created.

  **b.** Only extents that do not fill the current capacity of their LUN can be expanded.

  **c.** You cannot determine the size of the LUN with the vSphere client, only the size of the extent.

  **d.** You can determine both the size of the LUN and the size of the extent with the vSphere client.

**10.** Which of the following are true regarding expanding and extending VMFS datastores? (Choose two.)

  **a.** You can extend a VMFS datastore without taking it offline.

  **b.** You cannot extend a VMFS datastore without taking it offline.

  **c.** You can expand a VMFS datastore without taking it offline.

  **d.** You cannot expand a VMFS datastore without taking it offline.

**Foundation Topics**

## Supported NFS Versions

As I mentioned earlier, vSphere 6 makes NFS 4.1 available for the first time; however, only vSphere 6 hosts support it. In addition, because NFS 4.1 is not compatible with NFS 3, you will not be able to use both versions on the same storage array. This means that if you want to use NFS 4.1 on an NFS storage array, you should upgrade all the hosts that will connect to the array to vSphere 6.

## Configuring NFS Storage for vmdk Formatting

You can make an NFS share on an NFS server available to your host by mounting it to the host. You can liken mounting an NFS share to creating a mapped drive. In other words, there is a share in the network, and if you connect to that share with the correct permissions, you can access the data on the share. Based on this analogy, what information would you think that you might need for the connection? You guessed it. You would need the address of the share and the name. In essence, that is exactly what you need to mount an NFS datastore. Of course, the NFS server must first be set up somewhere in the network from which you can access it. After this is done, to mount the NFS datastore to your host, follow the steps outlined in Activity 9-1.

**Activity 9-1    Mounting an NFS Datastore**

1. Log on to your vSphere Web Client.

2. Click **Home** and then **Storage**.

3. Right-click the data center on which you want to create the datastore and select **Storage** and then **New Datastore**, as shown in Figure 9-1.

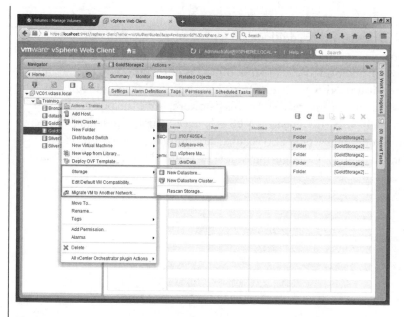

**Figure 9-1**   Creating a New Datastore

4.  Leave the data center that you selected and click **Next**.

5.  On Select Storage Type, select **NFS**, as shown in Figure 9-2, and then click
    **Next**. Choose **NFS 3** or **NFS 4.1**, and click **Next**.

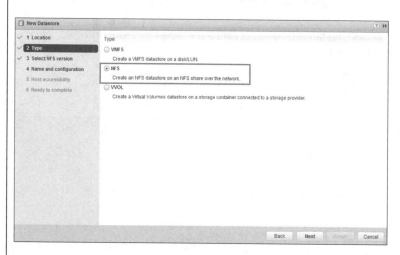

**Figure 9-2**   Mounting an NFS Datastore

**6.** Enter the datastore name and the IP address (IPv4 or IPv6), or the hostname of the NFS server. Enter additional addresses for multipathing with 4.1 and click **+**. Also, enter the folder name (case sensitive) where the shared files are stored. In addition, if you are mounting ISO files only, you may want to check the **Mount NFS as Read-Only** check box, as shown in Figure 9-3, but if you are planning to store VMs in this datastore, leave the box unchecked and then click **Next**. If you chose NFS 4.1, select whether to enable Kerberos authentication. (This would also require the additional configuration discussed in Chapter 8, "Configuring Software-Defined Storage.") Click **Next**.

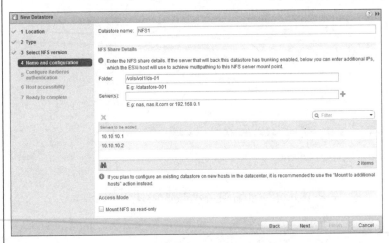

**Figure 9-3**   Addressing and Naming an NFS Datastore

**7.** Select the hosts that should have access to the new datastore and click **Next**, as shown in Figure 9-4.

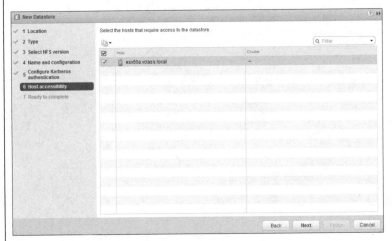

**Figure 9-4**   Selecting Host(s) for NFS Datastore Access

**8.** Review your settings and click **Finish**, as shown in Figure 9-5.

**Figure 9-5**   Reviewing Settings for a New NFS Datastore

Just as mounting an NFS datastore can be likened to mapping a drive, unmounting an NFS datastore can be likened to removing a mapped drive. The key point is that when you remove a mapped drive, you remove only your link to the data it contains, but you do not remove the data or the metadata. The same holds true for unmounting an NFS datastore. In other words, unmounting the NFS datastore does delete the datastore from your host, but it does not delete the data contained on the share or even its metadata. To unmount an NFS datastore, right-click the datastore that you want to unmount, select **Unmount Datastore**, and confirm your selection.

## Configuring Storage Multipathing (SAN)

Generally speaking, you do not have to change the default multipathing settings that your host uses for a specific storage device, because the host software is very good at making the right choice. VMware supports three native policies: Fixed, Most Recently Used, and Round Robin. Of the three, the only one that allows more than one path to be used during the same data transfer session is Round Robin. The others are availability policies used for fault tolerance and failover. The following is a brief description of each of these policies:

- **Fixed:** This is the default used with a SAN that is set to Active/Active. In this case, the preferred path is used whenever available. If the preferred path should fail, another path is used until the preferred path is restored, at which point the data moves back onto the preferred path. The disadvantage of this solution is that a flapping connection could cause the paths to "play ping-pong" with each other, a condition known as *thrashing*.

■ **Most Recently Used:** This is the default used with a SAN that is set to Active/Passive. With this policy, a path is chosen and continues to be used so long as it does not fail. If it fails, another path is used, and it continues to be used so long as it does not fail, even if the previous path becomes available again.

■ **Round Robin:** This is the only path selection policy that uses more than one path during a data transfer session. Data is divided into multiple paths, and the paths are alternated to send data. Even though data is sent on only one path at a time, this increases the size of "the pipe" and therefore allows more data transfer in the same period of time. If you decide to use Round Robin, the settings should be coordinated and tested between you and the storage administrator.

To show you where the settings are located, suppose that you have selected a Fixed Path Selection Policy (PSP) and you want to choose the preferred path instead of letting VMware do it for you. Follow the steps outlined in Activity 9-2.

### Activity 9-2   Selecting the Preferred Path for a VMFS Datastore

1. Log on to your vSphere Web Client.

2. Click **Home** and then **Datastores**.

3. Click the datastore that you want to configure, and then click **Manage**, **Settings**, and then **Connectivity and Multipathing**, as shown in Figure 9-6.

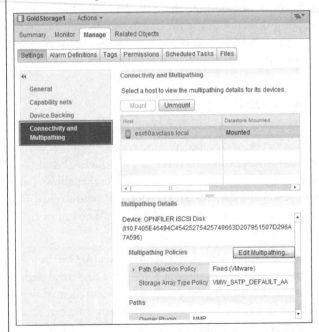

**Figure 9-6**   The Connectivity and Multipathing Link for a Host

4. Click the **Edit Multipathing** button, and then choose **Fixed (VMware)**. Then right-click your preferred path and select **Preferred**.

5. Note that the asterisk (*) under the Preferred column denotes the preferred path, as shown in Figure 9-7. Click **OK** to confirm.

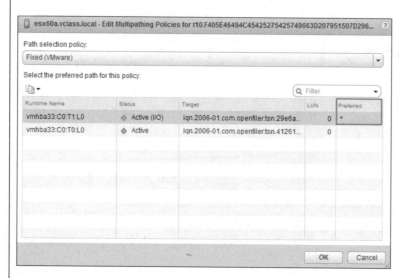

**Figure 9-7**  Choosing a Fixed Policy and a Preferred Path

### Disabling a Path to a VMFS Datastore

You might wonder why you would want to disable a path to a datastore. What if you wanted to make changes to the underlying components in that path, such as the switches or cables that connect the host to the datastore? In that case, you might want to temporarily disable that path so that the system would not use it or even try to rely on it for fault tolerance. You should make sure that there is another path available, but, as a precaution, the system will not allow you to disable a path if it is the only path to the datastore, as shown in Figure 9-8. To disable a path to a VMFS datastore, follow the steps outlined in Activity 9-3.

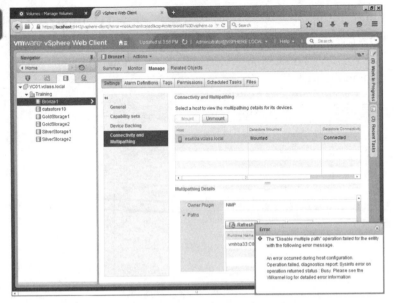

**Figure 9-8**  An Attempt to Disable the Only Path to a Datastore

**Activity 9-3   Disabling a Path to a VMFS Datastore**

1. Log on to your vSphere Web Client.

2. Click **Home** and then **Datastores**.

3. Click the datastore that you want to configure, and click the **Connectivity and Multipathing** link in the blue area.

4. Expand **Paths** at the bottom of the dialog box.

5. Choose the path that you want to disable and select **Disable**, as shown in Figure 9-9.

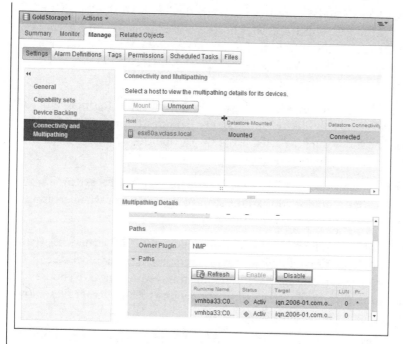

**Figure 9-9**   Disabling One Path to a Datastore

# Determining VMFS Requirements

As mentioned previously, your datastores are logical containers that are analogous to the file systems within them. In other words, datastores hide the specifics of a storage device and provide a uniform model for storing VMs. As you know, you can also use them for storing ISO images, VM templates, and even floppy images. I also mentioned that a good practice is to name your datastores based on what you are using them for, such as Production, Test-Dev, ISO_Library, and so on.

Therefore, the number of datastores that you need will be based on how diversified you are with regard to their use. In other words, you may want to create different datastores for different types of VMs. This approach will be especially helpful if the underlying disk for the datastores also differs in performance, which is highly likely. In that regard, you can group datastores into folders based on what types of VMs they contain. This makes it possible to assign permissions and alarms at the folder level, thereby reducing administrative effort. In addition, it is now possible to create storage profiles to make sure that your VMs are connecting to the appropriate datastore.

Whereas ESX/ESXi 3.5 and 4.x hosts can use only the legacy version of VMFS referred to as VMFS-3, ESXi 5.0 and later hosts can use the latest and current version referred to as VMFS-5. In fact, you can create only VMFS-5 datastores in vSphere 6. You can upgrade VMFS-3 to VMFS-5, but you cannot create new VMFS-3 datastores.

VMFS-5 has capabilities that exceed the legacy version and allow for more efficient use of storage and greater flexibility for the storage administrator and the vSphere administrator. The following is a partial list of the capabilities of VMFS-5 and the benefit that each new capability provides:

- Support for greater than 2 TB storage devices for each VMFS extent. This increases the flexibility for you and the storage administrator when creating and using LUNs. You can create and use up to 64 TB extents.

- Standard 1 MB file system block size with support of 62 TB virtual disks (with Version 10 or later VMs). Previous versions required a larger block size to store larger files. This meant that the administrator would have to choose between more efficient file storage or the capability to store larger files. Now you can have both at the same time.

- Support of greater than 2 TB disk size for RDMs in physical compatibility mode. You can use physical compatibility RDMs up to 64 TB in size.

- Online, in-place upgrade capability. You can upgrade VMFS-3 datastores to VMFS-5 without any disruption to your hosts or VMs.

## Configuring and Managing VMFS Extents

Generally speaking, to create a VMFS datastore, you mount a logical volume (the datastore) to one or more logical unit numbers (LUNs) that are local or on a storage area network (SAN). After the LUN is mounted to the VMFS datastore, it's also referred to as an *extent*. Therefore, a datastore mounted to only one LUN still has one extent.

You can use the tools included in vCenter to quickly create, rename, delete, or unmount VMFS datastores. To create a datastore, you should start the wizard, name the datastore, and choose the LUNs to be used for the datastore. You can use only LUNs that do not currently have a VMFS datastore on them. To create a new VMFS datastore, follow the steps outlined in Activity 9-4.

## Activity 9-4   Creating a VMFS Datastore

1. Log on to your vSphere Web Client.

2. Click **Home** and then **Datastores**; then select the data center on which you want to create the datastore.

3. Click the **Related Objects** tab.

4. In the upper-right corner, click the **New Datastore** icon, as shown in Figure 9-10.

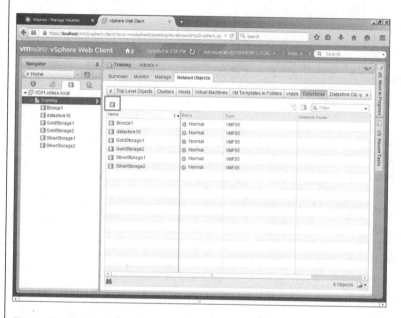

**Figure 9-10**   The New Datastore Icon

5. Select **Next** to accept the current data center, and then choose **VMFS**, as shown in Figure 9-11.

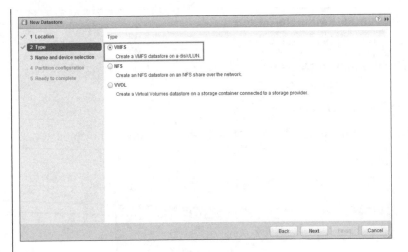

**Figure 9-11**  Adding a New VMFS Datastore

6. Type a name for your new datastore, and then select the host and the LUN from which to create the datastore, as shown in Figure 9-12. (Only the LUNs that are visible to the host that you select will be listed.) Click **Next**.

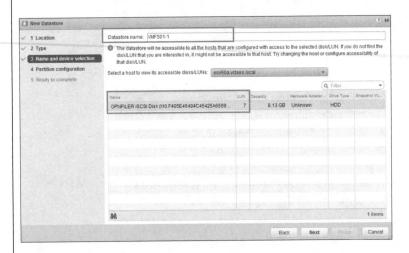

**Figure 9-12**  Naming the Datastore and Selecting a LUN

7. In the Partition configuration box, choose the partition configuration and datastore size for your datastore, as shown in Figure 9-13, and click **Next**.

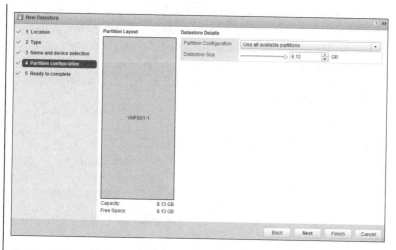

**Figure 9-13** Configuring the Partitions

**8.** On the Ready to Complete page, review the Disk layout and File system information and ensure that it's what you wanted, and then click **Finish**, as shown in Figure 9-14.

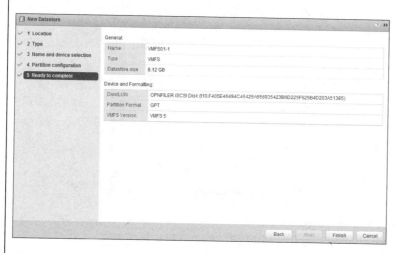

**Figure 9-14** The Ready to Complete Page

**9.** Monitor the Recent Tasks pane and your Storage link for the creation of your new datastore.

In general, you should name your datastores based on their purpose. In most cases, their purpose should be to store a particular type of VM, an ISO file library, templates, and so on. As you know, organizational goals and directions change over time, thereby redefining the purposes of your datastores. When this happens, you should consider changing their names. To change the name of your datastore, follow the steps outlined in Activity 9-5.

### Activity 9-5   Renaming a VMFS Datastore

1. Log on to your vSphere Web Client.

2. Click **Home** and then **Datastores**.

3. In the Navigator, right-click the datastore that you want to rename, and click **Rename**, as shown in Figure 9-15.

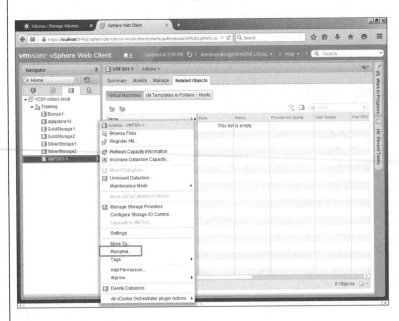

**Figure 9-15**   Selecting a Datastore to Rename

4. Type the new name for your datastore, as shown in Figure 9-16. Click **OK**.

**Figure 9-16**    Entering the New Name for Your Datastore

> 5. Ensure that the Identification of the datastore is changed.

If you decide that you no longer need a VMFS datastore, you can choose to delete it. You should be aware that deleting a VMFS datastore is a "permanent" action that deletes all the metadata on the LUNs in the SAN. In other words, there is no "going back" in any normal sense. Because of this, you should make absolutely sure that there is no data on the datastore that you will need. You can use Storage vMotion to migrate a VM's files, or you can cold migrate VM files to other datastores before deleting the datastore if you need to keep them. You should also move or back up any ISO files that you may need later. (Chapter 17, "Migrating Virtual Machines," covers Storage vMotion and cold migration.) To delete a VMFS datastore, follow the steps outlined in Activity 9-6.

**Activity 9-6    Deleting a VMFS Datastore**

> 1. Log on to your vSphere Web Client.
>
> 2. Click **Home** and then **Datastores**.
>
> 3. Right-click the datastore that you want to delete and select **Delete Datastore**, as shown in Figure 9-17.

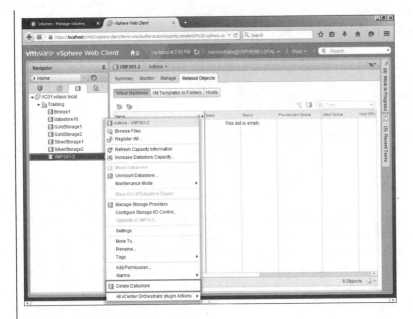

**Figure 9-17**   Deleting a VMFS Datastore

4. On the Confirmation page, select **Yes**, as shown in Figure 9-18 (but think first).

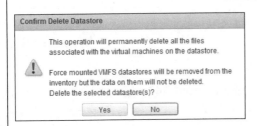

**Figure 9-18**   Confirming Deletion of a VMFS Datastore

5. Monitor the Recent Tasks pane and the Storage link to ensure that the datastore is deleted.

As you can see, deciding to delete a datastore can require a significant amount of thought and work. Sometimes, it might be better to just disconnect the datastore from the LUNs but leave the data on the LUNs intact. In earlier versions of vSphere, this was not possible with a VMFS datastore. With vSphere 5.0 and later, it is possible, but a lot of conditions must be met before it is possible.

The following is a list of conditions that you must address before unmounting a VMFS datastore:

- No registered VMs can reside in the datastore.

- The datastore cannot be part of a datastore cluster.

- The datastore cannot be managed by Storage DRS.

- Storage I/O Control must be disabled.

- The datastore cannot be used for vSphere HA Heartbeat.

As you can see, this limits the number of your VMFS datastores that can be successfully unmounted. Think about it this way, though. If you had a VMFS datastore that was used exclusively for ISO files, chances are good that you could meet these criteria and unmount the datastore from one host while leaving the ISO files in place on the datastore for later use, or available to connect to another host. To unmount a VMFS datastore, follow the steps outlined in Activity 9-7.

**Activity 9-7   Unmounting a VMFS Datastore**

1. Log on to your vSphere Client.

2. Click **Home** and then **Datastores**.

3. Right-click the datastore that you want to unmount, and select **Unmount Datastore**, as shown in Figure 9-19.

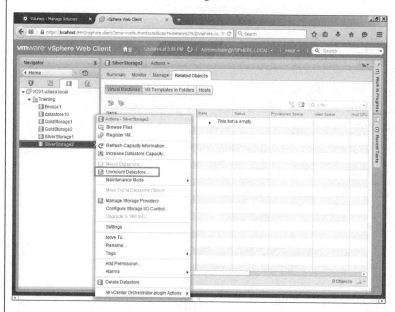

**Figure 9-19**   Unmounting a VMFS Datastore

4. On the Unmount page, choose the host or hosts from which you want to unmount the datastore. The system will verify that your datastore meets all the requirements to be unmounted, as shown in Figure 9-20. Click **OK** to continue.

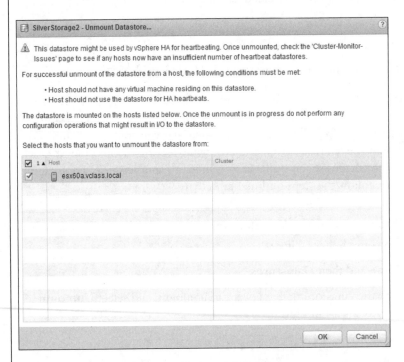

**Figure 9-20** Confirming VMFS Datastore Unmount

5. Monitor the Recent Tasks pane and the Storage link to ensure that the datastore is unmounted. The datastore will be grayed out and identified as inactive and unmounted, as shown in Figure 9-21.

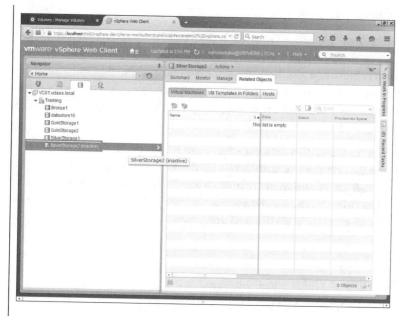

**Figure 9-21**   An Unmounted VMFS Datastore

## Extending/Expanding VMFS Datastores

As your organization continues to grow, so will your need for disk space. In the past, we had to tell users that the system would be offline for a while during the evening hours so that we could increase the storage capacity by adding LUNs or by increasing the size of the LUNs that we were using. Have you ever written or received an email with that message or something similar to it?

In our current world, where many organizations run 24/7, this is no longer an acceptable alternative. We now need to be able to expand the physical disk space and then expand the logical disk space right behind it, without having to take any servers offline or affect the user's functionality.

You might think that *extending* and *expanding* are just two words that essentially mean the same thing, but you should understand that this is not true with regard to VMFS datastores. In this section, I will discuss extending datastores, expanding datastores, and I will compare and contrast the two methods of growing your datastores. You should clearly recognize the differences between these two methods of adding datastore space.

## Extending VMFS Datastores

Extending a datastore means adding another LUN to it. In legacy versions of VMware software (prior to vSphere 4), this was the only option with regard to growing a datastore. Now you also have the option to expand the datastore (discussed next), but the option to extend might be the right choice depending on the situation. If your storage administrator is using only relatively small LUNs (500 GB and less), extending might be your best alternative.

For example, if you have a 10 GB datastore and want to grow it to 20 GB while maintaining all the data on the datastore, you could ask your storage administrator for another 10 GB LUN and then create an extent, which is basically a spanned volume between the two LUNs, thereby increasing your datastore to approximately 20 GB. To create an extent on a VMFS datastore, follow the steps outlined in Activity 9-8.

**Activity 9-8   Extending a VMFS Datastore**

1. Log on to your vSphere Web Client.

2. Click **Home** and then **Datastores**.

3. Right-click the datastore that you want to extend, and click **Increase Datastore Capacity**, as shown in Figure 9-22.

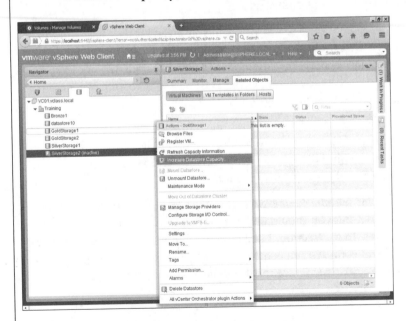

**Figure 9-22**   Adding an Extent to a Datastore

**4.** Select the LUN that you will use for the extent, as shown in Figure 9-23. Click **Next**.

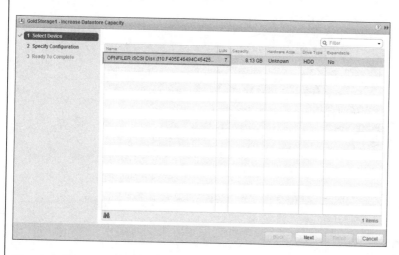

**Figure 9-23**    Viewing Datastore Extents

**5.** Select **Use All Available Partitions**, and then select the entire amount or a portion of the LUN (Extent Device), as shown in Figure 9-24. (It is typically best to use the whole LUN in the datastore.)

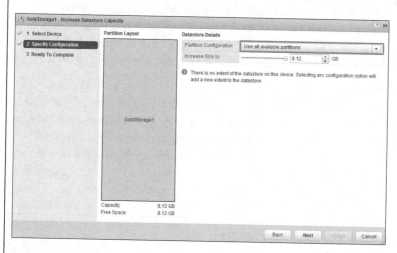

**Figure 9-24**    Selecting the Portion of the Extent Device to Use

6. On the Ready to Complete page, review your settings and click **Finish**, as shown in Figure 9-25.

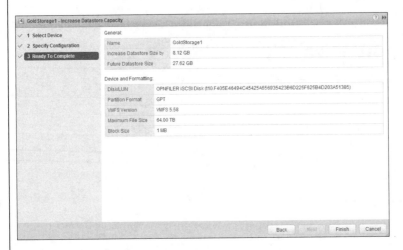

**Figure 9-25** Confirming the Creation of an Extent

### Expanding VMFS Datastores

Suppose that you do not want to add a LUN to your datastore to increase its size. Suppose instead that you just want to ask the storage administrator to increase the size of the LUN that you already have, and then you will increase the size of the datastore within the same LUN. In that case, you would not be creating an extent, but instead you would be *expanding* the datastore into the newly expanded LUN.

For example, if you have a 5 GB datastore using one LUN, and you need a 10 GB datastore, you could ask the storage administrator to increase the size of your LUN to 10 GB. After this is done, you could increase the size of your datastore within the same LUN. If your storage administrator is willing to increase the LUNs to whatever size you need, this might be your best alternative for increasing the size of the datastore. To expand your datastore after the storage administrator has increased the size of the LUN, follow the steps outlined in Activity 9-9.

### Activity 9-9  Expanding a VMFS Datastore

1. Log on to your vSphere Web Client.

2. Click **Home** and then **Datastores**.

3. Right-click the datastore that is on a LUN that is expandable, and click **Increase Datastore Capacity**, as shown in Figure 9-26.

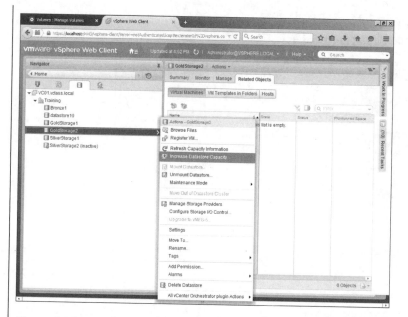

**Figure 9-26**   Increasing a Datastore

4. Choose an extent that is in use by the datastore but still has expandable capacity. You will see Yes under the column marked Expandable, as shown in Figure 9-27.

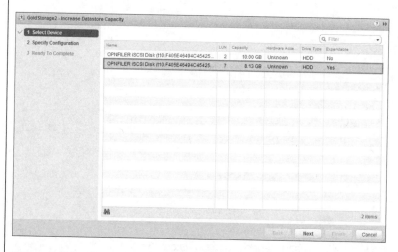

**Figure 9-27**   Choosing an Expandable Extent

5.  In Partition Configuration, choose to use the free space, as shown in Figure 9-28, and click **Next**.

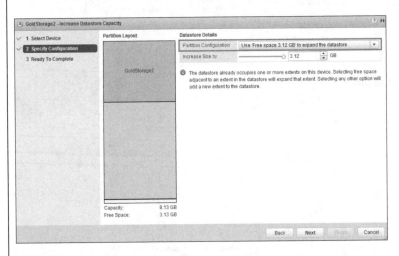

**Figure 9-28**   Increasing the Capacity of a Datastore

6.  From the Ready to Complete page, review your choices and note the increased capacity of the datastore, as shown in Figure 9-29, and then click **Finish**.

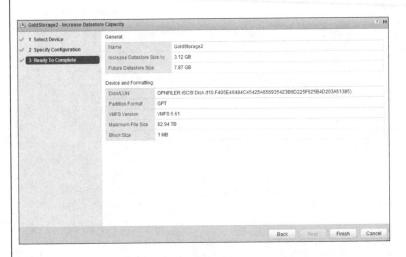

**Figure 9-29**   Confirming the Increased Capacity of a Datastore

## Summary

This chapter covered the following main topics:

- The two versions of NFS and their incompatibility with each other, and the configuration of NFS storage for virtual machine vmdks.

- The three different settings for multipathing: Fixed, MRU, and Round Robin, the differences between them, and how and where to configure them.

- How you can determine when to use VMFS datastores and how many to use, and how to configure and manage VMFS extents.

## Exam Preparation Tasks

## Review All the Key Topics

Review the most important topics from inside the chapter, noted with the Key Topic icon in the outer margin of the page. Table 9-2 lists these key topics and the page numbers where each is found.

**Table 9-2**  Key Topics for Chapter 9

| Key Topic Element | Description | Page Number |
|---|---|---|
| Activity 9-1 | Mounting an NFS Datastore | 204 |
| Bullet List | Native Multipathing Policies | 207 |
| Activity 9-2 | Selecting the Preferred Path for a VMFS Datastore | 208 |
| Figure 9-8 | An Attempt to Disable the Only Path to a Datastore | 210 |
| Activity 9-3 | Disabling a Path to a VMFS Datastore | 210 |
| Bullet List | VMFS-5 Capabilities | 212 |
| Activity 9-4 | Creating a VMFS Datastore | 213 |
| Activity 9-5 | Renaming a VMFS Datastore | 216 |
| Activity 9-6 | Deleting a VMFS Datastore | 217 |
| Bullet List | Conditions for Unmounting a VMFS Datastore | 219 |
| Activity 9-7 | Unmounting a VMFS Datastore | 219 |
| Activity 9-8 | Extending a VMFS Datastore | 222 |
| Activity 9-9 | Expanding a VMFS Datastore | 224 |

## Review Questions

The answers to these review questions are in Appendix A.

1. Which of the following are true with regard to NFS 4.1?

   a. vSphere 6 supports both NFS 3 and NFS 4.1.

   b. You can mount both NFS 3 and NFS 4.1 on the same array at the same time.

   c. NFS 3 is compatible with NFS 4.1.

   d. You will have to upgrade any legacy hosts to support NFS 4.1.

2. When you are creating an NFS share for storing VM files, which of the following are *not* true? (Choose two.)

   a. You should leave the default setting in regard to Mount NFS as Read-Only.

   b. You will need read and write permission to the share.

   c. You should check the box to Mount NFS as Read-Only.

   d. You should only need read permission to the share.

3. Which of the following are *not* true regarding configuring NFS for vmdk files in vSphere 6? (Choose two.)

   a. NFS 4.1 offers Kerberos Authentication.

   b. NFS 4.1 defaults to root authentication.

   c. NFS 3 is no longer supported.

   d. Configuring Kerberos Authentication requires only one check box and no other configuration on the host.

4. Which of the following multipathing options will be automatically configured by your host if it is connected to a SAN that is configured as Active/Passive?

   a. Fixed

   b. MRU

   c. Round-robin

   d. There is no autoconfiguration of multipathing.

**5.** Which of the following multipathing policies uses only one path during a data transfer session?

  **a.** Only MRU

  **b.** Only round-robin

  **c.** Fixed and MRU

  **d.** All multipathing policies use only one path during a data transfer session.

**6.** Which of the following are *not* true regarding VMFS-3 in vSphere 6? (Choose two.)

  **a.** vSphere 6 supports upgrading VMFS-3 to VMFS-5.

  **b.** You can create both VMFS-3 and VMFS-5 datastores in vSphere 6.

  **c.** VMFS-5 datastores can contain 64 TB extents.

  **d.** VMFS-5 can support only 2 TB virtual disks.

**7.** Which of the following are *not* true regarding VMFS extents? (Choose two.)

  **a.** A datastore with only one LUN will have one extent.

  **b.** A datastore with only one LUN can have no extents.

  **c.** Adding a new extent to a datastore requires another LUN.

  **d.** You can add an extent to a datastore on the same LUN.

**8.** Which of the following are *not* true regarding expanding a datastore in vSphere 6? (Choose two.)

  **a.** You always expand a datastore by adding to one of its current extents.

  **b.** You can expand a datastore by adding an extent.

  **c.** Datastores can be both expanded and extended.

  **d.** Datastores cannot be both expanded and extended.

**9.** Which of the following are *not* true regarding expanding an extent for a VMFS datastore? (Choose two.)

  **a.** All extents can be expanded, regardless of how they were created.

  **b.** Only extents that do not fill the current capacity of their LUN can be expanded.

  **c.** You cannot determine the size of the LUN with the vSphere client, only the size of the extent.

  **d.** You can determine both the size of the LUN and the size of the extent with the vSphere client.

**10.** Which of the following are *not* true regarding expanding and extending VMFS datastores? (Choose two.)

    **a.** You can extend a VMFS datastore without taking it offline.

    **b.** You cannot extend a VMFS datastore without taking it offline.

    **c.** You can expand a VMFS datastore without taking it offline.

    **d.** You cannot expand a VMFS datastore without taking it offline.

**This chapter covers the following subjects:**

- Capabilities of Virtual Machine Hardware Versions
- Methods to Access and Use Virtual Machine Console
- Virtual Machine Clones and Templates
- Virtual Machine Requirements for DirectPath I/O Passthrough
- Configuring and Deploying a Guest OS into a New Virtual Machine
- Configuring/Modifying Virtual CPU and Memory Resources

None of the virtual networking or the datastores would be necessary if it weren't for the fact that you want to create and deploy virtual machines (VMs). In other words, everything else discussed in this book, besides the VMs themselves, is just a "life support system" for the VMs. This section covers creating, deploying, managing, and administering VMs. You learn about the various capabilities of different virtual machine versions and how to configure them properly for your organization.

## CHAPTER 10

# Creating and Deploying Virtual Machines

## "Do I Know This Already?" Quiz

The "Do I Know This Already?" quiz allows you to assess whether you should read this entire chapter or simply jump to the "Exam Preparation Tasks" section for review. If you are in doubt, read the entire chapter. Table 10-1 outlines the major headings in this chapter and the corresponding "Do I Know This Already?" quiz questions. You can find the answers in Appendix A, "Answers to the 'Do I Know This Already?' Quizzes and Chapter Review Questions."

**Table 10-1** "Do I Know This Already?" Section-to-Question Mapping

| Foundation Topics Section | Questions Covered in This Section |
|---|---|
| Capabilities of Virtual Machine Hardware Versions | 1, 2 |
| Methods to Access and Use Virtual Machine Console | 3 |
| Virtual Machine Clones and Templates | 4 |
| Virtual Machine Requirements for DirectPath I/O Passthrough | 5 |
| Configuring and Deploying a Guest OS into a New Virtual Machine | 6 |
| Configuring/Modifying Virtual CPU and Memory Resources | 7, 8, 9, 10 |

1. What is the maximum amount of memory that can be assigned to a Version 11 virtual machine?

   a. 2 TB

   b. 256 GB

   c. 1 TB

   d. 4 TB

2. Which of the following are *not* supported on a Version 11 virtual machine? (Choose two.)

   a. 12 vnics

   b. 50 serial ports

   c. USB

   d. Hot add memory

3. Which of the following are valid methods to access a VM console?

   a. Right-click the VM and select **Open Console**.

   b. Right-click the VM, select **Guest OS**, and then **Open Console**.

   c. Launch **Console** from the Manage tab.

   d. Launch **Console** from the Summary tab.

4. Which of the following best describes a template?

   a. A snapshot of a VM that contains only part of the configuration

   b. An exact copy of another VM

   c. A master copy of a VM that is used to create new VMs and thereby establish a standard build

   d. A separate portion of a VM that can be added to provide more features

5. Which of the following *cannot* be used if a VM is using DirectPath I/O Passthrough? (Choose two.)

   a. HA

   b. Local datastores

   c. DRS

   d. SMP

6. You are attempting to deploy a new OS into a VM. You have added an ISO to the CD-ROM, but when you power on the VM you see a PXE boot instead of a loading ISO. Which of the following might be the cause? (Choose two.)

   a. You have not checked the **Connected** box for the ISO.

   b. You have not loaded an ISO that has a bootable OS.

   c. You have too many CPUs configured for the VM.

   d. You have not checked the **Connect at Power On** box for the ISO.

**7.** If you create a VM with one vCPU on a host that is Quad Core 3 GHz, what is the maximum processing power for the VM?

   **a.** 12 GHz

   **b.** 6 GHz

   **c.** 3 GHz

   **d.** .75 GHz

**8.** Which of the following are true regarding CPU hot add? (Choose two.)

   **a.** To configure the setting, the VM must be powered down.

   **b.** It should function well once set, regardless of the OS on the VM.

   **c.** You enable it by checking a box.

   **d.** You enable it by changing an Advanced Setting.

**9.** Which of the following are true regarding memory hot plug?

   **a.** The VM must be powered down to configure the setting.

   **b.** The VM can be configured while still powered up, as long as the OS supports it.

   **c.** All guest OSs will immediately recognize the new memory.

   **d.** The guest operating systems on the system compatibility list for CPU hot plug will recognize the new memory.

**10.** Which of the following is the correct description of the memory setting for a VM?

   **a.** The amount of memory that the guest OS will be told it can have

   **b.** The total amount of RAM that will be reserved for the guest OS

   **c.** The minimum amount of all types of memory that is guaranteed to the guest OS

   **d.** The minimum amount of RAM that is guaranteed to the guest OS

**Foundation Topics**

# Capabilities of Virtual Machine Hardware Versions

You should understand that a virtual machine (VM) is a computer. In fact, it's every bit as much of a computer as is a physical machine. The difference is that the VM exists in a software state rather than a hardware state. The software state of the VM exists on one host or another, but the resources that it uses with regard to networking and storage can be spread across the network. In fact, some of them can be anywhere in the world!

This section focuses on deploying VMs. I start by identifying the capabilities of VMs based on their virtual hardware versions. In addition, I discuss specialized software developed to match the hardware and installed OS, called VMware Tools. Methods used to access and use the VM console and the VM storage resources are also covered. Finally, I discuss the many aspects of configuration, installation, modification, and upgrading that you will be required to know to manage your own environment and pass the exam.

The first concept that you need to understand is that of VM hardware. These are the components that make up the VM and allow it to perform computing and communication. It's kind of funny that we call it "VM hardware," because it's really software. This software connects to hardware on the host or somewhere else in the network. It can generally be divided into four categories:

- CPU
- Memory
- Disk
- Network

Although the basic components haven't changed in the past several years, their capabilities have been greatly expanded, thereby expanding the capabilities of the average VM.

Each time a new version of ESX/ESXi has been introduced, it has brought with it a new virtual hardware version for the VMs intended for that type of host. Each new virtual hardware version has increased the capabilities of the VM in many ways. This section focuses primarily on the last four versions, because any before then would now be considered legacy. As you will see, the changes in just the past four versions have been dramatic.

A little history: When vSphere 4.0 was first introduced in 2009, it included a new virtual hardware version called Version 7 hardware. It represented a dramatic improvement over the Version 4 hardware that came with ESX/ESXi 3.5 hosts and vCenter 2.5. Later, vSphere 5.0 was introduced with its new Version 8 hardware, which has proven to be far superior to the Version 7 hardware of vSphere 4.x. Most recently, vSphere 5.1 and ESXi 5.1 introduced Version 9 hardware, vSphere 5.5 brought us Version 10 hardware, and finally (so far) vSphere 6 ushered in Version 11 hardware.

As mentioned, you can divide VM hardware into four categories: CPU, memory, disk, and network. Each of the categories can have one or more components of VM hardware. The major improvements in these categories generally involve higher configuration maximums or additional support of a new component. Table 10-2 illustrates many aspects of VM hardware and the capabilities of each version.

**Table 10-2**   Virtual Machine Hardware Versions

|  | Version 8 | Version 9 | Version 10 | Version 11 |
|---|---|---|---|---|
| **# of vCPUs for SMP** | 1–32[1] | 1–64[1] | 1–64[1] | 1–128[1] |
| **Maximum memory** | 1 TB | 1 TB | 1 TB | 4 TB |
| **Video (with VMware Tools)** | SVGA, 3D graphics[2] | SVGA, 3D graphics[2] | SVGA, 3D graphics[2] | SVGA, 3D graphics[2] |
| **Audio** | HD[2] | HD[2] | HD[2] | HD[2] |
| **IDE** | 1 controller, 4 devices | 1 controller, 4 devices | 1 controller, 4 devices | 1 controller, 4 devices |
| **Max. parallel ports** | 3 | 3 | 3 | 3 |
| **Max. serial ports** | 4 | 4 | 4 | 32 |
| **USB support** | Supported | Supported | Supported | Supported |
| **Floppy drives** | 1 controller, 2 drives | 1 controller, 2 drives | 1 controller, 2 drives | 1 controller, 2 drives |
| **Mouse** | Supported | Supported | Supported | Supported |
| **Keyboard** | Supported | Supported | Supported | Supported |
| **vNICs** | 1–10 | 1–10 | 1–10 | 1-10 |
| **SCSI adapters** | 1–4 SCSI adapters, 1–15 devices per adapter | 1–4 SCSI adapters, 1–15 devices per adapter | 1–4 SCSI adapters, 1–15 devices per adapter | 1–4 SCSI adapters, 1–15 devices per adapter |

|  | Version 8 | Version 9 | Version 10 | Version 11 |
|---|---|---|---|---|
| **Hot add capability** | Disk only | Disk, Ethernet controller, SCSI device, memory, CPU[3] | Disk, Ethernet controller, SCSI device, USB, memory, CPU[3] | Disk, Ethernet controller, SCSI device, USB, memory, CPU[3] |
| **SATA** | Not Supported | Not Supported | Supported | Supported |

[1] Supported CPUs are license-level dependent.

[2] Requires support on the device running the vSphere Client.

[3] Requires supported OS and first must be enabled with VM powered down.

### Identifying VMware Tools Device Drivers

The operating system (OS) that you install in a VM can have a dramatic effect on how the virtual hardware will be used. When you create a VM, a typical installation attempts to choose the correct components to complement the OS and version that you are intending to run on the VM. This is only one part of customizing or "tweaking" the installation. The other part is installing the correct device drivers for the virtual hardware after the OS is installed. For this step, VMware provides VMware Tools. These are specialized device drivers that can be installed after the OS is installed. They enhance the performance of the VM in many ways. The following are some of the enhancements that VMware Tools device drivers can provide your VM:

- **SVGA display:** Without VMware Tools, a VM has Video Graphics Array (VGA) graphics (640×480). With VMware Tools, VMs can have Super Video Graphics Array (SVGA) graphics (800×600), and often even better.

- **vmxnet–vmxnet3 vNIC drivers:** With VMware Tools installed, the virtual network interface card (vNIC) driver support is expanded to support most operating systems using specialized drivers created by VMware.

- **Balloon driver for memory management (vmmemctl):** This driver provides for efficient memory allocation between VMs.

- **Sync driver for quiescing I/O:** This driver can be especially important for features, such as vMotion and Storage vMotion, and obtaining clean snapshots.

- **Improved mouse support:** Without VMware Tools, the mouse is often slow and not properly responsive to commands. Also, the mouse cannot seamlessly move in and out of a VM console. With VMware Tools, the mouse operates as expected.

- **VM Heartbeat:** Especially useful for the High Availability (HA) feature called VM monitoring. VMware can detect that the OS has failed and can restart the VM to attempt to correct the problem.

- **Time synchronization:** VMware Tools make it easy to synchronize the VM time with that of the host on which it resides.

- **Ability to shut down the VM:** With VMware Tools installed, you can gracefully shut down the VM guest OS without first logging on.

## Methods to Access and Use Virtual Machine Console

Because the VM exists in the "virtual world," but you exist in the "physical world," you need a door or portal through which you can access and control the VM. The VM console on your vSphere Web Client provides this portal. To access the VM console, you right-click a VM and select **Open Console,** or click the **Open Console** icon, as shown in Figure 10-1. From the VM console, you can log on to the VM or use the tools at the top of the console to control the VM. These tools enable you to power on, power off, shut down, add ISOs, and so on.

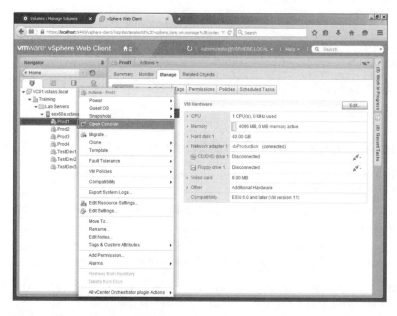

**Figure 10-1**   Opening a VM Console by Right-Clicking

Another method of accessing the console of your VM is by launching it from the Summary tab for the VM, as shown in Figure 10-2. This method also offers the same File menu options. From this section, you can also download and use the Virtual Machine Remote Console (VMRC) plug-in, which VMware has developed to support the latest versions of the Google Chrome browser.

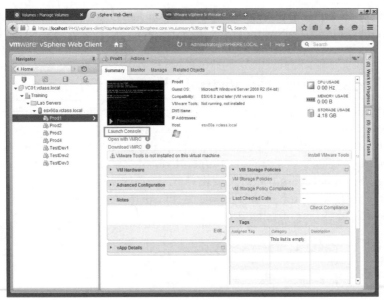

**Figure 10-2**    Launching a Console from the Summary Tab

## Virtual Machine Clones and Templates

When you create your first VMs, you will likely use the wizard and create them "from scratch," what I call "the old-fashioned way." You could continue to create all your VMs in this manner, but that would be what I call "the hard way." Instead, you could leverage the tools in the vSphere to create VMs faster and with more accuracy than with the wizard. Your vCenter Server and the ESXi hosts to which it is connected offer an array of tools and the power to build out your virtual data center.

One tool that you could use is a template, which is basically a master copy of a VM that is not intended for use itself as a VM but can be used to create other VMs that are just like it, and thereby establish a standard build. In contrast, you could make an exact copy of a VM the way it is at any time by cloning it. This may be the fastest method of creating a new VM, but it doesn't really establish a standard. Chapter 12, "Managing Virtual Machine Clones and Templates," discusses in great detail these faster and more efficient ways to create VMs using clones and templates.

# Virtual Machine Requirements for DirectPath I/O Passthrough

In general, virtualization is tied to the sharing of resources on hosts. All VMs on the same host start with the same priority to all of the resources available through the host. This includes the network cards, graphics cards, sound cards, and so on. You can use Resource Pools and shares, which are discussed in Chapter 16, "Creating and Administering Resource Pools," to give more priority to more important or more "resource hungry" VMs. This ensures that shared features such as Distributed Resource Scheduler (DRS), High Availability (HA), and so on, are available for all machines.

In some extreme "one-off" circumstances, you may want a VM to monopolize a specific physical card. You can do this by first enabling the card for DirectPath I/O Passthrough and then configuring the connection to the enabled card as virtual hardware on the VM. The requirements for the VM in regard to DirectPath I/O Passthrough are as follows:

- VM hardware must be version 7 or later.

- VM must be on a host with Intel Virtual Technology or Directed I/O (VT-d) or AMD I/O Virtualization Technology (IOMMU) enabled.

- A VM cannot be directly connected to more than eight devices at a time.

- PCI devices must be connected to the host and marked for passthrough. You can explore the PCI devices connected to your host by clicking on the host, then on **Manage**, **Settings**, and **PCI Devices**, as shown in Figure 10-3.

It should be noted that when you configure a VM to use DirectPath I/O Passthrough, you give up the capability to use many features, such as vMotion, DRS, HA, snapshots, FT, and hot add and removing of many devices. This is one of the reasons that it should be considered an unusual "one-off" setting.

**Figure 10-3**   The PCI Devices Setting

## Configuring and Deploying a Guest OS into a New Virtual Machine

As part of creating a VM, you can install a guest OS. Note that I said *can* and not *must*. In other words, a VM is a VM even without any guest OS or applications. It is a "box" that is made of software, called virtual hardware, that can support a guest OS. It's very important to understand that distinction.

As part of the installation of a VM, you can elect to install a Guest OS from a file or a datastore on which you have previously stored the required files. For example, you can install it from a connected ISO file, as shown in Figure 10-4.

If you choose this option, be sure to check **Connect at Power On**. Because many experienced professionals miss this option, it is highlighted in Figure 10-5.

When you click **Finish** and then power on the VM, you should see an installation beginning that you can continue or have automated with an unattended installation file. If you see a PXE boot installation instead, you should carefully check the **Connect at Power On** setting and also ensure that you have connected to an ISO that can boot an OS installation.

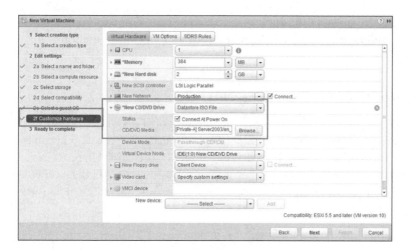

**Figure 10-4** Installing the Guest OS from an ISO File

**Figure 10-5** The Connect at Power On Check Box

# Configuring/Modifying Virtual CPU and Memory Resources

With full virtualization, the guest OS on your VM has no idea that it is running on a VM. It has not been altered in any way. It "believes" that it is running on a physical machine, and therefore that everything you "tell it" is a physical resource is actually a physical resource. When you first configure a VM, you should configure the CPU and the memory based on what the application needs to run. This section first covers CPU configuration and modification, followed by memory configuration and modification.

### Configuring and Modifying Virtual Machine CPU

When you create the VM and you configure the number of vCPUs, you obtain a maximum of one "core's worth" of processing power for each vCPU that you configure. In other words, if you have a host that has a Quad Core 2.5 GHz processor, you will obtain a maximum of 2.5 GHz of processing power per vCPU that you create on a VM. The VMkernel load balances over multiple cores, but this will be the numeric result.

Generally, you should not create VMs with more than one vCPU unless the application that will be running on them requires more than one vCPU or would truly run much faster with more than one. In fact, if you use a typical installation, the default setting is one vCPU. Most applications these days are single threaded, so a VM that is dedicated to them and has one vCPU with at least 2 GHz of processing power is more than enough. In some cases, with multithreaded high-performance applications (such as SQL, Exchange, or Java), you can gain performance advantages by creating VMs with more than one vCPU. In those cases, take care as to where you place those VMs, as discussed in more detail in Chapter 16.

In addition, with the right operating system and a little configuration beforehand, you can add vCPUs to a running VM. This process might not be as simple as it sounds, because you must have everything just right, but it is possible. To make it possible for you, you must use a supported guest OS, and you must select to **Enable CPU Hot Add** in the CPU hardware settings for the VM with the VM powered down. Figure 10-6 shows normal CPU settings and the check box to enable CPU Hot Add.

When this setting is enabled, with the right OS, you can add another vCPU to the VM and have the guest OS recognize it and use it. With some guest OSs, you can add vCPU to the virtual hardware, but the guest OS won't recognize it without a reboot. Is that truly a hot plug? You decide. At the time of this writing, there were more than 100 guest OSs that supported hot add vCPU for vSphere. You can obtain the latest list at http://www.vmware.com/resources/compatibility/search.php.

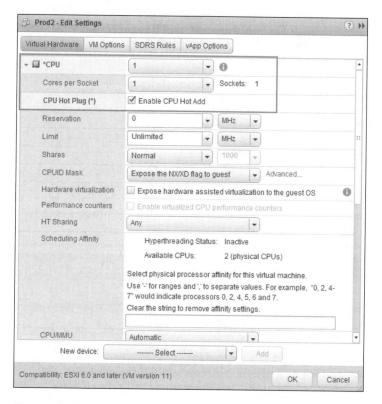

**Figure 10-6**   CPU Hot Add

## Configuring and Modifying Virtual Machine Memory

You should also configure the VM with the right amount of memory for the application that you will be running on it. During the installation of a VM on the Web Client, VMware will "suggest" the default amount of memory to use for the VM based on the OS that you choose, but you can decide to choose a different amount of memory, as shown in Figure 10-7.

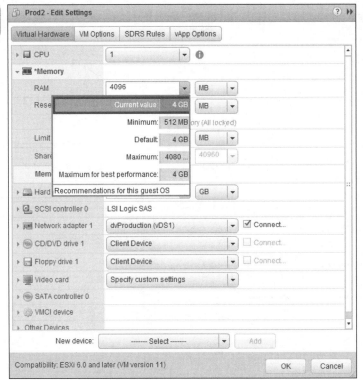

**Figure 10-7**   Setting Memory for a VM

By clicking the arrow to the left of Memory, you can choose many more settings, such as Reservations, Limits, and Shares, but for now I will focus on the general memory setting, as shown in Figure 10-8.

The important point to remember is that this is not a guarantee to the OS for a certain amount of physical RAM; instead, it's what you are telling the guest OS that it has in memory. In other words, you could still provide this memory from disk using a swap file, which is discussed in Chapter 13, "Administering Virtual Machines and vApps."

As with CPU, you can hot add memory on a VM as long as the guest OS supports it and you have configured it in advance. You must first enable **Memory Hot Plug** in the Advanced Hardware settings for the VM with the VM powered down, as shown in Figure 10-8.

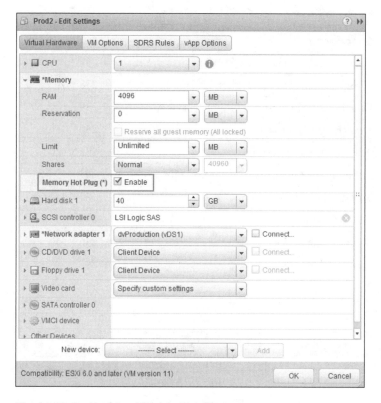

**Figure 10-8**   Enabling Memory Hot Plug

After this setting is enabled, you can add memory and have the guest OS recognize it and use it. Some guest OSs require a restart, but many do not. At the time of this writing, more than 100 guest OSs supported hot add memory. You can obtain the latest list at http://www.vmware.com/resources/compatibility/search.php.

## Exam Preparation Tasks

## Review All the Key Topics

Review the most important topics from the chapter, noted with the Key Topic icon in the outer margin of the page. Table 10-3 lists these key topics and the page numbers where each is found.

**Table 10-3**   Key Topics for Chapter 10

| Key Topic Element | Description | Page Number |
|---|---|---|
| Table 10-2 | Virtual Machine Hardware Versions | 237 |
| Bullet List | VMware Tools Device Drivers | 238 |
| Figure 10-1 | Opening a VM Console by Right-Clicking | 239 |
| Figure 10-2 | Launching a Console from the Summary Tab | 240 |
| Figure 10-3 | The PCI Devices Setting | 242 |
| Figure 10-4 | Installing the Guest OS from an ISO File | 243 |
| Figure 10-5 | The Connect at Power On Check Box | 243 |
| Figure 10-6 | CPU Hot Add | 245 |
| Figure 10-7 | Setting Memory for a VM | 246 |
| Figure 10-8 | Enabling Memory Hot Plug | 247 |

## Review Questions

The answers to these review questions are in Appendix A.

1. What is the maximum amount of vCPUs that can be assigned to a Version 11 virtual machine?

    a. 10

    b. 32

    c. 64

    d. 128

2. Which of the following are *not* supported on a Version 11 virtual machine? (Choose two.)

    a. 10 vnics

    b. 32 serial ports

    c. 5 parallel ports

    d. 6 SCSI adapters

**3.** Which of the following are *not* valid methods to access a VM console?

    **a.** Right-click the VM and select **Open Console**.

    **b.** Right-click the VM, select **Guest OS**, and then **Open Console**.

    **c.** Launch **Console** from the Manage tab.

    **d.** Launch **Console** from the Summary tab.

**4.** Which of the following best describes a clone?

    **a.** A snapshot of a VM that contains only part of the configuration

    **b.** An exact copy of another VM

    **c.** A master copy of a VM that is used to create new VMs and thereby establish a standard build

    **d.** A separate portion of a VM that can be added to provide more features

**5.** Which of the following can still be used if a VM is using DirectPath I/O Passthrough? (Choose two.)

    **a.** HA

    **b.** Remote Datastores

    **c.** DRS

    **d.** SMP

**6.** You are attempting to deploy a new OS into a VM. You have added an ISO to the CD-ROM, but when you power on the VM you see a PXE boot instead of a loading ISO. Which of the following might be the cause? (Choose two.)

    **a.** You have not checked the **Connected** box for the ISO.

    **b.** You have not loaded an ISO that has a bootable OS.

    **c.** You have too many CPUs configured for the VM.

    **d.** You have not checked the **Connect at Power On** box for the ISO.

**7.** If you create a VM with two vCPUs on a host that is Quad Core 3 GHz, what is the maximum processing power for the VM?

    **a.** 12 GHz

    **b.** 6 GHz

    **c.** 3 GHz

    **d.** .75 GHz

**8.** Which of the following are *not* true regarding CPU hot add? (Choose two.)

 **a.** To configure the setting, the VM must be powered down.

 **b.** It should function well once set, regardless of the OS on the VM.

 **c.** You enable it by checking a box.

 **d.** You enable it by changing an Advanced Setting.

**9.** Which of the following are *not* true regarding memory hot plug?

 **a.** The VM must be powered down to configure the setting.

 **b.** The VM can be configured while still powered up, as long as the OS supports it.

 **c.** All guest OSs will immediately recognize the new memory.

 **d.** The guest operating systems on the system compatibility list for CPU hot plug will recognize the new memory.

**10.** Which of the following is the correct best practice for the vCPU setting for VMs?

 **a.** Generally speaking, the more vCPUs per VM, the better.

 **b.** The vCPU setting defaults to 1 and should remain there unless the application is truly multithreaded and could benefit from having more processing power.

 **c.** You should configure more vCPUs, but set the GHz setting to a lower number to conserve resources.

 **d.** The vCPU setting on a VM has no effect on its performance.

**This chapter covers the following subjects:**

- vApp Requirements
- Creating/Cloning/Exporting a vApp
- Adding Objects to an Existing vApp
- Configuring and Editing vApp Settings

A vApp is not just a fancy way of saying *virtual appliance*. It's really much more. For a long time, we have known that it's sometimes better to use more than one server to provide an application for the end user. For example, a high-performance database might be provided to the user by using an application server and a separate database server, not to mention a separate domain controller. This was true in our data centers before virtualization. Now, with virtualization, you can package all three of those servers into one inventory object and use settings to control the way that they communicate with each other. Furthermore, you can export the entire package to other parts of your organization or to other organizations using the Open Virtualization Format (OVF).

## CHAPTER 11

# Creating and Deploying vApps

This chapter identifies the various vApp settings that are required when creating your vApps. In addition, you learn about creating, cloning, and exporting vApps. Finally, the chapter discusses editing the settings of a vApp that you already have.

## "Do I Know This Already?" Quiz

The "Do I Know This Already?" quiz allows you to assess whether you should read this entire chapter or simply jump to the "Exam Preparation Tasks" section for review. If you are in doubt, read the entire chapter. Table 11-1 outlines the major headings in this chapter and the corresponding "Do I Know This Already?" quiz questions. You can find the answers in Appendix A, "Answers to the 'Do I Know This Already?' Quizzes and Chapter Review Questions."

**Table 11-1** "Do I Know This Already?" Section-to-Question Mapping

| Foundation Topics Section | Questions Covered in This Section |
| --- | --- |
| vApp Requirements | 1, 2 |
| Creating/Cloning/Exporting a vApp | 3, 4, 5 |
| Adding Objects to an Existing vApp | 7 |
| Configuring and Editing vApp Settings | 6, 8, 9, 10 |

1. Which of the following are requirements to configure a vApp? (Choose two.)

    a. ESXi 5.5 or later hosts

    b. ESX 4.0 or later hosts

    c. Clusters enabled with HA

    d. Clusters enabled with DRS

2. In which of the following can you create a vApp? (Choose two.)

    a. vApp

    b. Resource pool

    c. Port group

    d. Virtual switch

3. Which of the following are true regarding cloning of vApps? (Choose two.)

    a. A cloned vApp is an exact copy of a vApp.

    b. You can modify the settings of a vApp while you clone it.

    c. You can modify the settings of a cloned vApp after you create it.

    d. You can clone a vApp that is powered on.

4. Which of the following best describes an OVF?

    a. A set of files in a package that can be exported and imported

    b. A single executable file that you can store on a USB drive

    c. A snapshot of a VM or several VMs working together

    d. A text file with configuration information about one or more VMs

5. Which of the following *best describes* an OVA?

    a. A set of files in a package that can be exported and imported

    b. A single executable file that you can store on a USB drive

    c. A snapshot of a VM or several VMs working together

    d. A text file with configuration information about one or more VMs

6. When you power off a vApp, which of the following happens?

    a. The vApp powers off but VMs remain powered on.

    b. The VMs in the vApp gracefully shut down based on their shutdown order.

    c. All the VMs in the vApp are powered off immediately.

    d. It is not possible to control the power of a vApp.

7. In which of the following can you view the VMs that are in a vApp? (Choose two.)

    a. The Related Objects tab for vApp

    b. Expand the vApp in the Navigator in Storage view

    c. Expand the vApp in the Navigator in Hosts and Clusters view

    d. On the vApps tab in the Related Objects for the vCenter

8. Which of the following are true regarding Application Properties settings for vApps? (Choose two.)

    a. If you have created the vApp for yourself, they will likely remain empty.

    b. They display non-editable product information from the vendor of the vApp.

    c. They should always be completed in order to run the vApp.

    d. They are editable settings about which you should consult your vApp vendor.

9. Which of the following IP schemes is the default for vApps?

    a. Static (manual) IPv4

    b. DHCP

    c. IP Pools

    d. Transient IP

10. Which of the following *best describes* the Start Order of vApp?

    a. Specifies when that vApp will be started in relation to other vApps on the same host

    b. Specifies when each VM in a vApp will be started in relation to the other VMs, on a VM by VM basis

    c. Specifies categories of VMs and when each category of VMs will be started in relation to the other categories

    d. Specifies when that vApp will be started in relation to other vApps on the same DRS cluster

**Foundation Topics**

## vApp Requirements

Creating a vApp is rather simple, as discussed next, but configuring all the settings on a vApp can be more complex. Because the purpose of the vApp is to allow the VMs to communicate more effectively with each other while securing them from other machines, all your settings should be configured with these goals in mind. You can create vApps for many uses when VMs need to communicate directly to each other as a group and you need to be able to control the whole group. For example, if you have taken a vSphere class recently, chances are good that the ESXi hosts, vCenter, and other VMs that you used for the labs were all part of the same vApp!

The requirements for creating a vApp are pretty simple. You need only one of the following:

- A standalone host running ESX 4.0 or later

  or...

- A host cluster that is enabled for DRS

With these components, you can add a vApp to a folder, standalone host, resource pool, cluster enabled for DRS, or even another vApp.

## Creating/Cloning/Exporting a vApp

To create a new vApp, you right-click in any place where you can create one, select **New vApp**, give the vApp a name, and populate it by creating new VMs or even dragging existing VMs into it. For example, to create a vApp named vApp-05, follow the steps outlined in Activity 11-1.

**Activity 11-1   Creating a vApp**

1. Log on to your vSphere Web Client.

2. Select **Home** and then **VMs and Templates**.

3. Right-click the folder in which you want to create the vApp (in this case I'm using a folder that I created named vApps) and select **New vApp** and then **New vApp** again, as shown in Figure 11-1.

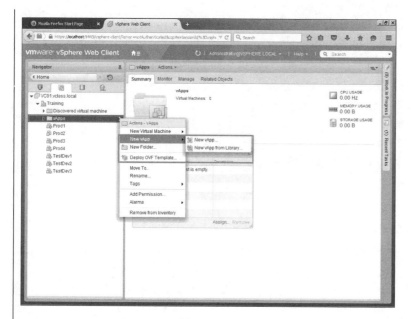

**Figure 11-1**   Creating a vApp

**4.** In the New vApp Wizard, select **Create a new vApp** and click **Next**, as
shown in Figure 11-2.

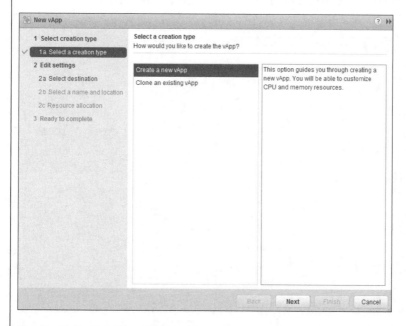

**Figure 11-2**   Selecting Create a New vApp

5. From **Select Destination**, select a cluster, host, resource pool, or vApp on which to run your vApp, as shown in Figure 11-3, and then click **Next**.

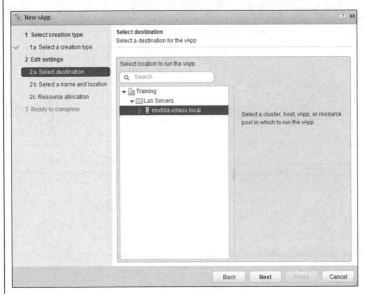

**Figure 11-3**    The Select Destination Page

6. Type the name of your vApp (in this case, **vApp-05**), as shown in Figure 11-4. Click **Next**.

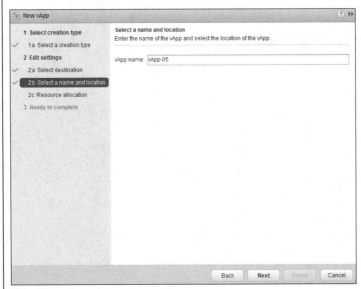

**Figure 11-4**    Naming Your vApp

**7.** Assign the appropriate CPU and Memory resources to your vApp, as shown in Figure 11-5. Click **Next**.

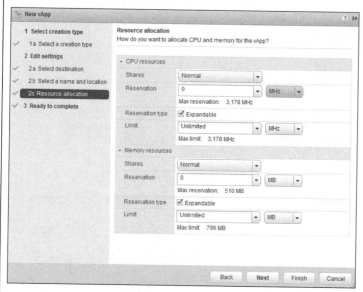

**Figure 11-5** Assigning Resources to Your vApp

**8.** Review the Ready to Complete page to confirm your settings, as shown in Figure 11-6. Click **Finish**.

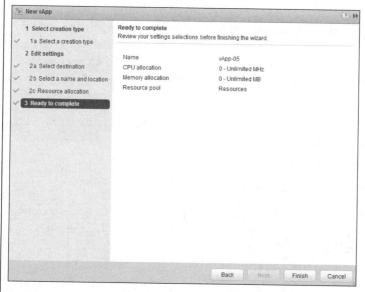

**Figure 11-6** Finishing a vApp

9. You can now view the new vApp in the folder in which you created it, as shown in Figure 11-7.

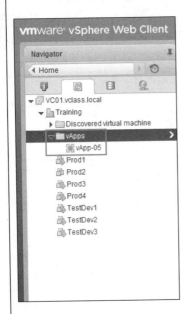

**Figure 11-7**   Viewing the New vApp

If you have a vApp that you really like and want another one just like it, you can clone the vApp (in other words, make an exact copy of it). You can also use the cloning technique to make an exact copy first and then configure only the changes that you want for your new vApp. This saves you configuration time and improves configuration accuracy. Note that the vApp must be powered off before cloning, which means that the VMs also need to be powered off. To clone a vApp, follow the steps outlined in Activity 11-2.

### Activity 11-2   Cloning a vApp

1. Log on to your vSphere Web Client.

2. Select **Home** and then **VMs and Templates**.

3. In the Navigator (the left pane), right-click the vApp that you want to clone, verify that it is powered off, select **Clone**, and then select **Clone** again, as shown in Figure 11-8.

**Figure 11-8**   Cloning a vApp

4. In the Clone vApp Wizard, click **Next** to accept to Clone an existing vApp, as shown in Figure 11-9, and then select the destination for your cloned vApp, as shown in Figure 11-10.

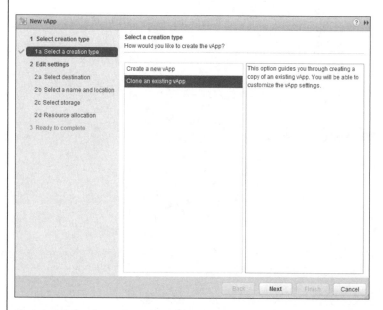

**Figure 11-9**   Cloning an Existing vApp

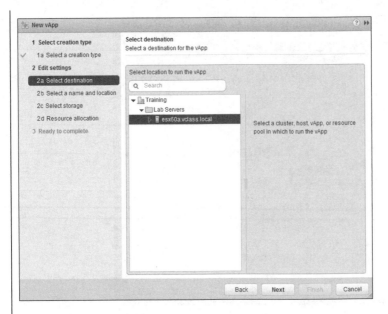

**Figure 11-10** Selecting the Destination for the Cloned vApp

5. On the Name and Location page, type a name for your new cloned vApp (in this case, **Clone of vApp-05**) and the inventory location (folder or data center) as shown in Figure 11-11, and then click **Next**.

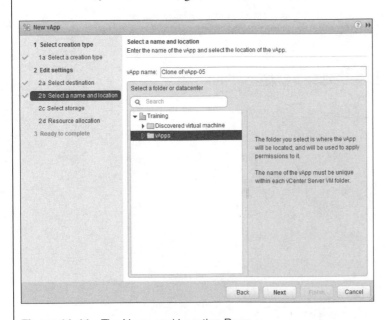

**Figure 11-11** The Name and Location Page

**6.** On the Datastore page, select the datastore where you want to store the vApp, as shown in Figure 11-12, and then click **Next**.

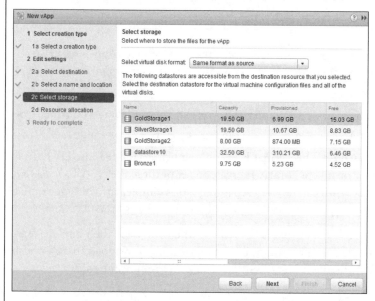

**Figure 11-12**    Selecting a Datastore for a vApp

**7.** On the Resource allocation page, configure the resource settings for your cloned vApp, as shown in Figure 11-13, and then click **Next**.

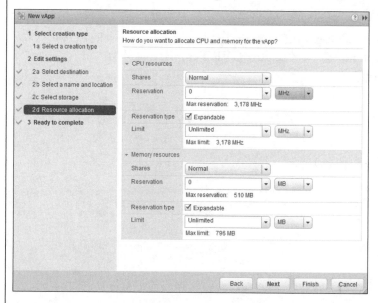

**Figure 11-13**    Configuring Resources for a Cloned vApp

8. On the Ready to Complete page, review your settings and then click **Finish**. A new vApp will be created with the same settings as the original and the same VMs as members of the vApp.

After you have created a vApp, you can export the state of that vApp as an OVF so that it can be imported at another location or division of your organization to be deployed as a vApp.

When you export the state of a VM or vApp, you can choose from two formats, as follows:

- **Folder of files (OVF):** This format is best if you plan to publish the OVF files to a web server or image library. It creates a set of three files (OVF, VMDK, and MF). These files can be used separately; for example, the package could be imported into a vSphere Client by publishing the URL to the OVF file.

- **Single file (OVA):** This format is best to use when you need the template represented as a single file. This might be used for explicit download from a website or to transport the file using a USB drive or other removable software device.

To export the state of a VM or vApp as an OVF or OVA, follow the steps outlined in Activity 11-3.

### Activity 11-3   Exporting an OVF of a vApp

1. Log on to your vSphere Web Client.

2. Right-click the powered-off vApp that you want to export, select **OVF Template**, and then select **Export OVF Template**, as shown in Figure 11-14.

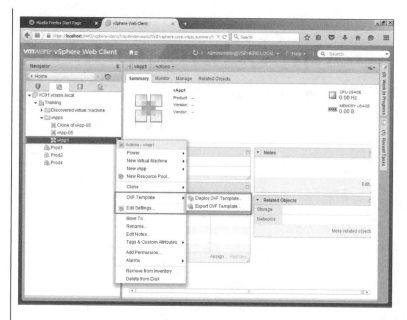

**Figure 11-14**   Exporting an OVF Template

3. In the Export OVF Template dialog box, type the name of the template, enter or browse for the directory that will contain the VM or vApp template, select **OVF** or **OVA**, and optionally enter a description (annotation) for the template, as shown in Figure 11-15.

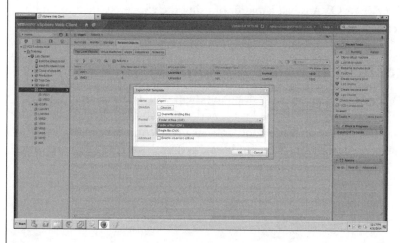

**Figure 11-15**   Selecting the Virtualization Format Type

4. Review all settings on the Ready to Complete page, as shown in Figure 11-16, and click **OK** to export the VM or vApp. Monitor your recent tasks and the export dialog box until complete.

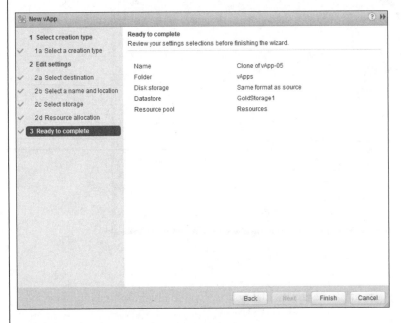

**Figure 11-16**    The Ready to Complete Page

Importing the OVF or OVA is just a matter of using the vSphere Client to find it and then selecting to deploy your new vApp from it.

## Adding Objects to an Existing vApp

You can add VMs to a vApp by simply dragging them into it. In addition, if you right-click a vApp, as shown in Figure 11-17, notice that you can then select to add a new virtual machine, a new resource pool, or even a new vApp. Figure 11-18 shows the Related Objects tab for vApp-05 with three TestDev VMs ready to work with each other.

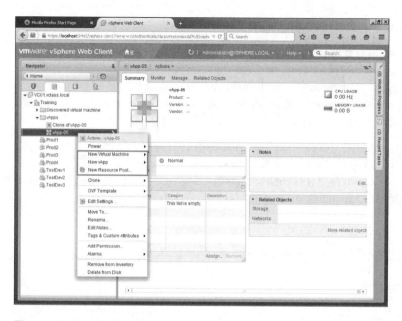

**Figure 11-17**    Adding Objects to a vApp

**Figure 11-18**    Viewing VMs Added to a vApp

# Configuring and Editing vApp Settings

As time goes by and you need to make changes to the vApp's settings, you don't need to re-create the vApp. Instead, you can right-click the vApp and select **Edit Settings**. Changing some settings will require that you power off the VM (such as Advanced properties), but there are many settings (such as Resources) that you can configure with the vApp powered on.

There are many settings you can configure for each vApp. You can access them by right-clicking the vApp and selecting **Edit Settings**. This brings up the Edit vApp dialog box. In it you will find three main sections: Application Properties, Deployment, and Authoring, as shown in Figure 11-19. This section discusses the details of each.

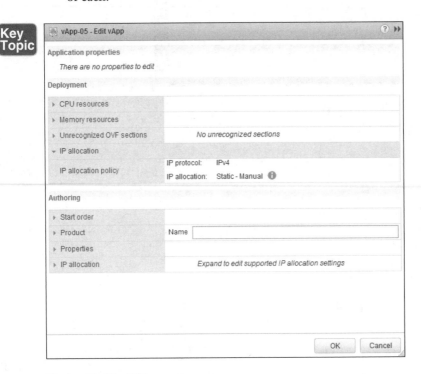

**Figure 11-19** Editing a vApp

## Application Properties

The Application Properties section displays non-editable product information from a vendor, such as the name of the vendor, the version of the software, and specified values for vApp custom properties. When you create your own vApps, this section will likely remain empty.

## Deployment

In general, the Deployment section of vApps allows you to configure Resources, Unrecognized OVF sections, and IP allocation policy. Because each setting is a subject on its own, they are listed separately so they can be discussed in greater depth. You should be able to identify each of these settings. Later chapters cover modifying some of these types of settings for troubleshooting and fine-tuning your virtual data center:

- **Resources:** As shown in Figure 11-20, this setting allows you to fine-tune the CPU and physical memory resources that will be allowed to the vApp and, therefore, the cumulative amount that the VMs in the vApp can use at any given time. (Chapter 12, "Managing Virtual Machine Clones and Templates," discusses these types of resource controls for vApps and VMs.)

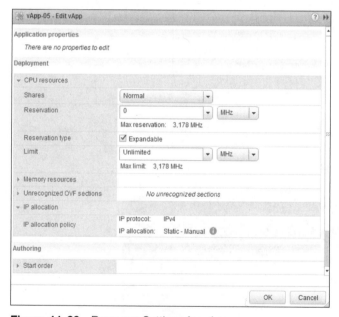

**Figure 11-20**   Resource Settings for vApps

- **Unrecognized OVF sections:** If your vApp is based on an OVF file that was not created in the vSphere Web Client, it might include some configuration information that is not recognized by vCenter Server. You can view this information to determine whether you may need to modify settings to "tweak" the vApp.

- **IP allocation policy:** As shown in Figure 11-21, this setting determines how the VMs in the vApp will receive their IP addresses. Settings in both the Deployment section and the Authoring section relate to each other. The default is a static (manual IPv4) scheme, but you can also configure IP Pools in this section, as shown in Figure 11-22.

Using the DHCP setting requires additional configuration that is not covered here. Configuring IP pools is covered later in Chapter 13, "Administering Virtual Machines and vApps."

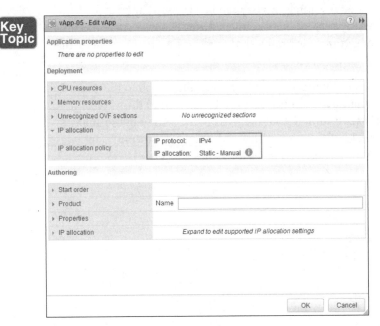

**Figure 11-21**   IP Settings for vApps

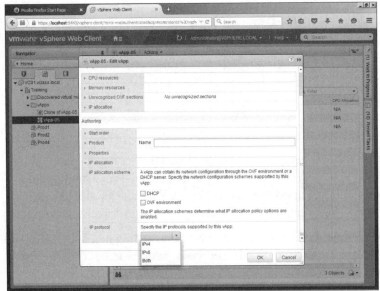

**Figure 11-22**   Configuring DHCP Settings for vApps

## Authoring

As shown in Figure 11-23, the Authoring setting allows you to note the Product Name, Version, Vendor, Vendor URL, and so on. There are also Properties settings that are used for the Open Virtualization Format (OVF) that will be created and can then be exported. You can define your own properties for a vApp if the properties you need are not already defined. This proves especially useful if you plan to use the vApp in other locations.

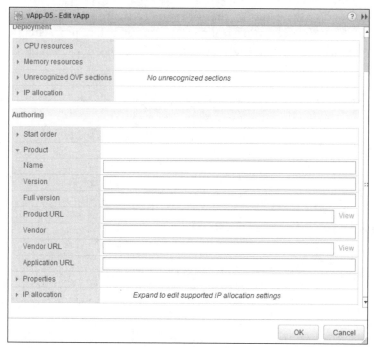

**Figure 11-23** Authoring Settings for vApps

## Start Order

Also included under Authoring is Start Order, but it is so different in regard to a setting that I'm giving it a section of its own. You might remember my earlier example of a database service being provided to the end user by three different VMs, an application server, a database server, and a domain controller. You might also remember that all the VMs in the vApp will be treated as one inventory object. That means that they will power on "as one" and power off "as one." If you think about that for a moment, you might see a potential issue. What if the database server powers up first and looks for the Active Directory, which is not there yet because the domain controller is lagging behind on its power up? What would happen is that the database server would likely register errors that you might have to address later.

To prevent this issue from occurring, you can use the Start Order screen to control the startup of the domain controller and the database server in such a way that the domain controller will always be up and ready with the Active Directory before the database server will be allowed to start. You can do this by placing the VMs into multiple startup groups, as shown in Figure 11-24, and then setting them so that one group must wait on another group. You can configure the number of seconds that a group must wait and/or the detection that VMware Tools are started and ready on the VM. All the VMs in the same group will be started before proceeding to the next group. Also, when you shut down the vApp, the system will use your settings in reverse order.

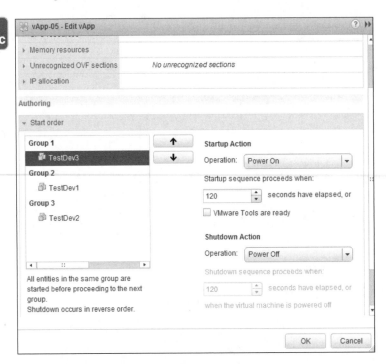

**Figure 11-24**   Start Order Settings for vApps

# Summary

This chapter covered the following main topics:

- The requirements for creating a vApp and in what locations you can create a vApp. You learned that you can create a vApp on a host, resource pool, folder, DRS cluster, or even another vApp.

- The creation, cloning, and exporting of vApps. You learned that vApps provide a flexible method of creating resources where you need them.

- The process of adding objects to the vApp. You learned that you can just drag and drop the objects, or you can right-click and select them.

- Configuring and editing vApp settings. You learned that there are three main groups of settings, but that there are many settings within some of the groups. Each can be controlled for the resources, connectivity, security, and so on, for each vApp.

## Exam Preparation Tasks

## Review All the Key Topics

Review the most important topics from the chapter, noted with the Key Topic icon in the outer margin of the page. Table 11-2 lists these key topics and the page numbers where each is found.

**Table 11-2**  Key Topics for Chapter 11

| Key Topic Element | Description | Page Number |
|---|---|---|
| Bullet List | Requirements for Creating a vApp | 256 |
| Activity 11-1 | Creating a vApp | 256 |
| Figure 11-7 | Viewing the New vApp | 260 |
| Activity 11-2 | Cloning a vApp | 260 |
| Bullet List | Exportable vApp Files | 264 |
| Activity 11-3 | Exporting an OVF of a vApp | 264 |
| Figure 11-17 | Adding Objects to a vApp | 267 |
| Figure 11-18 | Viewing VMs Added to a vApp | 267 |
| Figure 11-19 | Editing a vApp | 268 |

| Key Topic Element | Description | Page Number |
|---|---|---|
| Figure 11-20 | Resource Settings for vApps | 269 |
| Figure 11-21 | IP Settings for vApps | 270 |
| Figure 11-22 | Configuring DHCP Settings for vApps | 270 |
| Figure 11-23 | Authoring Settings for vApps | 271 |
| Figure 11-24 | Start Order Settings for vApps | 272 |

## Review Questions

The answers to these review questions are in Appendix A.

1. Which of the following are *not* requirements to configure a vApp? (Choose two.)

   a. vSphere 5.5 or later

   b. ESX 4.0 or later hosts

   c. Clusters enabled with FT

   d. Clusters enabled with DRS

2. In which of the following can you create a vApp? (Choose two.)

   a. Host

   b. DRS-enabled cluster

   c. VM

   d. Virtual switch

3. Which of the following are *not* true regarding cloning of vApps? (Choose two.)

   a. A cloned vApp is an exact copy of a vApp.

   b. You can modify the settings of a vApp while you clone it.

   c. You can modify the settings of a cloned vApp after you create it.

   d. You can clone a vApp that is powered on.

4. With which types of files can you export an OVF? (Choose two.)

   a. OVA

   b. iso

   c. OVF

   d. vmtx

5. Which of the following files are included in an exported OVF package? (Choose three.)

   a. OVF

   b. OVA

   c. VMDK

   d. MF

   e. VMTX

6. When you power on a vApp, which of the following happens?

   a. The vApp powers on but VMs remain powered off.

   b. The VMs in the vApp each start based on the Start Order.

   c. All the VMs in the vApp are powered off immediately and must be restarted.

   d. It is not possible to control the power of a vApp.

7. You have created a vApp and now want to view the VMs it contains. Which of the following would allow you to view the individual VMs in the vApp? (Choose two.)

   a. The Related Objects tab for vApp

   b. Expand the vApp in the Navigator in Networking view.

   c. Expand the vApp in the Navigator in Hosts and Clusters view.

   d. On the vApps tab in the Related Objects for the vCenter.

8. Which of the following are *not* true regarding Application Properties settings for vApps? (Choose two.)

   a. If you have created the vApp for yourself, they will likely remain empty.

   b. They display non-editable product information from the vendor of the vApp.

   c. They should always be completed in order to run the vApp.

   d. They are editable settings about which you should consult your vApp vendor.

9. Which of the following is the purpose of Unrecognized OVF Sections in vApp settings?

   a. Used for additional advanced IP settings

   b. Contains information that may not be recognized by your vCenter Server when the vApp was created in the vSphere Web Client

   c. Used for advanced resource settings

   d. Contains information that may not be recognized by your vCenter Server when the vApp was *not* created in the vSphere Web Client

10. Which of the following *best describes* the Shutdown Order of vApp?

    a. Specifies when that vApp will be shut down in relation to other vApps on the same host

    b. Specifies when each VM in a vApp will be shut down in relation to the other VMs, on a VM by VM basis

    c. Specifies categories of VMs and when each category of VMs will be shut down in relation to the other categories

    d. Specifies when that vApp will be shut down in relation to other vApps on the same DRS cluster

**This chapter covers the following subjects:**

- Cloning and Template Options
- Configuring Virtual Machine Options
- Adding/Removing Virtual Machines
- Creating a Template from an Existing Virtual Machine
- Deploying a Virtual Machine from a Template
- Updating Existing Virtual Machine Templates
- Configuring CPU and Memory Reservations and Shares

If you have a VM that you like and you want another one identical to it, you can clone the VM. The catch is that a clone is an exact copy, and you might not want an exact copy. For example, it's unlikely that you want the same NetBIOS name, IP address, or SID, especially if you are planning to continue to use the VM that you cloned. In these cases (with VMs using a Microsoft guest OS), you can use Sysprep to provide customization while you are creating the clone.

## CHAPTER 12

# Managing Virtual Machine Clones and Templates

Suppose that you don't want just one copy of a VM that you currently have running. Assume instead that you are in charge of standardizing the OS and applications that will be used for a certain type of VM. In that case, you might want to create a template that will thereafter be used by anyone who creates that type of VM. A template is a VM that cannot be powered on but that can be used as a master copy to create VMs that can be powered on. By enforcing the use of the template to create certain VMs, you will improve not only the speed at which VMs can be created but also the accuracy of their creation.

In this chapter, you learn about your options in regard to virtual machine clones and templates, and why you might choose one over the other. In addition, I discuss configuring the VMs that you have and adding more or removing those that you don't need. Finally, I discuss the process of deploying VMs from templates, updating existing templates, and configuring resources, such as CPU and memory reservations and shares.

## "Do I Know This Already?" Quiz

The "Do I Know This Already?" quiz allows you to assess whether you should read this entire chapter or simply jump to the "Exam Preparation Tasks" section for review. If you are in doubt, read the entire chapter. Table 12-1 outlines the major headings in this chapter and the corresponding "Do I Know This Already?" quiz questions. You can find the answers in Appendix A, "Answers to the 'Do I Know This Already?' Quizzes and Chapter Review Questions."

**Table 12-1**   "Do I Know This Already?" Section-to-Question Mapping

| Foundation Topics Section | Questions Covered in This Section |
|---|---|
| Cloning and Template Options | 1, 2 |
| Configuring Virtual Machine Options | 3, 4 |
| Adding/Removing Virtual Machines | 5 |
| Creating a Template from an Existing Virtual Machine | 6, 7 |
| Deploying a Virtual Machine from a Template | 8 |
| Updating Existing Virtual Machine Templates | 9 |
| Configuring CPU and Memory Reservations and Shares | 10 |

1. Which of the following are true regarding the cloning of a VM? (Choose two.)

    a. You must power a VM off before cloning it.

    b. You can clone a VM that is powered on.

    c. You can clone a VM that is powered off.

    d. Cloning a VM that is powered off will likely take much longer than cloning one that is powered on.

2. Which of the following are true regarding a VM clone? (Choose two.)

    a. Without customization, a clone is an exact copy of a VM.

    b. You cannot customize a VM while you clone it.

    c. You can customize a VM while you clone it.

    d. Customizing Microsoft VMs is not possible.

3. Which tab under Edit Settings for a VM contains the categories of VMware Tools and Power Management?

    a. Virtual Hardware

    b. VMware Tools

    c. General Options

    d. VM Options

**4.** Which of the following are configurable under VMware Tools? (Choose two.)

  **a.** Power Operations

  **b.** VMware Tools Scripts

  **c.** Memory Management (vmmemctl)

  **d.** Swap file location

**5.** If you removed a VM by selecting **Delete from Disk**, how can you recover the VM?

  **a.** Restore the VM from the new datastore that was automatically created during the deletion of the VM from its original disk.

  **b.** Restore the files from the datastore in which the VM was originally created.

  **c.** Restore the VM from your latest backup.

  **d.** You cannot restore the VM because to save space, deleting the disk will also delete any backups of the VM.

**6.** Which of the following are true regarding converting a VM to a template? (Choose two.)

  **a.** The VM can be powered on or off.

  **b.** The VM must be powered off.

  **c.** The VM and the template will exist in the inventory afterward.

  **d.** Only the template will exist in the inventory afterward.

**7.** Which of the following are true regarding the cloning of VM to a template? (Choose two.)

  **a.** The VM may be powered off or powered on.

  **b.** A VM and a template will exist in the inventory afterward.

  **c.** The VM must be powered off.

  **d.** Only the cloned template will exist in the inventory afterward. The VM will be deleted.

8. Which of the following are true regarding deploying a VM from a template? (Choose two.)

   a. You can deploy the VM only on the host on which the template exists.

   b. You can deploy a VM anywhere in the vCenter from a template on any host connected to the vCenter.

   c. You must select the compute resource as you deploy the VM.

   d. You can delay selecting a compute resource until you first want to start the VM.

9. Which of the following are *true* regarding VM templates? (Choose two.)

   a. You can edit the settings of VM templates, just like VMs.

   b. You cannot edit the setting of templates.

   c. You cannot power on a template.

   d. You can power on a template as long as the VM to which it is connected is powered on.

10. Which of the following are true regarding CPU and memory reservations for VMs? (Choose two.)

   a. It is not possible to change the CPU and memory reservations and shares on individual VMs.

   b. It is not recommended to change the CPU and memory reservations and shares on individual VMs.

   c. Resource pools provide the best environment to control CPU and memory reservations, not VMs.

   d. VMs provide the best environment to control CPU and memory resources, not resource pools.

## Foundation Topics

# Cloning and Template Options

Suppose that you have a VM that you want to clone. Can you clone it with it powered on, or do you have to power it off first? The answer is "yes," you can clone it with it powered on, but you could also clone it with it powered off; it's your choice. The trade-off is that cloning with the VM powered on might be more convenient because the users can continue to use it, but cloning with it powered off will definitely be a bit faster. To clone an existing VM, follow the steps outlined in Activity 12-1.

---

**Activity 12-1   Cloning an Existing Virtual Machine**

1. Log on to your vSphere Web Client.

2. Select **Home** and then **VMs and Templates**.

3. Right-click the VM that you want to clone and click **Clone**, and then select **Clone to Virtual Machine**, as shown in Figure 12-1. (The VM can be powered off or on; in this case, the VM is powered on.)

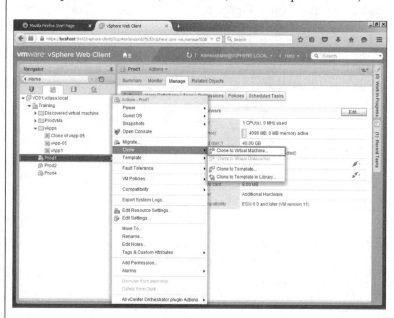

**Figure 12-1**   Cloning a VM

---

4. From Name and Location, give your new VM a name and select the inventory location, as shown in Figure 12-2, and then click **Next**.

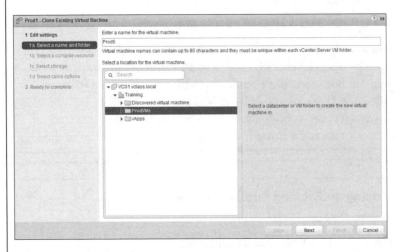

**Figure 12-2** Entering the Name and Selecting the Folder

5. Select the host, vApp, or resource pool in which you want to run the cloned VM, and click **Next**, as shown in Figure 12-3.

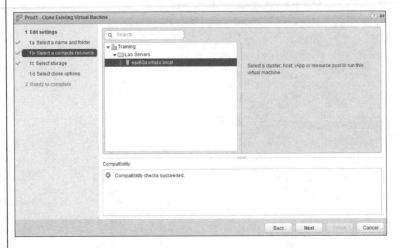

**Figure 12-3** Selecting the Compute Resource

**6.** In Storage, select the datastore that you will use for the VM, and click **Next**, as shown in Figure 12-4.

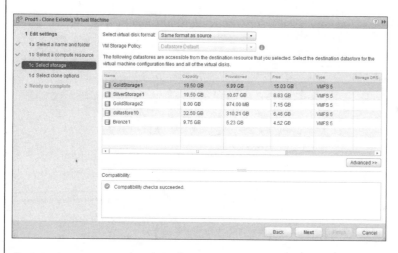

**Figure 12-4**   Selecting Storage Location

**7.** In clone options, you can choose to customize the operating system based on a standard that you have created, or choose not to customize (in this case, do not use customization) and click **Next**. (You can also choose to customize this VM's hardware or power on the VM after creation.) See Figure 12-5.

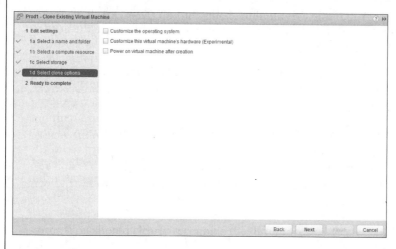

**Figure 12-5**   Selecting Clone Options

**8.** Review your settings and click **Finish**, as shown in Figure 12-6. Monitor the Recent Tasks pane and your inventory to see your new VM.

**Figure 12-6** Reviewing Ready to Complete

## Configuring Virtual Machine Options

Now you have another VM that is just like the one that you cloned. In this case, Prod5 is identical to Prod1. Chances are good that you don't need both to be absolutely identical, so you might want to change the options of the VM after you have cloned it from the other one. With a little knowledge, you can make the needed changes with minimal effort.

You might have noticed that when you right-click a VM and then click **Edit Settings**, there are multiple tabs, each with its own set of configuration settings, as shown in Figure 12-7.

One of these tabs is the **VM Options** tab, on which you can configure VM options. Also note that the version of the VM and its compatibility with regard to hosts is indicated in the bottom-left corner; in this case, we are viewing a Version 11 VM's settings. The options for a Version 11 VM are organized into the following categories:

- General

- VMware Remote Console

- VMware Tools

- Power Management

- Boot Options

- Advanced

- Fibre Channel NPIV

**Figure 12-7**   Edit Setting for VMs

This section briefly overviews the settings in each of the categories.

## General Options

There are many settings and areas of information on the General Options page, as shown in Figure 12-8. On the first section at the top, the VM name is listed. This is the only parameter on this page that can be changed with the VM powered on. The VM name listed here is also referred to as the display name. It is the name that the VM will be represented by in your vCenter inventory. Still further down, the VM's configuration file and working location are listed. The names of these files will start with the display name. The last setting is that of the OS on the VM. Based on this setting, the system updates the VM with the latest drivers and VMware Tools. This setting should always match the actual OS that starts when you power on your VM.

**Figure 12-8**    General Options

## VMware Remote Console Options

This option controls the behavior of a remote connection or connections to the VM. Specifically, you can configure the VM to lock the guest OS when the last remote user disconnects (remember that this is a server), and you can limit the number of simultaneous connections to the VM, as shown in Figure 12-9.

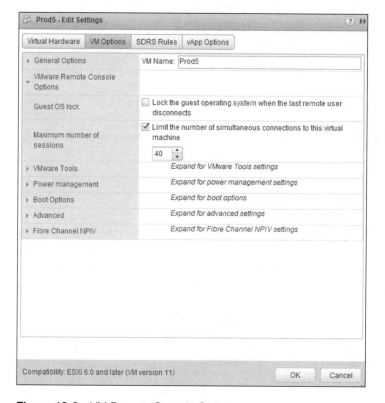

**Figure 12-9**   VM Remote Console Options

## VMware Tools

The VMware Tools options are organized into four categories, as shown in Figure 12-10:

- Power Operations
- Run VMware Tools Scripts
- Tools Upgrades
- Time

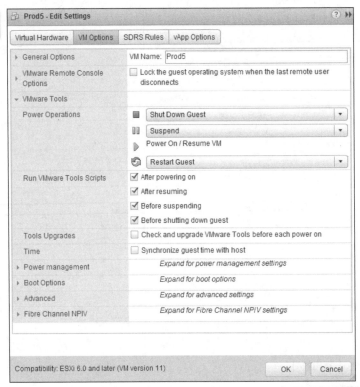

**Figure 12-10** VMware Tools Options with VM Powered Off

The default setting of Power Operations provides for a graceful shutdown of the guest OS, suspend, and restart guest. These default settings should be fine for most VMs. Below that, the Run VMware Tools Scripts controls when the scripts are run. These are optional scripts installed in a VM along with VMware Tools that do things like answer the annoying Windows Server 2008 "Why are you shutting down?" question. If the tools have changed, running the scripts takes a short period of time, but the trade-off is that you have the latest options. You can decide whether you want that to happen when changing power states or before shutting down the guest OS. The VM represented in Figure 12-10 is powered off; therefore, all options are available. Changing most of these settings requires powering down the VM; otherwise, many of the settings would be grayed out (dimmed) and unavailable, as shown in Figure 12-11 with the same VM power on.

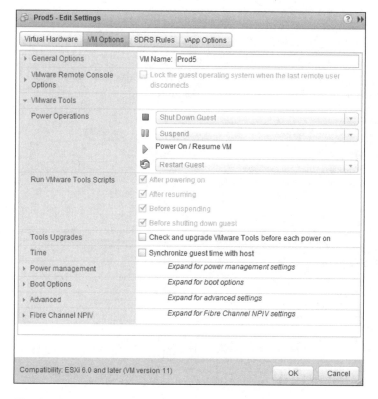

**Figure 12-11**   VMware Tools Options with VM Powered On

## Power Management

The Power Management setting determines how the VM will respond when the guest OS is placed into standby mode. It is set by default to leave the VM powered on. The section "Configuring Virtual Machine Power Settings" discusses configuration options for this setting.

**NOTE**   Don't worry, I'm not forgetting about Boot Options. I will cover those in a few sections within a section called "Configuring Virtual Machine Boot Options."

## Advanced Options

As you can see from Figure 12-12, the options such as debugging settings, swap file location, and other configuration parameters that are included under the Advanced category can usually be left at their defaults. They are configurable for the unusual "one-off" situation when you might need to make a change.

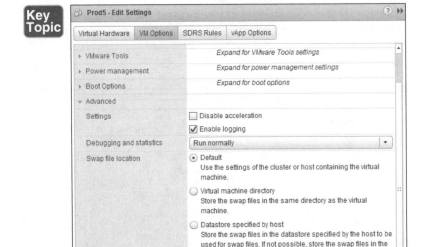

**Figure 12-12**  Advanced Options

## Fibre Channel NPIV

This option enables you to examine worldwide names (WWNs) for individual VMs running on hosts that are using Fibre Channel hardware. These WWNs are normally assigned by the host of the vCenter for VMs that are enabled for NPIV. The details of this option are beyond the scope of this book.

### Configuring Virtual Machine Power Settings

As mentioned previously, you can set the power management options for a VM on the VM Options tab. The default setting is that the VM will remain powered on even when the OS is placed into standby mode. For servers, this is usually the appropriate setting.

If you elect to suspend the VM, the VM will have to be resumed to be used when the guest OS comes out of standby mode. Because standby mode was originally created to save energy and reduce the amount of heat that a computer puts into a room, and because this does not apply to a VM, it might be best to let the VM's guest OS go into standby mode but keep the VM powered on, as shown in Figure 12-13. Changing this setting requires first powering down the VM.

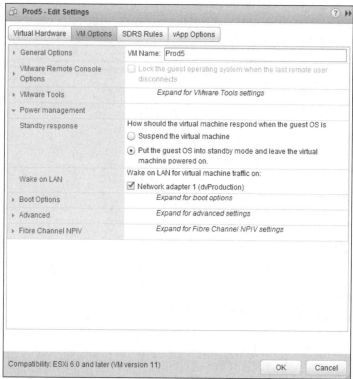

**Figure 12-13**   Power Management Settings

## Configuring Virtual Machine Boot Options

You can configure VM boot options in four categories, as shown in Figure 12-14:

- **Firmware:** Allows you to specify the boot firmware for your VM, but changing to a setting that does not match your capabilities may render the VM unbootable. You should use this setting if your host supports EFI.

- **Boot Delay:** Allows you to specify a number of milliseconds between the time that POST is finished and the OS begins to load. This can give you time to press the appropriate key (such as F2) to enter setup. This might be useful, for example, to change the boot sequence to recognize a CD-ROM drive, but it will delay the start of the VM every time you power it on.

- **Force BIOS Setup:** This is a run-once type of setting that will clear itself automatically after you use it.

- **Failed Boot Recovery:** Used to configure the action of the VM if it should fail to find a boot device. This could be especially helpful if you are attempting to boot and install an operating system through a network, which can cause a delay in the VM's sensing the boot device.

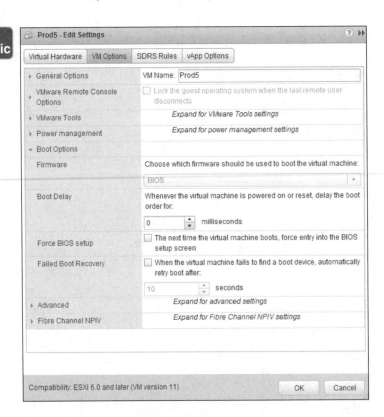

**Figure 12-14**   Advanced Boot Options

## Configuring Virtual Machine Troubleshooting Options

Troubleshooting is a process of isolating an issue. To isolate an issue, what you need more than anything is information (in other words, *logs*). Normal logging of events and tasks associated with a VM is enabled by default. You can see this by logging on to your vSphere Client, choosing a VM, and examining the advanced options, as shown in Figure 12-15. You can disable logging on this setting, but that is not a recommended practice. In addition, if you are troubleshooting a VM and you want verbose debugging information or statistics, you can change this setting to force the system to record the information that you want. The information that is collected might also be useful to VMware technical support.

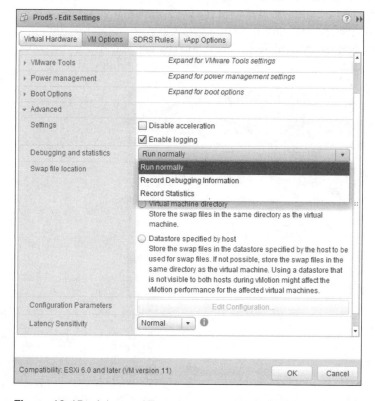

**Figure 12-15**   Advanced Troubleshooting Options

# Adding/Removing Virtual Machines

There are many ways to add a virtual machine (VM) to your host and your vCenter inventory. In fact, we have already discussed many of them. You can add the VM by building it "from scratch," cloning, deploying from a template, or just acquiring a virtual appliance and installing it. Regardless of how you have added the VM, you can manage it with all the same tools as you manage the others. Many of these tools are covered in the coming chapters of this book.

In contrast, there are only two ways to remove a VM from your vCenter inventory. You can remove it from the inventory but leave the files on the datastore, so you can add it back later as needed, as shown in Figure 12-16. As an alternative, you can completely delete the VM from the datastore at the same time that you remove it from your vCenter inventory, as shown in Figure 12-17. If you choose this option, the VM is said to be "permanently" deleted, but if you change your mind, you could still restore it with your latest backup. You did make a backup, didn't you?

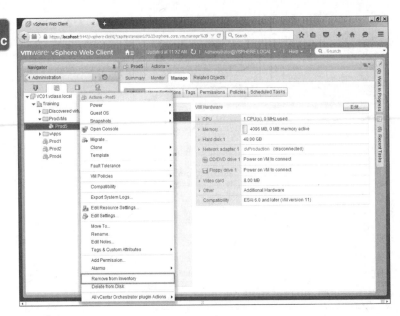

**Figure 12-16** Removing a VM from Inventory

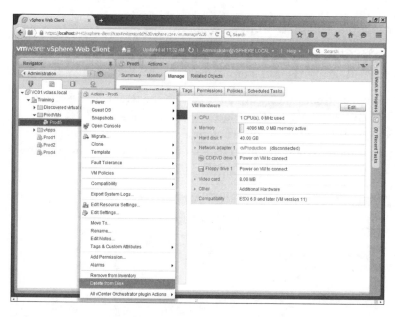

**Figure 12-17**   "Permanently" Deleting a VM

# Creating a Template from an Existing Virtual Machine

As mentioned earlier, you might use a template to create a new standard that you want everyone to use in the future. In that case, the VM that you are using for the template might not even be in your production environment. In that situation, the easiest and fastest way to create a template from the VM would be to convert the VM into the template. Of course, then you wouldn't have your VM anymore until you created a new VM from the template or converted it back. The upside of this method is that it happens almost instantaneously.

Another method of creating the template would be to clone the template from the running VM. As you can imagine, this takes longer to do; however, it allows the users to continue to use the VM while the template is being created, possibly with minor loss in performance. Either way, you end up with a template. However, cloning the template from the running VM results in your ending up with a template and still retaining the VM from which you created the template.

To create a template from an existing VM, follow the steps outlined in Activity 12-2.

**Activity 12-2  Creating a Template from an Existing VM**

1. Log on to your vSphere Web Client.

2. Select **Home** and then **VMs and Templates**.

3. Right-click the VM from which you want to create the template and select **Clone**. Then choose **Clone to Template**, as shown in Figure 12-18. The VM can be powered off or on if you are cloning. If you are converting, the VM must be powered off. In this case, I am cloning the template with the VM powered off.

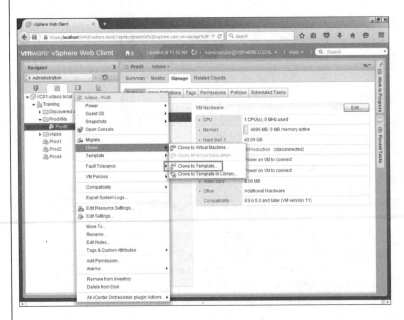

**Figure 12-18**   Creating a Template

4. Give your new VM a name and select the inventory location, as shown in Figure 12-19, and then click **Next**.

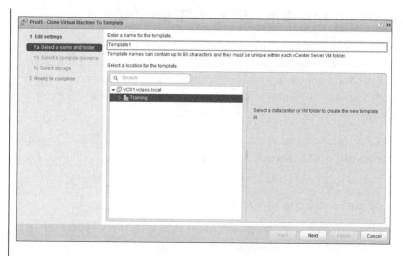

**Figure 12-19**   Naming a Template

5. Select a host for the new VM, as shown in Figure 12-20, and click **Next**. The system performs a compatibility check.

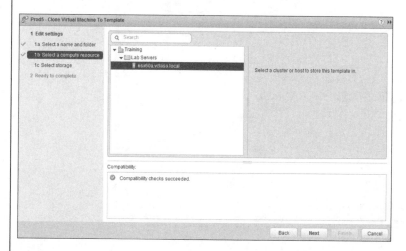

**Figure 12-20**   Selecting a Host for a Template

6. From Datastore, select the datastore that you will use for the VM and the VM disk format, and click **Next**.

7. Review your settings and click **Finish**. Monitor the Recent Tasks pane and your inventory to see your new template.

# Deploying a Virtual Machine from a Template

Of course, the reason that you made the template is not just to have a template, but to be able to deploy VMs more quickly and accurately by using the template. After you have created the template, you can deploy VMs from it and create them anywhere in your vCenter. To deploy a VM from your template, follow the steps outlined in Activity 12-3.

**Activity 12-3    Deploying a VM from a Template**

1. Log on to your vSphere Web Client.

2. Select **Home** and then **VMs and Templates**.

3. Right-click the template from which you want to deploy the VM and select **Deploy VM from this Template**, as shown in Figure 12-21.

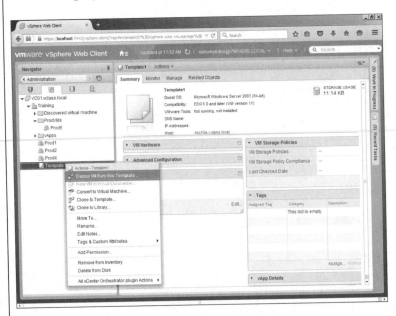

**Figure 12-21**    Deploying a VM from a Template

4. From Name and Location, give your new VM a name and select the inventory location, as shown in Figure 12-22, and then click **Next**. The location can even be a different data center in the same vCenter.

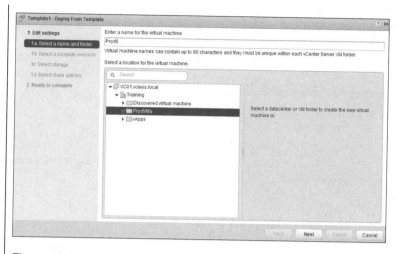

**Figure 12-22**   Naming the New VM

5. From Host/Cluster, select the host for the new VM.

6. Select the host, vApp, or resource pool to which you want to deploy the new VM, as shown in Figure 12-23, and then click **Next**.

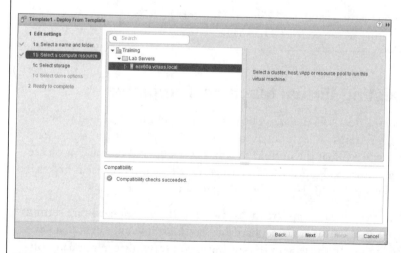

**Figure 12-23**   Selecting a Host, Resource Pool, or vApp

7. From Datastore, select the datastore that you will use for the VM and the VM disk format, and click **Next**.

8. From **Select Clone Options**, select whether you want to use a custom group of settings that you have previously created (in this case, do not use customization), as shown in Figure 12-24, and then click **Next**.

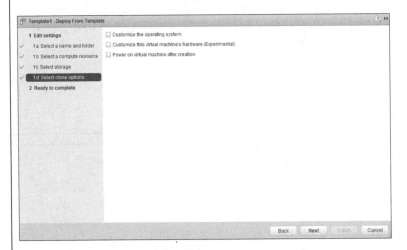

**Figure 12-24**    The Select Clone Options Section

9. Review your settings and click **Finish**. Monitor the Recent Tasks pane and your inventory to see your new template.

## Updating Existing Virtual Machine Templates

Not only is a template a VM that can't be powered on, but it's a VM on which you can't change settings, at least not as long as it's a template. If you right-click a template, you will see that the options to edit its settings and to power it on are not available, as shown in Figure 12-25. This is actually good, because it makes it unlikely that someone could change your template by accident.

However, what if you need to update the software or the virtual hardware settings on the template? In the case of virtual hardware settings, it would seem that you don't have the option. In the case of the software, you certainly can't update software on a VM that you can't power on, so what is the solution to this problem?

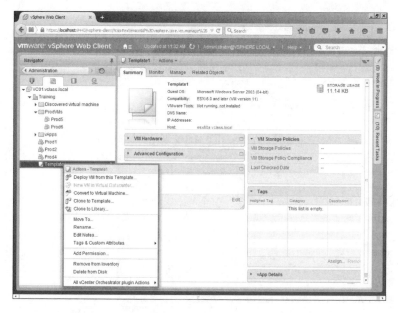

**Figure 12-25**   Templates Cannot Be Powered On

If you look again at Figure 12-25, you will see that you can convert the template back to a VM. After you have converted the template to a VM, you can apply the updates and convert the VM back to a template to use the updates for future VMs created with the template. To convert a template into a VM, follow the steps outlined in Activity 12-4.

---

**Activity 12-4   Converting a Template to a VM**

1. Log on to your vSphere Client.

2. Select **Home** and then **VMs and Templates**, right-click the template that you want to convert to a VM, and select **Convert to Virtual Machine**, as shown in Figure 12-26.

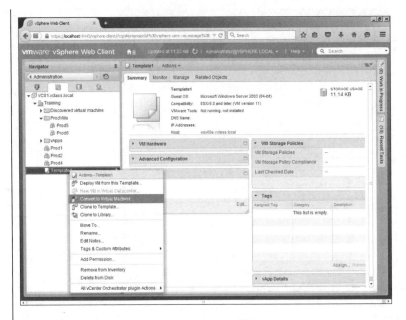

**Figure 12-26**    Converting a Template to a VM

3.  Select the host, vApp, or resource pool for the new VM, as shown in Figure
    12-27, and click **Next**.

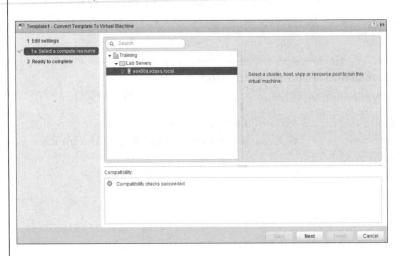

**Figure 12-27**    Selecting the Compute Resource for the New VM

4. From Ready to Complete, review your settings and click **Finish**, as shown in Figure 12-28. Monitor the Recent Tasks pane and your inventory for your converted VM.

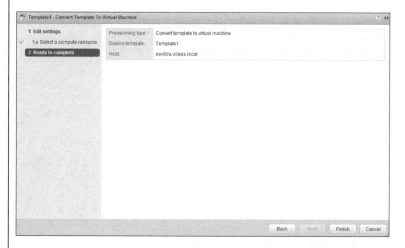

**Figure 12-28**   Confirming Your Selections to Convert a Template to a VM

**NOTE**   You can also use software, such as VMware Update Manager, to automate much of this process. You learn about Update Manager in Chapter 19, "Updating ESXi and Virtual Machines."

## Configuring CPU and Memory Reservations and Shares

Strictly speaking, it's not usually a best practice to configure CPU and memory reservations for individual VMs. This is because a reservation that is configured arbitrarily too high can prevent a VM from starting up. However, if you really need to configure these on a VM, you can find them on the Virtual Hardware tab of the VM's settings, as shown in Figure 12-29.

So, you might be wondering where you should configure these settings instead of on the VM itself. The best place to use CPU reservations and shares is in conjunction with resource pools for VMs. Chapter 16, "Creating and Administering Resource Pools," covers the best practices related to CPU and memory reservations and shares.

**Figure 12-29**    Configuring CPU and Memory Settings for a VM

## Summary

This chapter covers the following main topics:

- The options for configuring virtual machines, clones, and templates.

- Adding and removing virtual machines in your inventory.

- Creating templates, deploying VMs from templates, and updating VM templates.

- You learned that it's not a best practice to configure individual CPU and memory reservations on VMs and that you should use resource pools instead.

## Exam Preparation Tasks

## Review All the Key Topics

Review the most important topics from inside the chapter, noted with the Key Topic icon in the outer margin of the page. Table 12-2 lists these key topics and the page numbers where each is found.

**Table 12-2**  Key Topics for Chapter 12

| Key Topic Element | Description | Page Number |
|---|---|---|
| Activity 12-1 | Cloning an Existing Virtual Machine | 283 |
| Bullet List | Options for Version 11 VMs | 286 |
| Figure 12-7 | Edit Setting for VMs | 287 |
| Figure 12-8 | General Options | 288 |
| Figure 12-9 | VM Remote Console Options | 289 |
| Figure 12-10 | VMware Tools Options with VM Powered Off | 290 |
| Figure 12-11 | VMware Tools Options with VM Powered On | 291 |
| Figure 12-12 | Advanced Options | 292 |
| Figure 12-13 | Power Management Settings | 293 |
| Figure 12-14 | Advanced Boot Options | 294 |
| Figure 12-15 | Advanced Troubleshooting Options | 295 |
| Figure 12-16 | Removing a VM from Inventory | 296 |
| Figure 12-17 | "Permanently" Deleting a VM | 297 |
| Activity 12-2 | Creating a Template from an Existing VM | 298 |
| Activity 12-3 | Deploying a VM from a Template | 300 |
| Activity 12-4 | Converting a Template to a VM | 303 |

## Review Questions

The answers to these review questions are in Appendix A.

1. Which of the following are *not* true regarding the cloning of a VM? (Choose two.)

   a. You must power a VM off before cloning it.

   b. You can clone a VM that is powered on.

   c. You can clone a VM that is powered off.

   d. Cloning a VM that is powered off will likely take much longer than cloning one that is powered on.

**2.** Which of the following are *not* true regarding a VM clone? (Choose two.)

    **a.** Without customization, a clone is an exact copy of a VM.

    **b.** You cannot customize a VM while you clone it.

    **c.** You can customize a VM while you clone it.

    **d.** Customizing Microsoft VMs is not possible.

**3.** Which tab under Edit Settings for a VM contains the categories of VMware Remote Console and Fibre Channel NPIV?

    **a.** Virtual Hardware

    **b.** VMware Tools

    **c.** Boot Options

    **d.** VM Options

**4.** Which of the following are configurable under VMware Tools? (Choose two.)

    **a.** Tools Upgrades

    **b.** Time Synchronization

    **c.** Memory Management (vmmemctl)

    **d.** Swap file location

**5.** If you removed a VM by selecting **Remove from Inventory**, how can you recover the VM?

    **a.** Restore the VM from the new datastore that was automatically created during the deletion of the VM from its original disk.

    **b.** Restore the files from the datastore in which the VM was located.

    **c.** Restore the VM from your latest backup.

    **d.** You cannot restore the VM, because deleting the disk will also delete any backups of the VM, to save space.

**6.** Which of the following are *not* true regarding converting a VM to a template? (Choose two.)

    **a.** The VM can be powered on or off.

    **b.** The VM must be powered off.

    **c.** The VM and the template will exist in the inventory afterward.

    **d.** Only the template will exist in the inventory afterward.

**7.** Which of the following are *not* true regarding the cloning of VM to a template? (Choose two.)

   **a.** The VM may be powered off or powered on.

   **b.** A VM and a template will exist in the inventory afterward.

   **c.** The VM must be powered off.

   **d.** Only the cloned template will exist in the inventory afterward. The VM will be deleted.

**8.** Which of the following are *not* true regarding deploying a VM from a template? (Choose two.)

   **a.** You can only deploy the VM on the host on which the template exists.

   **b.** You can deploy a VM anywhere in the vCenter from a template on any host connected to the vCenter.

   **c.** You must select the compute resource as you deploy the VM.

   **d.** You can delay selecting a compute resource until you first want to start the VM.

**9.** Which of the following are *not* true regarding VM templates? (Choose two.)

   **a.** You can edit the settings of VM templates, just like VMs.

   **b.** You cannot edit the setting of templates.

   **c.** You cannot power on a template.

   **d.** You can power on a template as long as the VM that it's connected to is powered on.

**10.** Which of the following are *not* true regarding CPU and memory reservations for VMs? (Choose two.)

   **a.** It is not possible to change the CPU and memory reservations and shares on individual VMs.

   **b.** It is not recommended to change the CPU and memory reservations and shares on individual VMs.

   **c.** Resource Pools provide the best environment to control CPU and memory reservations, not VMs.

   **d.** VMs provide the best environment to control CPU and memory resources, not resource pools.

**This chapter covers the following subjects:**

- Files Used by Virtual Machines
- Locations for Virtual Machine Configuration Files and Virtual Disks
- Common Practices for Securing Virtual Machines
- Configuring IP Pools
- Configuring and Managing a Content Library

The word *administering* covers a lot of ground and means many things. To effectively administer VMs and vApps, you first have to know what they are made up of and where to find their components. Also, you need to understand common practices for keeping them secure. In addition, you need to know how to connect them to the environment with IP pools. Finally, you may want to create a central location for VM and vApp templates to further standardize your configurations. This section focuses on administering VMs and vApps.

## CHAPTER 13

# Administering Virtual Machines and vApps

## "Do I Know This Already?" Quiz

The "Do I Know This Already?" quiz allows you to assess whether you should read this entire chapter or simply jump to the "Exam Preparation Tasks" section for review. If you are in doubt, read the entire chapter. Table 13-1 outlines the major headings in this chapter and the corresponding "Do I Know This Already?" quiz questions. You can find the answers in Appendix A, "Answers to the 'Do I Know This Already?' Quizzes and Chapter Review Questions."

**Table 13-1**  "Do I Know This Already?" Section-to-Question Mapping

| Foundation Topics Section | Questions Covered in This Section |
|---|---|
| Files Used by Virtual Machines | 1, 2 |
| Locations for Virtual Machine Configuration Files and Virtual Disks | 3, 4 |
| Common Practices for Securing Virtual Machines | 5, 6 |
| Configuring IP Pools | 7 |
| Configuring and Managing a Content Library | 8, 9, 10 |

1. Which of the following is the extension of a text file that describes a VM that is marked to never be powered on?

    a. .vmtx

    b. .vmx

    c. -flat.vmdk

    d. There is no such file.

**2.** Which of the following is the extension of a special pointer file that allows the VM to see a LUN instead of using data from a VMFS or NFS?

   **a.** .vmx

   **b.** .vmdk

   **c.** -flat.vmdk

   **d.** -rdmp.vmdk

**3.** Which of the following is the default setting on a cluster regarding the location of VM swap files?

   **a.** There is no setting on the cluster regarding VM swap files.

   **b.** Virtual machine directory

   **c.** Datastore specified by the host

   **d.** Use SSD when available.

**4.** Which of the following is the default setting on a host regarding VM swap files?

   **a.** Virtual machine directory

   **b.** Datastore specified by the host

   **c.** There is no setting on the cluster regarding VM swap files.

   **d.** Use SSD when available.

**5.** Which of the following are *true* in regard to securing VMs? (Choose two.)

   **a.** A VM is not inherently secure because of the many files that it shares with other VMs.

   **b.** A VM is inherently secure in regard to its isolation from other VMs.

   **c.** There are configuration steps and best practices that you can follow to add to the inherent security of your VMs.

   **d.** There is nothing else that you can do to make a VM more secure than it is by default.

**6.** Which of the following are *not* true in regard to securing VMs? (Choose two.)

   **a.** The more virtual hardware you have on a VM, the more secure it will be.

   **b.** VMs do not require antivirus because they are immune to viruses.

   **c.** You should never copy sensitive data into the clipboard on the OS of a VM.

   **d.** You should not change the file size for the informational messages to the host.

7. Which of the following are true regarding IP pools? (Choose two.)

   a. vApps always use IP pools for their IP address assignments.

   b. vApps use IP pools when they are set to use Transient IP allocation.

   c. You cannot configure IP pools for vSphere 6 on the Windows-based vSphere Client.

   d. You can configure IP pools for vSphere 6 on the Windows-based vSphere Client.

8. If you want to create a library to which you can add OVFs and other files, which type of library should you create?

   a. Local

   b. Subscribed

   c. Local or subscribed

   d. Shared

9. Which of the following should be able to use the templates stored in a local library?

   a. Only administrators on the same vCenter as content library.

   b. All administrators in all vCenters and all Single Sign-On domains.

   c. All administrators in all vCenters on the same Single Sign-On domain as the content library.

   d. Only administrators of the same hosts to which the content library is assigned.

10. Which of the following are true regarding a subscribed content library?

   a. The administrator can change the options to download all content or just metadata.

   b. The administrator can add content to the original library as needed.

   c. The administrator can change the required password that will be used to connect to the library.

   d. The administrator can choose to automatically synchronize all new content.

## Foundation Topics

## Files Used by Virtual Machines

As previously mentioned, a VM is a VM even without an OS or applications installed on it. A VM is a "box" that is made of software that we call *virtual hardware*. The virtual hardware is constructed using many files. Each file takes the place of what would otherwise be hardware or firmware on a physical machine. It's important that you understand the main files that make up each of your VMs and what they do on the VM. Table 13-2 shows the main files that make up a VM, their naming convention, and their purpose.

**Table 13-2**   Virtual Machine Files

| File | Filename | Description |
|---|---|---|
| Configuration file | [VM_name].vmx | A text file that describes the VM and all its configuration settings. |
| Swap file | [VM_name].vswp | A file that is created by the VMkernel when the VM is powered on and deleted when powered off. The size of this file is equal to the available (configured) memory minus any reservation. The file can be as large as available memory if there is no reservation. |
| BIOS file | [VM_name].nvram | A file that takes the place of BIOS (Basic Input Output System). This is important with full virtualization because the guest OS on the VM might need to address something that looks to it like BIOS. |
| Log files | vmware.log | Files that keep a record of events and tasks that have occurred on the VM, its OS, and its applications. These files might be useful for troubleshooting. |
| Disk descriptor files | [VM_name].vmdk | A small file for each virtual disk on a VM that describes the virtual disk, such as how large it is, thick or thin, and where it is located. |
| Disk data files | [VM_name]-flat.vmdk | Typically, a rather large file for each virtual disk on a VM that represents the actual preallocated space that has been allowed on the datastore for this virtual disk. |
| Suspend state file | [VM_name]. vmss | A file that holds the state of a VM when the VM is suspended (only CPU activity). |

| File | Filename | Description |
|---|---|---|
| Snapshot data file | [VM_name].vmsd | A centralized file for storing information and metadata about snapshots. |
| Snapshot state file | [VM_name].vmsn | A descriptor file for each snapshot capturing the state of the VM at a particular point in time. |
| Snapshot disk file | [VM_name].00000x.vmdk This six-digit number is based on the snapshot files that exist in the directory and does not consider the number of disks attached to the VM. It starts with 000001 and is incremented by 1 when each additional snapshot is taken. | A file that contains a linear list of all changes to a VM after a snapshot is taken. This file is used along with the descriptor files to return a VM to a previous state. |
| Template file | [VM_name].vmtx | A text file describing a VM that has been converted or cloned to a template. The file cannot be used to power on a VM. |
| Raw device map file | [VM_name]-rdmp.vmdk if physical compatibility or rdm.vmdk if virtual compatibility | A special pointer file that can allow a VM to see the raw LUN instead of using data from a VMFS or NFS datastore. |

## Locations for Virtual Machine Configuration Files and Virtual Disks

The locations for the VM files and the VM disks are "on the datastores," so what does this topic mean? Well, here's the question: "Should you store your VM swap file for a particular VM in the same location that you store the rest of its files?" The answer, of course, is "It depends."

As a best practice, you should store all the files for a VM in the same location whenever possible. This will make it easier for you to administer the VM, and it will generally increase the speed of migrating the VM during vMotion.

However, a relatively new technology called solid state drives (SSD) is changing this practice. If you have SSDs on your host, you might very well want to consider placing the VSWP files for the VMs on the SSDs. This would ensure that the swap file could still give the best performance technologically available and allow for even more memory overcommitment. (These resources are discussed in detail in Chapter 16, "Creating and Administering Resource Pools.")

You might be wondering when you get this choice and how you can easily separate the VSWP file from the other VM files. Actually, there are multiple places in the virtual data center where you can configure this option. Following is a brief description of each as well as an illustration of where you can configure this setting.

You can configure the location for VM swap files in the cluster and then accept this setting as a default throughout the data center, as shown in Figure 13-1. Alternatively, you can configure this setting on each host, as shown in Figure 13-2, or you can even configure this setting on each VM, as shown in Figure 13-3. In other words, you can take the easy way out and configure the setting for all VM swap files at the cluster level and then accept the cluster settings everywhere else. However, if you have SSDs or some other reason that you want to use a different location (purchased storage, and so on), you can choose a different location for any host or VM.

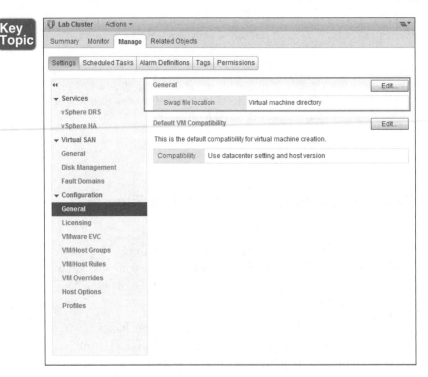

**Figure 13-1**   Configuring the VM Swap File Location in the Cluster Settings

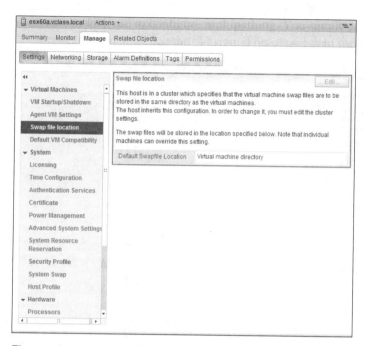

**Figure 13-2**   Configuring the VM Swap File Location on the Host

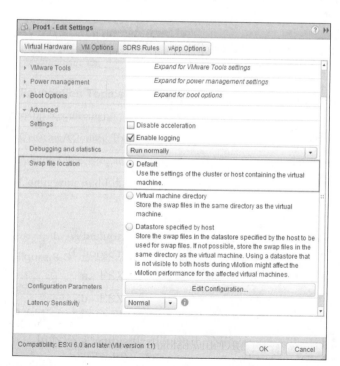

**Figure 13-3**   Configuring the VM Swap File Location on the VM

To identify the datastores that a VM is using, you can examine the Related Objects panel in the Summary tab of the VM, as shown in Figure 13-4.

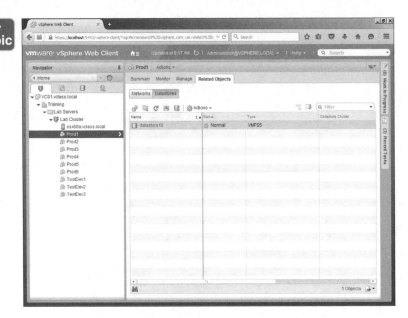

**Figure 13-4**    Identifying VM Storage

From there, you can click the datastore and then click the **Files** tab to see the actual files associated with the VM, as shown in Figure 13-5.

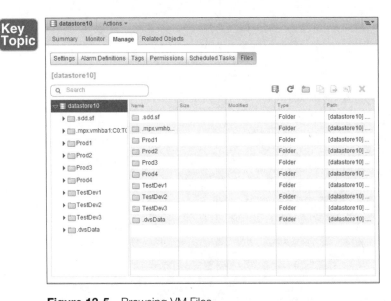

**Figure 13-5**    Browsing VM Files

# Common Practices for Securing Virtual Machines

In general, a VM is inherently very secure. By its design, each VM is isolated from all the other VMs, even if it's running on the same host. This isolation allows the VM to run securely, even though it is sharing physical hardware with other VMs. Permission granted to a user for a VM's guest OS does not allow that user to access any other VMs, even if the user has administrative permission. Also, because VMs are isolated from each other, a failure in one VM will not cause a "domino effect" failure in other VMs.

However, VMware recommends some precautions when administering VMs. Some of these precautions are the same as if the machine were a physical machine, whereas others are specific to the virtual environment. The following is a list of general precautions that you should take when administering security for the VMs:

- **Use antivirus software:** It is generally good practice to have antivirus protection on all computers, whether they are virtual or physical. Remember, however, that installed antivirus software does take resources, and you should balance the need for security against the need for performance. This might mean that some systems that are used only in a lab environment and not used in production will not require antivirus software. Alternatively, you could use a VMware product called vShield Endpoint to offload the key antivirus and anti-malware functions to a security VM and improve the guest OS performance of your VMs by eliminating the antivirus footprint on each of them. Yes, vShield Endpoint is still supported with vSphere 6. (See Knowledge Base article 2110078.)

- **Limit exposure of sensitive data copied to the clipboard:** Because it could be possible to copy data from a guest OS to the remote console, you should limit this by training administrators. By default, the capability to copy from a VM's guest OS to remote console is disabled. Although it is possible to enable this function, the best practice is to leave it disabled.

- **Remove unnecessary hardware devices:** Because users without administrative privileges can connect and disconnect hardware devices, such as CD-ROM drives and network cards, you should make sure that there is no virtual hardware on VMs that is not being used. Hardware that is "out of sight, out of mind" to the administrator makes a perfect tool for the experimentation of an attacker.

- **Limit guest OS writes to host memory:** The guest OS processes sometimes send informational messages to the host through VMware Tools. There is nothing wrong with a little of this, but an unrestricted amount could open the door for a denial-of-service (DoS) attack. For this reason, the configuration file for these messages is limited to 1 MB of storage. Although it's possible to change this parameter, it's not a recommended practice.

- **Configure logging levels for the guest OS:** VMs can write troubleshooting information into a log file stored on the VMFS. Over time, these log files can become large and cause problems in performance. To prevent this from happening, you can modify the parameters for the total size of the log files and for the total number of log files. VMware recommends saving 10 log files, each one limited to 100 KB.

- **Secure your fault-tolerance logging traffic:** When you enable and configure fault tolerance (FT), VMware Lockstep captures inputs and events that occur on the Primary VM and sends them to the Secondary VM, which is running on a different host. This logging traffic is then sent from the Primary VM to the Secondary VM in an unencrypted format. Because the traffic could potentially include sensitive information, such as passwords in clear text, you should use methods such as IPsec to encrypt data sent between hosts. You learn about FT in Chapter 15, "Planning and Implementing VMware Fault Tolerance."

## Configuring IP Pools

You can use IP pools to provide a network identity to your vApp. After you have configured an IP pool, the vApp can leverage vCenter to automatically provide an IP configuration to the VMs contained within it. The addresses from a pool will be configured for the VMs when the vApp is set to use Transient IP allocation. The easiest place at present to configure a new IP pool is the vSphere Windows Client, so I will illustrate this lab on the Windows Client. You can configure IP pool ranges with IPv4 or IPv6. To configure an IP pool for a vApp, follow the steps outlined in Activity 13-1.

**Activity 13-1   Configuring IP Pools**

1. Log on to your vSphere Web Client.

2. Select **Home** and then **Hosts and Clusters**.

3. Select the data center on which you want to configure the vApp, click the **Manage** tab, click the **Network Protocol Profiles** tab, and then click the green plus sign (+), as shown in Figure 13-6.

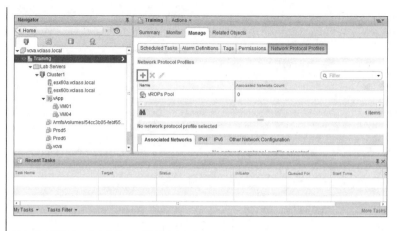

**Figure 13-6**  Adding an IP Pool

4. Provide a name for your new IP pool and a network to which it will be associated, as shown in Figure 13-7.

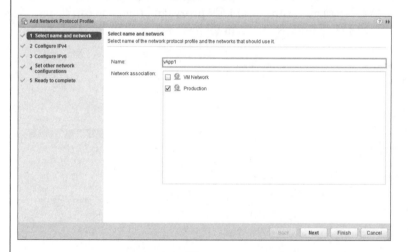

**Figure 13-7**  Naming and Associating a Network with the New IP Pool

5. Enter the IP subnet and gateway in their respective fields and (optionally) select **Enable IP Pool** to enter an IP address range, as shown in Figure 13-8. You can use a comma-separated list of host ranges in the Ranges field. The ranges must be within the subnet but must exclude the gateway address.

**Figure 13-8**  Configuring an IP Pool

6.  If necessary, you can configure IPv6 addressing and other network configurations, such as DNS search paths or HTTP proxy, and then you can review your settings and click **OK**, as shown in Figure 13-9.

**Figure 13-9**  Configuring IPv6 Addressing and Other Network Configurations

## Configuring and Managing a Content Library

In general, a content library is a place for you to store all your templates, vApps, ISOs, and so on, that is accessible to you and to which other users (admins) can sub-scribe as well, even if they are in a different vCenter! This type of sharing builds on consistency, efficiency, and potential automation of deploying workloads at scale. You create the library on one vCenter, but other vCenters can subscribe to it, as long as they are on the same Single Sign-On domain.

There are basically two types of libraries:

- **Local:** A local library is one that you create and use to store items that are to be used by your single vCenter Server instance.

- **Subscribed:** A subscribed library is one that has been published and to which you have connected.

After you create the library, you can store VM templates and vApp templates as OVF formats.

When you connect to a subscribed library, you can elect to download all content or only the metadata (list of the available content). Downloading only the metadata can save you space if some of the items in the library are something that you are never likely to use. In a library to which you are subscribed, you can view and use con-tent; but you cannot contribute to it. Only the administrator of the local library can change the content or delete the library. To create a content library, follow the steps outlined in Activity 13-2.

---

**Activity 13-2   Creating a Content Library**

1. Log on to your vSphere Web Client.

2. Select **Home** and then select **vCenter Inventory Lists** from the Web Client Navigator, as shown in Figure 13-10.

3. Double-click **Content Libraries**, as shown in Figure 13-11.

**Figure 13-10**   vCenter Inventory Lists

**Figure 13-11**   The Content Libraries Link

   **4.** Click the **Create a New Library** icon, as shown in Figure 13-12.

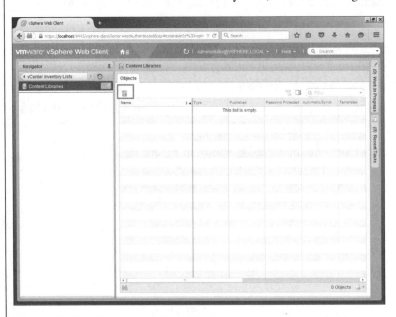

**Figure 13-12**   The Create a New Library Icon

**5.** Give your library a name and notes that define it, and choose the vCenter that will host it, as shown in Figure 13-13. Then click **Next**.

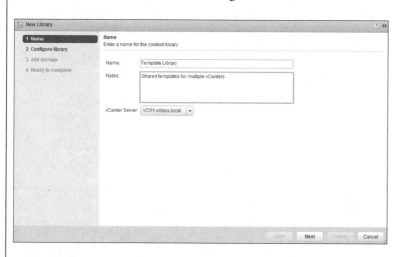

**Figure 13-13**   Naming a Content Library

**6.** Choose whether to create a local content library or subscribe to another library, and whether to enable authentication that will require additional credentials to connect to the library. In this case, I am creating a local library that will be published, with authentication required, as shown in Figure 13-14. Click **Next**.

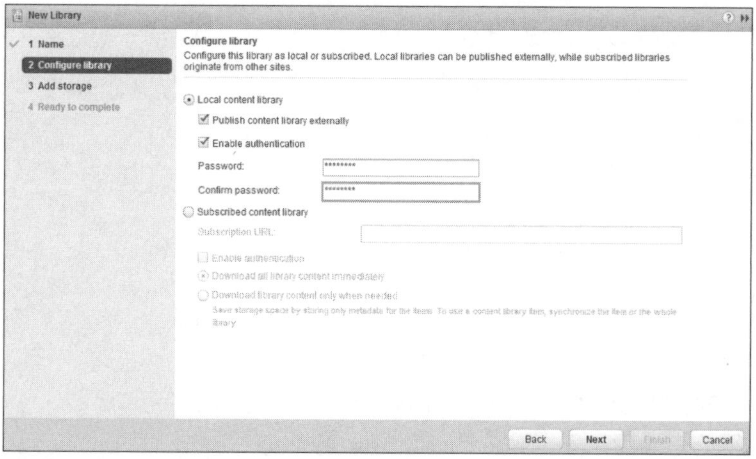

**Figure 13-14**   Creating a Local Library with Authentication Required

7. Enter the local file system path, or a URL to which others can connect to share your library, as shown in Figure 13-15, and click **Next**.

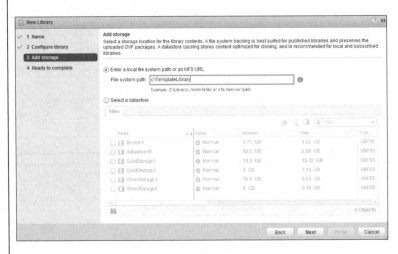

**Figure 13-15** Configuring the Connection to the Library

8. Review the Ready to complete page to confirm your settings, as shown in Figure 13-16, and click **Finish**.

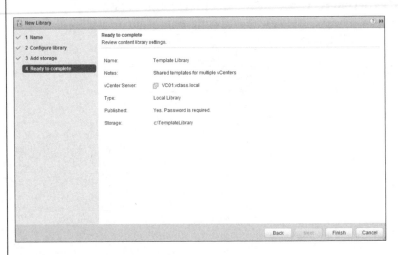

**Figure 13-16** Finishing and Reviewing Work

9. To add an OVF to your new library, use the **Import OVF Package or Other File Types** link, as shown in Figure 13-17.

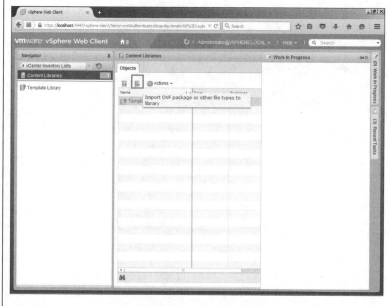

**Figure 13-17**    The Import OVF Package or Other File Types Link

To subscribe to a library that was created and shared, you select **Subscribed Content Library** and then enter the appropriate URL and credentials on the New Library configuration wizard. In this wizard, you can also elect whether to download all library content immediately or save space by downloading only the metadata, as shown in Figure 13-18. If storage is not lacking, you can even right-click the subscribed library and elect to automatically synchronize with the local library when changes are made, as shown in Figure 13-19.

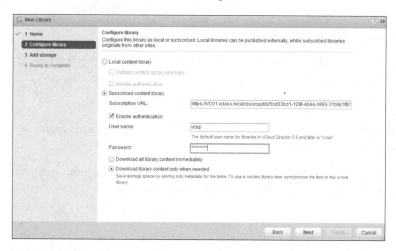

**Figure 13-18**    Options for Subscribed Content Libraries

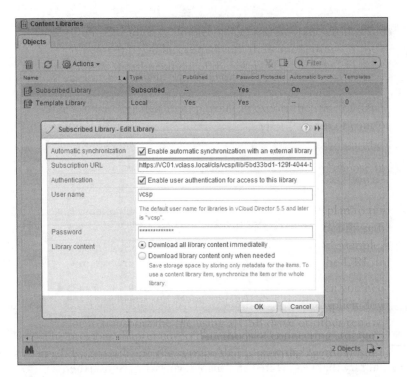

**Figure 13-19**   The Automatically Synchronize Option

## Summary

This chapter covers the following main topics:

- The files that are used by virtual machines and the purpose of each of the files. This is useful information for troubleshooting purposes.

- The various locations for virtual machine configuration files and especially for the swap files of VMs.

- Common practices to secure virtual machines and how to apply them.

- IP pools that you can use with vApps to provide for the proper assignment of IP addresses for their components.

- Configuring and managing a content library, including creating local libraries, as well as connecting to shared libraries using a subscription.

## Exam Preparation Tasks

## Review All the Key Topics

Review the most important topics from the chapter, noted with the Key Topic icon in the outer margin of the page. Table 13-3 lists these key topics and the page numbers where each is found.

**Table 13-3**   Key Topics for Chapter 13

| Key Topic Element | Description | Page Number |
|---|---|---|
| Table 13-2 | Virtual Machine Files | 314 |
| Figure 13-1 | Configuring the VM Swap File Location in the Cluster Settings | 316 |
| Figure 13-2 | Configuring the VM Swap File Location on the Host | 317 |
| Figure 13-3 | Configuring the VM Swap File Location on the VM | 317 |
| Figure 13-4 | Identifying VM Storage | 318 |
| Figure 13-5 | Browsing VM Files | 318 |
| Activity 13-1 | Configuring IP Pools | 320 |
| Activity 13-2 | Creating a Content Library | 323 |

## Review Questions

The answers to these review questions are in Appendix A.

1. Which of the following is the extension of a text file that describes the configuration of a VM?

   a. .vmtx

   b. .vmx

   c. -flat.vmdk

   d. There is no such file.

2. Which of the following is the extension of a file that is created only when the VM is powered on and that is always deleted with the VM is powered off?

   a. .vmx

   b. .vmdk

   c. .vswp

   d. .nvram

3. Which of the following is *not* a location on which you can configure the location of VM swap files?

   a. Cluster

   b. vApp

   c. VM

   d. Host

4. Which of the following is the default setting on a VM regarding VM swap files?

   a. Virtual machine directory

   b. Datastore specified by the host

   c. Use the settings of the cluster or host containing the virtual machine.

   d. Use SSD when available.

5. Which of the following are *not* true in regard to securing VMs? (Choose two.)

   a. A VM is not inherently secure because of the many files that it shares with other VMs.

   b. Using products such a vShield Endpoint puts more load on the VM during antivirus updates.

   c. There are configuration steps and best practices that you can follow to add to the inherent security of your VMs.

   d. There is nothing else that you can do to make a VM more secure than it is by default.

6. Which of the following are *not* true in regard to securing VMs? (Choose two.)

   a. The more virtual hardware you have on a VM, the more secure it will be.

   b. VMs do not require antivirus because they are immune to viruses.

   c. You should never copy sensitive data into the clipboard on the OS of a VM.

   d. You should not change the file size for the informational messages to the host.

**7.** Which of the following are *not* true regarding IP pools? (Choose two.)

   **a.** vApps always use IP pools for their IP address assignments.

   **b.** vApps use IP pools when they are set to use Transient IP allocation.

   **c.** You cannot configure IP pools for vSphere 6 on the Windows-based vSphere Client.

   **d.** The easiest place to configure IP pools for vSphere 6 is on the Windows-based vSphere Client.

**8.** If you want to connect to a previously created library that is managed by its own administrator, which type of library should you create?

   **a.** Local

   **b.** Subscribed

   **c.** Local or subscribed

   **d.** Shared

**9.** Which of the following will not be able to use templates stored in a content library?

   **a.** Administrators on the same vCenter as the content library

   **b.** All administrators in all vCenters and all Single Sign-On domains

   **c.** All administrators in all vCenters on the same Single Sign-On domain as the content library

   **d.** Only administrators on the same vCenter

**10.** Which of the following are *not* true regarding a subscribed content library?

   **a.** The administrator can change the options to download all content or just metadata.

   **b.** The administrator can add content to the original library as needed.

   **c.** The administrator can change the required password that will be used to connect to the library.

   **d.** The administrator can choose to automatically synchronize all new content.

**This chapter covers the following subjects:**

- DRS Virtual Machine Entitlement
- Creating/Deleting a DRS/HA Cluster
- Adding/Removing ESXi Hosts
- Adding or Removing Virtual Machines
- Configuring Storage DRS
- Configuring VM Component Protection
- Configuring Migration Thresholds for DRS and Virtual Machines
- Configuring Admission Control for HA and Virtual Machines
- Determining Appropriate Failover Methodology and Required Resources for HA

The good news that goes with enterprise data center virtualization is that you can use fewer physical machines because you can host many virtual servers on one physical machine. That's good news with regard to resource utilization, space utilization, power costs, and so on. However, it does mean that you have all, or at least a lot, of your "eggs in one basket." In other words, what would happen if your physical machine that is hosting many of your virtual servers should fail? You probably don't want to leave that up to chance. In this chapter, you learn about creating and administering clusters of physical servers that can keep watch over each other and share the load. In addition, you see how you can configure those clusters to share their resources so that all the VMs on them benefit.

## CHAPTER 14

# Creating and Configuring VMware Clusters

## "Do I Know This Already?" Quiz

The "Do I Know This Already?" quiz allows you to assess whether you should read this entire chapter or simply jump to the "Exam Preparation Tasks" section for review. If you are in doubt, read the entire chapter. Table 14-1 outlines the major headings in this chapter and the corresponding "Do I Know This Already?" quiz questions. You can find the answers in Appendix A, "Answers to the 'Do I Know This Already?' Quizzes and Chapter Review Questions."

**Table 14-1** "Do I Know This Already?" Section-to-Question Mapping

| Foundation Topics Section | Questions Covered in This Section |
|---|---|
| DRS Virtual Machine Entitlement | 1 |
| Creating/Deleting a DRS/HA Cluster | 2 |
| Adding/Removing ESXi Hosts | 3 |
| Adding or Removing Virtual Machines | 4 |
| Configuring Storage DRS | 5 |
| Configuring VM Component Protection | 6 |
| Configuring Migration Thresholds for DRS and Virtual Machines | 7 |
| Configuring Admission Control for HA and Virtual Machines | 8, 9 |
| Determining Appropriate Failover Methodology and Required Resources for HA | 10 |

1. Which of the following will occur on a cluster that is undercommitted for resources? (Choose two.)

   a. A VM will be capped only by its available memory setting.

   b. A VM will be capped by its available memory setting or its limit, whichever is higher.

   c. A VM will be capped by its available memory setting or its limit, whichever is lower.

   d. A VM with no limit will receive whatever it demands for memory.

2. Which of the following are true in regard to creating a DRS/HA cluster? (Choose two.)

   a. After you create a host outside of a cluster, you cannot join it to a cluster.

   b. You can join a host that is already on a vCenter to a cluster by dragging and dropping it.

   c. You can join a host to your vCenter and install it into the cluster at the same time.

   d. After you create a cluster, you must enable both HA and DRS at a minimum.

3. What does it mean to "graft in" a host's resource settings when you create a cluster?

   a. You are adding a host that is not ESXi 6.0.

   b. You are using DRS but not HA.

   c. You are maintaining the hierarchy that was set by the host's Resource Pools.

   d. You will add the host only for a temporary project.

4. If you have clicked on a cluster in the Navigator, which tab would you click next to expose the Virtual Machines tab?

   a. Manage

   b. Monitor

   c. Summary

   d. Related Objects

5. Which of the following is an optional parameter for Storage DRS configuration?

    a. Capacity

    b. I/O performance

    c. CPU

    d. Memory

6. Which of the following are true regarding storage event types? (Choose two.)

    a. A PDL occurs when a storage array issues a SCSI sense code that informs the host that the storage array is down.

    b. An APD occurs when a storage array issues a SCSI sense code that informs the host that the storage array is down.

    c. Only PDLs have a timeout setting, not APDs.

    d. Only APDs have a timeout setting, not PDLs.

7. Which of the following are true regarding configuring migration thresholds in DRS?

    a. A setting that is too conservative may cause the VMs to move more often than might be necessary.

    b. A setting that is too aggressive may cause the VMs to move more often than might be necessary.

    c. The most aggressive setting is 5, farthest to the right.

    d. The least aggressive setting is 5, farthest to the right.

8. Which of the following are true regarding HA Admission Control settings? (Choose two.)

    a. Percentage of Cluster Resources Reserved as Failover Spare Capacity uses a slot size that might allow fewer VMs to be started versus other options.

    b. Specify failover hosts is the best practice preferred method because it uses passive standby hosts.

    c. You can specify a different percentage for CPU versus memory when you use the Define Failover Capacity by Reserving a Percentage of the Cluster Resources setting.

    d. The Define Failover Capacity by Reserving a Percentage of the Cluster Resources method can be configured from 1 to 31 hosts.

9. Which of the following are true regarding admission control for HA?

   a. In most cases you should use the Do Not Reserve Failover Capacity setting.

   b. You should use the Do Not Reserve Failover Capacity setting only as a temporary override.

   c. The Do Not Reserve Failover Capacity setting will free up resources that would otherwise be reserved.

   d. The Do Not Reserve Failover Capacity setting has no effect on resources available to start VMs.

10. Which of the following is true regarding the various methods of Admission Control Policy?

   a. Disabling Admission Control frees up the most resources and should be used whenever possible.

   b. Host failures that a cluster will tolerate can be constricting to resources because of its conservative slot size.

   c. Disabling Admission Control should be used only as a temporary override to another policy.

   d. Percentage of cluster resources can be constricting to resources because of its conservative slot size.

## Foundation Topics

When you decide to create a cluster by combining the resources of two or more hosts (physical servers), you are generally doing it primarily for one or both reasons: Distributed Resource Scheduler (DRS) and/or High Availability (HA). This section discusses many aspects of both of these vSphere features and how they can improve the reliability, performance, and survivability of your VMs. In particular, you learn about DRS VM entitlement, creating and deleting DRS/HA clusters, and adding/removing VMs from a cluster. In addition, you learn about features that were new to vSphere 5.x and some that are new to vSphere 6 that ensure the survivability and continued performance of your VMs. Finally, enabling and configuring the many aspects of DRS and HA are covered so that you can take advantage of automatic restarts of VMs when needed and load balancing of VMs on an ongoing basis.

**NOTE** Even though the hosts in my lab environment are named with a somewhat legacy name of "esx," rest assured that they are all vSphere 6 ESXi hosts. Old habits die hard!

## DRS Virtual Machine Entitlement

All the VMs that are in the same cluster are using everything at their disposal to fight for the RAM (physical memory from the hosts) that they need to satisfy the expectations of their guest OS and applications. When a cluster is undercommitted (has plenty of physical memory), each VM's memory entitlement will be the same as its demand for memory. It will be allocated whatever it asks for, which will be capped by its configured limit if that is lower than its available memory setting.

Now, what happens if the cluster becomes overcommitted (less physical memory than demand)? That's an important question to answer, because when there isn't enough physical RAM to go around, some VMs are going to have to use their swap file (at least in some portion), which means their performance will take a hit because using memory from a disk is much slower than using physical RAM. So, how does the VMkernel decide which VMs take priority and which VMs will be forced to use their swap file?

When the cluster is overcommitted, DRS and the VMkernel work together to allocate resources based on the resource entitlement of each VM. This is based on a variety of factors and how they relate to each other. In a nutshell, it is based on configured shares, configured memory size, reservations, current demands on the VMs and the Resource Pools that contain them, and on the working set (active utilization of the VM at a particular point in time). In Chapter 20, "Performing Basic Troubleshooting of ESXi and vCenter Server," you learn much more about DRS and its capability to control and balance resources while providing you with troubleshooting information.

## Creating/Deleting a DRS/HA Cluster

After you have connected to your vCenter Server with your vSphere Client, creating a cluster is simply a matter of adding the Cluster inventory object, dragging your ESXi hosts into it, and configuring the options that you need. You can independently configure options for DRS, HA, and other related settings. To create a DRS/HA cluster, follow the steps outlined in Activity 14-1.

**Activity 14-1   Creating a DRS/HA Cluster**

1. Log on to your vSphere Web Client.

2. Select **Home** and then **Hosts and Clusters**.

3. Right-click your data center and select **New Cluster**, as shown in Figure 14-1.

**Figure 14-1**   Creating a New Cluster

4. Enter a name for your new cluster and then select to **Turn ON vSphere HA** and/or **Turn ON DRS**, and then click **OK**, as shown in Figure 14-2. You can also enable EVC and vSAN.

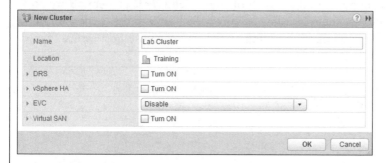

**Figure 14-2**   Naming a Cluster and Enabling HA/DRS

5. You can then select what else to configure in the left pane by opening each arrow. Separate settings will be available for each feature of your cluster.

## Adding/Removing ESXi Hosts

After you have created a cluster, you can use the tools to add hosts to your cluster, or you can drag and drop the hosts into the cluster. Adding a host to a cluster is like creating a "giant computer."

**NOTE**   Before the host was in the cluster, you might have established a hierarchy of Resource Pools on the host. In this case, when you add the host to a cluster, the system asks if you want to "graft" that hierarchy into the cluster or start a new hierarchy in the new cluster. This is an important decision and not just one regarding what the inventory will look like when you get done. If you have created Resource Pools on your host, and you want to retain that hierarchy, you will need to "graft" it in; otherwise, all the Resource Pools will be deleted when you add the host to the cluster.

To add a new host to a new cluster, follow the steps outlined in Activity 14-2.

**Activity 14-2   Adding a Host to a Cluster**

1. Log on to your vSphere Web Client.

2. Select **Home** and then **Hosts and Clusters**.

3. Right-click your cluster and select **Add Host**, as shown in Figure 14-3.

4. Enter the IP address or fully qualified domain name (FQDN) of the host that you want to add, as shown in Figure 14-3. If the host is not currently in your vCenter, this will likely be a root account or an account with root privileges. If the host is already member of your vCenter, the credentials are not required, and you could just drag and drop the host into the cluster. In this case, I am assuming that I'm adding a newly created host, host esx60a, to my newly created Lab Cluster.

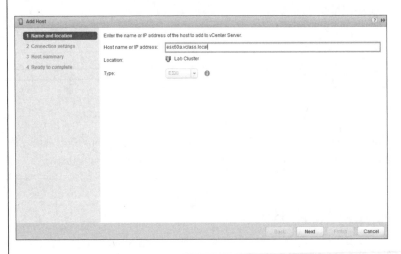

**Figure 14-3**   Adding a Host to a Cluster

5. Enter the credentials for the host as it sits right now, out of the cluster (in this case "root"), as shown in Figure 14-4. Click **Next**.

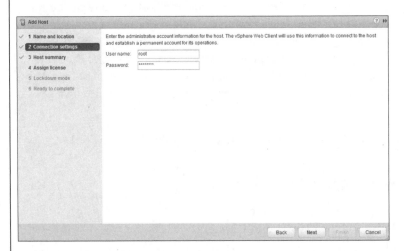

**Figure 14-4**   Entering Host Credentials

6. Verify that you are adding the right host, as shown in Figure 14-5. Click **Next**.

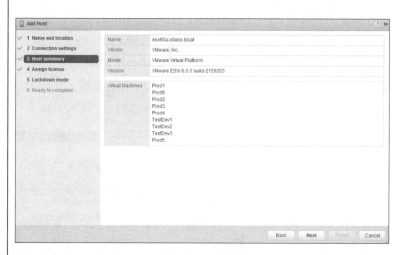

**Figure 14-5**  Host Summary Information

7. In the Assign License screen, you can assign a license that you have already entered or add a new license. You can also elect to use the 60-day evaluation mode, as shown in Figure 14-6.

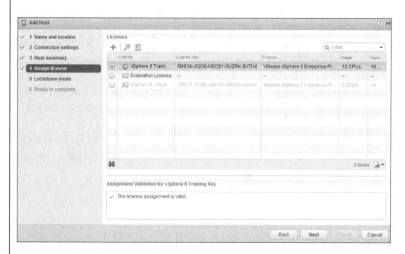

**Figure 14-6**  Assigning a License

8. Choose whether or not to enable lockdown mode. Beginning with vSphere 6, you have two levels of lockdown mode from which to choose—normal or strict—as shown in Figure 14-7.

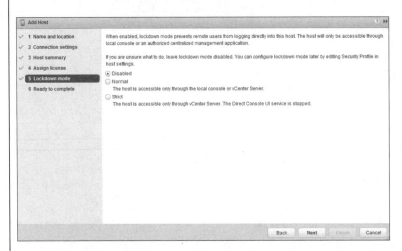

**Figure 14-7** Configuring Lockdown Mode

9. Review the Ready to Complete page and click **Finish**, as shown in Figure 14-8.

**Figure 14-8** The Ready to Complete Page

You might think that removing a host from a cluster would be as simple as dragging it out, but that would not be wholly correct. If you have been using a host within a cluster for any time at all, you will likely have VMs on the host. You will first need to either migrate all the VMs off the host or shut them down. You can begin this process by entering Maintenance Mode.

When you place a host in Maintenance Mode, you are in essence telling the rest of the hosts in the cluster that this host is "closed for new business" for now. When a host enters Maintenance Mode, no VMs will be migrated to that host, you cannot power on any new VMs, and you cannot make any configuration changes to existing VMs. With the proper configuration of DRS (which is discussed later in the section "Configuring Automation Levels for DRS and Virtual Machines"), all the VMs that can use vMotion to "automatically migrate" will immediately do so. You then decide whether to shut down the others and move them to another host, or just leave them on the host that you are removing from the cluster. Figure 14-9 shows a newly configured two-host cluster.

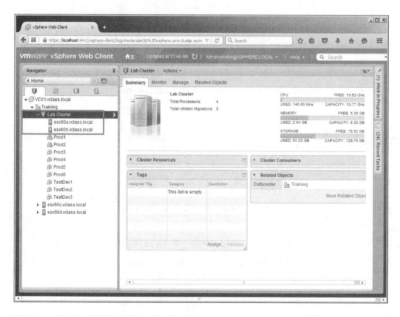

**Figure 14-9**   A Two Host Cluster

After you have made these preparations, it is a matter of reversing the steps covered earlier. In fact, the easiest way to remove a host from a cluster after the host is in Maintenance Mode is to drag the host object back to the data center. More specifically, to remove a host from an existing cluster, follow the steps outlined in Activity 14-3.

## Activity 14-3 Removing a Host from a Cluster

1. Log on to your vSphere Client.

2. Select **Home** and then **Hosts and Clusters**.

3. Right-click the host that you want to remove and select **Enter Maintenance Mode**, as shown in Figure 14-10.

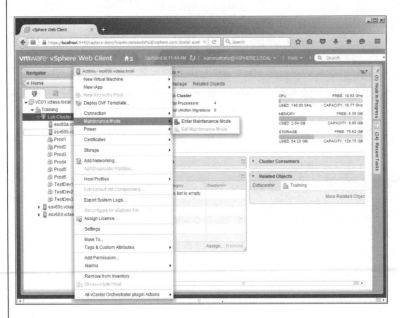

**Figure 14-10** Entering Maintenance Mode

4. Confirm that you want to enter Maintenance Mode, and select whether you want to also move powered-off and suspended VMs to other hosts in the cluster, and then click **OK**, as shown in Figure 14-11. If you choose not to move the VMs, they will be "orphaned" while the host is in Maintenance Mode because they will logically remain on that host.

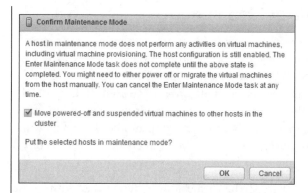

**Figure 14-11**   Maintenance Mode Confirmation

5. Click and hold the host that you want to remove from the cluster and drag the host to another inventory object, such as your data center or a folder that is higher in the hierarchy than the cluster. Figure 14-12 shows esx60b.vclass. local in Maintenance Mode.

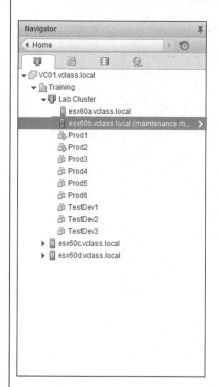

**Figure 14-12**   Maintenance Mode Icon

# Adding or Removing Virtual Machines

As I said earlier, after you have created a cluster, in essence you have a giant computer that combines the aggregate resources of the hosts in the cluster. Notice that I didn't say "super computer." You can't total up all the resources in a large cluster and assign them all to one VM and then play *Jeopardy* with it! In fact, a VM will always take all its CPU and memory from one host or another, depending on where it is powered on and whether it has been migrated to another host. You will, however, have larger pools of resources from which you can create more VMs or larger VMs.

Adding or removing a VM with regard to the cluster is no different than with a host. In other words, you can start by dragging and dropping the VM to the appropriate place in your hierarchy, whether that place happens to be a host in a cluster or a host that is not in a cluster. In Chapter 17, "Migrating Virtual Machines," this is discussed in much greater depth.

To determine which of your VMs are in a specific cluster, you can click the cluster in the Navigator (left pane), then on the Related Objects tab, and finally on the Virtual Machines tab, as shown in Figure 14-13.

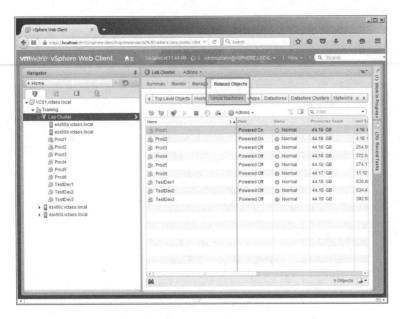

**Figure 14-13**   Determining the VMs on a Cluster

# Configuring Storage DRS

As your network grows, you need to use your resources in the most efficient manner, so having a tool that balances the loads of VMs across the hosts is very useful. If you've configured it properly, DRS does a wonderful job of balancing the loads of the VMs by using algorithms that take into account the *CPU* and the *memory* of the VMs on each host. This has the effect of strengthening two of the critical resources on each VM, namely *CPU* and *memory*.

If CPU and memory were the only two resources on your VMs, this would be the end of the story, but you also have to consider *network* and *storage*. Because networking was covered in Chapters 4 and 5, we'll focus on storage. As you know, the weakest link in the chain will determine the strength of the chain. By the same logic, if you took great care to provide plenty of CPU and memory to your VMs, but you starved them with regard to storage, the end result might be poorly performing VMs.

Too bad you can't do something with storage that's similar to what DRS does with CPU and memory; but wait, you can! What if you organized datastores into *datastore clusters* made of multiple datastores with the same characteristics? Then, when you created a VM, you would place the VM into the datastore cluster, and the appropriate datastore would be chosen by the system based on the available space on the logical unit numbers (LUNs) of each datastore and on the I/O performance (if you chose that, too). Better yet, in the interim, the datastore cluster would monitor itself and use Storage vMotion whenever necessary to provide balance across the datastore cluster and to increase the overall performance of all datastores in the datastore cluster.

This is what Storage DRS (SDRS) can do for your virtual data center. When you set it up, you choose whether to take I/O into consideration with regard to automated Storage vMotions, and it always takes the available storage into consideration. After you have configured it, SDRS runs automatically and, in a very conservative way (so as not to use Storage vMotion resources too often), maintains balance in the datastore clusters that you have configured. This results in an overall performance increase in "storage" for your VMs to go right along with the performance increases in CPU and memory that DRS has provided—a nice combination.

To configure SDRS, you first create the datastore clusters. This configuration includes selecting the automation level and runtime rules for the cluster, as well as selecting the datastores that you will include in the cluster. The datastores should have equal capabilities so that one is "as good as the other" to the SDRS system. To create an SDRS datastore cluster, follow the steps outlined in Activity 14-4.

## Activity 14-4   Creating and Configuring an SDRS Datastore Cluster

1. Log on to your vSphere Web Client.

2. Select **Home** and then **Storage**, as shown in Figure 14-14.

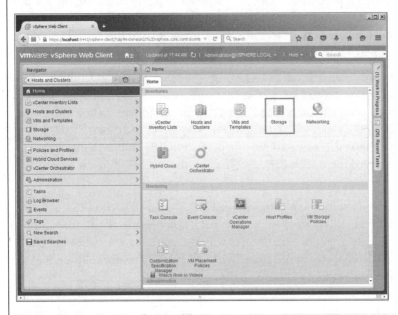

**Figure 14-14**   Entering Storage View

3. Right-click the data center in which you want to create the datastore cluster and select **Storage** and then **New Datastore Cluster**, as shown in Figure 14-15.

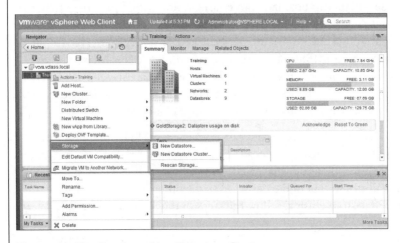

**Figure 14-15**   Creating a New Datastore Cluster

4. On the General page, enter a name for your datastore cluster and leave the check box selected to **Turn ON Storage DRS**, as shown in Figure 14-16, and click **Next**. (If you are creating the datastore cluster for future use but not for immediate use, you can uncheck the **Turn ON Storage DRS** box.)

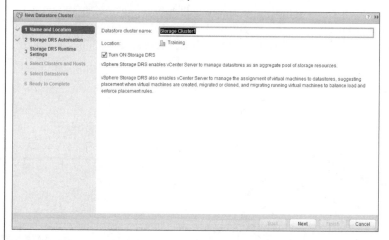

**Figure 14-16**   Enabling SDRS in a Datastore Cluster

5. From SDRS Automation, select the automation level for your datastore cluster in regard to space, I/O balance, rules, policy enforcement, and VM evacuation, and click **Next**, as shown in Figure 14-17. Selecting No Automation will only provide recommendations and will not cause the system to use Storage vMotion on your VM files without your intervention. The Fully Automated setting will use Storage vMotion to migrate VM files as needed based on the loads and on the rest of your configuration.

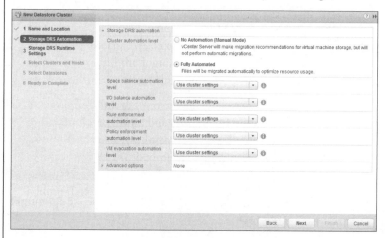

**Figure 14-17**   Selecting the SDRS Automation Level

6. From SDRS Runtime Rules, select whether you want to enable I/O Metric Inclusion. This is available only when all the hosts in the datastore cluster are at least ESXi 5.x. Select the DRS thresholds for **Utilized Space** and **I/O Latency**. You can generally leave these at their default settings, at least to get started. There is also an Advanced Options setting, as shown in Figure 14-18, that you can almost always leave at the default but that you can tweak if needed. When you are finished with all these settings, click **Next** to continue.

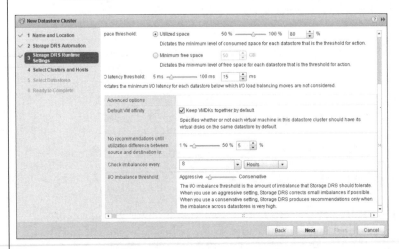

**Figure 14-18**  Configuring SDRS Runtime Rules

7. Select the Hosts and Clusters that you want to include in your datastore cluster, as shown in Figure 14-19, and click **Next**.

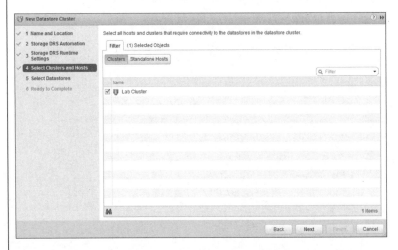

**Figure 14-19**  Selecting Hosts and Clusters for SDRS

**8.** Select the datastores that you want to include in your datastore cluster and click **Next**. The status of each datastore will be listed along with its capacity, free space, and so on. If the datastore does not have a connection to all the hosts you have chosen, it will be indicated in the Host Connection Status, as shown in Figure 14-20.

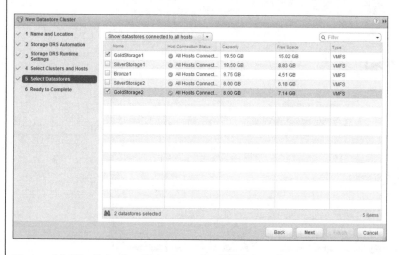

**Figure 14-20**   Selecting Datastores for SDRS Datastore Clusters

**9.** On the Ready to Complete page, you can review your selections, address any configuration issues, and then click **Finish**, as shown in Figure 14-21.

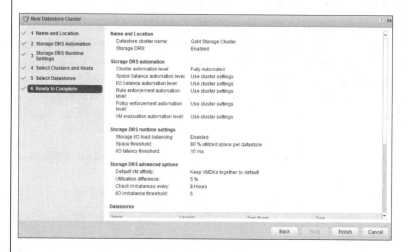

**Figure 14-21**   The Ready to Complete Page

10. Monitor your inventory and the Recent Tasks pane for the creation of your new datastore cluster, as shown in Figure 14-22.

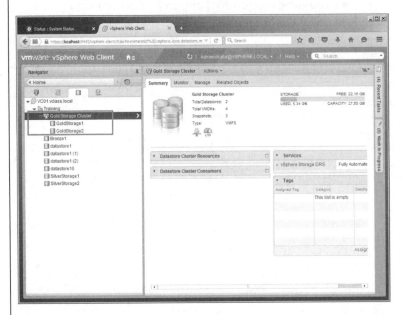

**Figure 14-22**    A New Datastore Cluster

## Configuring VM Component Protection

As you probably know, vSphere HA has always been good for restarting your VMs on a new host when the current host is down or has lost connectivity to the network. However, what if the host is not down and has not lost connectivity to the network but has lost connectivity to the storage that it was providing the VM? Earlier versions of vSphere provided some configuration for this event on the command line only, but vSphere 6 makes this additional protection available with a single click, as shown in Figure 14-23.

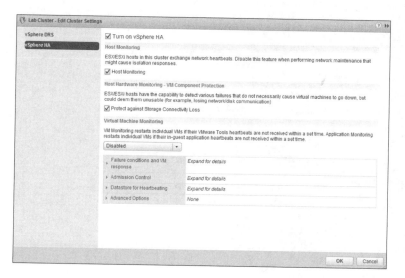

**Figure 14-23**    Configuring VMCP

There are two types of storage events for which VM Component Protection can monitor and react, each of which could cause a VM to be unusable because it can no longer reach its storage:

- **Permanent Device Loss (PDL):** A PDL occurs when a storage array issues a SCSI sense code informing that the device is unavailable. This might happen if a LUN were to fail on a storage array or if an administrator inadvertently removed critical storage configuration, such as a WWN from a zone configuration. When a host receives this type of code, it ceases sending I/O requests to that array.

- **All Paths Down (APD):** An APD event is different from a PDL because the host cannot reach the storage, but no PDL SCSI code is received either. For this reason, the host does not "know" whether the disconnection is temporary or whether it might continue for some time. The host will therefore continue to try the storage until a set timeout is reached. This timeout value is 140 seconds by default and can be changed using the Misc.APDTimeout advanced setting.

Now that you understand what could happen, you might be asking what VMCP is going to do about it. That's pretty much up to you and how you configure it. You can configure each type of event independently, in regard to whether it's enabled and what actions it will take for your VMs. When you change the configuration, a table is automatically created that illustrates your configuration and its result, as shown in Figure 14-24.

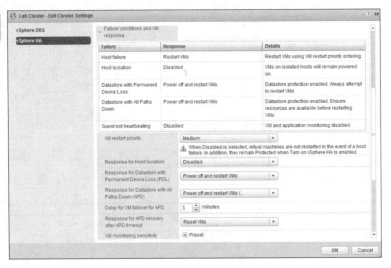

**Figure 14-24**  Settings for VMCP

Some of these settings require a little more explanation, so each of them is described separately.

- **Response for Datastore with Permanent Device Loss (PDL):** This setting has three options:

    - **Disabled** means that no action will be taken and no notification will be sent to the administrator.

    - The **Issue Events** setting will notify the administrator that a PDL has occurred, but no action will be taken for the VMs.

    - The **Power Off and Restart VMs** setting will attempt to restart the VMs on a host that still has connectivity to the storage device.

- **Response for Datastore with All Paths Down (APD):** This setting has four options:

    - **Disabled** means that no action will be taken.

    - **Issue events** will notify the administrator but take no further action.

    - **Power Off and Restart VMs (conservative)** will not attempt to restart the VMs until it has determined that there is another host that has the needed storage and the compute capacity to restart the VMs. It does this by communicating with the master host. If it cannot communicate with the master host, no further action will be taken. The assumption is that "the grass may not be greener on the other side of the fence."

- **Power Off and Restart VMs (aggressive)**, by contrast, will terminate the connection of the affected VMs in the "hopes" that another host that has the needed storage will have the compute capacity as well. The assumption is that "anyplace else is better than here."

- **Delay of VM Failover for APD:** This one is tricky because it's not the same as the timeout, but instead an additional timer is added to the timeout. As mentioned earlier, the default for the timeout value is 140 seconds. However, the default for the delay timer is an additional 3 minutes. The end result is (with default settings) that VMCP will not begin taking action in regard to an APD event for 5 minutes and 20 seconds—the sum of the timeout and the delay. This total figure is also known as the VMCP Timeout.

- **Response for APD Recovery After APD Timeout:** This is what you are configuring to happen if the storage event clears after the timeout expires but before the additional delay expires. There are two options. Disabled means that no **additional** action will be taken, with the assumption that the VMs will now be able to connect to the storage as before. Reset VMs will cause a hard reset of the VMs to ensure that they can connect the storage. This will cause a temporary outage that might not have been necessary if the VMs were able to connect without it, but it will ensure that they have the best chance going forward.

# Configuring Migration Thresholds for DRS and Virtual Machines

DRS uses algorithms to balance the loads of VMs based on the CPU and memory resources that they are using on a host. The main premise is that by balancing the resources across the hosts, you can improve the overall performance of all the VMs, especially when the physical resources of CPU and memory are much more heavily used on one host than on another. When this occurs, DRS can use vMotion to automatically move the state of one or more VMs on one host to another host. Moving the state of the VMs means moving them to another physical place (host). As an alternative, DRS can also just make recommendations to move the VMs, which you can then read and follow.

If you decide to let DRS in essence read its own recommendations and then automatically migrate the VMs (this is a called Fully Automated Mode, and it is discussed next), the question then becomes, "How far off balance does the resource usage have to be to create a situation where a migration is actually performed?" The answer to this question can be configured in the Migration Threshold setting for DRS on the cluster, as shown in Figure 14-25. If you configure this setting too conservatively, you might not get the balance that you desire, but if you configure it too aggressively, any imbalance might cause a system to use vMotion to migrate the VMs and thereby use resources needlessly.

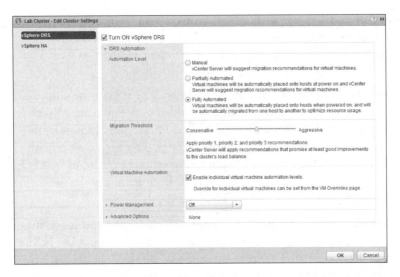

**Figure 14-25**  Configuring the DRS Automation Level and Migration Threshold

To help you make the right decision, the Migration Threshold slider control identifies five settings and the expected impact of that setting. You should read over each of the settings and make the choice that will work best for you. The settings on the Migration Threshold are as follows:

- **Setting 1:** This is the left-most setting on the slider and the most conservative. It will apply only the most important, Priority 1, recommendations. As indicated below the slider, these recommendations "must be taken to satisfy cluster constraints like affinity rules and host maintenance."

- **Setting 2:** One notch to the right from Setting 1, this will apply only Priority 1 and Priority 2 recommendations. These are deemed by the vCenter, based on its calculations, to "promise a significant improvement to the cluster's load balance."

- **Setting 3:** One more over to the right, this will apply Priority 1, 2, and 3 recommendations. These "promise at least good improvement to the cluster's load balance."

- **Setting 4:** One more to the right, as you can imagine, this one applies Priority 1, 2, 3, and 4 recommendations. These are expected to "promise even a moderate improvement to the cluster's load balance."

- **Setting 5:** Farthest to the right and most aggressive, this setting will apply recommendations that "promise even a slight improvement to the cluster's load balance."

## Configuring Automation Levels for DRS and Virtual Machines

You might think that this was already covered in the previous paragraphs, but that would not be totally correct. In addition to making the recommendations and decisions with regard to balancing cluster loads, DRS is involved with choosing the host to which the VM is powered on in the first place. This is referred to as *initial placement*. Because of this, there are three automation levels you can choose from when you configure DRS for your cluster. Each level addresses who will decide initial placement and, separately, who will decide on load balancing, you or DRS? The three possible DRS automation levels you can choose from, also shown in Figure 14-25, are the following:

- **Manual:** In this mode, vCenter will only make recommendations about initial placement and load balancing. You can choose to accept the recommendation, accept some of them (if there are more than one at a time), or ignore them altogether. For example, if vCenter makes a recommendation to move a VM and you accept it, DRS will use vMotion (if configured) to migrate the VM while it's powered on, with no disruption in service.

- **Partially Automated:** In this mode, vCenter will automatically choose the right host for the initial placement of the VM. There will be no recommendations with regard to initial placement. In addition, vCenter will make recommendations with regard to load balance in the cluster, which you can choose to accept, partially accept, or ignore.

- **Fully Automated:** As you might expect, this setting allows vCenter to make all the decisions on your behalf. These include initial placement and load balance. DRS uses algorithms to generate recommendations and then "follow its own advice" based on the Migration Threshold, as discussed earlier. This mode also ensures that all VMs that are compatible for vMotion will automatically migrate when you place your host in Maintenance Mode.

Now, you might be thinking that these cluster settings will be fine for most of your VMs, but that some VMs are different, and you need more flexibility in their settings. For example, what if you have a VM that is connected to a serial security dongle on a single host and, therefore, will need to stay on that host? If you are in Manual Mode, will you have to constantly answer those recommendations? If you are in Fully Automated Mode, can it ignore that one?

Thankfully, there are DRS settings for each of the VMs in your cluster. These Virtual Machine Options settings default to the cluster setting unless you change them, as shown in Figure 14-26. For example, the setting that would be best for the security dongle scenario would be **Disabled**, which does not disable the VM but rather disables DRS for the VM and therefore does not create recommendations. To make this available, you must first enable the option by checking the box labeled **Enable Individual Virtual Machine Automation Levels**, as shown previously in Figure 14-25. After this is done, you can configure the individual VMs in the **VM Overrides** section under **Manage**, **Settings** for the cluster, as shown in Figure 14-27.

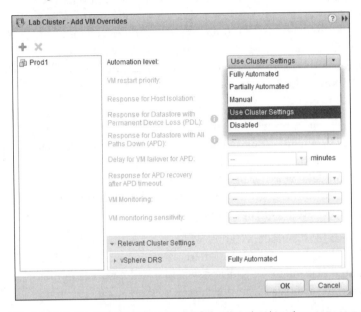

**Figure 14-26**  VM Overrides for DRS Automation Level

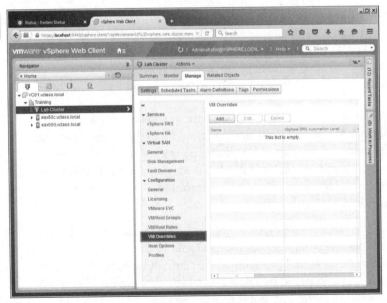

**Figure 14-27**  Accessing VM Overrides for DRS Automation Level

# Configuring Admission Control for HA and Virtual Machines

vSphere HA provides for the automatic restart of VMs on another host when the host on which they are running has failed or has become disconnected from the cluster. If you think about it, how could the other hosts help out in a "time of crisis" if they themselves had already given all of their resources to other VMs? The answer is, they couldn't! For this reason, Admission Control settings cause a host to "hold back" some of its resources by not allowing any more VMs to start on a host so that it can be of assistance if another host should fail. The amount of resources held back is up to you. In fact, this is the central question that you are answering when you configure Admission Control for HA.

This section discusses two topics: Admission Control and Admission Control Policy. As shown in Figure 14-28, Admission Control Policy can be configured in a few ways. First, Admission Control is discussed in general, followed by the finer points of configuring Admission Control Policy.

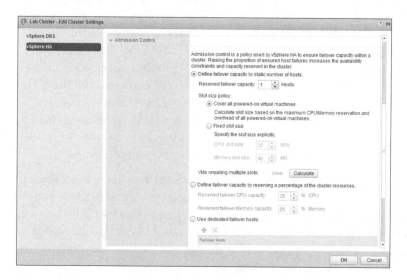

**Figure 14-28**   Admission Control Policy Settings

## Admission Control

In most cases, you want to make sure that Admission Control is enabled by your Admission Control Policy setting. In some unusual cases, when you need to start a critical VM and the system won't let you, you can use the **Do Not Reserve Failover Capacity** option to temporarily override the HA Admission Control and get the VM started. If you do this, you should address the real resource issue and enable Admission Control as soon as possible. It is not a best practice to leave Admission Control disabled.

### Admission Control Policy

You can choose between three options for Admission Control Policy. The central question is this: "If HA is supposed to make the hosts save enough resources so that VMs on a failed host can be restarted on the other hosts, how is it supposed to know how much to save?" When you configure Admission Control Policy, you answer two questions. First, how many hosts will I "allow" to fail and still know that the VMs on the failed hosts can be restarted on the remaining hosts? Second, how will I tell HA how to calculate the amount of resources to "hold back" on each host?

The following is a brief description of each of the three Admission Control Policies:

- **Define failover capacity by static number of hosts:** This setting is configurable from 1–31, although, in most cases, you probably wouldn't configure it any higher than 2. This policy is the oldest of the three and is sometimes used in organizations today, although it might no longer be considered the favorite. It relies on a "slot size," which is a calculation that it determines to be an estimate of CPU and memory needs for every VM in the cluster. A setting of 2 means that two hosts could fail at the same time in a cluster and all the VMs that are on the failed hosts could be restarted on the remaining resources of the other hosts in the cluster. You can imagine the additional resources that would have to be "held back" to allow for this setting. In most cases, organizations use a setting of 1, unless they are configuring very large clusters.

- **Define failover capacity by reserving a percentage of the cluster resources:** If you choose this method, you then set the percentages that you need for your organization. In addition, you can set a different percentage for CPU than you do for memory. After you have chosen your settings, HA continually compares the total resource requirements for all VMs with the total failover capacity that it has derived from your settings. When you are attempting to power on a VM that would cause the first calculation to become higher than the second, HA will prevent the VM from being powered on. How you derive the percentages is beyond the scope of this book, but know that this option should be used when you have highly variable CPU and memory reservations.

- **Use dedicated failover hosts:** If you choose this option, you then choose a host or hosts that are in your cluster that will become a passive standby host or hosts. Failover hosts should have the same amount of resources as any of the hosts in your cluster, or more. This option at first seems to violate all that HA stands for, because part of the goal is to provide fault tolerance without the need for passive standby hardware, but there is a reason that it's there, as you'll see very soon when I discuss determining the most appropriate methodology to use.

Finally, as with DRS, you have options, through VM Overrides with regard to each VM that can be different from what is set for the cluster, as shown in Figure 14-29.

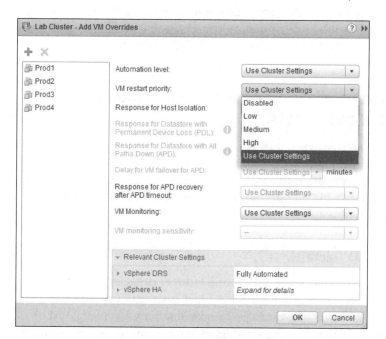

**Figure 14-29**   Virtual Machine Overrides for HA

These options do not have anything to do with admission control, or at least not directly. However, they do have an impact on what happens to each VM when HA is used. The list that follows provides a brief description of each of these two settings.

- **VM Restart Priority:** The default configuration in the cluster is Medium. If you leave the default setting, all VMs will have the same priority on restart; in other words, no VMs will have any priority over any others. If there are some VMs that you want to have a greater priority (closer to the front of the line), you can change the restart priority on the specific VMs. Only by leaving the cluster setting at the default of Medium will you allow yourself the option to give each VM a priority that is lower or higher than the default setting. You can also change the default setting on the cluster, although it's not often needed.

- **Host Isolation Response:** This setting determines what the host does with regard to VMs when the host is not receiving heartbeats on its management network. The options are to leave it powered on, or power off, or gracefully shut down the VMs. The default setting in the cluster is Leave Powered On, but this can be set specifically for each VM in the cluster. In most cases, you do not want to power off a server that has applications running on it because it can corrupt the applications and cause a very long restart time. For this reason, you should generally use either the default setting of Leave Powered On or a setting of Shut Down VMs to shut down the servers gracefully and not corrupt the applications that they are running.

## Determining Appropriate Failover Methodology and Required Resources for HA

The main focus here is to analyze the differences between the three Admission Control methods. In addition, you learn about the use of each method and when one would be more appropriate than another. You should understand your options with regard to configuring HA and the impact of each possible decision on your overall failover methodology.

### Host Failures the Cluster Tolerates

To use this methodology, you choose the **Define failover capacity by static number of hosts** setting. Then, by default, HA calculates the slot size for a VM in a very conservative manner. It uses the largest reservation for CPU of any VM on each host in a cluster and then the largest reservation for memory plus the memory overhead. These numbers are used, in essence, to assume that every VM is that size, a value called *slot size*. This calculation is then used to determine how many "slots" each host can support; however, it's entirely possible that no VM may have both of those values, so the calculation can result in a much larger slot size than actually needed. This, in turn, can result in less capacity for VMs in the cluster.

You can use advanced settings to change the slot size, but that will be valid only until you create a VM that is even larger. The actual calculations to make advanced settings changes are beyond the scope of this book, but you should know how the default slot size is determined. The only factor that might make this option appropriate and simple is if your VMs all have similar CPU and memory reservations and similar memory overhead.

### Percentage of Cluster Resources as Failover Spare Capacity

To use this methodology, you choose the **Define failover capacity by reserving a percentage of the cluster resources** setting. Unlike the previous option, the Percentage of Cluster Resources as Failover Spare Capacity option works well when you have VMs with highly variable CPU and memory reservations. In addition, you can now configure separate percentages for CPU and memory, making it even more flexible and saving your resources. How you derive the percentages is beyond the scope of this book, but you should know that this option should be used when you have highly variable CPU and memory reservations. This method is generally most preferred now because it uses resources in an efficient manner and does not require the manipulation of slot sizes.

### Specify Failover Hosts

To use this methodology you select the **Use dedicated failover hosts** setting. If you think about it, part of the reason that you used HA rather than clustering was to avoid passive standby hosts, so why does VMware even offer this option? The main reason Specify Failover Hosts is an option is that some organizational policies dictate that passive standby hosts must be available. To provide flexibility in these instances, VMware offers this option, but it should not be considered a best practice.

## Exam Preparation Tasks

# Review All the Key Topics

Review the most important topics from the chapter, noted with the Key Topic icon in the outer margin of the page. Table 14-2 lists these key topics and the page numbers where each is found.

**Table 14-2**   Key Topics for Chapter 14

| Key Topic Element | Description | Page Number |
|---|---|---|
| Activity 14-1 | Creating a DRS/HA Cluster | 338 |
| Activity 14-2 | Adding a Host to a Cluster | 339 |
| Activity 14-3 | Removing a Host from a Cluster | 344 |
| Activity 14-4 | Creating and Configuring an SDRS Datastore Cluster | 348 |
| Figure 14-23 | Configuring VMCP | 353 |

| Key Topic Element | Description | Page Number |
|---|---|---|
| Bullet List | Storage Event Types | 353 |
| Figure 14-24 | Settings for VMCP | 354 |
| Bullet List | Configuration Options for VMCP | 354 |
| Bullet List | Migration Threshold Settings | 356 |
| Bullet List | Automation Level Settings | 357 |
| Figure 14-27 | Accessing VM Overrides for DRS Automation Level | 358 |
| Figure 14-28 | Admission Control Policy Settings | 359 |
| Bullet List | Admission Control Policy | 360 |
| Figure 14-29 | Virtual Machine Overrides for HA | 361 |
| Bullet List | Virtual Machine Overrides for HA | 361 |

# Review Questions

The answers to these review questions are in Appendix A.

1. Which of the following can you configure in the setting of a host cluster? (Choose two.)

   a. Virtual Machine Monitoring

   b. SDRS

   c. FT

   d. EVC

2. Which of the following can be used only on a host that is part of a cluster? (Choose two.)

   a. vMotion

   b. DRS

   c. Resource Pools

   d. HA

**3.** Which Admission Control method would be best for an organization that has many VMs with highly variable reservations?

    **a.** Specify failover hosts.

    **b.** Percentage of cluster resources reserved as failover spare capacity

    **c.** Host failures that the cluster tolerates

    **d.** Any of these methods would work fine.

**4.** Which of the following are true regarding SDRS? (Choose two.)

    **a.** I/O is always taken into consideration.

    **b.** Capacity is always taken into consideration.

    **c.** Datastores are managed through host clusters.

    **d.** Datastores are managed by adding similar datastores to datastore clusters.

**5.** Which of the following are storage events that can be monitored using VCMP?

    **a.** FT

    **b.** APD

    **c.** PDL

    **d.** SDRS

**6.** If the timeout value for VCMP APD is set to the default of 140 seconds and the delay is set to the default of 3 minutes, how long will it take for the system to act on the VM?

    **a.** 40 sec

    **b.** 140 sec

    **c.** 3 min

    **d.** 5 min 20 sec

**7.** Which of the following is a DRS Automation Level that will make recommendations but will not perform an action of any kind on VMs?

    **a.** Partial

    **b.** Manual

    **c.** Disabled

    **d.** Fully Automatic

8. Which of the following DRS Automation Levels will perform initial place-ment of VMs but will not move them to balance loads?

    a. Manual

    b. Partial

    c. Fully Automated

    d. Disabled

9. Which of the following is the default setting for Host Isolation Response in vSphere HA?

    a. Leave Powered On

    b. Shut Down

    c. Power Off

    d. Disabled

10. Which cluster setting of VM Restart Priority offers the greatest flexibility for VM overrides?

    a. High

    b. Medium

    c. Low

    d. Disabled

**This chapter covers the following subjects:**

- VMware Fault Tolerance Requirements

- Configuring VMware Fault Tolerance Networking

- Enabling/Disabling VMware Fault Tolerance on a Virtual Machine

- Testing an FT Configuration

- Determining Use Cases for Enabling VMware Fault Tolerance on a Virtual Machine

For some of your VMs, the option of restarting them when their host fails is not good enough. What you want is for them never to go down at all, even if their host fails. The only way this could be possible is if the VM was running on two different hosts at the same time. In essence, this is what VMware Fault Tolerance (FT) does. In this chapter, you learn about the requirements of FT, including the network configuration requirements. In addition, you see how you can enable, test, and disable FT for your critical VMs. Finally, you learn how to determine a use case for enabling FT on a VM.

## CHAPTER 15

# Planning and Implementing VMware Fault Tolerance

## "Do I Know This Already?" Quiz

The "Do I Know This Already?" quiz allows you to assess whether you should read this entire chapter or simply jump to the "Exam Preparation Tasks" section for review. If you are in doubt, read the entire chapter. Table 15-1 outlines the major headings in this chapter and the corresponding "Do I Know This Already?" quiz questions. You can find the answers in Appendix A, "Answers to the 'Do I Know This Already?' Quizzes and Chapter Review Questions."

**Table 15-1**  "Do I Know This Already?" Section-to-Question Mapping

| Foundation Topics Section | Questions Covered in This Section |
| --- | --- |
| VMware Fault Tolerance Requirements | 1–3 |
| Configuring VMware Fault Tolerance Networking | 4, 5 |
| Enabling/Disabling VMware Fault Tolerance on a Virtual Machine | 6, 7 |
| Testing an FT Configuration | 8 |
| Determining Use Cases for Enabling VMware Fault Tolerance on a Virtual Machine | 9, 10 |

1. You are attempting to configure vSphere 6 FT. You have a two-host cluster that is configured for vSphere 6 HA. The hosts meet the requirements for FT, and the appropriate networking is installed. What else will you need?

    a. An Enterprise Plus license

    b. To install DRS on the cluster

    c. Another vSphere 6 host

    d. To disable HA on the cluster

   **2.** What is the minimum number of network cards that are required on a host, just to support FT?

   **a.** 1

   **b.** 2

   **c.** 3

   **d.** 4

   **3.** Which of the following types of storage provisioning are supported with vSphere 6 FT?

   **a.** Eager Zero Thick only

   **b.** Thick and Thin

   **c.** Thin only

   **d.** Eager Zero Thick, Thick, and Thin

   **4.** Which of the following are recommend practices when configuring vSphere 6 FT? (Choose two.)

   **a.** Distribute each vmnic team over two physical switches to eliminate a single point of failure at Layer 2.

   **b.** Connect all vmnics in the same team to the same physical switch to avoid looping.

   **c.** Use a nondeterministic teaming policy, such as IP hash.

   **d.** Use a deterministic teaming policy, such as originating port ID.

   **5.** Which of the following are true regarding network configuration for vSphere 6 FT? (Choose two.)

   **a.** You should use one vSwitch with separate VLANs for vMotion and FT Logging traffic.

   **b.** You should use a separate vSwitch and VLAN for vMotion and FT Logging traffic.

   **c.** A minimum of three 10Gbps vmnics is required.

   **d.** A minimum of three 10Gbps vmnics is highly recommended.

6. Which of the following are true about vSphere 6 FT? (Choose two.)

   a. You can enable FT on a powered-on VM "on the fly" without disrupting the user session.

   b. You must power down a VM to enable FT.

   c. You will need to clone a copy of the VM that will be used as the secondary machine.

   d. When you enable FT, the Primary VM will use vMotion to make a copy of itself on another host to be used as the secondary VM.

7. Which of the following are *not* true regarding vSphere 6 FT? (Choose two.)

   a. The Primary VM will be used only if the Secondary VM fails.

   b. The Secondary VM is protected against a failure.

   c. The Primary VM is protected by the Secondary VM.

   d. Both VMs are protected against guest OS failure.

8. Which of the following would be the most appropriate method of testing FT on vSphere 6?

   a. Right-click the host on which the VM resides and click Test Failover.

   b. Right-click the host on which the VM resides and click Power and then Reboot.

   c. Right-click the VM that has been configured with FT and click Fault Tolerance and then Test Failover.

   d. Right-click the VM that has been configured with FT and click Fault Tolerance and then Reboot.

9. Which of the following would *not* be an appropriate use case for vSphere 6 FT? (Choose two.)

   a. A VM with an application that requires SMP with four vCPUs

   b. A VM with an application that requires SMP with eight vCPUs

   c. As a safeguard to ensure that the operating system on the VM can never fail

   d. As a safeguard to ensure that the failure of one host will not take the application away from the end user

**10.** Which of the following would be a good use case for vSphere 6 FT? (Choose two.)

    **a.** In a case where clustering cannot be used for an application

    **b.** As an "on-demand" service to protect an application from hardware failure while a time-sensitive project is running

    **c.** As an "on-demand" service to protect an application from software failure while a time-sensitive project is running

    **d.** For an important application that must be available at all times, even in the event of a guest operating system failure

## VMware Fault Tolerance Requirements

Based on my description of FT, you might have already decided that you want all or at least most of your VMs to take advantage of FT. Well, there are two sides to every story, and you should hear the other side of this one before you make any decisions. You will find that FT works best for only those critical VMs that absolutely need it, and that is what it's designed for anyway.

The requirements and limitations with regard to FT are many. I tell my students that this stuff is truly "rocket surgery!" Until vSphere 6, most people considered the biggest limitation of the earlier version of FT, now called Legacy FT, to be that it did not allow for VMs with more than one vCPU. Because most of your VMs don't need more than one, this may not seem like much of a limitation; however, many of your "critical" VMs (the kind on which you want to use FT) do perform better with more than one vCPU. For example, mission-critical VMs, such as MS Exchange and Java servers, can be used with one vCPU but will perform much better with more than one.

However, vSphere 6 supports FT for VMs with up to four vCPUs, so now you can provide a service that ensures zero downtime due to physical host failure for those machines that require higher performance standards. This means that more companies than ever before will be able to leverage it for their mission-critical applications. However, to leverage it, your hosts and network first have to meet the requirements. Figure 15-1 shows the architecture of vSphere 6 FT, which is described further in the following section.

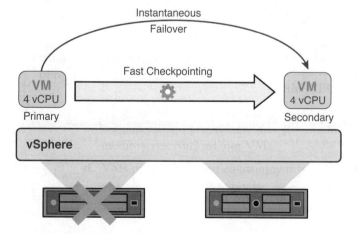

**Figure 15-1**   vSphere FT Architecture

There are many FT requirements with regard to networking, memory, and storage. Some of the requirements have changed from those of Legacy FT, but many of them are still the same. The following is a list of requirements and limitations of vSphere 6 FT:

- **vSphere configuration:** All host hardware must be certified for FT, and all hosts must have certificate checking enabled. You should have a minimum of three hosts in a cluster. You can check the compatibility lists at http://www.vmware.com/resources/compatibility/search.php for hardware with compatible feature sets.

- **Storage:** VMs must be provisioned with shared storage. As of vSphere 6, this can be eager zero thick, thick, or even thin storage. This storage can now be backed up in the normal manner that you back up any other storage, because each VM has its own VMDK in the shared storage.

- **Networking:** vSphere 6 FT requires a minimum of two 1-Gbps vmnics: one for vMotion and one for FT Logging; however two 10-Gbps vmnics are highly recommended. vMotion and FT Logging should be configured on separate virtual switches and on separate VLANs (subnets). Three or more vmnics are recommended. vSphere 6 FT uses a Fast Checkpointing technology that replaces the previous Record-Play technology used by vSphere 5.5 FT. This is a much more efficient method, but it still requires a more robust network to support it; especially when you are running VMs that have two or more vCPUs.

- **Processor:** Up to four vCPU VMs are now supported with Enterprise Plus licensing. The Standard license supports only two vCPUs on an FT VM. Host processors must be FT-compatible. VMs must be running a supported guest OS. Host processors must be compatible with one another. At the time of this publication, Intel Sandy Bridge and later were supported, as well as AMD Bulldozer and later.

- **Host BIOS:** Hosts must have Hardware Virtualization enabled. Hosts must run the same instruction set.

**NOTE**   VMware recommends that the hosts you use to support FT VMs have their BIOS power management settings turned to Maximum Performance or OS-Managed Performance.

## Configuring VMware Fault Tolerance Networking

As I mentioned earlier, the networking requirements for FT are that you must have at least two separate switches on two separate subnets: one for vMotion and at least one for FT Logging. The reason is that when you use FT, the VM in essence uses vMotion to copy itself to another host and then begins the FT Logging process using Fast Checkpointing technology from then on. Actually, there is a little more to configuring an FT network than just two vmnics. Each configuration will have its own challenges. The following is a list of guidelines that apply to FT networking:

- Distribute each vmnic team over two physical switches to eliminate a single point of failure at Layer 2.

- Use a deterministic teaming policy, such as originating port ID. This will ensure that specific traffic types stay on their own specific vmnics.

- When using active/standby policies, take into account the traffic types that would share a vmnic in the event of a failure.

- Configure all active adapters for a particular type of traffic (for example, FT Logging) to the same physical switch. The standby adapter should use the other switch.

## Enabling/Disabling VMware Fault Tolerance on a Virtual Machine

This section discusses what really happens when you enable FT on a VM. What you are looking for is a way to run the VM in two places at the same time. That way, a physical failure of a host won't mean that the server goes down, because it is running on another host as well. This means that the VM needs to make a copy of itself and place it on another host. This, in essence, is what happens when you enable FT on a VM. The VM on which you enabled FT becomes the Primary VM and uses vMotion to copy itself to another host, with one important exception.

Whereas the Primary VM continues to operate normally, the new Secondary VM does not connect to the network normally; instead, it is connected to the Primary VM using the FT Logging connection and Fast Checkpoint technology. Everything that happens on the Primary VM will therefore happen on the secondary VM only milliseconds later. The Secondary VM is always "up to speed" so that if the host on which the Primary VM resides should fail, the system needs only to connect the Secondary VM to the main network. If that happens, the Secondary VM becomes the new Primary VM, and it creates a new Secondary VM on yet another (third) host. In addition, if the Secondary VM should fail, it will be replaced by another Secondary VM to maintain the fault tolerance of the Primary VM.

As of vSphere 6, you can even enable FT on a VM that is powered on. To enable FT on a VM, after the hosts have been properly configured, follow the steps outlined in Activity 15-1.

## Activity 15-1   Enabling Fault Tolerance on a Virtual Machine

1. Log on to your vSphere Web Client.

2. Select **Home** and then **VMs and Templates**.

3. Right-click the VM on which you want to enable FT and select **Fault Tolerance**, **Turn On Fault Tolerance**, as shown in Figure 15-2. Note that the VM can be powered on or off.

**Figure 15-2**   Enabling FT for a VM on a Configured Cluster

4. Confirm by clicking **Yes**, and then monitor the Recent Tasks pane and your inventory to see the changes. You will then be able to view and test your primary and secondary VM and migrate your secondary VM as needed.

## Testing an FT Configuration

After FT is enabled for a VM, you can test to verify that it works if the host should fail. Now, shutting down the host on which the VM resides would definitely kick off a test, but you might not want to get that drastic. If you have other VMs on the same host, and you want to perform as safe and nondisruptive a test as possible, you can right-click the VM that is protected by FT and select **Fault Tolerance** and then **Test Failover**.

## Determining Use Case for Enabling VMware Fault Tolerance on a Virtual Machine

Now that you have seen the advantages and drawbacks of FT, it's up to you to decide where, or even whether, it fits into your virtual data center. For example, if you have VMs that are critical to the point that lives or millions of dollars are on the line, you might consider using FT to provide for zero disruption in the event of a physical failure of a host. You will need to evaluate the need for FT in your own organization. In general, organizations use FT for the following reasons:

- Important applications that need to be available at all times, even in the event of a hardware failure.

- Custom applications that are not cluster aware and therefore have no other way of being protected from a physical failure.

- Cases where clustering might be used but the complexity of configuring and maintaining it is beyond the capabilities of the administrators.

- In cases where a critical transaction is happening, such as the transfer of a large database or the creation of an important and time-sensitive report. In this case, FT can be enabled "on demand" for the servers used in this event and can be disabled when the transaction is finished.

## Summary

This chapter covered the following main topics:

- The concept of VMware Fault Tolerance (FT) and the host requirements for its use.

- The configuration requirements for networking and storage.

- How to enable and disable fault tolerance on a VM and test failover without disrupting your environment.

- Scenarios in which you might benefit from FT.

## Exam Preparation Tasks

## Review All the Key Topics

Review the most important topics from the chapter, noted with the Key Topic icon in the outer margin of the page. Table 15-2 lists these key topics and the page numbers where each is found.

**Table 15-2**   Key Topics for Chapter 15

| Key Topic Element | Description | Page Number |
|---|---|---|
| Figure 15-1 | vSphere FT Architecture | 373 |
| Bullet List | Requirements and Limitations of vSphere FT | 374 |
| Bullet List | Guidelines Regarding FT Networking | 375 |
| Activity 15-1 | Enabling Fault Tolerance on a Virtual Machine | 376 |
| Bullet List | Use Cases for FT | 377 |

## Review Questions

The answers to these review questions are in Appendix A.

1. You are attempting to configure vSphere 6 FT for VMs with four vCPUs. You have a three-host cluster that is configured for vSphere 6 HA. The hosts meet the requirements for FT, and the appropriate networking is installed. In addition, you have a Standard license. What else will you need?

    a. An Enterprise Plus license

    b. To install DRS on the cluster

    c. Another vSphere 6 host

    d. To disable HA on the cluster

**2.** What of the following are *not* best practices in regard to vSphere 6 FT? (Choose two.)

   **a.** Configure active and standby adapters on the same physical switches to prevent loops.

   **b.** Configure all active adapters on the same physical switch, and configure all standby adapters on the other.

   **c.** Use a nondeterministic load-balancing method, such as IP hash.

   **d.** Use a deterministic load-balancing method, such as originating source port.

**3.** Which of the following types of storage provisioning is *not* supported with vSphere 6 FT?

   **a.** Eager Zero Thick

   **b.** Thick

   **c.** Thin

   **d.** All types of storage provisioning are supported with vSphere 6 FT.

**4.** What of the following are *not* recommend practices when configuring vSphere 6 FT? (Choose two.)

   **a.** Distribute each vmnic team over two physical switches to eliminate a single point of failure at Layer 2.

   **b.** Connect all vmnics in the same team to the same physical switch to avoid looping.

   **c.** Use a nondeterministic teaming policy, such as IP hash.

   **d.** Use a deterministic teaming policy, such as originating port ID.

**5.** Which of the following are *not* required for vSphere 6 FT? (Choose two.)

   **a.** An Enterprise Plus license

   **b.** A minimum of three hosts

   **c.** A minimum of three 1Gbps vmnics

   **d.** A minimum of three 10Gbps vmnics

6. Which of the following are *not* true about vSphere 6 FT? (Choose two.)

   a. You can enable FT on a powered VM on-the-fly without disrupting the user session.

   b. You must power down a VM to enable FT.

   c. You will need to clone a copy of the VM that will be used as the secondary machine.

   d. When you enable FT, the Primary VM will use vMotion to make a copy of itself on another host to be used as the secondary VM.

7. Which of the following are true regarding vSphere 6 FT? (Choose two.)

   a. The Primary VM will be used only if the Secondary VM fails.

   b. The Secondary VM is protected against a failure.

   c. The Primary VM is protected by the Secondary VM.

   d. Both VMs are protected against guest OS failure.

8. Which of the following are true regarding vSphere 6 FT? (Choose two.)

   a. FT can protect against OS failures.

   b. FT can protect against application failures.

   c. FT can protect critical VMs against hardware failures.

   d. FT requires a minimum of three hosts, two vmnics, and a Standard license.

9. Which of the following are appropriate use cases for vSphere 6 FT? (Choose two.)

   a. A VM with an application that requires SMP with four vCPUs

   b. A VM with an application that requires SMP with eight vCPUs

   c. As a safeguard to ensure that the operating system on the VM can never fail

   d. As a safeguard to ensure that the failure of one host will not take the application away from the end user

10. Which of the following would *not* be a good use case for vSphere 6 FT? (Choose two.)

    a. In a case where clustering cannot be used for an application

    b. As an "on-demand" service to protect an application from hardware failure while a time-sensitive project is running

    c. As an "on-demand" service to protect an application from software failure while a time-sensitive project is running

    d. For an important application that must be available at all times, even in that event of a guest operating system failure

**This chapter covers the following subjects:**

- Resource Pool Hierarchies
- vFlash Architecture
- Creating/Removing a Resource Pool
- Configuring Resource Pool Attributes
- Adding/Removing Virtual Machines from a Resource Pool
- Creating and Deleting a vFlash Resource Pool
- Determining Resource Pool Requirements for a Given vSphere Implementation

The four resources that you manage for all your VMs are CPU, memory, disk, and network. You could manage each of these resources individually for every VM in your organization, but that would be doing it the hard way. Instead, you can combine VMs that share the same characteristics and resource needs into logical abstractions called Resource Pools and manage the aggregate total of the pools to satisfy the needs of the VMs they contain. In addition, you can use Resource Pools to establish relative priorities between groups of VMs and give some VMs more priority to physical resources just because they reside in the appropriate Resource Pool.

## CHAPTER 16

# Creating and Administering Resource Pools

In this chapter, you learn about the Resource Pool hierarchy and its relationship to managing resources in your organization. In addition, the chapter defines expandable reservations and discusses the advantages and disadvantages of configuring them. You learn how to create, configure, and remove a Resource Pool. Also, you learn how to add VMs to and remove them from a Resource Pool. I also assist you in determining Resource Pool requirements for a given vSphere implementation. Finally, you learn how to evaluate the appropriate shares, reservations, and limits for a Resource Pool based on VM workloads.

## "Do I Know This Already?" Quiz

The "Do I Know This Already?" quiz allows you to assess whether you should read this entire chapter or simply jump to the "Exam Preparation Tasks" section for review. If you are in doubt, read the entire chapter. Table 16-1 outlines the major headings in this chapter and the corresponding "Do I Know This Already?" quiz questions. You can find the answers in Appendix A, "Answers to the 'Do I Know This Already?' Quizzes and Chapter Review Questions."

**Table 16-1**  "Do I Know This Already?" Section-to-Question Mapping

| Foundation Topics Section | Questions Covered in This Section |
|---|---|
| Resource Pool Hierarchies | 1, 2 |
| vFlash Architecture | 3 |
| Creating/Removing a Resource Pool | 4 |
| Configuring Resource Pool Attributes | 5, 6 |
| Adding/Removing Virtual Machines from a Resource Pool | 7 |
| Creating and Deleting a vFlash Resource Pool | 8 |
| Determining Resource Pool Requirements for a Given vSphere Implementation | 9, 10 |

1. Which of the following would be appropriate to use as the root of your Resource Pool hierarchy? (Choose two.)

    a. A standalone host

    b. A cluster enabled for HA but not for DRS

    c. A cluster enabled for HA and DRS

    d. A parent resource pool

2. Which of the following is *not* a container in which you could place a resource pool?

    a. Host

    b. Resource pool

    c. DRS-enabled cluster

    d. Folder

3. An administrator is attempting to create a vFlash resource, and the container is not available. Which of the following could cause this issue? (Choose two.)

    a. The resource is in use by VSAN.

    b. The resource has a VMFS volume on it.

    c. vSphere does not support the use of vFlash.

    d. vFlash requires a specific vFlash license.

4. Which of the following is required before creating a resource pool?

    a. You must create the VMs that will be placed into the resource pool.

    b. You must set aside the CPU and memory resources that the resource pool will use.

    c. You must define the range for the resource pool in the overall hierarchy.

    d. None of the above are required before creating a resource pool.

5. Which of the following can be used to establish relative priority between resource pools?

    a. Reservations

    b. Limits

    c. Shares

    d. All of these options apply.

6. An administrator is attempting to start a VM but is not able to because there are not enough resources in its resource pool. Which of the following might allow the VM to start? (Choose two.)

   a. Increase the reservation of the VM.

   b. Increase the limit assigned to the resource pool.

   c. Decrease the limit assigned to the resource pool.

   d. Decrease the reservation assigned to the VM.

7. Which of the following must be done before you can add a VM to a resource pool?

   a. The resource pool must be powered on.

   b. The resource pool must be added to the hierarchy.

   c. The resource pool must be registered in the vCenter.

   d. You must assign resources to the resource pool for the VM to use.

8. An administrator is creating a vFlash Resource Pool. He has already right-clicked the host in the vSphere Web Client and selected Settings/Virtual Flash Resource Management. What does he need to select next?

   a. Create

   b. Add Capacity

   c. Register

   d. Manage

9. An administrator created two resource pools and gave one low shares and the other high shares. She then placed VMs in each of the resource pools without changing the default shares of the VMs. Which of the following are true? (Choose two.)

   a. The VMs in the pool with high shares will always use more resources than the VMs in the pool with low shares.

   b. The VMs in the pool with high shares will be entitled to more resources than the VMs in the pool with low shares.

   c. The share settings will always matter, even if there is no contention for a scarce resource.

   d. The share settings will matter only if there is contention for a scarce resource.

**10.** Which of the following are true about resource pools? (Choose two.)

    **a.** VMs in a resource pool do not have to compete for resources.

    **b.** VMs in a resource pool do have to compete for resources.

    **c.** You can assure that a specific VM will get more resources, just by putting it into a resource pool.

    **d.** The resource available to a VM in a resource pool will depend upon the resources assigned to the resource pool and on all the other VMs in the resource pool that are competing for the same resources.

## Foundation Topics

# Resource Pool Hierarchies

The root of the Resource Pool hierarchy can be a standalone host or a DRS cluster. This "invisible" point of reference establishes the top of your Resource Pool hierarchy. When you create your first Resource Pool on a host or a DRS cluster, it extends the hierarchy and is called a *parent pool*. You can create multiple parent pools, as needed for your organization to identify departments or functions that you want to differentiate. In addition, you can create a Resource Pool within a Resource Pool, called a *child pool*. If you create multiple child pools within the same parent pool, they are referred to as *siblings*. Seriously! I know, I know. Figure 16-1 will help you make sense of all this.

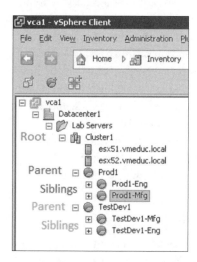

**Figure 16-1**   The Resource Pool Hierarchy

Establishing a hierarchy of Resource Pools allows you to manage your VMs in a much more organized fashion than without Resource Pools. If you plan this properly for your organization, you will be able to take full advantage of the benefits offered by Resource Pools. The specific benefits offered vary by organization, but in general these Resource Pool hierarchies allow the following:

- Flexible hierarchical organization.

- Isolation of resources between pools and sharing of resources within pools.

- Access control and delegation.

- Separation of resources from hardware.

- Management of sets of VMs running a multitier service. These VMs need each other and therefore need the same priorities to resources.

### Defining the Expandable Reservation Parameter

The expandable reservation parameter will make a lot more sense toward the end of this section, after discussion of shares, reservations, and limits for Resource Pools. Suffice it to say that an expandable reservation allows a pool to borrow resources from a pool that is higher in the hierarchy; for example, a child pool can borrow from a parent pool, and a parent pool can borrow from the root pool.

## vFlash Architecture

While we are on the subject of resources, it makes sense to discuss a relatively new resource that can have a significant impact on host and VM performance, namely SSDs (also known as flash memory). Because SSDs are much faster than magnetic "spinning" disks, and because many hosts now contain one or more SSDs "out of the box," it makes sense to leverage those disks to improve performance on the host itself as well as the VMs on it. To do this, you can set up a virtual flash resource on which you add SSDs for the exclusive use of the virtual flash. The SSDs will then be dedicated to use on the virtual flash resource, and you will not be able to use them with any other vSphere service, such as vSAN. Also, the vFlash container cannot already be formatted with VMFS or contain a VMFS volume. Later in this chapter, you learn the steps that you take to create a resource pool with vFlash storage.

## Creating/Removing a Resource Pool

A Resource Pool is a logical container that allows you to control resources in a larger setting than just each individual VM at a time. You can create a Resource Pool by "pretending like it exists already." In other words, because you are creating only a logical abstraction, you can create the object in the inventory, name it, configure it, and immediately begin to use it. To create a Resource Pool, follow the steps outlined in Activity 16-1.

**Activity 16-1   Creating a Resource Pool**

1. Log on to your vSphere Web Client.

2. Select **Home** and then **Hosts and Clusters**.

3. Right-click the host or DRS cluster on which you want to create the Resource Pool and select **New Resource Pool**. In this case, because the host

is already a member of a cluster, the capability to create Resource Pools on the host itself has been removed (grayed out), as shown in Figure 16-2.

Create a Resource Pool in the cluster by right-clicking the cluster and selecting **New Resource Pool**, as shown in Figure 16-3.

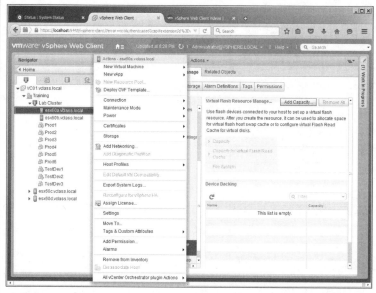

**Figure 16-2**    Resource Pool Creation on Clustered Hosts Is Disabled

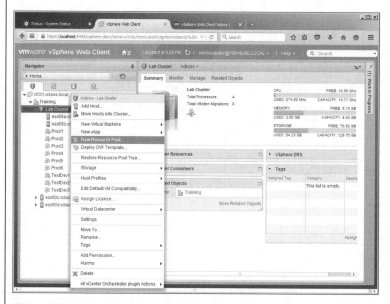

**Figure 16-3**    Creating a Resource Pool in a Cluster

4. Type a name for your new Resource Pool and then set CPU Resources and Memory Resources if necessary. Then click **OK**, as shown in Figure 16-4.

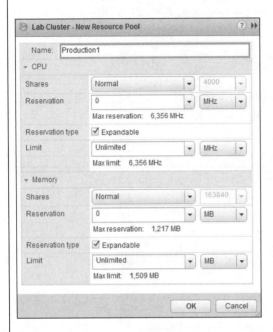

**Figure 16-4**   Naming a Resource Pool

5. Monitor your Recent Tasks pane and your vCenter inventory for the creation of your new Resource Pool. You should see your new resource pool under the cluster on which you created it, as shown in Figure 16-5.

**NOTE**   To remove a resource pool, you can right-click it and select Delete, as shown in Figure 16-6. You should remove any VMs or resource pools that are in it before you delete it.

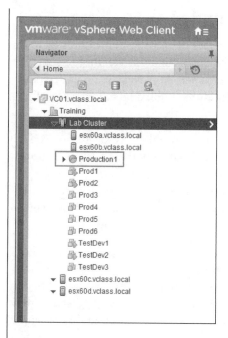

**Figure 16-5**   A Newly Created Resource Pool

**Figure 16-6**   Deleting a Resource Pool

## Configuring Resource Pool Attributes

Resource Pools allow you to manage the aggregate totals of resources allowed to the VMs in the pool. You can control the CPU Resources and the Memory Resources with regard to shares, reservation, limit, and expandability. You should understand the impact of each of these options on your Resource Pool. The following briefly explains each Resource Pool attribute:

- **Shares:** These establish relative priority between sibling Resource Pools. They are both relative and proportional. They are relative in their settings of Low, Normal, High, and Custom. They are proportional in that how much of the physical resource they receive depends on how many other sibling Resource Pools are competing for the same physical resource. (The section "Determining Resource Requirements for a Given vSphere Implementation" discusses each setting for shares and their impact on the whole environment.

- **Reservation:** This is a guarantee that a fixed amount of a certain resource is to be given to this Resource Pool. With this guarantee, the VMs in this pool do not have to compete using their shares for these resources. In essence, they are given a "head start" or advantage over the VMs in pools that do not have a reservation.

- **Limit:** This is a cap on the aggregate physical resources that can be consumed by the VMs in this Resource Pool. It might be useful if there are many large VMs that can "take turns," but you don't want all of them taking resources from the root at the same time. The limit "chokes" back the resources that the pool can use, even if the resources are not being consumed by other VMs in other pools. Because of this, be careful using limits.

- **Expandable Reservation:** As I mentioned earlier, this refers to whether the Resource Pool can borrow the resources from its parent. The impacts of this setting are covered in the section "Determining Resource Pool Requirements for a Given vSphere Implementation."

## Adding/Removing Virtual Machines from a Resource Pool

After you have created a Resource Pool, you can add VMs to it by dragging and dropping. Any VMs that are added to a Resource Pool will then share in the resources of the pool as configured in the Resource Pool's attributes. To remove a VM from a Resource Pool, drag it to another appropriate object (Resource Pool, host, cluster, or data center) and drop it. In the case of an object higher in the hierarchy, you might have to answer the question as to which host you want to use for the VMs resources.

# Creating and Deleting a vFlash Resource Pool

As discussed earlier in the section on vFlash Architecture, you can create a resource pool from SSD storage that will give you significantly better performance than traditional spinning disk storage. To create a vFlash resource pool, you should do the following:

1. Right-click a host and click **Settings**.

2. In the details pane (on the right), click **Virtual Flash Resource Management** and click **Add Capacity**, as shown in Figure 16-7.

3. From the list of available SSDs, select one or more SSDs to use for virtual flash. Click **OK**.

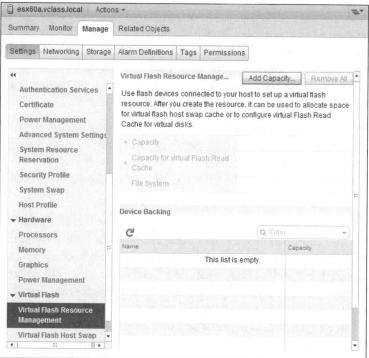

**Figure 16-7**   Creating a vFlash Resource Pool

After the Flash Resource Pool is created, you can assign flash resources to a VM through the advanced settings on its virtual disks. You should understand that the system will create the flash resource for the VM when it is powered on and destroy it when it is powered down. The flash read cache will then support write-through or read caching as configured. Not every workload will benefit from flash read cache, because the performance boost will depend on workload pattern and working set sizes, but many systems will realize a pronounced performance boost.

## Determining Resource Pool Requirements for a Given vSphere Implementation

Remember that the purpose of Resource Pools is to establish relative priorities within the same host or cluster of your vSphere. For most organizations, this will be a real-world advantage. For example, the capability to give production VMs an edge when competing for physical resources with testing and development VMs could assist you in managing your resources. Of course, you could also put the two types of VMs on entirely different clusters, but that requires that you use more hosts.

In practice, each organization will define its own needs and uses for Resource Pools. By understanding what is possible, you will be able to see how you can use these configuration options to your advantage. For example, evaluate the following scenario and then consider how you might use the same principles in your own organization. I'm going to use as few numbers and values as possible so that you can concentrate on the "philosophy" and not on the math.

Your cluster has multiple hosts and multiple VMs on each host. Your VMs can be divided into categories based on their function. Some of your VMs are servers that are used by end users for normal daily production. Others are servers used for testing and development, an important role, but not as urgent a function as the production servers.

To begin to control the resources given to your servers, you create two Resource Pools named Production and TestDev. You then drag each of your VMs into their respective Resource Pools. You configure the CPU and memory Shares on Production to High and the CPU and memory Shares on TestDev to Low. This gives Production an advantage for any resources for which it must compete with TestDev. Giving the Resource Pool an advantage will give all the VMs in the Resource Pool a potential advantage, as well, but it also depends on how many VMs are in the same pool and competing for resources.

In addition, so that Production has some CPU and memory guaranteed to it for which it does not have to compete, you give Production a reservation in each category of CPU and memory. This reservation is a guarantee to the aggregate total of all VMs running in the Production Resource Pool.

Now, here's the really good thing. Even though Production is guaranteed those reservations, the resources are not "locked" to Production and only Production.

In other words, if the VMs in Production are not using the resources, the VMs in TestDev can have them. This means that the resources won't be wasted, no matter what happens.

Your VMs that are in TestDev are powered on and off for testing purposes. Some of them are rather large and, if too many of them were to be powered on and run at the same time, they might have a negative effect on Production. Please don't misunderstand this concept. Production would still get its reservation and, due to its high shares, it would win the competition for the rest of resources more often than TestDev. However, TestDev might put up quite a fight for those resources. Because of this, you decide to throttle back the capability of TestDev by placing a limit on the amount of CPU and memory for which it's allowed to compete. You do this by setting a limit on CPU and memory in the settings of TestDev.

As you can see, the purpose in this scenario was to provide an appropriate balance of physical resources to VMs, not an equal one. Your organization might have the same needs (or different needs), so you should understand how you can use the Resource Pool configuration settings to your advantage. The math involved will be specific to the individual scenario, and it's all yours!

## Summary

The main topics covered in this chapter are as follows:

- A discussion and examination of the concept of a resource pool. You learned how to create a resource pool hierarchy by adding resource pools to hosts, DRS clusters, and other resource pools.

- vFlash architecture and how it has changed some of the decisions that you make in regard to storage locations and storage hardware. You learned how to create a vFlash resource pool.

- Creating resource pools and configuring their attributes. You learned how to set shares, limits, and reservations for resource pools.

- How to determine resource pool requirements and in what type of scenarios you should consider using resource pools. You learned the practical best practices associated with using resource pools in your environment.

## Exam Preparation Tasks

## Review All the Key Topics

Review the most important topics from inside the chapter, noted with the Key Topic icon in the outer margin of the page. Table 16-2 lists these key topics and the page numbers where each is found.

**Table 16-2**   Key Topics for Chapter 16

| Key Topic Element | Description | Page Number |
| --- | --- | --- |
| Figure 16-1 | The Resource Pool Hierarchy | 387 |
| Bullet List | Benefits of Resource Pools | 387 |
| Activity 16-1 | Creating a Resource Pool | 388 |
| Figure 16-6 | Deleting a Resource Pool | 391 |
| Bullet List | Resource Pool Attributes | 392 |
| Numbered List | Steps to Create and Delete a vFlash Resource Pool | 393 |
| Figure 16-7 | Creating a vFlash Resource Pool | 393 |

## Review Questions

The answers to these review questions are in Appendix A.

1. Which of the following are considered as advantages to using Resource Pools? (Choose two.)

   a. Flexible hierarchical organization

   b. Management of sets of VMs running a multitier service

   c. Creates more overall total resources to be consumed

   d. Speeds up the creation of VMs and templates

2. Which of the following is the best definition of the Expandable Resource Parameter for a resource pool?

   a. Allows a host to borrow resources from a VM

   b. Allows a VM to borrow resources from another VM

   c. Allow a parent pool to expand its resources using child pools

   d. Allows a pool to borrow from a parent resource

3. An administrator is attempting to create a vFlash resource, and the container is not available. Which of the following are least likely to be the cause of this issue? (Choose two.)

   a. The resource is in use by VSAN.

   b. The resource has a VMFS volume on it.

   c. vSphere does not support the use of vFlash.

   d. vFlash requires a specific vFlash license.

4. An administrator attempts to create a resource pool on a host, but the option to create the resource pool is grayed out. Which of the following is the most likely cause of this issue?

   a. The host does not have the proper license to use the resource pool.

   b. A resource pool has already been created on the host.

   c. The host has lost its connection to the vCenter Server.

   d. The host is part of a DRS cluster.

5. Which of the following establishes a cap on the aggregate total of resources that can be consumed by VMs in a resource pool?

   a. Reservation

   b. Limit

   c. Shares

   d. All of the above

6. An administrator is attempting to start a VM but is not able to because there are not enough resources in its resource pool. Which of the following might allow the VM to start?

   a. Increase the limit of the VM.

   b. Increase the limit assigned to the resource pool.

   c. Decrease the shares assigned to the resource pool.

   d. Decrease the reservation assigned to the VM.

7. Which of the following must be done before you can add a VM to a resource pool?

   a. The resource pool must be powered on.

   b. The resource pool must be added to the hierarchy.

   c. The VM must be powered on.

   d. The resource pool must be registered to its parent pool.

8. An administrator is creating a vFlash Resource Pool. He has already right-clicked the host in the vSphere Web Client and selected Settings/Virtual Flash Resource Management. What does he need to select next?

   a. Configure

   b. Add Capacity

   c. vFlash

   d. Continue

9. An administrator created two resource pools and gave one low shares and the other high shares. She then placed VMs in each of the resource pools without changing the default shares of the VMs. Which of the following are *not* true? (Choose two.)

   a. The VMs in the pool with high shares will always use more resources that the VMs in the pool with low shares.

   b. The VMs in the pool with high shares will be entitled to more resources than the VMs in the pool with low shares.

   c. The share settings will always matter, even if there is no contention for a scarce resource.

   d. The share settings will matter only if there is contention for a scarce resource.

**10.** Which of the following are true about resource pools? (Choose two.)

    **a.** Resource pools do not compete with other resource pools.

    **b.** VMs in a resource pool do have to compete for resources.

    **c.** Placing VMs in resource pools can dramatically increase the amount of total available resources in your vSphere environment.

    **d.** The resource available to a VM in a resource pool will depend upon the resources assigned to the resource pool and on all the other VMs in the resource pool that are competing for the same resources.

**This chapter covers the following subjects:**

- ESXi Host and Virtual Machine Requirements for vMotion and Storage vMotion

- Enhanced vMotion Compatibility CPU Requirements

- Long Distance vMotion

- Snapshot Requirements for vMotion and Storage vMotion Migration

- Migrating Virtual Machines Using vMotion/Storage vMotion

- Migrating a Powered-Off or Suspended Virtual Machine

When you think about it, *migration* is not a technical term; in fact, even birds migrate. To migrate means to move from one place to another. So, what is actually moving with regard to our studies? What is moving is either the state of the VMs, the files that the VMs use, or both. These moves can be done with the VMs powered off or powered on.

## CHAPTER 17

# Migrating Virtual Machines

When the VMs are powered off, we refer to the moving of their state and their files as *cold migration*. When they are powered on, we refer to the moving of their state as *vMotion* and the moving of their files as *Storage vMotion*. There are advantages and disadvantages to each option. To facilitate any option, you must have your vSphere configured properly.

This chapter first identifies the ESXi host and VM requirements for vMotion, Storage vMotion, and the newest type of vMotion called Enhanced vMotion or Cross-Host vMotion. Next are the requirements for Enhanced Storage vMotion and Long Distance vMotion. The new requirements (or actually lack of requirements) with regard to snapshots and vMotion/Storage vMotion are also discussed. In addition, you learn how you can configure the VM swap file location. Finally, the chapter covers utilizing Storage vMotion techniques for other creative uses, such as changing the disk type, changing the provisioning, and renaming the VM folders.

## "Do I Know This Already?" Quiz

The "Do I Know This Already?" quiz allows you to assess whether you should read this entire chapter or simply jump to the "Exam Preparation Tasks" section for review. If you are in doubt, read the entire chapter. Table 17-1 outlines the major headings in this chapter and the corresponding "Do I Know This Already?" quiz questions. You can find the answers in Appendix A, "Answers to the 'Do I Know This Already?' Quizzes and Chapter Review Questions."

**Table 17-1**  "Do I Know This Already?" Section-to-Question Mapping

| Foundation Topics Section | Questions Covered in This Section |
|---|---|
| ESXi Host and Virtual Machine Requirements for vMotion and Storage vMotion | 1–3 |
| Enhanced vMotion Compatibility CPU Requirements | 4 |
| Long Distance vMotion | 5 |
| Snapshot Requirements for vMotion/Storage vMotion Migration | 6–8 |
| Migrating Virtual Machines Using vMotion/Storage vMotion | 9 |
| Migrating a Powered-Off or Suspended Virtual Machine | 10 |

**1.** An administrator uses vMotion to migrate a VM. Which of the following will occur? (Choose two.)

   **a.** The state of the VM will move from one datastore to another datastore.

   **b.** The VMs files will remain on the same datastore.

   **c.** The state of the VM will move from one host to another host.

   **d.** The VM files will move from one datastore to another one.

**2.** An administrator of a vSphere network with a Standard license attempts to migrate a VM using vMotion but receives an error message indicating that vMotion is not enabled. Which of the following could be the cause of this message?

   **a.** There is no shared storage configured.

   **b.** The VMkernel port intended for vMotion is not enabled for vMotion.

   **c.** There is not enough memory to provide for vMotion.

   **d.** The CPUs are the same on both source and destination hosts.

**3.** Which of the following would prevent an administrator from using Storage vMotion?

   **a.** The VMkernel port is not enabled for vMotion.

   **b.** The vSphere uses a Standard license.

   **c.** The host does not have visibility to the destination datastore.

   **d.** The CPU of the host is not compatible with Storage vMotion.

**4.** An administrator attempts to configure EVC on a cluster but does not meet the requirements. Which of the following would prevent EVC from succeeding?

   **a.** Hosts are a mixture of vSphere 4, 5, and 6.

   **b.** Host CPUs are a mixture of Intel and AMD.

   **c.** All hosts are in the same host cluster.

   **d.** All hosts are configured for vMotion.

**5.** Which of the following would prevent long-distance vMotion from operating properly? (Choose two.)

   **a.** RTT of 50 ms

   **b.** A vSphere Standard license

   **c.** RTT of 200 ms

   **d.** A common Layer 2 environment

**6.** Which of the following is not a part of a snapshot?

   **a.** Settings state

   **b.** Disk state

   **c.** Memory state

   **d.** Power state

**7.** Which of the following are true in regard to vMotion and Storage vMotion with vSphere 6? (Choose two.)

   **a.** You can migrate a VM using vMotion when it contains snapshots.

   **b.** You cannot migrate a VM's files using Storage vMotion if the VM contains snapshots.

   **c.** You cannot migrate a VM using vMotion if the VM contains snapshots.

   **d.** You can migrate the files of a VM using Storage vMotion when the VM contains snapshots.

**8.** Which of the following would prevent a VM from using vMotion?

   **a.** An internal switch on its host, to which the VM is not connected

   **b.** A snapshot that has not been deleted

   **c.** A swap file that is local to a host

   **d.** An ISO mounted on the local host, to which the VM is connected

**9.** Which of the following are true regarding vMotion? (Choose two.)

    **a.** By definition, you cannot vMotion a VM that is powered off.

    **b.** You can vMotion a VM, whether it is powered on or off.

    **c.** vMotion will always move the files of a VM to another location.

    **d.** Just vMotion will never move the files of a VM to another location.

**10.** Which of the following are true? (Choose two.)

    **a.** To cold migrate a VM's files, you must first power off the VM.

    **b.** You can cold migrate a VM's files with a VM powered on or off.

    **c.** The cold migration of the state of a VM is referred to as vMotion.

    **d.** Cold migration of the state of a VM happens with the VM is powered off.

## Foundation Topics

# ESXi Host and Virtual Machine Requirements for vMotion and Storage vMotion

Identifying ESXi host and virtual machine requirements is too big a "bite to chew" all at once. We'll break this into two discussions: one for vMotion and the other for Storage vMotion. Although some of the requirements are the same for both, not all the requirements are the same.

### ESXi and VM Requirements for vMotion

As you might remember, vMotion means moving the state of the VM from one host to another without disrupting the user. You may be wondering, "What exactly is the *state* of the VM?" The state of the VM consists of three components:

- **Settings:** These are the settings that you will see on all the tabs if you right-click the VM and select **Edit Settings**. These are also the configuration settings as defined in the VMX file. These settings describe the VM and all its attributes and virtual hardware.

- **Disk:** These are all the VMDK files and virtual compatibility RDMs that make up the source volumes for the VM.

- **Memory:** This is the active memory on the VM at the time that you are performing the vMotion.

Each component of the state of the VM is handled in a different manner. The Settings state is simple to move, or actually re-create, on another host. The Disk state cannot be re-created in the short amount of time allowed; therefore, we have to use shared storage. The Memory state must be gradually copied over to the destination host so that when the guest OS on the VM is quiesced, the OS "wakes up" on the destination host with the same memory it had on the source host.

We are in essence fooling the guest OS on the VM into thinking that it hasn't migrated. This means that all the components of the host and the VM must be configured properly to pull off the trick. The requirements for the host with regard to vMotion are as follows:

- Source and destination hosts must both have visibility to shared storage used by the VM on Fibre Channel, iSCSI, or NAS (for original vMotion).

- All hosts must have access to at least a 1 Gbps Ethernet network.

- Source and destination hosts must have access to the same physical network or the same VLAN or VXLAN.

- Source and destination hosts must have VMkernel ports configured on a vSS or a vDS that are enabled for vMotion and have a proper IP configuration. It is possible to vMotion from one vDS to another with vSphere 6. This is called *cross-switch vMotion*.

- Host CPUs must be the same vendor and family (for example, Intel Xeon) and must share the same CPUID unless configured otherwise in Advanced settings or by using EVC. (These options are discussed in the next section.)

Just as the hosts must be configured properly for vMotion, the VMs must also be configured properly. If you remember what you are trying to pull off here, you will see that you can't have anything that the VM can "see" on the source host that it won't be able to "see" when it gets to the destination host. With that in mind, the following are the VM requirements with regard to vMotion:

- VMs must not have a connection to an internal switch (zero uplink adapters).

- VMs must not have a connection to a virtual device with a local image mounted (locally mounted CD, floppy drive, or ISO).

- VMs must not have CPU affinity configured.

- If the VM's swap file is not accessible to the destination host, vMotion must be able to create a swap file accessible to the destination host before migration can begin. (This option can be advantageous when using SSD hard drives locally on a host.)

- If the VM uses an RDM, the RDM must be accessible to the destination host as well.

### ESXi and VM Requirements for Storage vMotion

The main thing about Storage vMotion that you should understand is that the VM's state doesn't move at all! What moves (or rather, is copied) are the files that the VM is using. In other words, when you use Storage vMotion, you have a running VM (in our case, a server) that continues to operate while the files that it requires to operate are moved to another physical location. When the migration happens, the OS on the running server is unaware that it has taken place at all. The advantages of this technology are as follows:

- You can perform storage maintenance and reconfiguration without VM downtime.

- You can redistribute storage loads without VM downtime.

- You can evacuate physical storage about to be retired and perform storage tiering, without VM downtime.

Another cool fact is that Storage vMotion is completely storage type independent. That means that you can move files that are on Fibre Channel SAN LUNs to NAS (for an extreme example) while the server is running without disruption to the OS or the user. This is just the beginning, and you learn some other creative things that you can do with Storage vMotion later in this section. The bottom line is that having to tell users that they won't be able to get onto the system because you have to do some hardware maintenance to the drives should now be a thing of the past.

### Enhanced vMotion (Cross-Host vMotion)

VMware originally named it Enhanced vMotion, but too many people were confusing that term with Enhanced vMotion Compatibility (EVC), which (as you see in the next section) is not at all the same thing. So, for lack of a better term, VMware decided to call it Cross-Host vMotion instead. This term doesn't really describe what is different about it, because vMotion is always going "cross host"! However, what is so different about Cross-Host vMotion that it should deserve its own name?

Cross-Host vMotion can do two things that the original vMotion cannot. The first, in my opinion, is cool, but the second has the potential to be a game changer. The two things that Cross-Host vMotion can do that the original vMotion cannot are as follows:

- **Migrate the state of a VM to a new host at the same time that the files are migrating to another datastore:** This, in my opinion, is cool because it ranks high on the "cool factor" and makes me change my story when I'm teaching class, but I don't see myself having to use it much in real life because I am generally performing only one or the other of those actions. Figure 17-1 shows the capability to migrate a powered-on VM's state to another host while simultaneously migrating its files to another datastore.

- **Perform a migration of a VM from one host to another without having a shared datastore between the hosts:** This also causes me to change my story in class, but it has the potential to be a game changer. At present, DRS and SDRS do not take advantage of this option, but if they do some day, will that change some data center design options? Make no mistake, shared storage is always best, and we are coming up with more and new ways to have shared storage, but this might offer a "one-off" solution of the future.

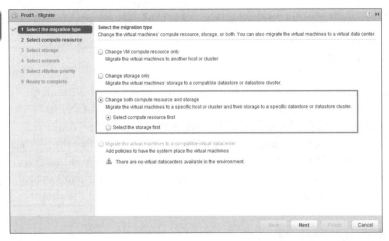

**Figure 17-1**   Migrating a VM's Host and Datastore at the Same Time

## Enhanced vMotion Compatibility CPU Requirements

When you initiate the use of vMotion or a migration of a suspended machine (still running a CPU instruction set), the wizard checks the destination host for compatibility. The CPU feature set that was detected when the VM was powered on to the source host is checked against what will be available on the destination host. The CPU feature set includes all of the following:

- Host CPU vendor, family, and model

- Settings in the BIOS that might disable CPU features

- ESX/ESXi version running on the host

- VM's virtual hardware version (for example 7, 8, 9, 10, or 11)

- VM's guest OS

If the feature set is determined to be different on the destination host than on the source host, the system lets you know with a detailed error message if there are compatibility problems that will prevent the successful migration of the VM. You can hide some of the instruction set from the guest OS and satisfy the wizard by masking the CPUID in the CPU settings of each VM on the host, as shown in Figure 17-2.

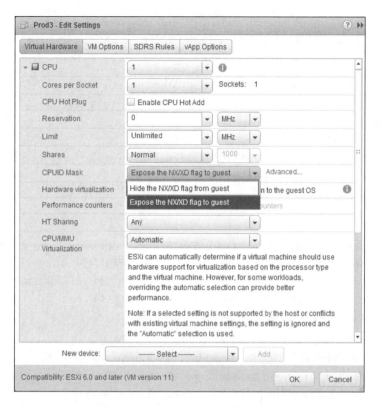

**Figure 17-2**   Hiding the Host's NX/XD Flag from the Guest OS

An easier way to improve CPU compatibility between hosts of varying feature sets is to configure Enhanced vMotion Compatibility (EVC) on your cluster. EVC ensures that all hosts in your cluster present the same feature set to VMs, even if the actual CPUs on the host differ from each other. When you configure EVC, you are telling all host processors to present a feature set of the baseline processor. This feature set is referred to as the *EVC mode*. As you might remember, you can configure EVC in your cluster, but only if certain compatibility requirements are met first. The following are the compatibility requirements for EVC:

- All VMs that are running on the cluster with a feature set greater than that of the EVC mode you intend to enable must be powered off or migrated out of the cluster before EVC is enabled.

- All hosts in the cluster must have CPUs from a single vendor, either AMD or Intel (not both).

- All hosts in the cluster must be running ESX/ESXi 3.5 Update 2 or later.

- All hosts in the cluster must be connected to the vCenter System.

- All hosts in the cluster must have advanced CPU features, such as hardware virtualization support (AMD-V or Intel VT) and AMD No eXecute (NX) or Intel eXecute Disable (XD), enabled in the BIOS if they are available.

- All hosts in the cluster should be configured for vMotion.

- All hosts in the cluster must have supported CPUs for the EVC mode you want to enable.

Any new host that is added to the cluster after EVC is enabled must also meet these requirements.

## Long-Distance vMotion

When I first started teaching about vMotion with ESX 3.5 hosts and Virtual Center 2.5, the "magic" pretty much stopped in the local-area network (LAN). In other words, the technology worked within the "walls" of the LAN, but how could it possibly be extended to the WAN? After all, it required shared storage and a shared Layer 2 network, right?

Technologies have progressed, and we now have shared storage on the "cloud" as a common resource. In addition, VMware has made advancements that allow for vMotion in environments that do not have shared storage and that have higher latencies than what was possible in the past. This, combined with the newer technologies such as VXLAN (which is beyond the scope of this text), allow us to create a Layer 2 network that stretches across multiple Layer 3 networks.

For these reasons, it's now possible to vMotion VMs from New York to California! That's right, intracontinental long-distance vMotion is supported with vSphere 6! Now, to take advantage of this option, your network must meet the following criteria:

- You must have an Enterprise Plus vSphere license.

- Latency must be a round-trip time (RTT) of 150 milliseconds or less.

- Both hosts must exist in the same Layer 2 environment, which means that a VXLAN-based technology such as NSX must be used.

## Snapshot Requirements for vMotion/Storage vMotion Migration

Basically, a *snapshot* is a capture of the state of a VM at a specific point in time. As you should remember, the state can include settings, disk, and memory. Until vSphere 5.0, it was important to know that you could use vMotion to migrate VMs that had VM snapshots but that you could not use Storage vMotion to move VM files. The reason was that the technologies that worked with VM snapshots and those that worked with Storage vMotion were "oil and water"; in other words, they didn't "blend" well together. Starting with vSphere 5.0, the technologies and methods used for Storage vMotion VM files have changed completely, so on vSphere 6.0 you can use Storage vMotion on VMs that have snapshots. If you think about it, this had to be done if Storage DRS was going to be used. Otherwise, how would the system automatically move VM files from one datastore to another on a datastore cluster if the administrator was using snapshots at the same time?

# Migrating Virtual Machines Using vMotion/Storage vMotion

As mentioned earlier, this objective about migrating virtual machines is broken up into two objectives to stress that these are two different features in vSphere. First you learn about the process of migrating VMs using vMotion, and then the process of migrating VM files using Storage vMotion is covered.

### Migrating a VM Using vMotion

When I say that we are migrating the VM, I am saying that the state of the VM is moving from one host to another host. When you do this with the VM powered on, by definition, it's vMotion. I've heard some people use this term improperly by saying, "We vMotioned them, but we powered them down first." You should understand clearly that what they did was a cold migration, not an actual vMotion.

However, you know that DRS uses vMotion to balance loads automatically, but what if you want to initiate the process yourself? If your hosts, your VMs, and your network meet all the requirements for vMotion, the process is easy. For example, to vMotion a VM from one host to another on the same cluster, follow the steps outlined in Activity 17-1.

---

**Activity 17-1   Migrating a VM Using vMotion**

1. Log on to your vSphere client.

2. Select **Home** and then **Hosts and Clusters**.

3. Right-click the powered-on VM that you want to vMotion and select **Migrate**, as shown in Figure 17-3.

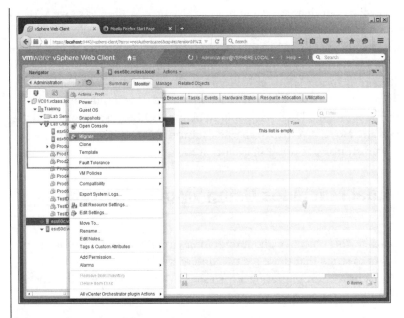

**Figure 17-3**    Migrating a VM with vMotion

4. On the Select Migration Type page, select the option button for **Change VM Compute Resource Only**, as shown in Figure 17-4, and then click **Next**.

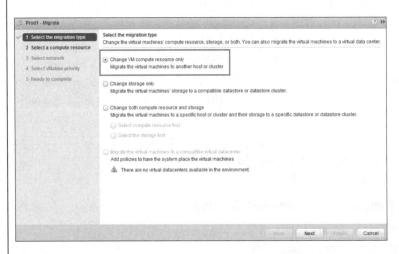

**Figure 17-4**    Selecting to Migrate the State of the VM to a Different Compute Resource

5. Choose the host, cluster, resource pool, or vApp to which you want to migrate the VM, in this case esx60a.vclass.local; verify compatibility, as shown in Figure 17-5; and click **Next**.

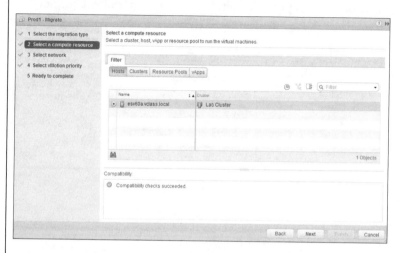

**Figure 17-5**    Destination Choice and Compatibility Check

6. Select the destination network to which you want to connect the VM, as shown in Figure 17-6, and click **Next**. (In vSphere 6, you can select Advanced to migrate to another vDS.)

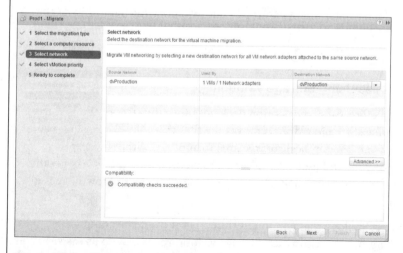

**Figure 17-6**    Choosing the Destination Network

7. Choose between reserving CPU resources first or performing with available CPU resources, as shown in Figure 17-7, and click **Next**. The first (default) option is almost always the right choice because you are performing this manually as a step in a process; therefore, you want it to work (or not) right now!

**Figure 17-7**   Choosing Whether to Perform with Reserved CPU or Without

8. Review your settings, and click **Finish**.

9. Monitor your Recent Tasks pane and your inventory for the results of the vMotion.

### Migrating a VM's Files Using Storage vMotion

As I mentioned before, Storage vMotion does not move the state of the VM from one host to another. Storage vMotion moves the files that the VM is using, while it's using them, from one physical storage area to another, without disrupting your VM's OS or your end users. As discussed earlier, migrating this way greatly enhances your flexibility when making changes to storage due to growth, ages of disk, and so on.

It's such a cool technology that you might think that it would be complicated to use, but you would not be correct. In fact, Storage vMotion is as easy to use as vMotion. To Storage vMotion a VM's files from one datastore connected to your vSphere to another, follow the steps outlined in Activity 17-2.

## Activity 17-2   Migrating a VM's Files Using Storage vMotion

1. Log on to your vSphere Web Client.

2. Select **Home** and then **Hosts and Clusters**.

3. Right-click the powered-on VM that you want to Storage vMotion and select **Migrate**.

4. On the Select Migration Type page, select the option button for **Change Storage Only**, as shown in Figure 17-8, and then click **Next**. Note that the option Change Both Host and Datastore at the same time is available on the vSphere Web Client, even though it's grayed out on the Windows-based vSphere Client. Isn't that interesting?

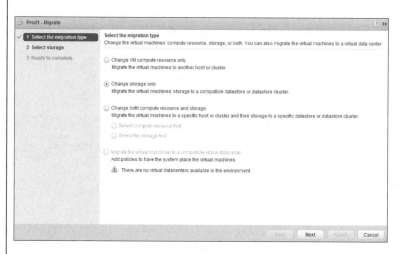

**Figure 17-8**   Selecting to Migrate the VM's Files to a Different Datastore

5. Select the destination datastore or datastore cluster on your inventory and the disk format for the datastore, wait for validation of compatibility, as shown in Figure 17-9, and click **Next**. Note that you can also specify a specific VM Storage Policy.

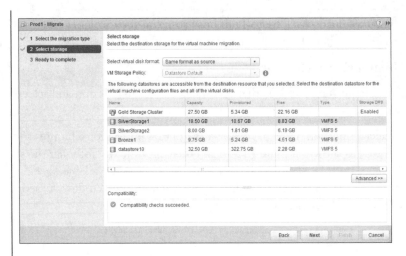

**Figure 17-9**    Selecting the Destination Datastore

> **6.** Review your settings, as shown in Figure 17-10, and click **Finish**.

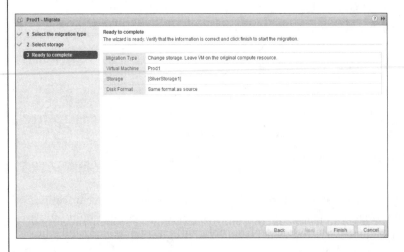

**Figure 17-10**    The Review Selections Page

> **7.** Monitor your Recent Tasks pane and your inventory for the results of the Storage vMotion.

## Configuring Virtual Machine Swap File Location

This might seem like a funny place to discuss the VM swap file, but there is a method to my madness, and it's not just because of the exam blueprint this time. The VM swap file is created when a VM is powered on and deleted when a VM is powered off. Its size is equal to the available memory of the VM (what the guest OS is told that it has) minus the reservation assigned to the VM.

So, what does the VM swap file have to do with vMotion? For vMotion to succeed, the VM swap file that was created by the source host must be visible to the destination host (shared) or must be created on the destination host before the migration can begin. This usually means that the VM swap file is stored in the same location with the other VM files. Now, you might think that having to create a new swap file would slow down migration significantly, and you would be right, unless you used the right kinds of drives for the VM swap files. What is slower than RAM but still much faster than conventional disk? That's right, solid state drives (SSDs).

If you are using local SSDs, you might want to allow the host to provide the swap file locally. This could provide better performance in the event that the swap file is used when memory is in serious contention. If you are using a conventional disk, make sure that the datastore containing the swap file is shared by the source and destination hosts; otherwise, your vMotion performance might be degraded. You can configure this option on the cluster as a default and then you can make changes further down in your hierarchy by configuring it on the host and even on the individual VM. Figures 17-11, 17-12, and 17-13 show the three places where you can configure the location of your VM swap files.

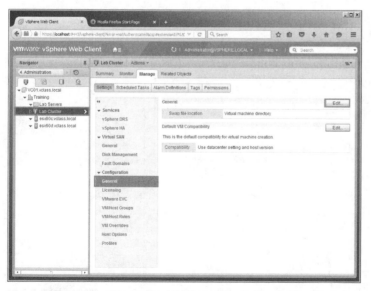

**Figure 17-11**   Configuring the VM Swap File Setting in the Cluster

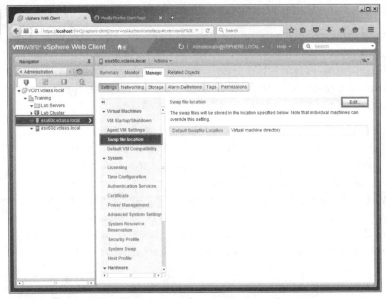

**Figure 17-12**    Configuring the VM Swap File Setting on the Host

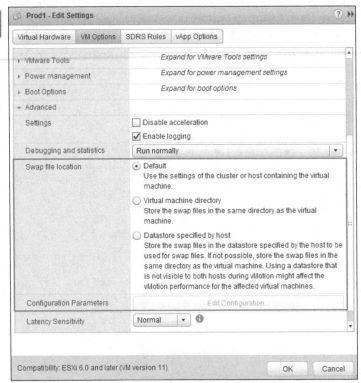

**Figure 17-13**    Configuring the VM Swap File Setting on the VM

# Migrating a Powered-Off or Suspended Virtual Machine

Again, migrating a powered-off or suspended virtual machine is really two objectives, but they are similar enough this time that I'll handle them as one. The main thing you should realize is that a suspended VM is still running a CPU instruction set and therefore must meet the CPU compatibility requirements just like a VM that is being vMotioned. Other than that, migrating a VM that is powered off or suspended is incredibly simple, and there are very few limitations. You can even migrate a VM's state to another host at the same time you migrate its files to another datastore (on either client), as shown in Figure 17-14.

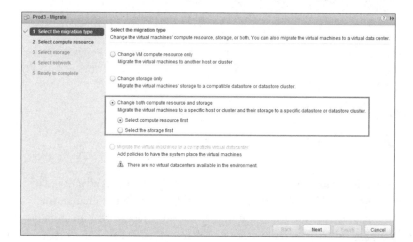 

**Figure 17-14**   Cold Migrating the VM Host and Datastore at the Same Time

### Utilizing Storage vMotion Techniques

I already discussed the main reason that Storage vMotion was created: to make it easier to move the VM's files from one datastore to another while the VM was powered on. This is likely the main reason that you will use Storage vMotion in your vCenter. However, you might find that some of the options that are given to you when you Storage vMotion can come in handy if you need to make a change but really don't need to move the VM's files at all. In addition, one of the side effects might interest you as well.

As you might have noticed when we did the Storage vMotion exercise earlier in this chapter, you were given the choice of virtual disk format on the Storage page of the wizard, as shown in Figure 17-15. What if you just want to change the virtual disk on a VM from thick-provisioned eager-zeroed to thin-provisioned (for example)? Could you move the VM files to another location just to make that change? Yes, you could; in fact, any change in disk provisioning is possible. Then, if you want them back where they were, you can Storage vMotion again. Remember that you are not disrupting the user, at least not directly.

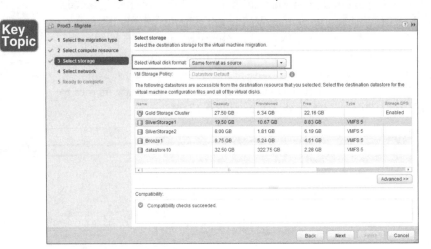

**Figure 17-15**    Changing Disk Format During Storage vMotion

Here's another example of using Storage vMotion creatively by taking advantage of a side effect of moving the VM files. Suppose that you have decided to change the display name of a VM so that it shows up differently in your inventory. You should know that just changing the display name does not change the VM filenames that are in the datastore. However (as of vSphere 5.5), if you Storage vMotion the VM files to another datastore, the VM's folder name and the files within it are changed to match that of the new display name that you've given the VM. Now, the NetBIOS name and hostname are not changed, and you are on your own there. In fact, that's a good reason to seriously consider your options before you change a display name on a VM.

## Summary

This chapter covered the following main topics:

- The requirements for vMotion and Storage vMotion. In addition, EVC, snapshots, and swap files as they relate to vMotion were discussed. You examined the capabilities of Storage vMotion with regard to changing virtual disk type and renaming VMs. I addition, you learned about the newest capabilities of vMotion, such as Long Distance and Cross-Switch vMotion.

- The capabilities of Storage vMotion with regard to changing virtual disk type and renaming VMs. Finally, you learned about Cross-Host vMotion and its additional capabilities.

## Exam Preparation Tasks

## Review All the Key Topics

Review the most important topics from the chapter, noted with the Key Topic icon in the outer margin of the page. Table 17-2 lists these key topics and the page numbers where each is found.

**Table 17-2**   Key Topics for Chapter 17

| Key Topic Element | Description | Page Number |
| --- | --- | --- |
| Bullet List | Components in the state of a VM | 405 |
| Bullet List | Host Requirements for vMotion | 405 |
| Bullet List | VM Requirements for vMotion | 406 |
| Bullet List | Advantages of Storage vMotion | 406 |
| Bullet List | Capabilities of Enhanced vMotion | 407 |
| Figure 17-1 | Migrating a VM's Host and Datastore at the Same Time | 408 |
| Bullet List | Components of a CPU Feature Set | 408 |
| Figure 17-2 | Hiding the Host's NX/XD Flag from the Guest OS | 409 |
| Bullet List | Compatibility Requirements for EVC | 409 |
| Bullet List | Requirements for Long-Distance vMotion | 410 |
| Activity 17-1 | Migrating a VM Using vMotion | 411 |
| Activity 17-2 | Migrating a VM's Files Using Storage vMotion | 415 |
| Figure 17-11 | Configuring the VM Swap File Setting in the Cluster | 417 |
| Figure 17-12 | Configuring the VM Swap File Setting on the Host | 418 |
| Figure 17-13 | Configuring the VM Swap File Setting on the VM | 418 |
| Figure 17-14 | Cold Migrating a VM Host and Datastore at the Same Time | 419 |
| Figure 17-15 | Changing Disk Format During Storage vMotion | 420 |

## Review Questions

The answers to these review questions are in Appendix A.

1. An administrator uses Storage vMotion to migrate a VM. Which of the following will occur? (Choose two.)

   a. The state of the VM will remain on the same host.

   b. The VMs files will remain on the same datastore.

   c. The state of the VM will move from one host to another host.

   d. The VM files will move from one datastore to another one.

2. An administrator of a vSphere network with a Standard license attempts to vMotion a VM but receives an error message indicating the vMotion is not enabled. Which of the following could be the cause of this message?

   a. There is no shared storage configured.

   b. The VMkernel port intended for vMotion is not enabled for vMotion.

   c. There is not enough memory to provide for vMotion.

   d. vMotion requires an Enterprise Plus license.

3. Which of the following would prevent an administrator from using vMotion? (Choose two.)

   a. The VMkernel port is not enabled for vMotion.

   b. The vSphere uses a Standard license.

   c. The host does not have visibility to the destination datastore.

   d. The CPU of one host is not compatible with the other.

4. Which of the following are part of a CPU feature set? (Choose two.)

   a. Host CPU vendor, family, and model

   b. VM CPU vendor, family, and model

   c. ESXi version running on the host

   d. Power state of VM

5. Which of the following would prevent long-distance vMotion from operating properly? (Choose two.)

   a. RTT of 50ms

   b. A vSphere Enterprise Plus license

   c. RTT of 160 ms

   d. No common Layer 2 environment

6. Which of the following is *not* a part of a snapshot?

    a. Settings state

    b. Disk state

    c. Memory state

    d. VM backup

7. Which of the following are *not* true in regard to vMotion and Storage vMotion with vSphere 6?

    a. You can vMotion a VM that contains snapshots.

    b. You cannot Storage vMotion a VM that contains snapshots.

    c. You cannot vMotion a VM that contains snapshots.

    d. You can Storage vMotion a VM that contains snapshots.

8. Which of the following would prevent a VM from using vMotion?

    a. An internal switch on its host, to which the VM is not connected

    b. A snapshot that has not been deleted

    c. A swap file that is shared between the hosts

    d. A VMkernel port that is not enabled for vMotion

9. Which of the following are true regarding Storage vMotion? (Choose two.)

    a. By definition, you cannot Storage vMotion a VM that is powered off.

    b. You can Storage vMotion a VM, whether it is powered on or off.

    c. Storage vMotion will always move the files of a VM to another location.

    d. Storage vMotion will never move the files of a VM to another location.

10. Which of the following are *not* true? (Choose two.)

    a. To cold migrate a VM's files, you must first power off the VM.

    b. You can cold migrate a VM's files with a VM powered on or off.

    c. The cold migration of the state of a VM is referred to as vMotion.

    d. Cold migration of the state of a VM happens with the VM is powered off.

**This chapter covers the following subjects:**

- Snapshot Requirements

- VMware Data Protection Requirements and Sizing Guidelines

- VMware Data Protection Version Offerings

- vSphere Replication Architecture

- Creating/Deleting/Consolidating Virtual Machine Snapshots

- Installing and Configuring VMware Data Protection

- Creating a Backup Job with VMware Data Protection

- Installing, Configuring, and Upgrading vSphere Replication

- Configuring Replication for Single/Multiple VMs

- Recovering a VM Using vSphere Replication

- Performing a Failback Operation Using vSphere Replication

- Determining an Appropriate Backup Solution for a Given vSphere Implementation

Here's a question for you. What percentage of your VMs are software? I hope you answered 100%. Because 100% of your VMs are software, and because they are the type of software that you really don't want to take a chance on losing, you should perform regular backups of your VM files. This chapter discusses many aspects regarding backing up and restoring VMs.

## CHAPTER 18

# Backing Up and Restoring Virtual Machines

It begins by identifying snapshot requirements as they relate to backing up and restoring VMs. You learn how to create, delete, and consolidate VM snapshots. In addition, you learn about VMware Data Protection (VDP), which is a backup appliance designed primarily for small- to medium-sized companies. You also learn how to install and configure VDP and how to create a backup job using the VDP appliance and an add-on named File Level Restore (FLR). The chapter also discusses a new way to create another copy of your VMs for disaster recovery, called vSphere Replication. Finally, you learn about your options with regard to backups and how to determine the most appropriate backup solution for your vSphere implementation.

## "Do I Know This Already?" Quiz

The "Do I Know This Already?" quiz allows you to assess whether you should read this entire chapter or simply jump to the "Exam Preparation Tasks" section for review. If you are in doubt, read the entire chapter. Table 18-1 outlines the major headings in this chapter and the corresponding "Do I Know This Already?" quiz questions. You can find the answers in Appendix A, "Answers to the 'Do I Know This Already?' Quizzes and Chapter Review Questions."

**Table 18-1**   "Do I Know This Already?" Section-to-Question Mapping

| Foundation Topics Section | Questions Covered in This Section |
|---|---|
| Snapshot Requirements | 1 |
| VMware Data Protection Requirements and Sizing Guidelines | 2 |
| VMware Data Protection Version Offerings | 3 |
| vSphere Replication Architecture | 4 |
| Creating/Deleting/Consolidating Virtual Machine Snapshots | 5 |
| Installing and Configuring VMware Data Protection | 6 |
| Creating a Backup Job with VMware Data Protection | 7 |
| Installing, Configuring, and Upgrading vSphere Replication | 8 |
| Configuring Replication for Single/Multiple VMs | 9 |
| Recovering a VM Using vSphere Replication | 10 |
| Performing a Failback Operation Using vSphere Replication | 11 |
| Determining an Appropriate Backup Solution for a Given vSphere Implementation | 12 |

1. As the administrator of a virtual data center, you are using snapshots. Which of the following are true? (Choose two.)

    a. You are using snapshots to replace the need for backups.

    b. You should delete the snapshots when you no longer need them.

    c. You might use snapshots as part of a backup solution.

    d. Snapshots should never be deleted because they are used as part of the restore process.

2. You are the administrator in charge of a virtual data center that has about 50 server VMs and 5 hosts. Which of the following are true? (Choose two.)

    a. You cannot use VDP because your environment is too large.

    b. You cannot use the VADP API because your environment is too small.

    c. You can use VDP with your current license.

    d. You can have a maximum of 2 TB worth of deduplicated data storage.

3. You have installed VDP 6.0 on your Standard licensed vSphere environment. Which of the following are true? (Choose two.)

   a. You need to upgrade to Enterprise Plus to use the advanced features of VDP.

   b. You need to upgrade your VDP option to use the advanced features.

   c. Your current license supports the use of advanced VDP features.

   d. Your current VDP version supports the use of advanced features.

4. You have just installed vSphere Replication for your two-site infrastructure. Which of the following are true? (Choose two.)

   a. You installed only one instance of vSphere Replication: which was then connected to your remote site.

   b. You installed two instances of vSphere Replication: one on the primary site and a second at the secondary site.

   c. After the appliance is installed at each location, it will require extensive configuration and testing before it can be used effectively.

   d. After the appliance is installed at each location, it is ready to go without further configuration, but it can be "tweaked" on the VAMI if necessary.

5. Which of the following files is essentially "frozen" when you take the first snapshot of a VM?

   a. -delta.vmdk

   b. .vsmn

   c. .vswp

   d. -flat.vmdk

6. As an administrator of a small virtual data center, you have just installed VDP. Which of the following are true? (Choose two.)

   a. You need to install a plug-in to your vSphere Client to configure the software.

   b. You can configure the appliance through its web interface.

   c. You can connect to the appliance at the address that was provided by DHCP at the time of the installation.

   d. You need to connect to the appliance at the static address that you supplied during the installation.

7. You have just installed and configured VDP and now want to perform a backup. Which of the following are true? (Choose two.)

   a. You use the same web interface that you used to configure the appliance to perform the backup.

   b. You use the vSphere Web Client to perform the backup.

   c. You should find the VDP plug-in under the Administration section of the vSphere Web Client.

   d. You should find the VDP plug-in under the Solutions and Applications section of the vSphere Web Client.

8. Which of the following are true regarding vSphere Replication in vSphere 6.0?

   a. vSphere Replication is included in the base installation of vSphere 6.0 and only needs to be activated.

   b. You can install vSphere Replication by deploying an OVA.

   c. vSphere Replication can be configured only through the vSphere Client, just as SRM can be configured.

   d. You can configure vSphere Replication through the VAMI.

9. Which of the following are true regarding configuring vSphere Replication for VMs?

   a. Only the primary site needs to be a vSphere data center.

   b. The primary and secondary site must each be a vSphere data center.

   c. You can configure an RPO as tight as 5 minutes.

   d. The RPO setting will determine how up-to-date the secondary VM will stay on an ongoing basis.

10. You are the administrator of a small network that uses vSphere Replication. A VM on the primary site has just failed, and you want to recover to the secondary VM. Which of the following are true? (Choose two.)

    a. You need to use the thick vSphere Client and connect to SRM to manage replication.

    b. You use the vSphere Web Client to connect to vSphere Replication through the Home site.

    c. You can attempt to synchronize the secondary VM with the primary VM.

    d. You will not be given the option to synchronize the secondary VM with the primary VM.

11. Which of the following are true regarding failback of a VM in vSphere Replication? (Choose two.)

    a. Failback is typically not needed and therefore not supported.

    b. Failback is simply configuring replication to occur again in the reverse direction.

    c. You need to unregister the VM from the primary site before you configure the reverse direction replication.

    d. Unregistering the VM from the primary site is not necessary.

12. You are an administrator of an Enterprise Plus virtual data center with 100 hosts and 2000 VM servers. You are considering options such as VDP and vSphere Replication. Which of the following are true? (Choose two.)

    a. Your organization can still take advantage of the VADP API, even if you elect not to use VDP.

    b. You can use vSphere Replication to create a hot site for some selected VMs.

    c. Your organization is much too large to use vSphere Replication, VADP, or VDP in any manner.

    d. vSphere Replication is not supported at your license level.

## Foundation Topics

### Snapshot Requirements

First, you should understand that, even though we are discussing snapshots in a section regarding backups, *snapshots* should never be regarded as *backups*. However, backup software often takes a snapshot as part of the process of creating a backup. The reason is that backing up the snapshot is efficient and allows for a static image of the VM. In addition, vSphere can provide an incremental backup mechanism called *changed block tracking*, which saves backup time and disk storage space. Typically, after a backup is performed from the snapshot, the snapshot is deleted.

### VMware Data Protection Requirements and Sizing Guidelines

VMware has never really been in the "backup business" for enterprise. Most large companies have opted for a third-party solution that suits their backup needs and might very well use the API that VMware has provided for data protection (VADP). However, for small- to medium-size companies, VMware has provided a backup appliance that is included with all vSphere editions except for Essentials. The appliance works along with vCenter and the vSphere Web Client to provide a backup solution, as illustrated in Figure 18-1. The name of this appliance is VMware Data Protection (VDP).

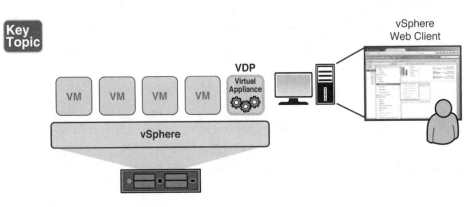

**Figure 18-1**   The Components of VDP

The requirements to install VDP are as follows:

- VMware vCenter Server 5.1 or later
- vSphere Web Client
- Web Browser with Adobe Flash Player
- ESX/ESXi 4.0 or higher hosts

### VMware Data Protection Sizing Guidelines

You can use VDP to create backups of VMs without interrupting their use. It also supports deduplication to remove redundant data and make more efficient use of disk space. In vSphere 6.0, new compression algorithms are used to improve performance and save space.

VDP is integrated with vCenter Server using the vSphere Web Client, allowing you to centralize the scheduling of backup jobs. The deduplication datastores can be virtual machine disks (VMDKs), Raw Device Mappings (RDMs), or Common Internet File System (CIFS) shares. You can have a maximum of 2 TB of deduplicated data storage. Each backup job can contain a maximum of 100 VMs, but you can back up only 8 VMs simultaneously. In addition, each vCenter can manage up to 10 VDP appliances, each with 100 VMs.

VDP can be installed in three configurations—basically small, medium, and large, as outlined in Table 18-2.

**Table 18-2**  Minimum System Requirements for VDP

|  | **.5 TB** | **1 TB** | **2 TB** |
|---|---|---|---|
| **Processors** | Minimum four 2 GHz | Minimum four 2 GHz | Minimum four 2 GHz |
| **Memory** | 4 GB | 4 GB | 4 GB |
| **Disk Space** | 873 GB | 1,600 GB | 3,100 GB |

You should take care to make the right decision, because after you deploy your VDP, you cannot change the size. Some of the factors that you should consider are the following:

- **Number of VMs:** On average, you can support about 25 VMs per TB of capacity.
- **Types of VMs:** For example, do the VMs contain a large database?
- **Your retention period:** Daily, weekly, monthly, yearly.
- **Typical change rate:** Changed Block Tracking will help tremendously when the change rate is low.

## VMware Data Protection Version Offerings

Before vSphere 6.0 and vSphere Data Protection 6.0, there were two editions of vSphere Data Protection: vSphere Data Protection, included with vSphere, and vSphere Data Protection Advanced, which was sold separately. However, with the release of vSphere Data Protection 6.0, all vSphere Data Protection Advanced functionality has been consolidated into vSphere Data Protection 6.0 and included with vSphere 6.0 Essentials Plus Kit and higher editions. These advancements include new compression algorithms and the capability to have automated test restores.

## vSphere Replication Architecture

The vSphere Replication appliance provides all the components required to perform vSphere Replication. These include a plug-in to the vSphere Client, an embedded database, a vSphere Replication Management Server, and a vSphere Replication Server. You deploy one instance of the appliance at your primary site and another one at your secondary site.

After the appliances are deployed, the vSphere Replication is ready to go without further configuration. However, there is a Virtual Appliance Management Interface (VAMI) that connects to the vSphere Replication appliance for additional configuration if needed. For example, you can use the VAMI to change security settings, change network settings, and configure an external database. Figure 18-2 shows the architecture of vSphere Replication.

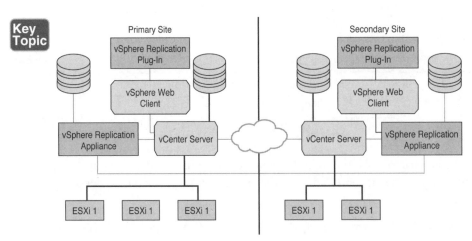

**Figure 18-2**   vSphere Replication Architecture

# Creating/Deleting/Consolidating Virtual Machine Snapshots

If you wanted to perform all the backup steps yourself, rather than use third-party backup software, you could. You would first have to understand how to create snapshots. After you created them, you could copy the snapshots for the backup and finally delete them. In this section, you learn about the process of creating, deleting, and consolidating snapshots. You can use what you learn here for snapshots used for backups or just to create snapshots when testing software.

When you create a snapshot, you create a static capture of the VM at a specific point in time. The -flat.vmdk file on your VM is in essence "frozen," and a delta.vmdk file begins to record changes. Every time you take another snapshot, a descriptor is used to note the amount of the delta.vmdk file that should be used in addition to the -flat.vmdk file to revert to a specific point. The -flat.vmdk file and a portion of the delta.vmdk file can then be used to revert to any point in time as defined by the descriptor file with an extension of .vmsd. If you have chosen to include VM memory in your snapshot, another file with an extension of .vmsn is also created. Including memory with a snapshot takes longer, but you can then revert the VM to a previous state without it having to be powered off and restarted. If you don't have memory included in a snapshot, when you revert to a previous state, the VM will power down and "make its own memories" when you power it back up.

Now that you have a brief understanding of what happens when you take a snapshot, you'll look at the process of taking one. You can use this same process to take snapshots for backups or for any other use. To create a snapshot of your VM, follow the steps outlined in Activity 18-1.

---

**Activity 18-1   Creating a VM Snapshot**

1. Log on to your vSphere Web Client.

2. Select **Home** and then **VMs and Templates**.

3. Right-click the VM that you want to snapshot and select **Snapshots**, and then **Take Snapshot**, as shown in Figure 18-3.

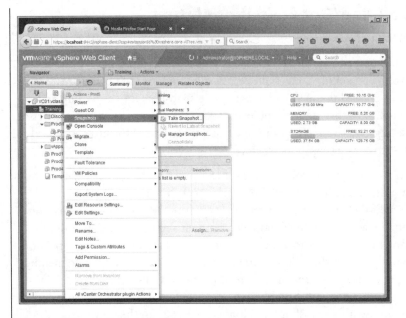

**Figure 18-3**    Taking a VM Snapshot

4. Type a name and description for your snapshot (usually defined by its purpose), and then choose whether to snapshot the VM memory and quiesce (quiet or pause) the guest file system. It's best to quiesce the guest file system if the snapshot will be used as part of a backup, because it will allow you to get a static image of the VM. You must have VMware tools installed on the VM to use this option. Finally, click **OK**, as shown in Figure 18-4.

**Figure 18-4**   Naming a Snapshot and Selecting Options

5. Monitor the progress of your snapshot in the Recent Tasks pane, as shown in Figure 18-5. Snapshots with memory will take longer to complete, but you can revert to them without restarting the VM.

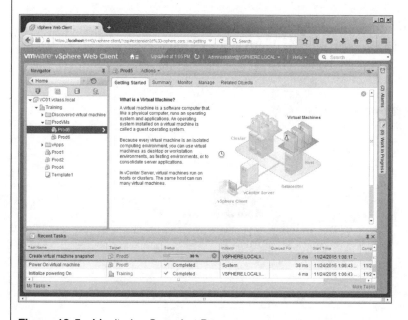

**Figure 18-5**   Monitoring Snapshot Progress

6. When the snapshot is complete, right-click the same VM and select **Snapshots**, **Manage Snapshots**, as shown in Figure 18-6.

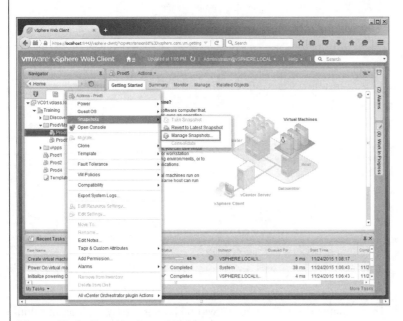

**Figure 18-6** Entering Snapshot Manager

7. In Snapshot Manager, you can view the snapshots that you've taken and their relationship to each other, as shown in Figure 18-7.

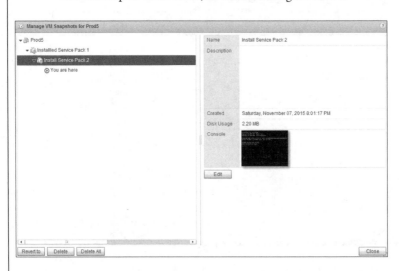

**Figure 18-7** Snapshot Manager

Now that you know how to create snapshots, it's important that you know how to delete them. Leaving snapshots on a VM for long periods of time can consume the rest of your disk because the delta.vmdk file will continue to grow with every activity that happens on the disk and can take up all the unallocated space on the drive. Because of this, it's important that you know how to delete snapshots and how to consolidate them when necessary.

You might think that deleting a snapshot would be as simple as selecting it and selecting **Delete**, and you would be half right. You should understand that what really happens to the effect of the snapshot depends on where the You Are Here indicator is when you delete the snapshot. The You Are Here indicator is the current state of the VM, and its position relative to the snapshot makes all the difference. To illustrate this point, see the series of snapshots in Figure 18-8.

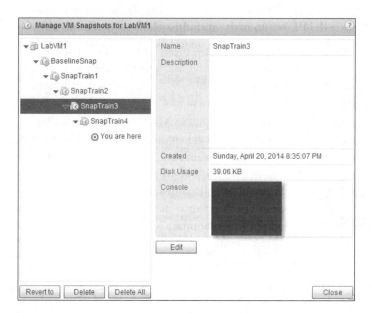

**Figure 18-8**   A Series of Snapshots

In this example, I took four snapshots of LabVM1 in addition to my BaselineSnap snapshot, SnapTrain1—SnapTrain4. I made subtle changes to the configuration before I took each snapshot in succession. The specific changes that I made are not important, just the fact that I made some changes. (If you were doing this, maybe you added some software or changed a setting.) For contrast, both the base image and SnapTrain1 included the memory, as indicated by the green arrow. Snap-Train2 through SnapTrain4 did not include the memory. After I took SnapTrain4, I reverted back to SnapTrain3 by selecting it and clicking **Revert To** and then restarting LabVM1.

Now, if I were to position my mouse pointer on SnapTrain4 and select **Delete**, what would happen? You may have guessed that SnapTrain4 would be deleted. Because it is after the You Are Here indicator, you would be right. SnapTrain4 would be gone and forgotten. Any configuration that it and only it contained would be lost.

Now, if I were to position my mouse pointer on any of the snapshots before the You Are Here indicator and select **Delete**, what would happen with them? The answer is, the snapshots would be gone, but their effect would still be committed to the current state of the VM. In fact, if I were to select **Delete All**, no matter where my mouse pointer happened to be, all the snapshots would be deleted, but the ones after the You Are Here indicator would be deleted and forgotten while the ones before the You Are Here indicator would be deleted but "remembered." In other words, any configuration changes that they included would have already been rolled in to the current state of the VM. Just deleting the snapshot would not change that fact.

I hope this simple scenario has helped you to see the true nature of VM snapshots and realize that they are not meant to be kept around like a template. In fact, because of a known issue that causes a VM's snapshots to fail to commit and therefore do away with the delta.vmdk file, you have a new tool in vSphere that you can use to consolidate the snapshots. To determine whether a VM has snapshots that need consolidating, you can add the column to your Virtual Machines tab, as shown in Figure 18-9.

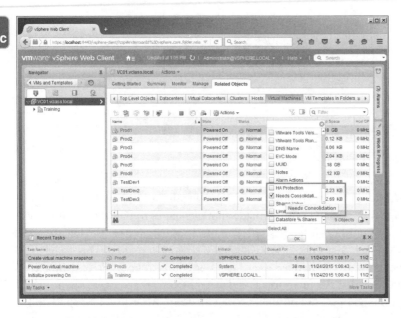

**Figure 18-9** Adding a Needs Consolidation Column to the Virtual Machines Tab

The new column will indicate whether consolidation is required. If a VM indicates that it needs consolidation, you can take the appropriate action. To consolidate snapshots on the VM, right-click and select **Snapshots**, **Consolidate**, as shown in Figure 18-10. Note that if a VM's snapshots do need consolidation, the Consolidate option will not be grayed out.

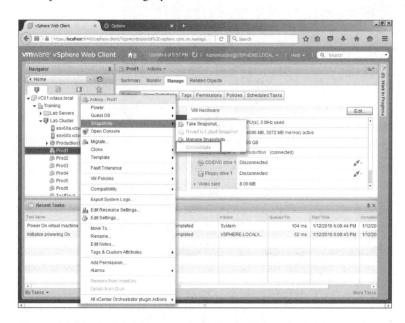

**Figure 18-10**  Consolidating the VM's Snapshots

# Installing and Configuring VMware Data Protection

The installation of VDP can be described in three major steps, as follows:

1. Acquire and deploy the VDP appliance .ova package.

2. Configure the appliance through its web interface.

3. Add a hard disk to the backup appliance, if needed. You can download an ISO or OVA file from http://www.vmware.com and burn a CD with all the files that you need. To deploy VDP, follow the steps outlined in Activity 18-2.

---

**Activity 18-2    Deploying VDP**

1. Log on to your vSphere Web Client.

2. Select **Home** and then **VMs and Templates**.

3. Right-click your data center and click **Deploy OVF Template**, as shown in Figure 18-11.

**Figure 18-11**   Deploying an OVF Template

4. If prompted, allow the installation of the VMware Client Integration Plug-In, as shown in Figure 18-12.

**Figure 18-12**   Loading the Client Integration Plug-In

5. Browse to the source of the VDP Appliance OVA package to load the OVA.

6. Accept any EULAs and click **Next**.

7. Enter the name of the VDP Appliance that matches the DNS server name (hostname) that you have assigned in DNS. Click **Next**.

8. On Select a Resource, select the host for the VDP appliance. Click **Next**.

9. On Select Storage, select the virtual disk format and location for your VDP appliance. Click **Next**.

10. On Setup Networks, select the destination network. Click **Next**.

11. On Customize, specify the hostname, static IP, and subnet mask for the VDP. The VDP does not support DHCP. Click **Next**.

12. On Ready to Complete, confirm that all options are correct. Check **Power On After Deployment** and click **Finish**.

## Creating a Backup Job with VMware Data Protection

After you have completed the installation and configuration of VDP, you are ready to create a backup job. You should find VDP under Solutions and Applications in your Home panel. From there, it's just a matter of connecting to the virtual appliance and selecting the VMs to back up. When you have properly installed the VDP appliance and then connected to it with your vSphere Client and the enabled plug-in, you can choose VMs on the network to back up, just as you would any other files, as shown in Figure 18-13.

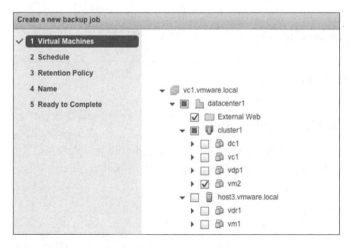

**Figure 18-13**  Backing Up VMs with VDP

# Installing, Configuring, and Upgrading vSphere Replication

vSphere Replication was introduced with vSphere 5.1. It is designed to help an organization augment its recovery capability by continually replicating a running virtual machine to another location. That location can be local or remote to the site of the running VM. It does not replace other more sophisticated products, such as Site Recovery Manager (SRM), but it can provide the replication engine that they use. It is provided at no charge as a component of all vSphere licenses from the Essentials Plus edition on up though Enterprise Plus. It is managed by the vSphere Web Client. In addition, it is fully integrated with Microsoft VSS to ensure the MS SQL and Exchange databases are quiescent and consistent when replica data is being generated.

The vSphere Replication appliance provides all the components that vSphere Replication needs, including the following:

- A plug-in to the vSphere Web Client that provides a user interface for vSphere Replication

- An embedded database that stores replication configuration and management information

- The vSphere Replication management server

- The vSphere Replication server

You can begin using vSphere Replication immediately after deploying the appliance. The virtual appliance management interface (VAMI) enables you to configure the appliance and change settings, such as security settings, network settings, external database, and so on.

To deploy the appliance, follow the steps outlined in Activity 18-3.

**Activity 18-3   Deploying vSphere Replication**

1. Log on to your vSphere Web Client.

2. Select **Home** and then **Hosts and Clusters**.

3. Right-click the cluster or host on that you want to deploy the template and select **Deploy OVF Template,** as shown in Figure 18-14. Click **Next.**

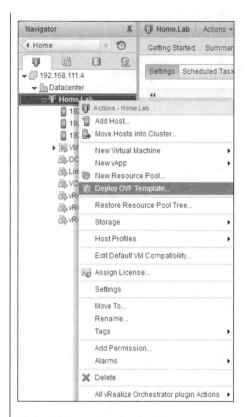

**Figure 18-14**    Deploy OVF Template

4. Browse for the OVF file and load it for installation.

5. Accept the EULA. Click **Next**.

6. Accept the default name and destination folder, or provide a new destination. Click **Next**.

7. In the configuration settings, select 2 vCPU or 4 vCPU, as shown in Figure 18-15. Click **Next**.

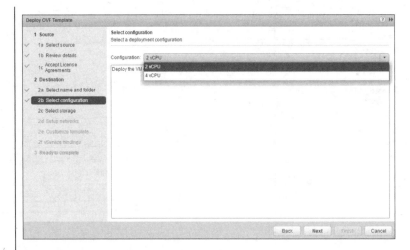

**Figure 18-15**    Configuration Settings

> **8.** Select the storage datastore. Click **Next**.
>
> **9.** Select the network. Click **Next**.
>
> **10.** On Customize Template, set the password (eight characters minimum), NTP server, and IP address (Static IP selected), as shown in Figure 18-16. Click **Next**.

**Figure 18-16**    Customize Template

11. Review the vService bindings and vCenter Extension Service, as shown in Figure 18-17. Click **Next**.

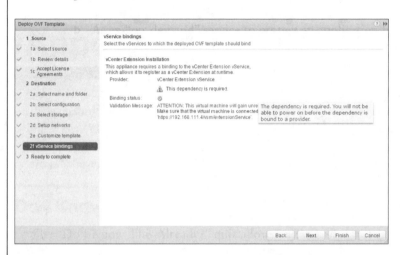

**Figure 18-17**   Review vService Bindings and vCenter Extension Service.

12. Select **Power On After Deployment**. Click **Finish**.

13. Register the vSphere Replication Appliance with vCenter Single Sign-On (SSO) by going to https://Your-VR-Appliance-Address:5480.

14. Log in with your credentials set when deploying the appliance.

15. Click the **Configuration** tab and in the **LookupService Address** box, enter the FQDN or IP address where the lookup service runs.

16. Enter vCenter SSO credentials and click **Save and Restart Service**, as shown in Figure 18-18. Ensure VRM service is running, as shown in Figure 18-18.

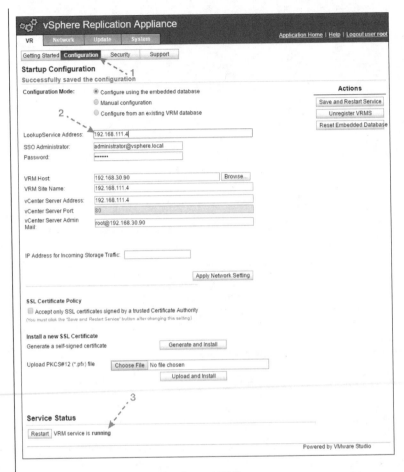

**Figure 18-18**   Replication Appliance VAMI

17. Finally, log off the vSphere Web Client and then back on, ensure that vSphere Replication is present on the Home screen, and repeat the procedure to install vSphere Replication to the target site.

# Configuring Replication for Single/Multiple VMs

To replicate VMs from source to target, both source and target must have a vSphere data center and the necessary resources to support VMs. In addition, the source and target machines must be able to connect to each other. When that is accomplished, configuring replication is a straightforward process. To configure replication for a single VM, you should do the following:

1. Right-click the VM and select **All vSphere Replication Actions** and then **Configure Replication**, as shown in Figure 18-19.

2. Select the target site.

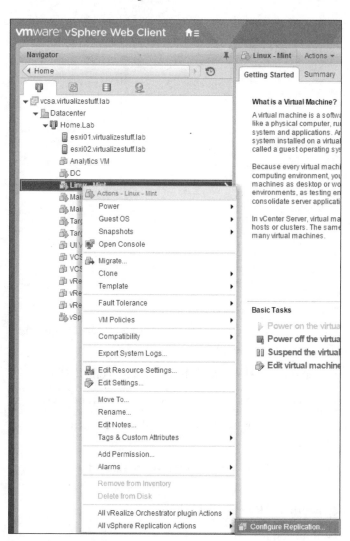

**Figure 18-19**  Configure Replication

3. Set the RPO using the slider. This range is from 15 minutes to 24 hours and will determine how up-to-date the VM will stay on an ongoing basis, as shown in Figure 18-20.

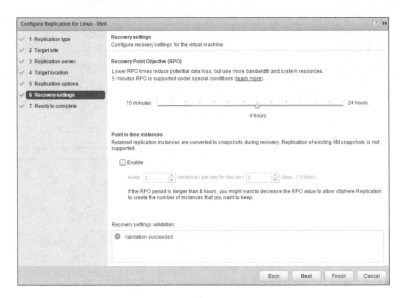

**Figure 18-20**   RPO Settings

4. Review the settings and click **Finish**.

You can also configure replication on multiple VMs using the multi-VM replication wizard. To configure replication for multiple VMs, you should do the following:

1. Select your data center and then select the **Related Objects** tab.

2. Click **Virtual Machines** and select multiple VMs using the Ctrl or Shift keys.

3. Right-click the group of VMs, click **All vSphere Replication Actions**, and then **Configure Replication**.

4. Acknowledge the number of VMs to replicate and verify validation. Click **Next**.

5. Select the target site and then RPO for all machines.

6. Review your settings and click **Finish**.

## Recovering a VM Using vSphere Replication

Having a target machine isn't much good if you can't restore it. Therefore, vSphere Replication is designed to make locating and restoring a target machine as simple as a few clicks. To restore a failed machine, you should do the following:

1. Log in to the target site with your vSphere Web Client and click **Home**, **vSphere Replication**, and then **Monitor**, as shown in Figure 18-21.

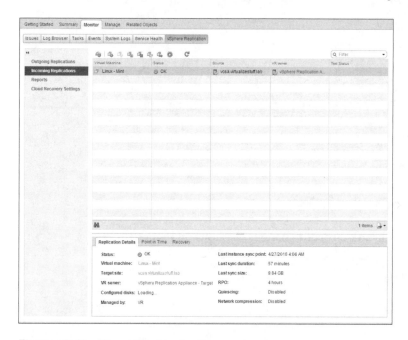

**Figure 18-21**   Target Site Monitor tab

2. On the Incoming Replications tab, right-click the VM to recover and select **Recover**, as shown in Figure 18-22.

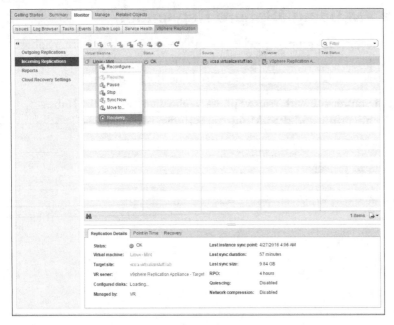

**Figure 18-22**   Target Site Incoming Replications

3. Select **Synchronize recent changes**, as shown in Figure 18-23.

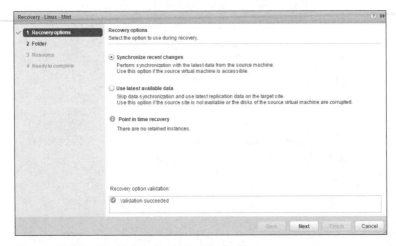

**Figure 18-23**   Target Site Configure Replication

4. Select the recovery folder. Click **Next**.

5. Select the target compute resource. Click **Next**.

6. Check the box if you would like to power on the VM after recovery, and click **Finish**.

## Performing a Failback Operation Using vSphere Replication

You can also perform a failback in vSphere Replication as a manual process. Basically, after performing a successful recovery from the primary site to the secondary site, you manually configure a new replication in the reverse direction—that is, from the secondary site to the primary site. The disks on the primary site are used as replication seeds so that vSphere Replication synchronizes only the changes made to the .vmdk files. However, before you configure the reverse replication, you must manually unregister the virtual machine from the inventory on the primary site.

## Determining an Appropriate Backup Solution for a Given vSphere Implementation

If your organization has more than 100 server VMs, the chances are good that you are using some type of third-party backup solution. There are a good number of them, and they usually offer some nice features, such as data deduplication, sometimes even at the source. VMware is more than happy to offer the application programming interfaces (APIs), such as vStorage API for Data Protection (VADP), so that you can use all the latest backup software that is designed for VMs. However, if you have a small organization with fewer than 100 server VMs, VDP might be just the tool for you to provide a relatively inexpensive backup solution that includes deduplication of data at the destination. vSphere Replication is also a great and inexpensive (really free) tool that you can use if you do not have a more complex and sophisticated system of creating a hot or warm site for your data center.

## Summary

This chapter covered the following main topics:

- A brief discussion of snapshots as they relate to backups. You learned that snapshots are often used as part of a backup process but that snapshots should never be considered a backup in and of themselves.

- The requirements for installing VMware Data Protection (VDP) and the sizing guidelines. You learned that VDP is primarily designed for small- to medium-size companies and that larger companies might opt for a third-party solution that used the VADP API provided by VMware. In addition, you learned that each VDP appliance can back up only 100 VMs simultaneously.

- There are no longer two editions of VDP as of vSphere 6.0. Instead, the elements that were earlier considered "advanced" have been rolled into the main product. These include new compression algorithms and the capability to do periodic automated test restores.

- vSphere Replication architecture. You learned that you install one instance of vSphere Replication at your primary site and another instance at your secondary site. Also, after installing vSphere Replication, you can make configuration changes using the Virtual Appliance Management Interface (VAMI).

- A general understanding of how to work with snapshots as they relate to backups. You learned how to create, delete, and consolidate snapshots.

- The installation of VDP, including the deployment of the OVA and the general configuration of the product. After that we walked through creating a simple backup job with VDP.

- How to install and configure the vSphere Replication product for single and multiple VMs. In addition, you learned how to recover a VM using vSphere Replication and how to fail back a VM when the primary site is working again.

- How to determine whether VDP and vSphere Replication are the appropriate tools for your organization. You learned that VDP is included with all vSphere kits higher than Essentials now, as is vSphere Replication. If your organization has fewer than 100 server VMs and is not complex, these "essentially free" services might provide what you need for backed-up data, functionality, and a form of disaster recovery.

## Exam Preparation Tasks

## Review All the Key Topics

Review the most important topics from inside the chapter, noted with the Key Topic icon in the outer margin of the page. Table 18-3 lists these key topics and the page numbers where each is found.

**Table 18-3**   Key Topics for Chapter 18

| Key Topic Element | Description | Page Number |
|---|---|---|
| Figure 18-1 | The Components of VDP | 430 |
| Table 18-2 | Minimum System Requirements for VDP | 431 |
| Figure 18-2 | vSphere Replication Architecture | 432 |
| Activity 18-1 | Creating a VM Snapshot | 433 |
| Figure 18-8 | A Series of Snapshots | 437 |

| Key Topic Element | Description | Page Number |
|---|---|---|
| Figure 18-9 | Adding a Needs Consolidation Column to the Virtual Machines Tab | 438 |
| Figure 18-10 | Consolidating the VMs' Snapshots | 439 |
| Activity 18-2 | Deploying VDP | 439 |
| Figure 18-13 | Backing Up VMs with VDP | 441 |
| Activity 18-3 | Deploying vSphere Replication | 442 |
| Numbered List | Configuring Replication for Single/Multiple VMs | 447 |
| Numbered List | Recovering a VM Using vSphere Replication | 449 |

## Review Questions

The answers to these review questions are in Appendix A.

1. As the administrator of a virtual data center, you are performing a backup using a third-party backup software. Which of the following are true? (Choose two.)

   a. You can use a snapshot as part of a backup solution.

   b. You should keep the snapshot for at least as long as you keep the backup.

   c. You can use snapshots instead of backups.

   d. Backup software will typically delete the snapshot for you after the backup is completed.

2. You are the administrator in charge of a virtual data center that has about 50 server VMs and 4 hosts. Which of the following are true? (Choose two.)

   a. You cannot use VDP because your environment is too large.

   b. You cannot use the VADP API because your environment is too small.

   c. You can use VDP with your current license.

   d. You can have a maximum of 2 TB worth of deduplicated data storage.

3.  You have installed VDP 6.0 on your Essentials Plus licensed vSphere environment. Which of the following are true? (Choose two.)

    a.  You need to upgrade to Enterprise Plus to use the advanced features of VDP.

    b.  You need to upgrade your VDP option to use the advanced features.

    c.  Your current license supports the use of advanced VDP features.

    d.  Your current VDP version supports the use of advanced features.

4.  You have just installed vSphere Replication for your two-site infrastructure. Which of the following are true? (Choose two.)

    a.  You installed only one instance of vSphere Replication, which was then connected to your remote site.

    b.  You installed two instances of vSphere Replication: one on the primary site and a second at the secondary site.

    c.  After the appliance is installed at each location, it will require extensive configuration and testing before it can be used effectively.

    d.  After the appliance is installed at each location, it is ready to go without further configuration but can be "tweaked" on the VAMI if necessary.

5.  Which of the following files is always created when you take the first snapshot of a VM?

    a.  -delta.vmdk

    b.  .vsmn

    c.  .vswp

    d.  -flat.vmdk

6.  As an administrator of a small virtual data center, you have just installed VDP. Which of the following are true? (Choose two.)

    a.  You need to install a plug-in to your vSphere Client to configure the software.

    b.  You can configure the appliance through its web interface.

    c.  You can connect to the appliance at the address that was provided by DHCP at the time of the installation.

    d.  You need to connect to the appliance at the static address that you supplied during the installation.

7. You have just installed and configured VDP and now want to perform a backup. Which of the following are true? (Choose two.)

   a. You will use the same web interface that you used to configure the appliance to perform the backup.

   b. You will use the vSphere Web Client to perform the backup.

   c. You should find the VDP plug-in under the Administration section of the vSphere Web Client.

   d. You should find the VDP plug-in under the Solutions and Applications section of the vSphere Web Client.

8. Which of the following are true regarding vSphere Replication in vSphere 6.0?

   a. vSphere Replication is included in the base installation of vSphere 6.0 and only needs to be activated.

   b. You can install vSphere Replication by deploying an OVA.

   c. vSphere Replication can only be configured through the vSphere Client, just as SRM can be configured.

   d. You can configure vSphere Replication through the VAMI.

9. Which of the following are true regarding configuring vSphere Replication for VMs?

   a. Only the primary site needs to be a vSphere data center.

   b. The primary and secondary site must each be a vSphere data center.

   c. You can configure an RPO as tight as 5 minutes.

   d. The RPO setting determines how up-to-date the secondary VM will stay on an ongoing basis.

10. You are the administrator of a small network that uses vSphere Replication. A VM on the primary site has just failed, and you want to recover to the secondary VM. Which of the following will be part of the process? (Choose two.)

    a. You need to use the thick vSphere Client and connect to SRM to manage replication.

    b. You use the vSphere Web Client to connect to vSphere Replication through the Home site.

    c. You can attempt to synchronize the secondary VM with the primary VM.

    d. You will not be given the option to synchronize the secondary VM with the primary VM.

**11.** Which of the following are true regarding failback of a VM in vSphere Replication? (Choose two.)

   **a.** Failback is typically not needed and therefore not supported.

   **b.** Failback is simply configuring replication to occur again in the reverse direction.

   **c.** You need to unregister the VM from the primary site before you configure the reverse direction replication.

   **d.** Unregistering the VM from the primary site is not necessary.

**12.** You are an administrator of a Standard licensed virtual data center with 10 hosts and 200 VM servers. You are considering options such as VDP and vSphere Replication. Which of the following are *not* true? (Choose two.)

   **a.** Your organization can still take advantage of the VADP API, even if you elect not to use VDP.

   **b.** You can use vSphere Replication to create a hot site for some selected VMs.

   **c.** Your organization is much too large to use vSphere Replication, VADP, or VDP in any manner.

   **d.** vSphere Replication is not supported at your license level.

**This chapter covers the following subjects:**

- Patching Requirements for ESXi Hosts and Virtual Machine Hardware/Tools

- Creating/Editing/Removing a Host Profile from an ESXi Host

- Importing/Exporting a Host Profile

- Attaching/Applying a Host Profile to an ESXi Host or Cluster

- Performing Compliance Scanning and Remediation of an ESXi Host Using Host Profiles

- Installing and Configuring vCenter Update Manager

- Configuring Patch Download Options

- Creating/Editing/Deleting an Update Manager Baseline

- Attaching an Update Manager Baseline to an ESXi Host or Cluster

- Scanning and Remediating ESXi Hosts and Virtual Machine Hardware/Tools Using Update Manager or Staging for Later

- Staging ESXi Host Updates

Someone once said that the only thing that remains constant is change. This certainly applies to anything in today's IT world, including your virtual data center. In this section, you learn about the two primary tools you can use to keep up with changes with regard to your ESXi hosts and your VMs: VMware Update Manager and Host Profiles. This chapter discusses many specific aspects of each tool and how you can use each of them to assist in managing your vSphere.

## CHAPTER 19

# Updating ESXi and Virtual Machines

More specifically, you learn about patching requirements for ESXi hosts and VMs, followed by how to create, edit, and remove a host profile from an ESXi host. In addition, the chapter covers attaching and applying a host profile to an ESXi host or cluster, which includes using a host profile to perform compliance scanning and remediation of an ESXi host.

Next is the VMware Update Manager (VUM). You learn about installing and configuring VUM, including configuring patch download options. In addition, creating, editing, and deleting an Update Manager baseline to an ESXi host or cluster is discussed. Finally, the chapter covers scanning and remediating ESXi hosts and VMs using VUM, as well as staging ESXi host updates to run at a predetermined time in the future.

## "Do I Know This Already?" Quiz

The "Do I Know This Already?" quiz allows you to assess whether you should read this entire chapter or simply jump to the "Exam Preparation Tasks" section for review. If you are in doubt, read the entire chapter. Table 19-1 outlines the major headings in this chapter and the corresponding "Do I Know This Already?" quiz questions. You can find the answers in Appendix A, "Answers to the 'Do I Know This Already?' Quizzes and Chapter Review Questions."

**Table 19-1**   "Do I Know This Already?" Section-to-Question Mapping

| Foundation Topics Section | Questions Covered in This Section |
|---|---|
| Patching Requirements for ESXi Hosts and Virtual Machine Hardware/Tools | 1 |
| Creating/Editing/Removing a Host Profile from an ESXi Host | 2 |
| Importing/Exporting a Host Profile | 3 |
| Attaching/Applying a Host Profile to an ESXi Host or Cluster | 4 |
| Performing Compliance Scanning and Remediation of an ESXi Host Using Host Profiles | 5 |
| Installing and Configuring vCenter Update Manager | 6 |
| Configuring Patch Download Options | 7 |
| Creating/Editing/Deleting an Update Manager Baseline | 8 |
| Attaching an Update Manager Baseline to an ESXi Host or Cluster | 9 |
| Scanning and Remediating ESXi Hosts and Virtual Machine Hardware/Tools Using Update Manager or Staging for Later | 10 |

1. As the administrator of a virtual data center, you are concerned with how often you should update your VMs. Which of the following are true? (Choose two.)

   a. You should not upgrade your VMs unless you have an upgraded license.

   b. You should upgrade your VMware Tools with every host upgrade.

   c. You should update your VM hardware with every host upgrade.

   d. You should update your VM hardware if there is an option or feature that you want to use and that is not supported with your current VM hardware.

2. You are the administrator in charge of a virtual data center with a Standard license. You are considering using Host Profiles. Which of the following are true? (Choose two.)

   a. Your current license level will not support the use of Host Profiles.

   b. Host Profiles enable you to create a reference host and then remediate other hosts to be configured with the same general settings.

   c. Host Profiles are only for initial configuration and cannot assist with ongoing compliance.

   d. Host Profile information is stored only in the hosts themselves and not in the vCenter, for security purposes.

**3.** You are the administrator of a virtual data center with a Standard vSphere license. You are considering the option of importing a host profile that was used on another host for a new host. Which of the following are true? (Choose two.)

   **a.** You will need to upgrade to Enterprise Plus to use Host Profiles.

   **b.** You will need to upgrade to at least Enterprise to use Host Profiles.

   **c.** You can import a profile by copying the .vmdk file of the host.

   **d.** You can import a profile by browsing for a .vpf file.

**4.** You are considering using Host Profiles on your vSphere Enterprise Plus virtual data center. Which of the following are true? (Choose two.)

   **a.** Creating a Host Profile automatically attaches it to a host.

   **b.** Creating a Host Profile doesn't change anything until you attach/apply it to a host.

   **c.** You can only attach a profile to a single host at a time, not to a cluster of hosts.

   **d.** You can attach a Host Profile to a single host, multiple hosts, or a cluster of hosts, as needed.

**5.** Which of the following are true regarding compliance scanning and remediation with Host Profiles? (Choose two.)

   **a.** You can check for host compliance in Hosts and Clusters view as well as VMs and Templates view.

   **b.** To check compliance of a host, a profile must first be attached to that host.

   **c.** Compliance checking requires a higher vSphere license level than just Host Profile usage for configuration does.

   **d.** Host compliance checking is always done in Hosts and Clusters view.

**6.** As an administrator of a small virtual data center, you have just installed VUM. Which of the following are true? (Choose two.)

   **a.** You will need to install a plug-in to your vSphere Client to configure the software.

   **b.** You can configure the appliance through its web interface.

   **c.** You can connect to the appliance at the address that was provided by DHCP at the time of the installation.

   **d.** You have not installed a new appliance, only a new service.

7. You have just installed and configured VUM and now want to configure patch download options. Which of the following are true? (Choose two.)

   a. You will use the same web interface that you used to install VUM.

   b. You can use the vSphere Web Client.

   c. You can configure VUM to update guest OSs and applications on VMs.

   d. There is no support of updating guest OSs and applications on VMs.

8. Which of the following types of baseline is used to enhance the capabilities of a host by installing additional VMware or third-party software?

   a. Host patch

   b. Host extension

   c. Host upgrade

   d. VA upgrade

9. Which of the following are true regarding baselines in vSphere Update Manager?

   a. Creating a baseline will automatically attach it to all hosts in a cluster.

   b. You will need to attach a baseline to a host or cluster after you create it.

   c. A baseline is a list of suggested settings for the administrator to consider.

   d. A baseline is a standard to which the host must measure up or else be considered out of compliance.

10. You are the administrator of a small network that uses VUM. You perform a scan of hosts against a baseline to which they are attached. Which of the following are true? (Choose two.)

   a. You will need to reattach the baseline before you can remediate the host.

   b. You can remediate the host after scanning it or stage the remediation for a later time.

   c. Remediation involves fixing the host to be in compliance with the attached baseline.

   d. Remediation involves fixing the baseline to be in compliance with the attached host.

## Foundation Topics

# Patching Requirements for ESXi Hosts and Virtual Machine Hardware/Tools

It's important to keep your ESXi hosts up to date with the latest patches. This gives you the most capability, and it also enhances the security of your systems. In addition, it's important to keep VMs up to date. In our context, most (if not all) of your VMs are servers, so keeping them up to date will enhance the user experience for many users. With this in mind, you should upgrade your VMware Tools with any host upgrade, and you should upgrade your virtual machine hardware if there is an option or feature on the newer hardware that you want to use and that is not supported on your current hardware.

# Creating/Editing/Removing a Host Profile from an ESXi Host

Installing the software for an ESXi host is the easy part, which was discussed in Chapter 3, "Installing and Configuring ESXi." After you have installed the host, the configuration steps that are required can be time-consuming and complicated. They might include configuration settings that relate to CPU, memory, storage, networking, licensing, DNS and routing, firewall settings, and so on. Because you want your ESXi hosts to be consistent, especially if they are in the same clusters, wouldn't it be nice to be able to configure a "reference host" and then use that as a baseline to configure the other hosts? This is exactly what you can do with Host Profiles in vSphere if you have an Enterprise Plus license. In addition, any fields that are specific to one host can be completed by prompting the user for input. After the user has supplied the information, an answer file is created and stored in the Auto Deploy cache and the vCenter Server host object.

After you have configured and tested your reference host, follow the steps outlined in Activity 19-1.

**Activity 19-1   Creating a Host Profile**

1. Log on to your vSphere Web Client.

2. Select **Home** and then, under Management, select **Host Profiles**, as shown in Figure 19-1. You must have an Enterprise Plus license to use Host Profiles.

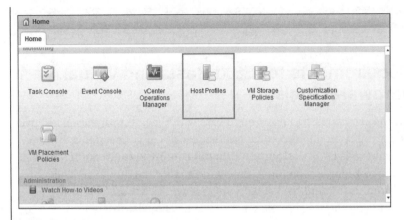

**Figure 19-1**    Using Host Profiles

   **3.** Click the **Extract Host Profile** link in the upper-left corner, as shown in
   Figure 19-2.

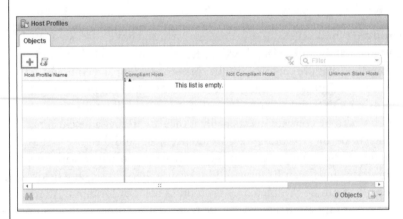

**Figure 19-2**    Creating a New Host Profile

4. Select the host from which you want to create the profile, as shown in Figure 19-3, and click **Next**.

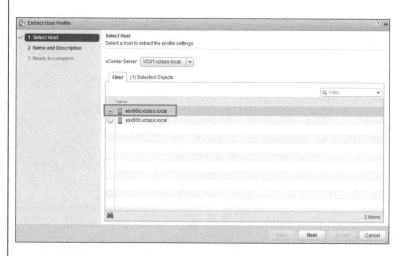

**Figure 19-3**   Creating a Profile from an Existing Host

5. Type the name and description for your profile, as shown in Figure 19-4, and click **Next**.

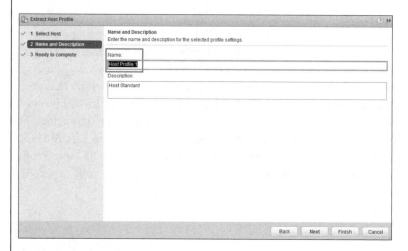

**Figure 19-4**   Naming a Profile

6. Review the summary information, as shown in Figure 19-5, and click **Finish**. Your new profile will appear on the list under Host Profiles.

**Figure 19-5**   Reviewing Profile Summary Information

## Importing/Exporting a Host Profile

You can also export a file from a host that is not directly part of your vSphere and then import the same profile to a host in your vSphere. This makes using profiles very convenient and flexible, but it could also introduce security risks. To prevent this from happening, passwords are not exported and must be reentered when a profile is imported. To export a profile, you should right-click the profile that you want to export and select **Export Host Profile**, as shown in Figure 19-6. The system exports the data to a .vpf file, which you can store in your selected location. The system also reminds you that passwords will not be saved, as shown in Figure 19-7. To import the exported .vpf file to its new environment, navigate to its Host Profile view, click the **Import Host Profile** link, and browse to location of your exported .vpf, as shown in Figure 19-8.

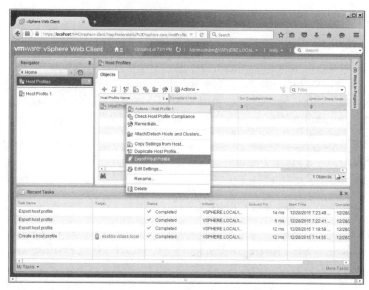

**Figure 19-6**   Exporting a Host Profile

**Figure 19-7**   Host Profile Security Reminder

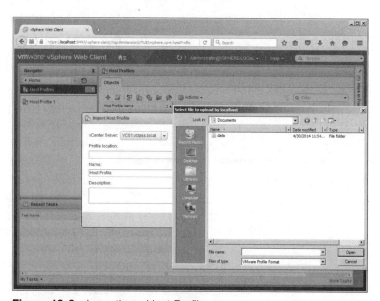

**Figure 19-8**   Importing a Host Profile

# Attaching/Applying a Host Profile to an ESXi Host or Cluster

Just creating a profile doesn't change anything; you have to attach it to a host or cluster and apply it for it to change the host. You should attach the profile to the host or cluster by opening Hosts and Cluster view first. To attach and apply your profile to a host or cluster, follow the steps outlined in Activity 19-2.

**Activity 19-2   Attach/Apply a Host Profile**

1. Log on to your vSphere Web Client.

2. Select **Home** and then **Hosts and Clusters**.

3. Right-click the host or cluster to which you would like to attach the profile (in this case, esx60a), select **Host Profiles**, and then **Attach Host Profile,** as shown in Figure 19-9.

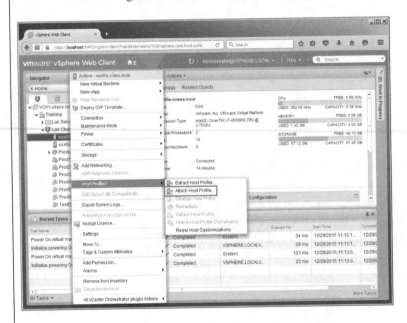

**Figure 19-9**   Attaching Host Profiles

After you have attached the host profile to a host or cluster, you can remediate the host or cluster to comply with the host profile by right-clicking it and then selecting Remediate, as shown in Figure 19-10.

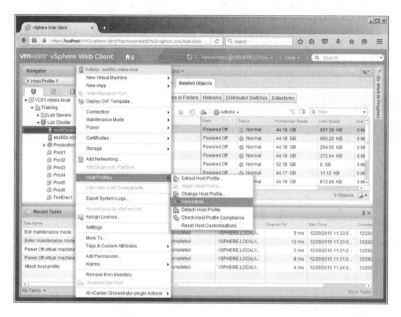

**Figure 19-10**    Remediating a Host

## Performing Compliance Scanning and Remediation of an ESXi Host Using Host Profiles

Even if Host Profiles could be used only for initial configuration of hosts, it would still be handy to have around, but you can also use it to ensure that hosts stay in ongoing compliance with a reference host or baseline. This means that errant configurations in your hosts can be quickly and easily remediated, even if the specific configurations are not discovered until after you run your Host Profile's compliance check.

To check whether a host is still in compliance with the profile to which it is attached, follow the steps outlined in Activity 19-3.

**Activity 19-3    Checking Host Compliance to an Attached Host Profile**

1. Log on to your vSphere Web Client.

2. Select **Home** and then **Hosts and Clusters**.

3. Right-click the host on which you would like to check compliance, select **Host Profiles**, and then **Check Host Profile Compliance**, as shown in Figure 19-11.

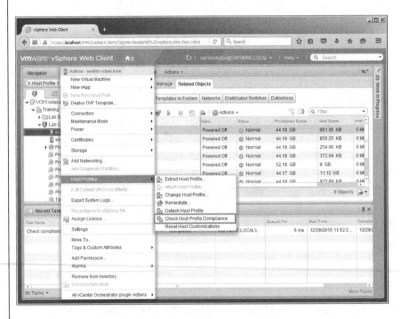

**Figure 19-11**   Checking a Host for Profile Compliance

4. Monitor the Recent Tasks pane for compliance status, as shown in Figure 19-12. If a host is still not in compliance with the attached profile, it will be indicated on the Summary tab of the host, as shown in Figure 19-13. You can also obtain more detailed information about host compliance/noncompliance on the Summary for the host profile, as shown in Figure 19-14.

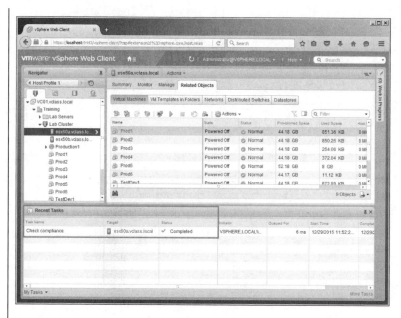

**Figure 19-12**   Verifying That Host Compliance Check Is Complete

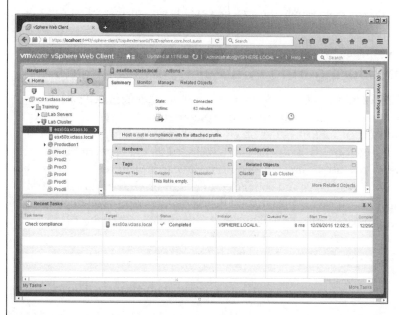

**Figure 19-13**   Summary Tab of Host Showing Host Is Not in Compliance

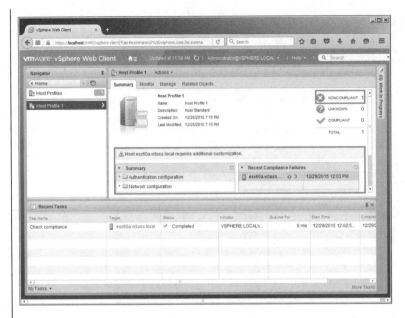

**Figure 19-14**   Summary Tab of Host Profile Showing Hosts Not in Compliance

   **5.** If necessary, you can reapply the attached profile to remediate the host.

## Installing and Configuring vCenter Update Manager

vCenter Update Manager (VUM) provides for centralized, automated patch and version management for your vSphere. It offers support for VMware ESX/ESXi hosts, VMs, and virtual appliances (VAs). Update Manager is fairly easy to install and configure for your needs. The software is included on the vSphere Installation Manager and can also be downloaded from VMware's website. VUM must be installed on a Windows Server and connected to a SQL or Oracle database. IBM DB2 is not supported as a VUM database. To install and perform basic configuration on vCenter Update Manager, follow the steps outlined in Activity 19-4.

### Activity 19-4    Installation and Basic Configuration of vSphere Update Manager

1. Log on to the computer on which you want to install the VUM.

2. Using the VIM Setup software and the vSphere Installer Package, click **VMware vSphere Update Manager** and click **Install**, as shown in Figure 19-15. If you do not have the prerequisites of Microsoft.NET 3.5 SP1 and Windows Installer 4.1, you can install them at this time, straight from the VIM Setup software.

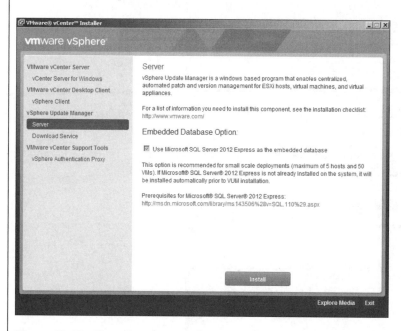

**Figure 19-15**   The vSphere Installer Package

3. Choose your installation language and click **OK**.

4. Click **Next** and accept the terms to begin the installation.

5. The default configuration option is to download updates immediately after installation, as shown in Figure 19-16. The updates that are downloaded are descriptions of the patches. The actual patch binary is never downloaded until you remediate an object that needs that patch.

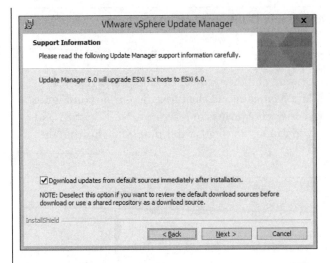

**Figure 19-16**  Default Installation Downloads Patches

6.  Enter your vCenter address and credentials, as shown in Figure 19-17, and click **Next**.

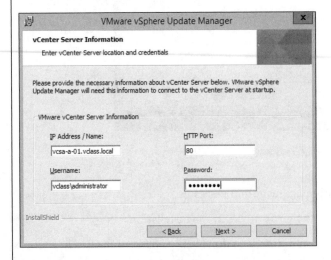

**Figure 19-17**  The vCenter Connection to VUM

7. Most of the time, you can accept the default ports, as shown in Figure 19-18, unless your network requires special considerations with regard to ports. Click **Next**.

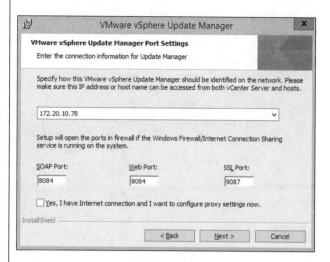

**Figure 19-18**   Default Ports Usually Suffice

8. Most of the time, you can accept the default locations for the installation packages, as shown in Figure 19-19, and click **Next**.

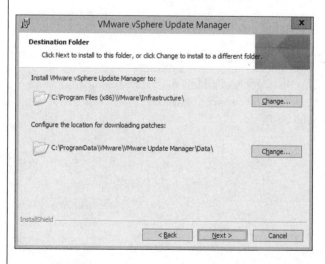

**Figure 19-19**   Default Installation Folders Usually Suffice

9. Click **Install** to begin the installation. The software installation begins by extracting many files and then will continue into a graphical installation.

10. After the installation finishes, log on to your vSphere Client and go to **Plug-Ins**, **Manage Plug-Ins** to download and install the Update Manager plug-in.

11. After the plug-in is downloaded and installed, the link will appear in the Home screen under Solutions and Applications, as shown in Figure 19-20.

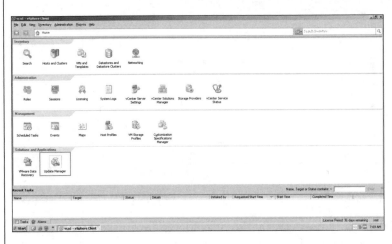

**Figure 19-20**  The VUM Link in Solutions and Applications

## Configuring Patch Download Options

After you have the software installed, you can add to the patch download options that are already configured by default by connecting to the Internet or to an optional server, as shown in Figure 19-21.

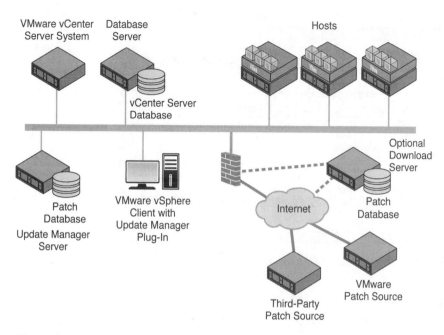

**Figure 19-21**  Options for vCenter Update Manager

Note that additional patch downloads are intended as enhancements to the host and to networking, storage, and so on. The VUM is no longer supported for patching guest OSs. To configure additional download options after you have installed VUM, follow the steps outlined in Activity 19-5.

**NOTE**  I am showing how this is done on the thick (Windows-based) vSphere Client. It can also now be accomplished on the vSphere Web Client with very similar steps.

### Activity 19-5  Configuring Patch Download Options

1. Log in to your vSphere Client.

2. Go to **Home**, **Solutions and Applications**, and click **Update Manager**.

3. Click the **Configuration** tab at the top of the screen. Then click **Download Settings** and finally **Add Download Source**, as shown in Figure 19-22.

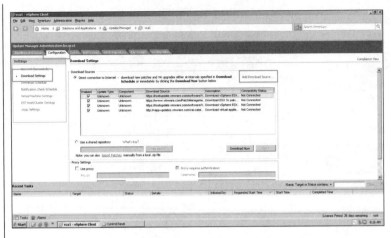

**Figure 19-22**    Adding Download Sources to VUM

4. You can then specify the Source URL and click **OK** to contact the third-party source for your patches.

# Creating/Editing/Deleting an Update Manager Baseline

After you have downloaded your patches, you can combine them to form groups of patches called *baselines*. To create a baseline, you first choose the type of baseline that you want to create, and then, based on your first choice, you choose the patches that will be part of the baseline. You can create five types of baselines:

- **Host patch:** VMware patches that can be applied to a host or a set of hosts

- **Host extension:** Plug-ins and other software from VMware or third parties that extend the capabilities of the host

- **Host upgrade:** Patches that are specifically for the purpose of upgrading the ESX/ESXi host to the next level

- **VA upgrade:** Updates that the virtual appliance vendors provide for upgrade of the VA

- **VM Upgrade:** Upgrades the VMware Tools and virtual hardware on VMs and templates

To create a baseline in VUM, follow the steps outlined in Activity 19-6.

**Activity 19-6    Creating a Baseline in VUM**

1. Log in to your vSphere Client.

2. Go to **Home**, **Solutions and Applications**, and click **Update Manager**.

3. Open the Baseline and Groups tab, choose between **Hosts** and **VMs/VAs**, and click the **Create** link next to Baselines, as shown in Figure 19-23.

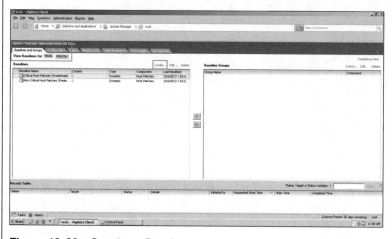

**Figure 19-23**    Creating a Baseline

4. On the Baseline Name and Type screen, type a name for your baseline and optionally a description, and then choose the applicable baseline type, as shown in Figure 19-24.

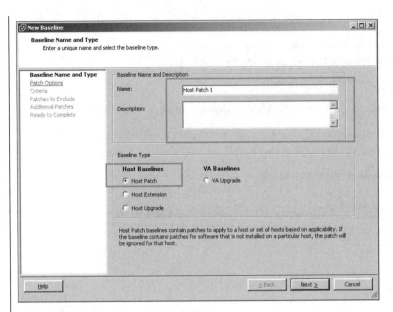

**Figure 19-24**  Naming and Describing a Baseline

5.  Choose whether the patches in this baseline will be the same every time it's applied (Fixed) or whether new patches that meet the criteria will be automatically added to enhance or replace the old patches (Dynamic), as shown in Figure 19-25, and then click **Next**.

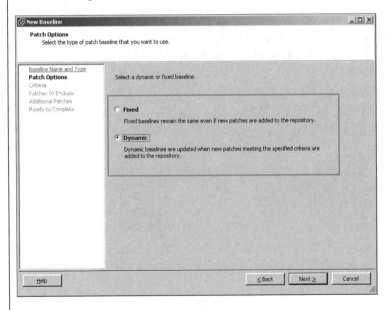

**Figure 19-25**  Choosing Patch Options

6. If you chose to create a dynamic baseline, enter the criteria such as vendor and severity of the issue that the patch fixes, and click **Next**.

7. List any patches that you want to exclude (if applicable), as shown in Figure 19-26. Then click **Next** and list any additional patches to be included (if you chose Dynamic).

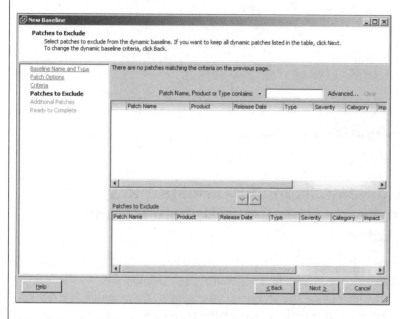

**Figure 19-26**    Patch Inclusion/Exclusion

8. On the Ready to Complete page, review your settings and click **Finish**.

## Attaching an Update Manager Baseline to an ESXi Host or Cluster

Just creating a baseline for a host or cluster does not change the host in any way; you have to attach the baseline to the host or cluster and then apply it to change the host or cluster. Attaching the baseline gives you a standard to which the host must measure up or be considered out of compliance. To attach your newly created baseline to a host, return to Hosts and Clusters view, click the host on which you would like to attach the baseline, click **Attach**, select your baseline, and confirm by clicking **Attach** in the dialog box, all shown on Figure 19-27.

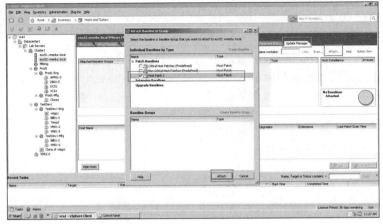

**Figure 19-27**   Attaching a VUM Baseline to an ESXi Host

## Scanning and Remediating ESXi Hosts and Virtual Machine Hardware/Tools Using Update Manager or Staging for Later

After you have created a baseline and attached it to a host, a cluster, a VM, or multiple VMs, you can scan the objects for compliance to the standard set by the baseline. If the objects that you scan are found to be noncompliant, they can then be remediated (fixed) to match the standard set by the baseline and its patches and settings. You can also elect to stage the patches for a later time when there is not as much demand on the resources, as shown in Figure 19-28.

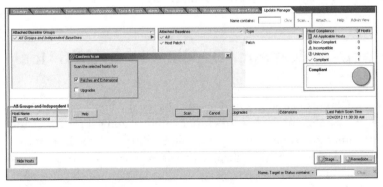

**Figure 19-28**   Scanning and Remediating an ESXi Host

## Summary

The main topics covered in this chapter are the following:

- Patching requirements for ESXi hosts and VMs. This included the creation, editing, and deletion of Host Profiles, as well as importing/exporting of host profiles. The chapter also covered attaching/applying a Host Profile to a single host or a cluster of hosts, followed by using Host Profiles for the purpose of compliance scanning and remediation of hosts.

- vCenter Update Manager (VUM) installation and configuration and the process of configuring patch download options and creating, editing, and deleting Update Manager Baselines. You learned how to attach baselines to scan and remediate ESXi hosts and VMs, and how to stage the update for a later time if needed.

## Exam Preparation Tasks

## Review All the Key Topics

Review the most important topics from the chapter, noted with the Key Topic icon in the outer margin of the page. Table 19-2 lists these key topics and the page numbers where each is found.

**Table 19-2**  Key Topics for Chapter 19

| Key Topic Element | Description | Page Number |
|---|---|---|
| Activity 19-1 | Creating a Host Profile | 463 |
| Figure 19-6 | Exporting a Host Profile | 467 |
| Figure 19-7 | Host Profile Security Reminder | 467 |
| Figure 19-8 | Importing a Host Profile | 467 |
| Activity 19-2 | Attach/Apply a Host Profile | 468 |
| Figure 19-10 | Remediating a Host | 469 |
| Activity 19-3 | Checking Host Compliance to an Attached Host Profile | 470 |
| Activity 19-4 | Installation and Basic Configuration of vSphere Update Manager | 473 |
| Figure 19-21 | Options for vCenter Update Manager | 477 |

| Key Topic Element | Description | Page Number |
|---|---|---|
| Activity 19-5 | Configuring Patch Download Options | 477 |
| Bullet List | Types of Baselines | 478 |
| Activity 19-6 | Creating a Baseline in VUM | 479 |
| Figure 19-27 | Attaching a VUM Baseline to an ESXi Host | 482 |
| Figure 19-28 | Scanning and Remediating an ESXi Host | 482 |

## Review Questions

The answers to these review questions are in Appendix A.

1. As the administrator of a virtual data center, you are concerned with how often you should update your VMs. Which of the following are true? (Choose two.)

   a. You should update your hosts as infrequently as possible to prevent security vulnerabilities.

   b. You should upgrade your VMware Tools with every host upgrade.

   c. You must update your VM hardware to update your VMware tools.

   d. You should update your VM hardware if there is an option or feature that you want to use and that is not supported with your current VM hardware.

2. You are the administrator in charge of a virtual data center with a vSphere Standard license. You are considering using Host Profiles. Which of the following are true? (Choose two.)

   a. Your current license level will not support the use of Host Profiles.

   b. Host Profiles enable you to create a reference host and then remediate other hosts to be configured with the same general settings.

   c. Host Profiles are only for initial configuration and cannot assist with ongoing compliance.

   d. Host Profile information is stored only in the hosts themselves and not in the vCenter for security purposes.

3. You are the administrator of a virtual data center with a Standard Enterprise license. You are considering the option of importing a host profile that was used on another host for a new host. Which of the following are true? (Choose two.)

    a. You will need to upgrade to Enterprise Plus to use Host Profiles.

    b. You will need to upgrade to at least Enterprise to use Host Profiles.

    c. You can import a profile by copying the .vmdk file of the host.

    d. You can import a profile by browsing for a .vpf file.

4. You are considering using Host Profiles on your vSphere Enterprise Plus virtual data center. Which of the following are *not* true? (Choose two.)

    a. Creating a Host Profile automatically attaches it to a host.

    b. Creating a Host Profile doesn't change anything until you attach/apply it to a host.

    c. You can attach a profile only to a single host at a time, not to a cluster of hosts.

    d. You can attach a Host Profile to a single host, multiple hosts, or a cluster of hosts as needed.

5. Which of the following are *not* true regarding compliance scanning and remediation with Host Profiles? (Choose two.)

    a. You can check for host compliance in Hosts and Clusters view as well as VMs and Templates view.

    b. To check compliance of a host, a profile must first be attached to that host.

    c. Compliance checking requires a higher vSphere license level than just Host Profile usage for configuration does.

    d. Host compliance checking is always done in Hosts and Clusters view.

6. As an administrator of a small virtual data center, you have just installed VUM. Which of the following are *not* true? (Choose two.)

    a. You will need to install a plug-in to your vSphere Client to configure the software.

    b. You can configure the appliance through its web interface.

    c. You can connect to the appliance at the address that was provided by DHCP at the time of the installation.

    d. You have not installed a new appliance, only a new service.

7. You have just installed and configured VUM and now want to configure patch download options. Which of the following are true? (Choose two.)

   a. You will use the same interface that you used to install VUM.

   b. You cannot use the vSphere Web Client.

   c. You cannot configure VUM to update guest OSs and applications on VMs.

   d. There is support for updating VMware tools or VM hardware.

8. Which of the following types of baselines is used to upgrade VMware Tools and virtual hardware of VMs and templates on a host?

   a. Host patch

   b. Host extension

   c. VA upgrade

   d. VM upgrade

9. Which of the following are *not* true regarding baselines in vSphere Update Manager?

   a. Creating a baseline will automatically attach it to all hosts in a cluster.

   b. You will need to attach a baseline to a host or cluster after you create it.

   c. A baseline is a list of suggested settings for the administrator to consider.

   d. A baseline is a standard to which the host must measure up or else be considered out of compliance.

10. You are the administrator of a small network that uses VUM. You perform a scan of hosts against a baseline to which they are attached. Which of the following are *not* true? (Choose two.)

   a. You will need to reattach the baseline before you can remediate the host.

   b. You can remediate the host after scanning it, or stage the remediation for a later time.

   c. Remediation involves fixing the host to be in compliance with the attached baseline.

   d. Remediation involves fixing the baseline to be in compliance with the attached host.

**This chapter covers the following subjects:**

- ESXi Host Troubleshooting Guidelines

- vCenter Troubleshooting Guidelines

- Troubleshooting Common Installation Issues

- Monitoring ESXi System Health

- Exporting Diagnostic Information

Troubleshooting is a process of isolating the components of a system from each other to systematically determine what works. That's right, I said "what works" and not "what doesn't work." If you can determine what does work in a system and how "far" it does work, then you can determine the point at which it begins to "not work."

## CHAPTER 20

# Performing Basic Troubleshooting of ESXi and vCenter Server

Just as with any other product or service, many things can go wrong with vSphere if they are not configured properly or if something unexpected and unaccounted for should happen. When you are a vSphere administrator, part of your job is to minimize the chance of these unexpected issues and to minimize their impact to your organization when they occur. The other part of your job is to understand how to work your way out of an issue to provide a solution for yourself and your servers with the least disruption possible to your users.

This chapter covers basic troubleshooting on your ESXi hosts and vCenter Servers. In addition, you learn basic troubleshooting for the features that put all these resources to work in an organized manner that makes the vSphere and the virtual data center possible. This chapter, and the next five chapters that follow it, will assist you in truly understanding more about your vSphere and not just in "having head knowledge" of its components. This understanding will help you troubleshoot your own systems and is essential to successfully navigate the troubleshooting questions on the exam.

## "Do I Know This Already?" Quiz

The "Do I Know This Already?" quiz allows you to assess whether you should read this entire chapter or simply jump to the "Exam Preparation Tasks" section for review. If you are in doubt, read the entire chapter. Table 20-1 outlines the major headings in this chapter and the corresponding "Do I Know This Already?" quiz questions. You can find the answers in Appendix A, "Answers to the 'Do I Know This Already?' Quizzes and Chapter Review Questions."

**Table 20-1**   "Do I Know This Already?" Section-to-Question Mapping

| Foundation Topics Section | Questions Covered in This Section |
|---|---|
| ESXi Host Troubleshooting Guidelines | 1, 2 |
| vCenter Troubleshooting Guidelines | 3, 4 |
| Troubleshooting Common Installation Issues | 5, 6 |
| Monitoring ESXi System Health | 7, 8 |
| Exporting Diagnostic Information | 9, 10 |

1. Which of the following tools is provided by VMware as a last resort to troubleshoot issues that cannot be resolved through more normal means?

    a. vCLI

    b. vSphere Web Client

    c. ESXi Shell

    d. PowerCLI

2. Which of the following should you select in the DCUI to review the system logs?

    a. View Support Information

    b. View System Logs

    c. Troubleshooting Options

    d. System Customization

3. You are in the process of installing vCenter server on Windows when the installation fails. What type of file can you easily create, just by following the wizard, on the desktop of the Windows machine to review the installation logs?

    a. .zip

    b. .tgz

    c. .inst

    d. .temp

**4.** Which two locations will contain log information in regard to vCenter setup? (Choose two.)

   **a.** c:\ProgramData\VMware\vCenter-Server\logs

   **b.** c:\ProgramData\vCenter\Install\logs

   **c.** c:\users\*username*\AppData\Local\Temp

   **d.** c:\users\administrator\LogData\Local\Temp

**5.** You have installed ESXi, but when you boot the physical server it continues to boot to the installation .iso instead of the installed software. Which of the following should you do?

   **a.** Reinstall ESXi to a different boot drive.

   **b.** Change the boot setting in the BIOS of the first VM that you install.

   **c.** Change the boot setting in the BIOS of the physical server.

   **d.** Reconnect the host to the vCenter Server.

**6.** You have installed ESXi on a physical server that has 32 logical CPUs. You attempt to install a key that allows for only 16 logical processors. Which of the following will occur?

   **a.** You will be able to install the key and enable only 16 processors.

   **b.** You will not be able to install the key on that host.

   **c.** You will be able to install the key and enable all 32 processors temporarily until you install another key.

   **d.** The evaluation mode will immediately terminate, and you will not be able to use the host.

**7.** Which of the following tabs on the vCenter Web Client contains the Hardware Status tab?

   **a.** Manage

   **b.** Administration

   **c.** Monitor

   **d.** Status

8. Which of the following technologies does ESXi use to gather and present data in host monitoring?

   a. SMASH

   b. IP

   c. NetBIOS

   d. CIM

9. You are working with VMware Support and want to create a bundle that contains multiple logs with the least administrative effort. Which of the following should you do?

   a. Generate a separate report for each type of log.

   b. Select the logs that you want to create and export.

   c. Export all information and let VMware build the logs.

   d. Generate a log bundle.

10. Which of the following tabs contains the System Logs to export?

    a. Administration

    b. Monitor

    c. Logs

    d. Export

## Foundation Topics

# ESXi Host Troubleshooting Guidelines

Your ESXi hosts are the most important physical resources in your virtual data center. They provide the platform on which all the VMs are supported and from which they obtain their resources. When there is a problem with an ESXi host, that problem will likely affect many VMs.

This section begins by identifying general troubleshooting guidelines for ESXi hosts. Then you learn how to troubleshoot common installation issues and how to avoid them.

### Learn How to Access Support Mode

Tech Support Mode (TSM) consists of a command-line interface that you can use to troubleshoot abnormalities on ESXi Hosts. You can access it by logging in to the Direct Console User Interface (DCUI) or by logging in remotely using Secure Shell (SSH). It is provided by VMware specifically for the purpose of troubleshooting issues that cannot be resolved through the use of more normal means, such as the vSphere Client, vCLI, or PowerCLI. It is generally used with the assistance of the VMware Technical Support Team.

To enable TSM from the DCUI, follow the steps in Activity 20-1.

---

**Activity 20-1   Enabling TSM from the DCUI**

1. Access the DCUI of your ESXi host.

2. Press **F2** and enter your username and password, and then press **F2** again to proceed, as shown in Figure 20-1.

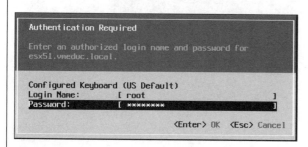

**Figure 20-1**   Logging On to the DCUI

---

3. Scroll to **Troubleshooting Options**, as shown in Figure 20-2, and press **Enter**.

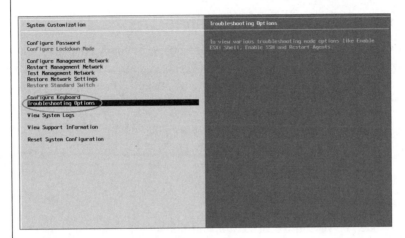

**Figure 20-2**   Selecting Troubleshooting Options

4. Select **Enable ESXi Shell** and press **Enter**. The panel on the right should now show that ESXi Shell is Enabled (see Figure 20-3).

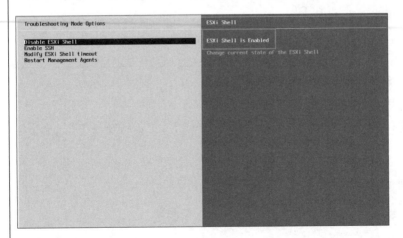

**Figure 20-3**   Enabling ESXi Shell

5. Select **Enable SSH** and press **Enter** to also enable remote TSM through SSH, and then press **Enter** and view the panel on the right to confirm the change.

6. Optionally, you can configure a timeout to enhance security if the logged-in user should walk away. To enable a timeout, select **Modify ESXi Shell Timeout**, press **Enter**, and configure your desired timeout value, as shown in Figure 20-4.

**Figure 20-4**  Modifying ESXi Shell Timeout

7. Press **Esc** three times to return to the main DCUI screen.

You can also enable TSM from the security profile of your vSphere Web Client. To illustrate how these are tied together, I am going to demonstrate that TSM is now enabled, and then you will disable it from the vSphere Web Client. To access the settings of the security profile of your ESXi host, follow the steps outlined in Activity 20-2.

### Activity 20-2    Configuring TSM from the vSphere Web Client

1. Log on to your vSphere Web Client and select **Hosts and Clusters**.

2. Select the host on which you want to configure TSM and (if necessary) open the **Summary** tab. Note the warnings that SSH and the ESXi Shell are enabled, as shown in Figure 20-5.

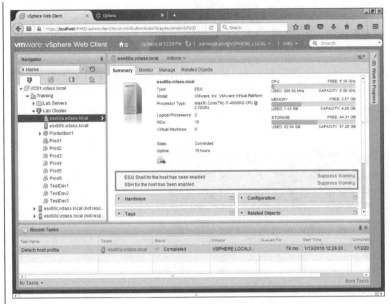

**Figure 20-5**   Confirming That SSH and ESXi Shell Are Enabled

3. Click the **Manage** tab, then the **Settings** tab, and select **Security Profile**. Scroll down to Services and note that the services of SSH and ESXi Shell are listed, which indicates that they can be controlled from here. Select **Edit** and then **ESXi Shell**; then click **Stop**, as shown in Figure 20-6. (You should also change the startup policy to **Start and Stop Manually**.)

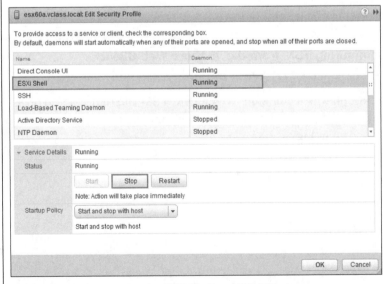

**Figure 20-6**   Configuring the ESXi Shell and SSH Services

4. Select **SSH**, click **Stop,** and then click **OK**.

5. Click the **Summary** tab for the host and note that the warnings are no longer there.

### Know How to Retrieve Host Logs

One thing that computers and networking components are good at is keeping up with what has happened to them, who or what made it happen, and when it happened. This information is stored in logs. Although there is generally no need for you to understand all the verbose information that is in every log, it is important that you know where to find logs and how to retrieve them when needed. In this section, you explore two different locations where you can access logs for your most essential vSphere components.

There are two locations on your ESXi hosts from which you can access logs: your DCUI and your vSphere Web Client. As mentioned earlier, it's not essential that you understand all the information in the log, but what's important is your ability to access it when working with a VMware Support person. The next section briefly describes how to access logs in each of these locations.

To access the logs from your DCUI, you should access your host's DCUI and then select **View System Logs**. From this screen, you can select from six logs, as shown in Figure 20-7 and described in the list that follows.

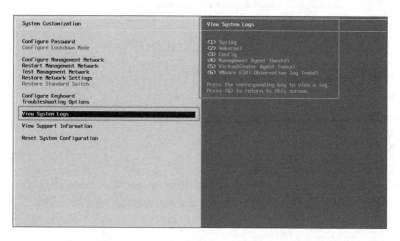

**Figure 20-7**   Viewing Logs on the DCUI

- **Syslog:** Logs messages from the VMkernel and other system components to local files or to the remote host

- **Vmkernel:** Used to determine uptime and availability statistics

- **Config:** Potentially useful in the case of a host hang, crash, or authentication issue

- **Management Agent (hostd):** Logs specific to the host services that connect your vSphere Client to your ESXi host

- **VirtualCenter Agent (vpxa):** Additional logs that appear when your ESXi host is connected to and managed by a vCenter

- **VMware ESXi Observation log (vobd):** Logs changes to the configuration of your host and their result

You can view each of these logs by pressing the number associated with it. For example, you can view the VMkernel log by pressing **2**. Figure 6-8 is an example of a VMkernel log. When you are finished viewing the log, press **Q** to return to the previous screen.

**Figure 20-8**   Viewing the VMkernel Log

To access your host's logs using the vSphere Web Client, select your host, click **Monitor**, and finally click **Log Browser**. Retrieve the logs for the host by clicking the **Retrieve Now** link, as shown in Figure 20-9. You can view hostd, VMkernel, shell logs, and others, as shown in Figure 20-9.

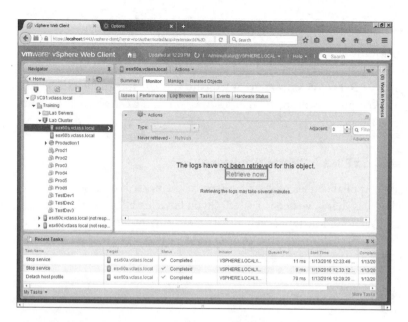

**Figure 20-9**   Retrieving Logs for a Single Host

# vCenter Troubleshooting Guidelines

As you know, your vCenter is a central component that enables you to manage multiple (up to 1,000) hosts and all the VMs associated with them. Your vCenter server also enables you to perform all the actions that are distributed across the hosts, such as vMotion, HA, DRS, and FT. Therefore, proper installation of your vCenter server is very important. Although many things could go awry during an installation and afterward, the most common of these can be detected and corrected by viewing the logs associated with them. You can sometimes interpret information from the logs, and sometimes you will have to refer users to VMware Support. In this section, you learn four ways to use logs as part of troubleshooting your vCenter server.

## Collect Installation Logs by Using the Installation Wizard

If an installation fails, a Setup Interruption page appears with the log collection boxes already checked. You can leave the boxes checked and click **Finish**. The installation log files will then be collected in a .zip file on your desktop that is named based on the time of the installation. You can retrieve the .zip file and read it to determine the cause of the installation failure.

### Retrieve Installation Logs Manually (Windows Installation)

If you continue past the Setup Interruption page and do not retrieve the logs, you do not have to try again to retrieve them. Instead, you can navigate to **c:\ProgramData\VMware\vCenterServer\logs** to retrieve the log files. They may also be stored temporarily in the **c:\users\\*username*\AppData\Local\Temp** folder of the administrator.

### Collect Deployment Log Files (vCenter Appliance)

If a vCenter Server Appliance fails to install correctly, the wizard informs you of the full path to the log files that have been created. If you have installed the vCenter Appliance from a Windows Machine, such as with a lab environment, you may also navigate to the **c:\users\Administrator\AppData\Local\VMware\CIP\ vcsaInstaller** folder.

### Export a vCenter Server Support Bundle

For ongoing troubleshooting, you can also create a support bundle in the form of a .tgz file to send to VMware Support. You can use the URL that is displayed in the direct console user interface. You should open a web browser and enter the URL that was displayed in the DCUI; then you can enter the username and password of the root user. The .tgz file will be created on the desktop of the Windows machine used for the vCenter server.

## Troubleshooting Common Installation Issues

For your hosts to function well in your vCenter, you must first install them properly. There are many different ways to install the software for an ESXi host, including interactive installation, USB key, scripted, or even loaded directly into the memory of the host. That makes this objective a very broad one indeed. With that in mind, I will list three of the most common installation issues and how you should address them. I also discuss much more troubleshooting in later chapters.

### Troubleshooting Boot Order

If you are installing ESXi, you might need to reconfigure BIOS settings. The boot configuration in BIOS is likely to be set to CD-ROM and then ordered by the list of drives available in your computer. You can change this setting by reconfiguring the boot order in BIOS or by selecting a boot device for the selection menu. If you change this in the BIOS, it affects all subsequent boots. If you change it in the boot selection menu, it affects only the current boot.

### Troubleshooting License Assignment

Suppose you have a vSphere key that allows for 16 processors. Now, suppose that you attempt to install that key on a host that has 32 processors. You might assume that the key would install but only enable the host to use the processors covered by the key. In fact, you will not be able to install the key on that host. In addition, you will not be able to install license keys that do not cover all the features that you have enabled for a host (for example, DRS, Host Profile, fault tolerance, and so on). To address the issue, you should do one of the following:

- Obtain and assign the appropriate key with a larger capacity.

- Upgrade your license edition to cover the features that you are using on your host.

- Disable the features that are not covered by the key that you are attempting to assign.

### Troubleshooting Plug-Ins

As you might know, plug-ins are used in vCenter, so it might seem unusual to discuss them under this heading. However, if you think about it, the services to the VMs are provided by the hosts and are only controlled by the vCenter. In addition, plug-ins that fail to enable can be frustrating, so troubleshooting them warrants discussion here.

In cases where plug-ins are not working, you have several troubleshooting options. You should first understand that plug-ins that run on the Tomcat server have extension.xml files that contain the URL of the application that can be accessed by the plug-in. These files are located in **C: \Program Files\VMware\Infrastructure\VirtualCenter Server\extensions**. If your vCenter Server and your vSphere Web Client are not on the same domain, or if the hostname of the plug-in server is changed, the clients will not be able to access the URL, and then the plug-in will not enable. You can address this issue by replacing the hostname in the extension file with the IP address of the plug-in server.

## Monitoring ESXi System Health

You can use your vSphere Client to monitor the state of your host hardware components. The host health monitoring tool allows you to monitor the health of many hardware components, including CPU, memory, fans, temperature, voltage, power, network, battery, storage, cable/interconnect, software, watchdog, and so on. Actually, the specific information that you will obtain will vary somewhat by the sensors available in your server hardware.

The host health monitoring tool gathers and presents data using Systems Management Architecture for Server Hardware (SMASH) profiles. SMASH (isn't that a fun acronym!) is an industry standard specification. You can obtain more information about SMASH at http://www.dmtf.org/standards/smash. You can monitor the host health status by connecting your vSphere Client directly to your host and selecting **Configuration** and then **Health Status**, as shown in Figure 20-10. As you might imagine, you are looking for a green check mark here. The status will turn yellow or red if the component violates a performance threshold or is not performing properly. Generally speaking, a yellow indicator signifies degraded performance, and a red indicator signifies that the component has either stopped or has tripped the highest (worst) threshold possible.

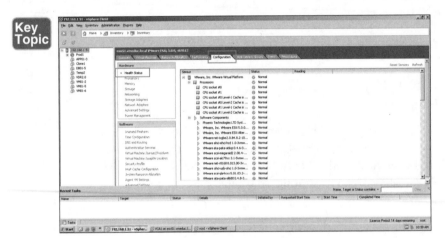

**Figure 20-10** Viewing Health Status on a Specific Host

You can also monitor your host's health by logging into the vSphere Web Client, selecting the host, and then clicking the **Monitor** tab and finally the **Hardware Status** tab, as shown in Figure 20-11.

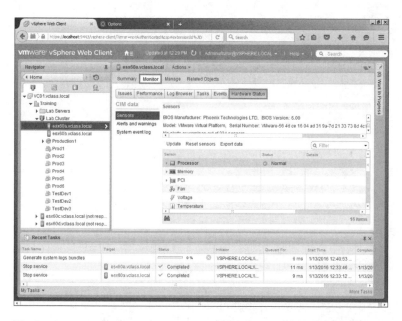

**Figure 20-11**    Viewing Hardware Status on a Host Through vCenter

## Exporting Diagnostic Information

If you have an issue that warrants contacting VMware technical support, the technicians might ask you to send them a log or two. If they want to see multiple logs, the easy way to send them "everything you've got" is to generate a diagnostic bundle. That sounds like more work for you, doesn't it? Actually, it's a very simple task that you can perform on your vCenter using the vSphere Web Client.

To export a diagnostic data bundle, you use either a host log-in, as detailed in Activity 20-3, or use a vCenter log-in, as detailed in Activity 20-4.

---

**Activity 20-3    Exporting Diagnostic Information from a Host Log-In**

1. Log on to your host with your vSphere Client.

2. Click your ESXi host in the console pane. Then select **File**, then **Export**, and finally **Export System Logs**, as shown in Figure 20-12.

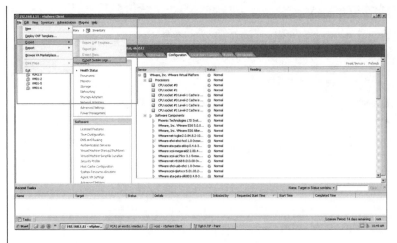

**Figure 20-12**   Exporting System Logs from a Single Host

3. Specify the system logs that you want to be exported, likely as directed by the VMware Support Team, as shown in Figure 20-13, and click **Next**.

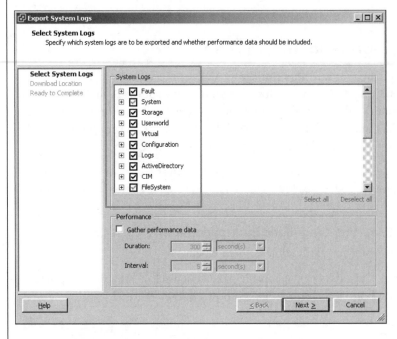

**Figure 20-13**   Selecting Logs to Export

4. Enter or select **Browse** to find the location to which you want to download the file, as shown in Figure 20-14.

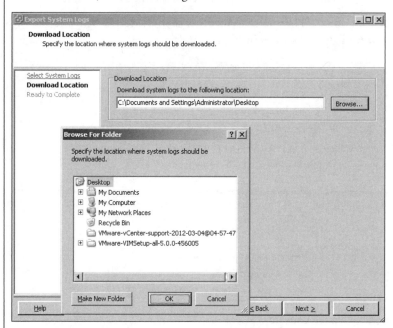

**Figure 20-14**   Selecting the Location for Exported Logs

5. You can view the progress of your System Log Bundle as it is downloaded to the destination, as shown in Figure 20-15.

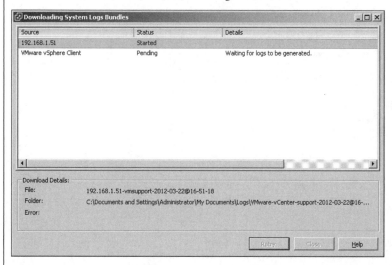

**Figure 20-15**   Viewing the Progress of a System Log Bundle on a Single Host

## Activity 20-4  Exporting Diagnostic Information from a vCenter Log-In

1. Log on to your vCenter using the vSphere Web Client.

2. Click your root object. Then select **Monitor**, then **System Logs**, and finally **Export System Logs**, as shown in Figure 20-16.

**Figure 20-16**  Exporting System Logs from vCenter

3. Specify the hosts that you want to include in the log bundle and whether you want to include the vCenter and Web Client logs as well, as shown in Figure 20-17, and click **Next**. These decisions will likely be directed by the VMware Support Team.

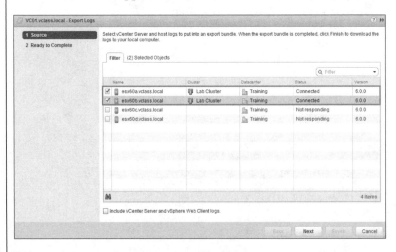

**Figure 20-17**  Specifying Hosts for Log Creation

**4.** Choose whether you want to gather performance data, as directed by the VMware Support Team, and select **Generate Log Bundle**, as shown in Figure 20-18.

**Figure 20-18**   Generating the Log Bundle

**5.** Select **Download Log Bundle** and choose the download destination for your logs, as shown in Figure 20-19.

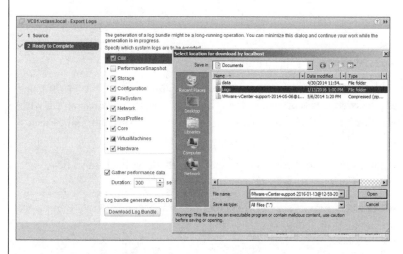

**Figure 20-19**   Selecting the Destination Location for Exported Logs

6. You can view your logs at the download destination, as shown in Figure 20-20.

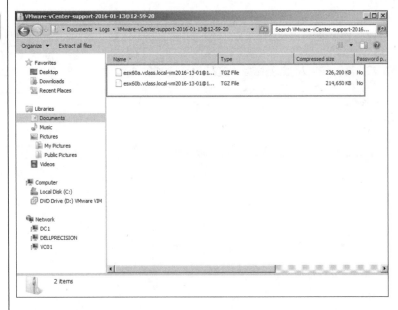

**Figure 20-20** Viewing the Download Destination

## Summary

This chapter covered the following main topics:

- Basic troubleshooting techniques for ESXi hosts and vCenter server. In particular, you learned how you can enable the tools that you can use along with the VMware Support Team as a last resort when more conventional tools are not working.

- How you can monitor an ESXi host's health on the host itself as well as through your vCenter.

- How you can easily export a diagnostic bundle to assist the VMware Support Team in assisting you.

## Exam Preparation Tasks

## Review All the Key Topics

Review the most important topics from the chapter, noted with the Key Topic icon in the outer margin of the page. Table 20-2 lists these key topics and the page numbers where each is found. Know how to perform basic troubleshooting on ESXi hosts, vSphere networks, vSphere storage, and HA/DRS clusters.

**Table 20-2**  Key Topics for Chapter 20

| Key Topic Element | Description | Page Number |
|---|---|---|
| Activity 20-1 | Enabling TSM from the DCUI | 493 |
| Activity 20-2 | Configuring TSM from the vSphere Web Client | 495 |
| Figure 20-7 | Viewing Logs on the DCUI | 497 |
| Bullet List | System Logs in DCUI | 498 |
| Figure 20-8 | Viewing the VMkernel Log | 498 |
| Figure 20-9 | Viewing Logs for a Single Host | 499 |
| Bullet List | Troubleshooting License Assignment | 501 |
| Figure 20-10 | Viewing Health Status on a Specific Host | 502 |
| Figure 20-11 | Viewing Hardware Status on a Host Through vCenter | 503 |
| Activity 20-3 | Exporting Diagnostic Information from a Host Log-In | 503 |
| Activity 20-4 | Exporting Diagnostic Information from a vCenter Log-In | 506 |
| Figure 20-20 | Viewing the Download Destination | 508 |

## Review Questions

The answers to these review questions are in Appendix A.

1. Which of the following tools is provided by VMware as a last resort to troubleshoot issues that cannot be resolved through more normal means?

   a. vCLI

   b. vSphere Web Client

   c. TSM

   d. PowerCLI

2. Which of the following are valid access paths for the TSM? (Choose two.)

   a. DCUI

   b. SSH

   c. vCLI

   d. PowerCLI

3. You are in the process of installing vCenter server on Windows when the installation fails. You choose to create a .zip file that contains logging information. Where on the Windows machine will you find the .zip file?

   a. On the desktop

   b. In My Documents

   c. On the root of C:

   d. In the Downloads folder

4. Which two locations will contain log information in regard to vCenter setup? (Choose two.)

   a. c:\ProgramData\VMware\vCenter-Server\logs

   b. c:\ProgramData\vCenter\Install\logs

   c. c:\users\*username*\AppData\Local\Temp

   d. c:\users\administrator\LogData\Local\Temp

5. You have installed ESXi, but when you boot the physical server it continues to boot to the installation .iso instead of the installed software. Which of the following should you do?

   a. Change the boot setting in the BIOS of the physical server.

   b. Change the boot setting in the BIOS of the first VM that you install.

   c. Reinstall ESXi and to a different drive that it recognizes.

   d. Reconnect the host to the vCenter Server.

6. You have installed ESXi on a physical server that has 16 logical CPUs. You attempt to install a key that allows for 32 logical processors. Which of the following will occur?

   a. You will be able to install the key and enable all 16 processors.

   b. You will not be able to install the key on that host.

   c. You will be able to install the key and enable all 32 processors temporarily until you install another key.

   d. The evaluation mode will immediately terminate, and you will not be able to use the host.

7. Which of the following tabs on the vCenter Web Client contains the Hardware Status tab?

   a. Hardware

   b. Monitor

   c. Manage

   d. Status

8. Which of the following technologies does ESXi use to gather and present data in host monitoring?

   a. DRS

   b. IP

   c. SMASH

   d. CIM

9. You are working with VMware Support and want to create a bundle that contains multiple logs with the least administrative effort. Which of the following should you do?

   a. Generate a log bundle.

   b. Select the logs that you want to create and export.

   c. Export all information and let VMware build the logs.

   d. Generate a separate report for each type of log.

10. Which of the following tabs contains the System Logs to export?

    a. Export

    b. Monitor

    c. Status

    d. Administration

**This chapter covers the following subjects:**

- Verifying Network Configuration
- Troubleshooting Common Storage Issues
- Troubleshooting Common VM Issues
- Verifying Correct Network Resources
- Troubleshooting Virtual Switch and Port Group Configuration Issues
- Troubleshooting Physical Network Adapter Configuration Issues
- Identifying and Detecting Common Knowledge Base Article Solutions

This chapter covers basic troubleshooting on your virtual networks and storage. In addition, you learn about troubleshooting common issues with VMs, port groups, and physical adapters. Finally, it covers using the VMware Knowledge base to learn from the experts about how to fix your issues. This understanding will help you troubleshoot your own systems and is essential to successfully navigate the troubleshooting questions on the exam.

## CHAPTER 21

# Performing Basic Troubleshooting of ESXi and vCenter Server Operations

## "Do I Know This Already?" Quiz

The "Do I Know This Already?" quiz allows you to assess whether you should read this entire chapter or simply jump to the "Exam Preparation Tasks" section for review. If you are in doubt, read the entire chapter. Table 21-1 outlines the major headings in this chapter and the corresponding "Do I Know This Already?" quiz questions. You can find the answers in Appendix A, "Answers to the 'Do I Know This Already?' Quizzes and Chapter Review Questions."

**Table 21-1** "Do I Know This Already?" Section-to-Question Mapping

| Foundation Topics Section | Questions Covered in This Section |
|---|---|
| Verifying Network Configuration | 1, 2 |
| Troubleshooting Common Storage Issues | 3, 4 |
| Troubleshooting Common VM Issues | 5, 6 |
| Verifying Correct Network Resources | 7 |
| Troubleshooting Virtual Switch and Port Group Configuration Issues | 8 |
| Troubleshooting Physical Network Adapter Configuration Issues | 9 |
| Identifying and Detecting Common Knowledge Base Article Solutions | 10 |

1. You are creating a management connection for your vSphere environment. Which of the following is a valid option?

   a. Create a VMkernel port and a separate VM port group that will each be used for management traffic.

   b. Create two VMkernel port groups that use the same vmnic.

   c. Create two VMkernel port groups that each use a separate vmnic.

   d. Create two VM port groups that are both for management and use two separate vmnics.

**2.** Which of the following are *not* true? (Choose two.)

    **a.** You can use VMkernel ports to enable vMotion.

    **b.** You can use VM port groups to enable vMotion.

    **c.** You can assign attributes to VM port groups.

    **d.** You cannot assign attributes to individual ports on a vDS.

**3.** You have clicked on Home/Storage. Which of the following might be visible in your Navigator pane? (Choose two.)

    **a.** Data centers

    **b.** Hosts

    **c.** Host Clusters

    **d.** Datastores

**4.** You want to view all hosts connected to a specific datastore. Which of the following is a valid option?

    **a.** Home, Hosts and Clusters, click on Host, Manage, Storage Devices

    **b.** Home, Storage, click on Datastore, Related Objects, Datastores

    **c.** Home, Storage, click on Datastore, Related Objects, Hosts

    **d.** Home, Hosts and Clusters, click on Host, Manage, Storage

**5.** Which of the following might improve the network performance of a VM? (Choose two.)

    **a.** Place VMs that communicate to each other frequently onto the same host on the same switch in the same subnet so they can communicate without using the external network at all.

    **b.** Change the speed and duplex settings on the vnic.

    **c.** Change the speed and duplex settings on the vmnic to which its port group is connected.

    **d.** Restart the guest operating system on the VM.

**6.** Which of the following are types of datastores? (Choose two.)

   **a.** VMFS

   **b.** RDM

   **c.** NFS

   **d.** iSCSI

**7.** Which of the following can you configure on a VM port group? (Choose two.)

   **a.** Security

   **b.** Default gateway

   **c.** NIC teaming

   **d.** IP subnet

**8.** Which of the following are true regarding vSwitch, port group, and port settings? (Choose two.)

   **a.** Settings for a vSS will override settings for port groups on it.

   **b.** Settings for port groups on a vSS will override settings for the vSwitch.

   **c.** Settings for a vDS will override settings for the port groups on it.

   **d.** Settings for a port on a vDS will override settings on the switch.

**9.** You want to view the point on the host at which the traffic moves out of the vSphere and into the physical network. Which terms might be used for this point of reference? (Choose two.)

   **a.** vmnic

   **b.** vnic

   **c.** Virtual port

   **d.** Physical NIC

**10.** Which of the following are valid search options on the VMware Knowledge Base? (Choose two.)

   **a.** Article ID

   **b.** Product

   **c.** Date

   **d.** Time

**Foundation Topics**

# Verifying Network Configuration

Your vSphere network should connect your VMs to each other and allow your VMs to connect to physical resources outside your vSphere. In addition, your network should provide a management port (or multiple management ports) that allows you to control your hosts and VMs. Finally, your network might very well be involved with your storage if you are using IP storage options such as Internet Small Computer System Interface (iSCSI), storage-area networking (SAN), or Network File System (NFS) datastores.

Because your vSphere network is such an integral part of your virtual data center, you should understand the network components and their correct configuration so that you can troubleshoot them when necessary. In this section, you learn how to verify and troubleshoot network configurations, including your VMs, port groups, and physical network adapters. In addition, you learn how to identify the root cause of a network issue based on troubleshooting information.

At the very least, your network configuration should include a VMkernel port for management; otherwise, you won't be able to control the host remotely. In fact, one is provided for you with the default installation of an ESXi host. If you are using vSSs, you will need at least one VMkernel management port on each host. If you are using a vDS, you will need at least one VMkernel management port on the vDS. Of course, it is possible to configure more than one management port, and that is certainly recommended on a vDS. Another option is to configure one VMkernel port but then configure it to use more than one physical NIC (vmnic). In addition, you might have additional VMkernel ports for a myriad of reasons, including an additional heartbeat network for high availability (HA), an additional port for IP storage (iSCSI or NFS), fault tolerance (FT) logging for vSphere fault tolerance, Virtual SAN, and vMotion.

Other than the VMkernel ports, the rest of the ports on a switch will be used for uplinks to the physical world or, for VM port groups, most will likely be used for VM port groups. The correct use of VM port groups enables you to get more options out of a single switch (vSS or vDS) by assigning different attributes to different port groups. As you know, with vDSs, you can even assign different attributes at the individual port level. VM port groups give you options on which to connect a VM.

Verifying your network configuration consists of viewing your network with an understanding of how all of these virtual components are linked together. Only by understanding how it should be connected will you be able to troubleshoot any configuration issue. Figure 21-1 shows one of the views you can use through your vSphere Web Client to manage the networking of your host.

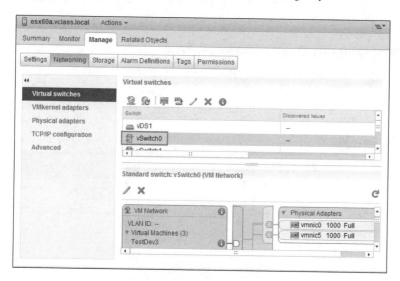

**Figure 21-1**   Managing the Networking of a vSS

## Troubleshooting Common Storage Issues

As you know, it's possible for a VM to be given visibility to its actual physical storage locations, as with a physical compatibility raw device mapping (RDM). However, it should not be the norm in your virtual data center. In most cases, you will use either a Virtual Machine File System (VMFS) datastore or an NFS datastore, either of which hides the specifics of the actual physical storage from the VM. Also, you may begin to use a Virtual SAN.

Regardless of what type of storage you use, you need to configure it properly to get your desired result. In this section, you learn about verifying storage configuration. Later, the chapter covers troubleshooting many aspects of storage, including storage contention issues, overcommitment issues, and iSCSI software initiator issues. In addition, storage reports and storage maps that you can use for troubleshooting are discussed. Finally, you learn how to identify the root cause of a storage issue based on troubleshooting information.

## Verifying Storage Configuration

Your vCenter includes two views that will assist you in verifying your storage configuration: the Manage, Storage link in Hosts and Clusters view and the Storage view. Each of these tools lists information about your storage, and there is some overlap with regard to what these tools list. If you are focusing on what a host can see, you might use the **Manage**, **Storage** link, as shown in Figure 21-2.

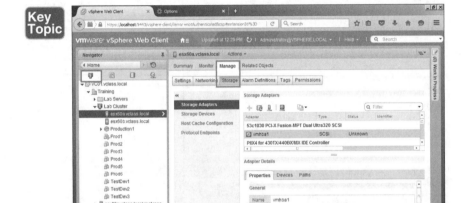

**Figure 21-2**  The Manage, Storage Link in Hosts and Clusters View

Click **Refresh** to make sure that you are seeing the latest information. You can use the **Manage**, **Storage** link to quickly identify the storage adapters and storage devices that are accessible to that host. In addition, you can view the status, type, capacity, free space, and so on, for each one. You can even customize what you show by right-clicking at the top of a column and selecting only what you want to see, as shown in Figure 21-3.

The Storage view allows you to see some of the same information as the Manage, Storage link, but also much more detail about datastores. You can determine which hosts are connected to each datastore, but that is not the primary focus. Instead, the primary focus is detailed information about the datastores to which the hosts are connected.

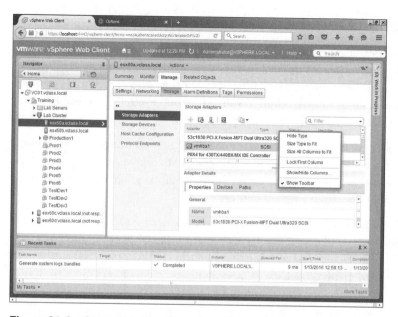

**Figure 21-3**  Customizing the Manage, Storage Link

You should click the **Refresh** link to make sure that you are seeing the latest information. Figure 21-4 shows the Storage view with a datastore selected in the Navigator (left pane) and the Summary tab selected in the details pane. As you can see, you can also show many more tabs.

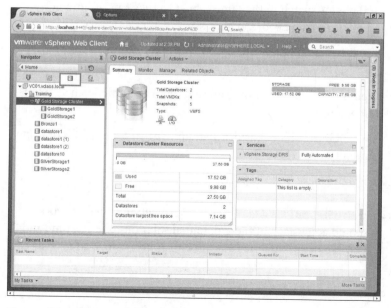

**Figure 21-4**  The Storage View Summary Tab

## Troubleshooting Common VM Issues

I've seen and written about many models of troubleshooting that look great on paper but might be overkill for the real world. Also, VMware doesn't subscribe to a certain five-step or seven-step model of troubleshooting with regard to the exam. Therefore, you should be able to "think through" a troubleshooting question based on what you know about virtual networking.

In general, a VM's network performance is dependent on two things: its application workload and your network configuration. Dropped network packets indicate a bottleneck in the network. Slow network performance could be a sign of load-balancing issues or the lack of load balancing altogether.

You'll know if you have high latency and slow network performance; there is no hiding that! How will you know if you have dropped packets? You can use the Advanced performance charts to examine dropped transmit (droppedTx) and dropped receive (droppedRx) packets. (These should be zero, or very close to it, if you don't have a bottleneck on this resource.)

If these utilities indicate that there is an issue, you can verify or adjust each of the following to address the issue:

- Verify that each of the VMs has VMware Tools installed.

- Verify that vmxnet3 vNIC drivers are being used wherever possible.

- If possible, place VMs that communicate to each other frequently onto the same host on the same switch in the same subnet so they can communicate without using the external network at all.

- Verify that the speed and duplex settings on your physical NICs are what you expected.

- Use separate physical NICs to handle different types of traffic, such as VM, iSCSI, VMotion, and so on.

- If you are using 1-Gbps NICs, consider upgrading to 10-Gbps NICs or using Link Aggregation Groups (LAGs).

- Use vNIC drivers that are TSO-capable

This is not an exhaustive list, but it's a good start toward better virtual network performance. You should apply each of these potential solutions one at a time and retest. In this way, you can determine the root cause of your network issue, even as you are fixing it.

Also, as you know, it's possible for a VM to be given visibility to its actual physical storage locations, as with a physical compatibility raw device mapping (RDM). However, it should not be the norm in your virtual data center. In most cases, you will use either a Virtual Machine File System (VMFS) datastore or an NFS datastore, either of which hides the specifics of the actual physical storage from the VM. Also, you may begin to use a Virtual SAN.

Regardless of what type of storage you use, you need to configure it properly to get your desired result. This includes verifying storage configuration and determining configurations in regard to connectivity and multipathing, iSCSI connections, and so on. Each of these is briefly discussed, along with how you can obtain information about them that is necessary for troubleshooting.

### Verifying Storage Configuration

Your vCenter includes two views that assist you in verifying your storage configuration: the Manage, Storage link in Hosts and Clusters view and the Storage view. Each of these tools lists information about your storage, and there is some overlap with regard to what these tools list. If you are focusing on what a host can see, you might use the **Manage**, **Storage** link, as shown in Figure 21-5.

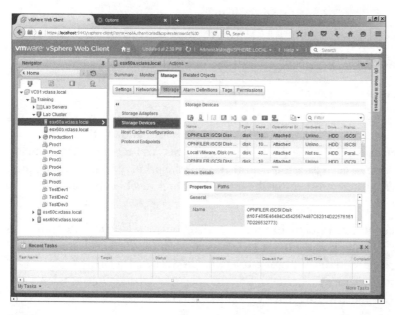

**Figure 21-5**  The Manage, Storage, Storage Devices Link in Hosts and Clusters View

Click **Refresh** to make sure that you are seeing the latest information. You can use the **Manage, Storage** link to quickly identify the storage adapters and storage devices that are accessible to that host. In addition, you can view the status, type, capacity, free space, and so on, for each one. You can even customize what you show by right-clicking at the top of a column and selecting only what you want to see, as shown in Figure 21-6.

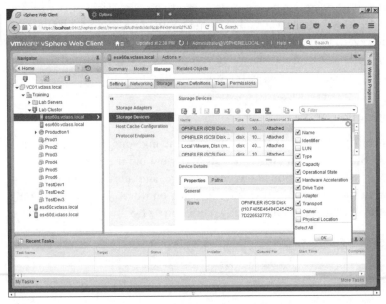

**Figure 21-6**    Customizing the Manage, Storage Link

The Storage view allows you to see some of the same information as the Manage, Storage link, but also much more detail about datastores. You can determine which hosts are connected to each datastore, but that is not the primary focus. Instead, the primary focus is detailed information about the datastores to which the hosts are connected.

You should click the **Refresh** link to make sure that you are seeing the latest information. Figure 21-7 shows the Storage view with a datastore cluster selected in the Navigator (left pane) and the Monitor tab selected in the details pane. As you can see, you can also show many more tabs. For example, the Related Objects tab in Figure 21-8 shows the hosts that have visibility to this datastore.

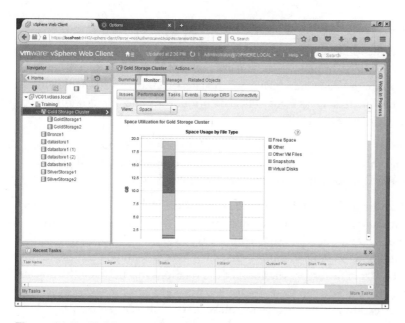

**Figure 21-7**  The Storage View Monitor Tab

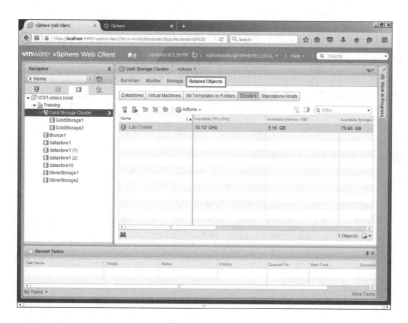

**Figure 21-8**  The Related Objects Tab

### Troubleshooting Storage Reports and Storage Maps

As you have already noticed, you can use a great number of reports and tools for troubleshooting vSphere. In most cases, you are going to be better off learning how to use the vSphere Web Client. Many of the latest features are available only through the Web Client, such as Cross-Host vMotion. Also, the Windows-based vSphere Client is on its way out.

However, there are a few exceptions. For example, at press time, you cannot view maps of any kind through the vSphere Web Client. Because of this, I will present this section on the Windows-based vSphere Client.

You can use the Storage Views tab on the vSphere Client in Reports view to gather a tremendous amount of data about your storage. You can get this same data from the vSphere Web Client, but vSphere Client offers just another location to see a lot of data. In addition, on your Windows-based vSphere Client, you can use the Maps view to see a graphical representation of the relationships between the objects in your vSphere. In fact, you can view storage reports and maps for every object in your data centers except for the networking objects, which have their own reports and maps. This section briefly discusses the use of these storage reports and maps.

### Storage Reports

Using your Storage Views tab, you can display storage reports to view storage information for any object except networking. For example, you can view datastores and LUNs used by a VM, the adapters that are used to access the LUN, and even the status of the paths to the LUNs. To access storage reports from the Storage Views tab, follow the steps outlined in Activity 21-1.

**Activity 21-1   Viewing Storage Reports**

1. Log on to your vCenter with your vSphere Client.

2. In the console pane, select the object on which you want to view connected storage (in this case, VM-02), and then open the Storage Views tabs and click the **Reports** button, as shown in Figure 21-9.

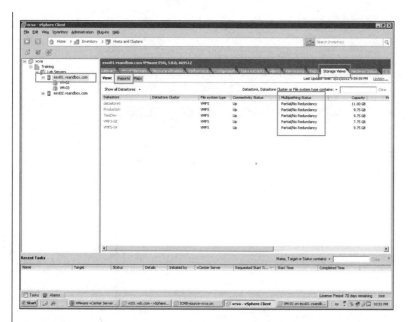

**Figure 21-9** The Storage Views Tab and Reports Button

3. Select **View** and then **Filtering** to display the **Show All** [*Category of Items*] or click the amazingly small drop-down arrow, as shown in Figure 21-10.

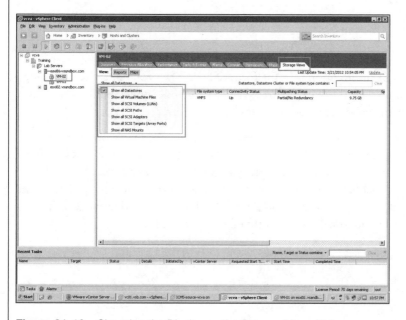

**Figure 21-10** Choosing the Display on the Storage Views Tab

**4.** Move the cursor over the column heading to the description of each attribute, as shown in Figure 21-11.

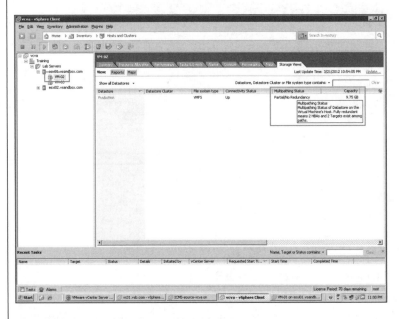

**Figure 21-11**   Viewing Column Descriptions

## Storage Maps

As you can see, Storage Reports can give you a lot of information about your data stores, but all the information is in the form of text. The problem is that we (people) don't think in text; we think in pictures. We can generally understand a situation better if someone will take the time to draw us a picture.

In essence, that's just what VMware has done with the Maps view of the Storage Views tab. You can use the view to display a graphical representation of every object that relates to your storage. For example, you can tell whether a specific VM has access to a host that has access to a storage processor that has access to a LUN, and whether or not there is a datastore on the LUN. To use your Maps view on your Storage Views tab, follow the steps outlined in Activity 21-2.

**Activity 21-2   Viewing Storage Maps**

1. Log on to your vCenter with your vSphere Client.

2. In the console pane, select the object on which you want to view connected storage objects (in this case, VM-03), and then open the Storage Views tab and click the **Maps** button, as shown in Figure 21-12.

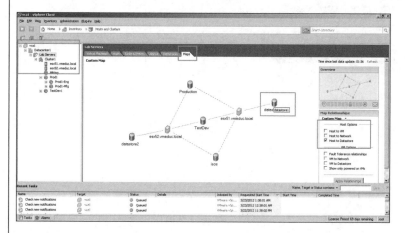

**Figure 21-12**   Viewing Maps in Storage Views

3. You can choose the objects that you would like to display on your map.

4. You can also hover your mouse pointer over an object for a few seconds to see the callout that gives a detailed description of that object.

## Verifying Correct Network Resources

As I mentioned earlier, port groups give you options on which to connect a VM. In my opinion, you can see this more clearly from the VM's standpoint. In Figure 21-13, I right-clicked a VM and then selected **Edit Settings**. As you can see, I have a list of port groups from which to choose for the virtual network interface card (vNIC) on this VM called **Network adapter 1**. These port groups are all VM port groups on this switch or on the vDS to which this host is connected. Also, note the Device Status check boxes at the top right of the screen. These should be selected on an active connection. When the VM is connected to the appropriate port group, it can be configured with the correct network resources. If it is not on the correct port group, many issues could result, including having the wrong security, traffic shaping, NIC teaming options, or even having a total lack of connectivity.

**Figure 21-13**  Viewing a VM's Network Configuration

## Troubleshooting Virtual Switch and Port Group Configuration Issues

Just connecting the VM to a port group does not guarantee that you get the desired configuration. What if the port group itself is not configured properly? You should understand that any configuration options on a vSS will be overridden by conflicting options on a port group of the same switch. In addition, any options on a port group of a vDS will be overridden by conflicting options on a specific port. These options were covered earlier in Chapter 6, "Configuring vSS and vDS Features," so this section does not go into great detail about security, traffic shaping, NIC teaming, and so on, but Figure 21-14 shows the general area in which you can find them on a vDS. The main point here is to verify that you have set the properties appropriately for the VMs that are connected to the port group.

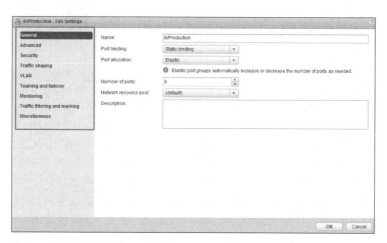

**Figure 21-14** Port Group Settings on a vDS

# Troubleshooting Physical Network Adapter Configuration Issues

It can't all be virtual! At some point, you have to connect your vSphere to the physical world. The point at which the data moves out of the host and into the physical world can be referred to as a physical network adapter, a vmnic, or an uplink. Because the configuration of this point of reference is for a piece of physical equipment, the available settings are what you might expect for any other physical adapter, namely speed, duplex, wake on LAN, and so on, as shown in Figure 21-15.

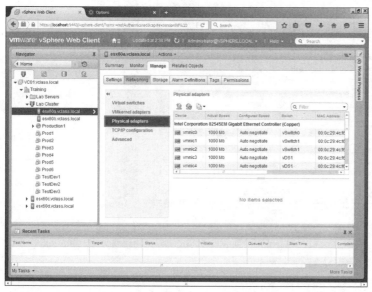

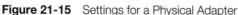

**Figure 21-15** Settings for a Physical Adapter

## Identifying and Detecting Common Knowledge Base Article Solutions

Everyone makes mistakes and has problems from time to time. The difference between the wise people and those who are not so wise is that the wise ones learn from the mistakes and problems of others, not just their own. This is the purpose of the VMware Knowledge Base. It is a quick resource that you can use to learn more about virtualization issues that you face on a daily basis. It works on the principle that whatever you are experiencing has most likely been experienced by someone before you and will be experienced again by someone after you.

You can access the VMware Knowledge Base at kb.vmware.com, as shown in Figure 21-16. There you can read the most popular documents, most recent documents, alerts, or type in the information for your own customized search. You can narrow it down by product or search by an Article ID to which you have been referred. There is even a Knowledge Base article (Article ID 878) about how to use the Knowledge Base! Using the Knowledge Base is free, so frequent use will help you stay up to date with the latest information from VMware in the most economical way possible.

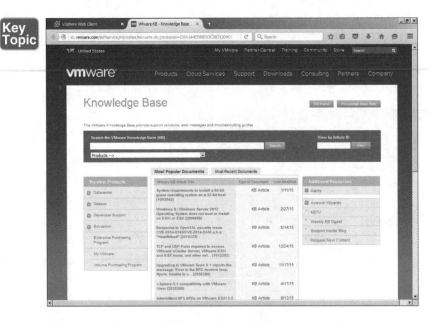

**Figure 21-16**   The VMware Knowledge Base

## Summary

This chapter covers the following main topics:

- Basic troubleshooting techniques for your network, storage, and VMs

- How you can verify that you have the correct network resources on the VMs so that you get the most performance from them

- Troubleshooting virtual connections as well as the physical connections of your hosts

- How you can learn from others by consulting the VMware Knowledge Base

## Exam Preparation Tasks

## Review All the Key Topics

Review the most important topics from the chapter, noted with the Key Topic icon in the outer margin of the page. Table 21-2 lists these key topics and the page numbers where each is found. Know how to perform basic troubleshooting on ESXi hosts, vSphere networks, vSphere storage, and HA/DRS clusters.

**Table 21-2**  Key Topics for Chapter 21

| Key Topic Element | Description | Page Number |
|---|---|---|
| Figure 21-1 | Managing the Networking of a vSS | 519 |
| Figure 21-2 | The Manage, Storage Link in Hosts and Clusters View | 520 |
| Figure 21-3 | Customizing the Manage, Storage Link | 521 |
| Figure 21-4 | The Storage View Summary Tab | 521 |
| Bullet List | VM Configuration for Network Performance | 522 |
| Figure 21-5 | The Manage, Storage, Storage Devices Link in Hosts and Clusters View | 523 |
| Figure 21-6 | Customizing the Manage, Storage Link | 524 |
| Figure 21-7 | The Storage View Monitor Tab | 525 |
| Figure 21-8 | The Related Objects Tab | 525 |
| Activity 21-1 | Viewing Storage Reports | 526 |
| Activity 21-2 | Viewing Storage Maps | 529 |

| Key Topic Element | Description | Page Number |
|---|---|---|
| Figure 21-13 | Viewing a VM's Network Configuration | 530 |
| Figure 21-14 | Port Group Settings on a VDS | 531 |
| Figure 21-15 | Settings for a Physical Adapter | 531 |
| Figure 21-16 | The VMware Knowledge Base | 532 |

## Review Questions

The answers to these review questions are in Appendix A.

1. You are creating a management port for your vSphere environment. Which of the following is a valid option?

    a. Create a VMkernel port and a separate VM port group that will each be used for management traffic.

    b. Create two VMkernel port groups that use the same vmnic.

    c. Create one VMkernel port group that uses two different vmnics.

    d. Create two VM port groups that are both for management and use two separate vmnics.

2. Which of the following are true? (Choose two.)

    a. You can use VMkernel ports to enable vMotion.

    b. You can use VM port groups to enable vMotion.

    c. You can assign attributes to VM port groups.

    d. You cannot assign attributes to individual ports on a vDS.

3. You want to quickly view all the storage options that are available to all the hosts in your vSphere with least administrative effort. Which of the following should you do?

    a. Click Home, Storage

    b. Click Home, Host and Clusters, Manage, Storage

    c. Click Search, Storage Options

    d. Click Storage Options, Hosts

4. You want to view all the datastores to which a specific host is connected. Which of the following is a valid option?

    a. Home, Hosts and Clusters, click on Host, Manage, Storage Devices

    b. Home, Hosts and Clusters, click on Host, Related Objects, Datastores

    c. Home, Storage, click on Datastore, Related Objects, Hosts

    d. Home, Hosts and Clusters, click on Host, Manage, Storage

5. Which of the following might improve the network performance of a VM? (Choose two.)

    a. Install VMware Tools.

    b. Use vmxnet3 vNIC drivers.

    c. Increase the throughput of the vNIC on the Network tab.

    d. Restart the guest operating system on the VM.

6. Which of the following are true regarding RDMs?

    a. You should use RDMs whenever possible, instead of datastores.

    b. A physical compatibility RDM gives the VM visibility to the actual storage location.

    c. VMFS and NFS datastores are generally preferable to RDMs.

    d. A physical compatibility RDM is just a pointer to a datastore.

7. Which of the following can you configure on a VM port group? (Choose two.)

    a. Security

    b. Traffic shaping

    c. Storage location

    d. IP subnet

8. Which of the following are true regarding vSwitch, port group, and port settings? (Choose two.)

    a. Settings for a vSS will override settings for port groups on it.

    b. Settings for port groups on a vSS will override settings for the switch.

    c. Settings for a vDS will override settings for the port groups on it.

    d. Settings for a port on a vDS will override settings on the switch.

9.  You want to view the point on the host at which the traffic moves out of the vSphere and into the physical network. Which terms might be used for this point of reference? (Choose two.)

    a.  vmnic

    b.  vnic

    c.  Virtual port

    d.  Uplink

10. Which of the following are on the Home page of the VMware Knowledge Base? (Choose two.)

    a.  Most Popular Documents

    b.  Most Recent Documents

    c.  Most Debated Documents

    d.  Most Interesting Documents

**This chapter covers the following subjects:**

- Troubleshooting Virtual Machine Resource Contention Issues

- Troubleshooting Storage Overcommitment Issues

- Troubleshooting iSCSI Software Initiator Configuration Issues

- Fault Tolerant VM Network Latency Issues

- Troubleshooting VMware Tools Installation Issues

- Troubleshooting VM States

- Virtual Machine Constraints

- Identifying the Root Cause of a Storage Issue

- Identifying Common Virtual Machine Boot Disk Errors

- Setting and Managing Settings in the vSphere Web Client

- Correcting Common Warnings and Alerts within the vSphere Web Client

This chapter discusses performing basic troubleshooting on your VMs. In addition, you learn how to troubleshoot common issues with FT latency, VM states, and VM constraints. The chapter also covers identifying the root cause of a storage issue and identifying and correcting common boot issues. Finally, you learn about managing in the vSphere Web Client, including "real world" information in regard to settings, properties, and warnings and alerts. This understanding will help you troubleshoot your own systems and is essential to successfully navigate the troubleshooting questions on the exam.

## CHAPTER 22

# Performing Basic Troubleshooting of Virtual Machine Operations

## "Do I Know This Already?" Quiz

The "Do I Know This Already?" quiz allows you to assess whether you should read this entire chapter or simply jump to the "Exam Preparation Tasks" section for review. If you are in doubt, read the entire chapter. Table 22-1 outlines the major headings in this chapter and the corresponding "Do I Know This Already?" quiz questions. You can find the answers in Appendix A, "Answers to the 'Do I Know This Already?' Quizzes and Chapter Review Questions."

**Table 22-1**  "Do I Know This Already?" Section-to-Question Mapping

| Foundation Topics Section | Questions Covered in This Section |
|---|---|
| Troubleshooting Virtual Machine Resource Contention Issues | 1 |
| Fault Tolerant Network Latency Issues | 2 |
| Troubleshooting VMware Tools Installation Issues | 3 |
| Troubleshooting VM States | 4 |
| Virtual Machine Constraints | 5 |
| Identifying the Root Cause of a Storage Issue | 6 |
| Identifying Common Virtual Machine Boot Disk Errors | 7 |
| Setting and Managing Settings in vSphere Web Client | 8, 9 |
| Correcting Common Warnings and Alerts Within the vSphere Web Client | 10 |

1. Which of the following can have a negative effect on virtual machine performance? (Choose two.)

    a. Excessive SCSI reservations

    b. Multipathing

    c. Path thrashing

    d. Adequate LUN queue depth

2. Which of the following could cause network latency issues on FT-enabled VMs? (Choose two.)

    a. Hosts with properly configured 1-Gbps vmnics

    b. Hosts with improperly configured 10-Gbps vmnics

    c. VMs with vmxnet3 vnics

    d. Hosts with properly configured 10-Gbps vmnics

3. You are attempting to install VMware tools without logging on to the VM first, but the installation is failing. Which of the following could be causing the issue?

    a. An antivirus software on the Guest OS is preventing the installation.

    b. It is not possible to install VMware tools without first logging on to the VM.

    c. You are performing an interactive installation.

    d. The VMware tools software is waiting for you to complete the wizard.

4. Which of the following could cause a VM to become orphaned?

    a. HA failover was unsuccessful for the VM.

    b. The VM was vMotioned to a host that was powered off.

    c. The host of the VM failed, and it was restarted on another host by HA.

    d. The parent resource pool of the VM was accidentally deleted.

5. Which of the following might result from setting Admission Control Policy in HA too conservatively? (Choose two.)

    a. You might not be able to start as many VMs as you had hoped.

    b. VMs might be vMotioned more frequently than you had planned.

    c. You might not be able to start a VM with high reservations.

    d. All VMs will run with restricted settings.

6. Which of the following are tools that you could use to identify the root cause of a storage issue? (Choose two.)

   a. Storage Maps in the vSphere Client

   b. Task Manager on a VMs OS

   c. The Storage Views tab in the vSphere Web Client

   d. The DCUI of a host

7. You have created a VM using the wizard and identified the OS as Windows Server 2008. You attempt to install an ISO on the VM that contains Windows Server 2003. Which of the following will result? (Choose two.)

   a. The ISO will install properly.

   b. The installation will fail.

   c. The boot disk on the VM will not be recognized.

   d. The boot disk will be recognized but will not contain the proper ISO to run Windows Server 2008, so the installation will fail.

8. You want to improve your user experience on your vSphere 6 Web Client that has a default installation. Which of the following should you do? (Choose two.)

   a. Move Recent Tasks to the bottom of the screen.

   b. Unpin the right side of the screen.

   c. Add a Summary tab to each of the objects that you use the most.

   d. Hide the Getting Started tabs.

9. What are two practical techniques you can use to make sure that you are using the screen space on your vSphere Web Client to your best advantage? (Choose two.)

   a. Leverage your browser tabs.

   b. Hide the Getting Started tabs.

   c. Log on as administrator@vsphere.local.

   d. Unpin the sides.

**10.** Which of the following occur when you choose to acknowledge an alarm in your vCenter? (Choose two.)

   **a.** Your credentials are recorded and you have taken the responsibility to fix the issue.

   **b.** The alarm is reset to green and therefore disabled.

   **c.** The inventory will no longer show the alert or warning on the object's icon.

   **d.** All actions associated with the alarm will be disabled.

## Foundation Topics

# Troubleshooting Virtual Machine Resource Contention Issues

This section focuses on troubleshooting storage issues on a VM. Storage is one of the "core four" resources that you need to know how to manage. The reason that I am focusing on storage in this section is that I have already discussed proper management and troubleshooting of the other three resources of the core four—namely, networking, CPU, and memory.

To troubleshoot storage contention issues, you should focus on the storage adapters that connect your hosts to their datastores. The settings for multipathing of your storage are in the Storage view. Click **Manage**, **Settings**, and then **Connectivity and Multipathing**; finally, click your host to show the Multipathing Details, as shown in Figure 22-1. You can change path selection policy after clicking **Edit Multipathing**, as shown in Figure 22-2.

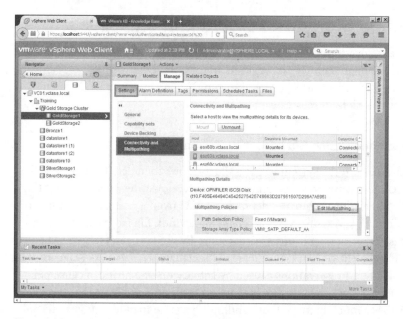

**Figure 22-1**  Settings for Multipathing of Storage

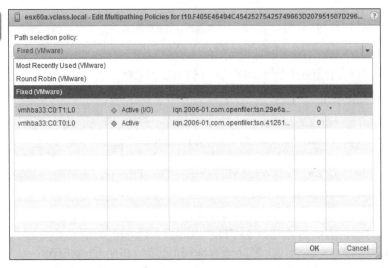

**Figure 22-2**    Configuring Multipathing in the Storage View

## Troubleshooting Storage Overcommitment Issues

As you continue to grow your vSphere, and your hosts and VMs are competing for the same resources, many factors can begin to affect storage performance. They include excessive SCSI reservations, path thrashing, and inadequate LUN queue depth. This section briefly discusses each of these issues.

### Excessive Reservations Cause Slow Host Performance

Some operations require the system to get a file lock or a metadata lock in VMFS. They might include creating or expanding a datastore, powering on a VM, creating or deleting a file, creating a template, deploying a VM from a template, creating a new VM, migrating a VM with vMotion, changing a vmdk file from thin to thick, and so on. These types of operations create a short-lived SCSI reservation, which temporarily locks the entire LUN or at least the metadata database. As you can imagine, excessive SCSI reservations caused by activity on one host can cause performance degradation on other servers that are accessing the same VMFS. Actually, ESXi 6.0 does a much better job of handling this issue than legacy systems did because only the metadata is locked and not the entire LUN.

If you have older hosts and you need to address this issue, you should ensure that you have the latest BIOS updates installed on your hosts and that you have the latest host bus adapter (HBA) firmware installed across all hosts. You should also consider using more small logical unit numbers (LUNs) rather than fewer large LUNs for your datastores. In addition, you should reduce the number of VM snapshots because they can cause numerous SCSI reservations. Finally, follow the Configuration Maximums document and reduce the number of VMs per LUN to the recommended maximum, even if you have seen that you can actually add more than that figure.

### Path Thrashing Causes Slow Performance

Path thrashing is most likely to occur on active-passive arrays. It's caused by two hosts attempting to access the same LUN through different storage processors. The result is that the LUN is often seen as not available to both hosts. The default setting for the Patch Selection Policy (PSP) of Most Recently Used will generally keep this from occurring. In addition, ensure that all hosts that share the same set of LUNs on the active-passive arrays use the same storage processor. Properly configured active-active arrays do not cause path thrashing.

## Troubleshooting iSCSI Software Initiator Configuration Issues

If your ESXi host generates more commands to a LUN than it can possibly handle, the excess commands are queued by the VMkernel. This situation causes increased latency, which can affect the performance of your VMs. It is generally caused by an improper setting of LUN queue depth, the setting of which varies by the type of storage. You should determine the proper LUN queue depth for your storage from your vendor documentation and then adjust your Disk.SchedNumReqOutstanding parameter accordingly.

## Fault Tolerant VM Network Latency Issues

For specific VMs on which you are using vSphere Fault Tolerance (FT), you might encounter issues related to FT that you need to address. If you encounter network latency issues with regard to FT-enabled VMs, you should ensure that 10-Gbps links are being used between the hosts and that the available bandwidth for FT is kept very high. There will be an associated overhead for the FT traffic, but it should still function well with sufficient bandwidth.

# Troubleshooting VMware Tools Installation Issues

VMware tools are highly recommended for every VM installation because they provide the drivers needed for advanced networking, efficient snapshotting, guest OS heartbeat, efficient memory handling, and much more. In most cases, you will just include VMware Tools as part of your template. In cases where you are installing the OS from the original software, you should install VMware Tools immediately after installing the OS on the VM.

Your Web Client will clearly inform you that VMware Tools are not installed on your VM, as shown in Figure 22-3. In general, VMware Tools are simple and "straightforward" to install. The one issue that you might encounter when installing VMware Tools if you choose to install them without logging onto the VM first is that you won't know how the installation is proceeding; or even if it is proceeding. To avoid this issue, you should install VMware Tools interactively. To do this, log on to the desktop of the VM first and then go to **VM, Guest, Install VMware Tools** from the logon. In this way, you will be able to monitor the installation of VMware Tools. Installing VMware Tools interactively will also enable you to ensure that no antivirus software on the VMs OS is preventing the installation of VMware Tools.

**Figure 22-3**   Summary Tab Showing VMware Tools Not Installed on VM

# Troubleshooting VM States

In rare cases, VMs that reside on an ESXi host connected to a vCenter server might become "lost" to the point that the VMs exist on the database of the vCenter but are not recognized by the host. This can happen if an HA failover is unsuccessful or if a VM is unregistered from the host instead of from the vCenter. In this case, you should right-click the VM, select to remove it from inventory, and then reregister the same VM by right-clicking its .vmx file and selecting to **Register VM**, as shown in Figure 22-4.

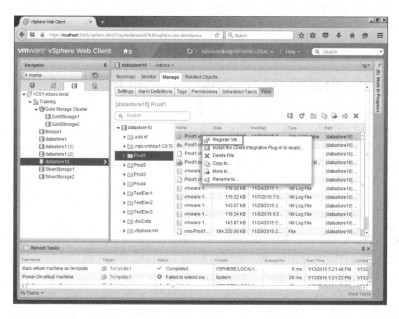

**Figure 22-4**   Reregistering an Orphaned VM

# Virtual Machine Constraints

As you know, Admission Control Policy in HA causes each host to reserve enough resources to recover VMs in the case of another host's failure on the same HA cluster. This means that if you set your Admission Control Policy too conservatively, you might not be able to start as many VMs as you may have thought possible. For example, changing from a policy that allows for only one host failure to one that allows two host failures can have a dramatic effect on the VM capacity of your cluster, especially in a small cluster. Therefore, the best thing you can do is verify that the settings that you expect to see are still there and that all the hosts you are counting on are still running.

## Identifying the Root Cause of a Storage Issue

After you have obtained information from the reports and maps provided by your vCenter, you can use your knowledge of your systems to compare what you are viewing to what should be occurring. One "catch-22" is that the time that you are most likely to need the information is also the time at which it is most likely to be unavailable. For this reason, consider printing a copy of your storage maps when everything is running smoothly to be kept on hand for a time when you need to troubleshoot. Then if you have access to the current maps, you can compare what you are seeing with what you have in print. However, if you can no longer use the tools, you have the printed map to use as an initial guide until you can access the current configuration.

## Identifying Common Virtual Machine Boot Disk Errors

This is kind of a funny topic because virtual machine boot disk errors are really no different from physical machine boot disk errors; the OS on the VM does not "know" that it's on a VM. However, if you attempt to boot a VM and it cannot recognize the disk at all, the chances are very good that the wrong type of controller is configured on the virtual machine.

This usually results from going outside of what the wizard selects for an installation of a controller based on the OS that you select. For example, Windows Server 2003 will not recognize LSI Logic SAS because it didn't exist when Windows Server 2003 was created. Therefore, for Windows Server 2003, you should use an "older" controller such as LSI Logic Parallel. If you follow the wizard during VM installation and make sure that the controller is appropriate for the OS, you should not have this issue; however, you can reconfigure the controller on a powered-off VM by editing the setting on the Virtual Hardware tab, as shown in Figure 22-5.

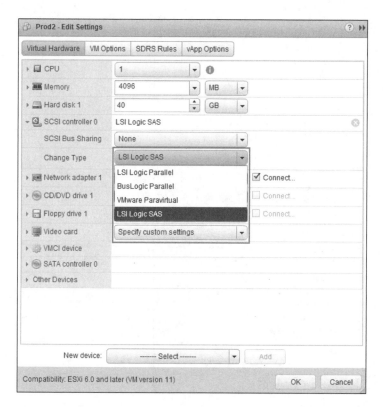

**Figure 22-5**   Changing Disk Controller on Virtual Hardware

Another much less common issue is when a VM has more than one virtual disk and the second disk contains only data and no OS. Chances are good that the data disk was created second and therefore will not be first in the boot order, so it should not cause an issue. However, if you are receiving an error that indicates that the disk can be read but does not contain an OS, then you should check the boot order in the BIOS of the VM, just as you would in a physical machine. You can make the BIOS settings available for a one-time boot by selecting the check box in the Option settings of the VM, as shown in Figure 22-6.

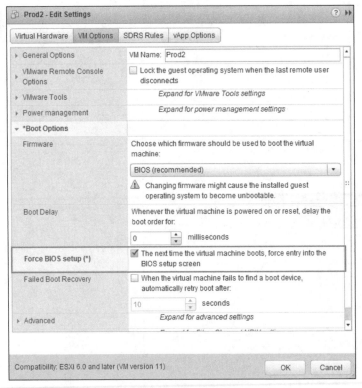

**Figure 22-6**   Forcing a VM to Boot to BIOS Settings

## Setting and Managing Settings in the vSphere Web Client

There is much to be said about the vSphere Web Client. It's a topic of heated discussion in many VMware circles. Some people are starting to like the Web Client, especially the latest version that comes with vSphere 6. Others may never like the vSphere Web Client and wish that VMware would just let everything run through the original desktop-based c## client. So, what settings can you change to get the most out of the vSphere Web Client? You can change many settings to improve your user experience, but following is a list of a few of my favorites.

- **Take off the training wheels:** Because you probably want to see the Summary tab when you select an object in the vSphere Web Client, you should hide the **Getting Started** pages as soon as possible. To do this, click **Help** in the upper-right corner of the client and click **Hide All Getting Started Pages**, as shown in Figure 22-7. You can bring them back by returning to the same area, but I'll bet you never will!

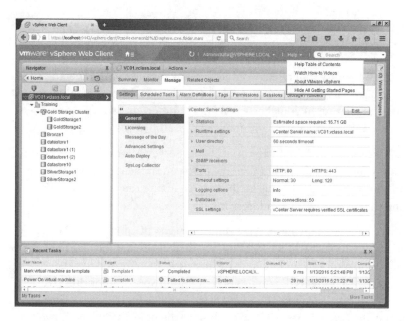

**Figure 22-7**   Hiding the Getting Started Pages

- **Unpin the right side:** Since VMware finally put the **Recent Tasks** back where
  they should have been all along, at the bottom of the client, you can now
  unpin the right side of the client and open it only when you want to grab
  a saved **Work in Progress**. This gives you significantly more desktop real
  estate, which is important if you are managing your vSphere from a laptop or a
  desktop that doesn't include a 36-inch monitor!

- **Leverage your browser tabs:** Because VMware seems to be dead set on making you manage your environment through your browser, you may as well
  take advantage of everything that type of configuration offers. In other words,
  don't forget about the tabs that you have open for your vCenter, VMs, and so
  on. Sometimes it's much easier to find a tab that is already open than it is to
  traverse the inventory again to find the same object. If you are not careful, you
  can end up with many objects open on your taskbar (Windows) that you have
  completely forgotten about. Leveraging the tabs on your browser, which are
  much more evident if you're looking for them, will keep you more organized.
  Try it, and you'll see what I mean.

# Correcting Common Warnings and Alerts Within the vSphere Web Client

As you are working in your vSphere environment, many monitors are "keeping an eye" on things to make sure that you can get the most from it. Many default alarms are built in to the installation of your hosts, vCenter, storage, and so on. As you know, you can also add custom alarms for your own specific needs.

In Chapter 24, "Creating and Administering vCenter Server Alarms," you learn how you can configure your own alarms, but for now this section focuses on what you can do when an alarm is triggered. This includes recognizing the warning or alert and then making the best decision to address it.

First, how will you know that an alarm has been triggered? In addition to the yellow or red icon that the object will be sporting, you will also see information about the triggered alarm in your logs and in your Events view. In addition, depending on how the alarm is configured, you or another administrator might receive an email or an SNMP trap. However, the best place to focus on triggered alarms is on the **Monitor**, **Issues**, **Triggered Alarms** link of the object itself, as shown in Figure 22-8. In this case, your vCenter has a Critical Issue in regard to Health Status Monitoring.

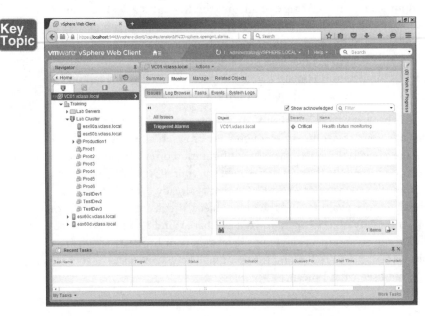

**Figure 22-8**   The Triggered Alarms Link

Now that you have found the alarm, what are your choices in regard to handling it? Well, you could ignore it and let someone else handle it, but you probably wouldn't have searched for it if you were going to ignore it. You could disable it, but that doesn't fix anything, and then you might forget about it entirely until the issue is even worse. Because neither of those are viable options, that means you have the following two options, as shown in Figure 22-9:

- **Reset to Green:** If you choose **Reset to Green** without actually fixing the issue that is triggering the alarm, there is a good chance that the alarm will be triggered again. Therefore, you should choose this option only after you have identified and corrected the issue that caused the alarm to trigger.

- **Acknowledge:** When you choose **Acknowledge**, you are taking the responsibility to work on the issue that is causing the alarm as soon as you find the opportunity. This will leave the "pretty colors" on the object in the inventory, but it will stop the other actions, such as emails and SNMP traps. It will also create a log entry that indicates that an administrator logged in with your credentials has acknowledged responsibility for addressing the issue.

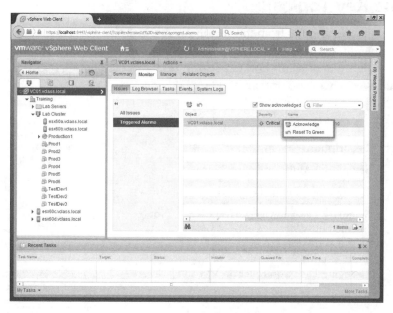

**Figure 22-9**   Resetting or Acknowledging Triggered Alarms

## Summary

This chapter covers the following main topics:

- Troubleshooting techniques for VM contention issues

- FT latency issues and VMware Tools installation issues

- Troubleshooting VM states, such as with orphaned VMs

- How to identify the root cause of a storage issue and how to correct the most common boot disk errors

- Managing the vSphere Web Client, including settings, properties, and alerts and warnings.

## Exam Preparation Tasks

## Review All the Key Topics

Review the most important topics from the chapter, noted with the Key Topic icon in the outer margin of the page. Table 22-2 lists these key topics and the page numbers where each is found. Know how to perform basic troubleshooting on ESXi hosts, vSphere networks, vSphere storage, and HA/DRS clusters.

**Table 22-2**   Key Topics for Chapter 22

| Key Topic Element | Description | Page Number |
| --- | --- | --- |
| Figure 22-1 | Settings for Multipathing of Storage | 543 |
| Figure 22-2 | Configuring Multipathing in the Storage View | 544 |
| Figure 22-3 | Summary Tab Showing VMware Tools Not Installed on VM | 546 |
| Figure 22-4 | Reregistering an Orphaned VM | 547 |
| Figure 22-5 | Changing Disk Controller on Virtual Hardware | 549 |
| Figure 22-6 | Forcing a VM to Boot to BIOS Settings | 550 |
| Bullet List | Settings to Improve User Experience on vSphere Web Client | 550 |
| Figure 22-7 | Hiding the Getting Started Pages | 551 |
| Figure 22-8 | The Triggered Alarms Tab | 552 |
| Figure 22-9 | Resetting or Acknowledging Triggered Alarms | 553 |

## Review Questions

The answers to these review questions are in Appendix A.

1. Which of the following can have a negative effect on virtual machine performance? (Choose two.)

   a. Excessive SCSI reservations

   b. Multipathing

   c. Lack of path thrashing

   d. Inadequate LUN queue depth

2. Which of the following would *not* cause network latency issues on FT-enabled VMs? (Choose two.)

   a. Hosts with properly configured 1 Gbps vmnics

   b. Hosts with improperly configured 10 Gbps vmnics

   c. VMs with vmxnet2 vnics

   d. VMs with e1000e vnics

3. Which of the following are true regarding an interactive installation of VMware tools? (Choose two.)

   a. It will enable you to detect whether an antivirus software package on the Guest OS is preventing the installation.

   b. It can be accomplished only by logging in to the VM first.

   c. You should perform a noninteractive installation and then an interactive installation.

   d. An interactive installation of VMware tools will always install more drivers than the noninteractive installation will.

4. Which of the following is true about a VM that is orphaned? (Choose two.)

   a. The VM files have been deleted from the datastore.

   b. The VM does not appear on the database of the vCenter.

   c. The VM is not recognized by its host.

   d. The VM files are in the datastore.

**5.** Which of the following might result from setting Admission Control Policy in HA too liberally?

  **a.** You might not be able to restart all the VMs on a host when it fails.

  **b.** VMs might be vMotioned more frequently than you had planned.

  **c.** You might not be able to start a VM with high reservations.

  **d.** All VMs will run with restricted settings.

**6.** Which of the following are tools that will not assist you in identifying the root cause of a storage issue? (Choose two.)

  **a.** Storage Maps in the vSphere Client

  **b.** Task Manager on a VMs OS

  **c.** The Storage Views tab in the vSphere Web Client

  **d.** The DCUI of a host

**7.** You have created a VM using the wizard and identified the OS as Windows Server 2003. You attempt to install an ISO on the VM that contains Windows Server 2008. Which of the following will result?

  **a.** The ISO will install properly, but your Summary tab will be wrong and your disk controller will not be optimal.

  **b.** The installation will fail.

  **c.** The boot disk on the VM will not be recognized.

  **d.** The boot disk will be recognized but will not contain the proper ISO to run Windows Server 2008, so the installation will fail.

**8.** You want to improve your user experience on your vSphere 6 Web Client that has a default installation. Which of the following should you do? (Choose two.)

  **a.** Add a Related Objects tab to the Manage Screen.

  **b.** Unpin the right side of the screen.

  **c.** Remove the Work In Progress feature from the software.

  **d.** Hide the Getting Started tabs.

**9.** What are two practical techniques you can use to make sure that you are getting the most efficient use of your vSphere Web Client? (Choose two.)

   **a.** Unpin both sides.

   **b.** Log on to your vCenter with the desktop client to compare.

   **c.** Log on to your vCenter as "root."

   **d.** Leverage the browser tabs.

**10.** Which of the following occur when you choose to acknowledge an alarm in your vCenter? (Choose two.)

   **a.** Your credentials are recorded, and you have taken the responsibility to fix the issue.

   **b.** The alarm is disabled.

   **c.** The inventory object will show a green "Acknowledged" icon.

   **d.** All actions associated with the alarm with be disabled.

**This chapter covers the following subjects:**

- Viewing Tasks and Events in vCenter
- Critical Performance Metrics
- Common Memory Metrics
- Common CPU Metrics
- Common Network Metrics
- Common Storage Metrics
- Comparing and Contrasting Overview and Advanced Charts
- Configuring SNMP for vCenter Server
- Configuring Active Directory and SMTP Settings for vCenter Server
- Configuring vCenter Server Logging Options
- Creating a Log Bundle
- Creating/Editing/Deleting a Scheduled Task
- Configuring/Viewing/Printing/Exporting Resource Maps
- Starting/Stopping/Verifying vCenter Server Status
- Starting/Stopping/Verifying ESXi Host Agent Status
- Configuring vCenter Server Timeout Settings
- Monitoring/Administering vCenter Server Connections
- Creating an Advanced Chart
- Determining Host Performance Using Guest Performance Monitor
- Given Performance Data, Identify the Affected vSphere Resource

As you know, there are four core resources in any computer system: CPU, memory, disk, and network. Which one is most important? The one that is giving you a problem—that's the one that is most important at any given time! Seriously, to get the most out of your vSphere implementation, you have to know which tools to use, what to look for, and what you expect to see. Then, by comparing what you see to what you should be seeing, you can make critical decisions and changes.

# Monitoring ESXi, vCenter Server, and Virtual Machines

You should first understand the metrics and measurements used, and then you should know which tools are appropriate to monitor each metric. In addition, you should know how to build specific log bundles to send to VMware Support. You should also be familiar with the process of stopping and starting critical services and configuring timeout settings for vCenter Server. In this chapter, I discuss the basics of monitoring your hosts, vCenter Server(s), and VMs.

## "Do I Know This Already?" Quiz

The "Do I Know This Already?" quiz allows you to assess whether you should read this entire chapter or simply jump to the "Exam Preparation Tasks" section for review. If you are in doubt, read the entire chapter. Table 7-1 outlines the major headings in this chapter and the corresponding "Do I Know This Already?" quiz questions. You can find the answers in Appendix A, "Answers to the 'Do I Know This Already?' Quizzes and Chapter Review Questions."

**Table 23-1**   "Do I Know This Already?" Section-to-Question Mapping

| Foundation Topics Section | Questions Covered in This Section |
|---|---|
| Viewing Tasks and Events in vCenter | 1 |
| Critical Performance Metrics | 2 |
| Common Memory Metrics | 3 |
| Common CPU Metrics | 4 |
| Common Network Metrics | 5 |
| Common Storage Metrics | 6 |
| Comparing and Contrasting Overview and Advanced Charts | 7 |
| Configuring SNMP for vCenter Server | 8 |
| Configuring Active Directory and SMTP Settings for vCenter Server | 9 |
| Configuring vCenter Server Logging Options | 10 |

| Foundation Topics Section | Questions Covered in This Section |
|---|---|
| Creating a Log Bundle | 11 |
| Creating/Editing/Deleting a Scheduled Task | 12 |
| Configuring/Viewing/Printing/Exporting Resource Maps | 13 |
| Starting/Stopping/Verifying vCenter Service Status | 14 |
| Starting/Stopping/Verifying ESXi Host Agent Status | 15 |
| Configuring vCenter Server Timeout Settings | 16 |
| Monitoring/Administering vCenter Server Connections | 17 |
| Creating an Advanced Chart | 18 |
| Determining Host Performance Using Guest Performance Monitor | 19 |
| Given Performance Data, Identify the Affected vSphere Resource | 20 |

1. Which of the following is *not* viewable on your vSphere Client when you are logged on directly to a host?

   a. The Events tab

   b. Recent Tasks

   c. The Tasks and Events tab

   d. The Performance tab

2. Which of the following memory technologies is most closely associated with ballooning technique?

   a. TPS

   b. vmmemctl

   c. Memory compression

   d. Swap

3. Which of the following memory conservation techniques is used by default, even when memory is *not* in contention?

   a. Ballooning

   b. Memory compression

   c. Swap file

   d. TPS

**4.** Which of the following are true about CPU Ready value on VMs? (Choose two.)

   **a.** The lower the CPU Ready value, the better.

   **b.** A CPU Ready value of 5% is considered high.

   **c.** A CPU Ready value of 5% is considered acceptable.

   **d.** The higher the CPU Ready value, the better.

**5.** You are examining your network and notice dropped packets. In general, what do dropped network packets indicate?

   **a.** A bottleneck in your network.

   **b.** Security protocols are in use.

   **c.** This is normal and healthy behavior.

   **d.** You have a physical network problem.

**6.** Which of the following are considered storage issues that need to be addressed? (Choose two.)

   **a.** VMkernel command latency of 5 ms

   **b.** VMkernel command latency of 1 ms

   **c.** Physical device command latency of 30 ms

   **d.** Physical device command latency of 10 ms

**7.** As an administrator of your vSphere environment, you want to create an Advanced Chart. Which of the following links will you need to select?

   **a.** Advanced

   **b.** Options

   **c.** Chart Options

   **d.** Details

**8.** For which of the following SNMP components is vCenter configured?

   **a.** MIB

   **b.** Server

   **c.** Trap

   **d.** Agent

**9.** Which of the following is the default User Directory Timeout value for vCenter?

    **a.** 5 sec

    **b.** 20 sec

    **c.** 30 sec

    **d.** 60 sec

**10.** Which of the following logging options is the default and recommended setting?

    **a.** Information

    **b.** None

    **c.** Warning

    **d.** Verbose

**11.** You have created a Log Bundle for VMware Support and stored it on your desktop. What extension will be on the files associated with the logs?

    **a.** .tgz

    **b.** .log

    **c.** .exe

    **d.** .vmx

**12.** Which of the following cannot be a scheduled task?

    **a.** Add a host to the data center.

    **b.** Delete a VM.

    **c.** Power off a VM.

    **d.** Create a snapshot.

**13.** You are the administrator of a vSphere 6 environment. Which of the following are true regarding your use of Resource Maps? (Choose two.)

    **a.** You can log in to your Windows-based vCenter Server with your vSphere 6 Windows-based client to view Resource Maps.

    **b.** You cannot log in to your vSphere 6 vCenter with your vSphere 6 client.

    **c.** The Resource Maps view is no longer available in the Windows-based client.

    **d.** Resource Maps are not available in your vSphere Web Client.

**14.** Which of the following are valid reasons to restart vCenter Server? (Choose two.)

   **a.** A new plug-in, for example VUM, is not starting.

   **b.** You have just added a new host.

   **c.** vCenter does not appear to be refreshing as normal.

   **d.** You have just added a new vDS.

**15.** You are the administrator of a vSphere 6 environment. You want to restart the host agent of one of your ESXi hosts. Where is the best place to restart the host agent?

   **a.** In the DCUI under Troubleshooting Options

   **b.** By logging on to your host with the vSphere Windows-based client and then going to Troubleshooting Options

   **c.** This can be done only in the vSphere Web Client under **Settings, Troubleshooting**.

   **d.** You will need to physically restart the host.

**16.** Which of the following is the default timeout setting for vCenter Server?

   **a.** 10 sec

   **b.** 20 sec

   **c.** 30 sec

   **d.** 60 sec

**17.** As an administrator of your vSphere environment, you have selected your vCenter and selected Manage/Sessions. If you select all the sessions that are active and then click Terminate Selected Sessions, which of the following will be the result?

   **a.** You will terminate your own session as well as others that you have selected.

   **b.** You can select specific sessions to terminate from this view.

   **c.** You will terminate the sessions that you selected, none of which will be yours.

   **d.** Only your session will be terminated, because this is an improper selection.

**18.** You are the administrator of a vSphere environment. You click on a host in Hosts and Clusters view, then on **Monitor**, and finally on **Performance**. You want to create an advanced chart. Which of the following will be the default Timespan of the chart?

    **a.** Last day

    **b.** Last week

    **c.** Last month

    **d.** Real-time

**19.** Which of the following Perfmon objects and their counters are available only after you install VMware Tools? (Choose two.)

    **a.** Aggregate CPU

    **b.** Available Bytes

    **c.** VM Memory

    **d.** VM CPU

**20.** Which of the following is *not* true regarding identifying the affected resource when troubleshooting vSphere?

    **a.** All resources are isolated from each other.

    **b.** You should change one thing at a time, and then test again.

    **c.** You should use all the tools at your disposal, as long as you know how to interpret the results.

    **d.** The strength of a whole system will usually be determined by strength of the weakest resource that it uses.

## Foundation Topics

# Viewing Tasks and Events in vCenter

Tasks and Events in vCenter is a flexible system of tools. You can view tasks and events that are associated with a single object or all objects in your vSphere inventory. So, what is the difference between a task and an event? Well, basically, an event is an indication of an occurrence in vCenter that was part of running vCenter. In contrast, a task is an indication that an administrator has performed an action. In essence, you could say that a task is an event that an administrator caused to happen. Because you can monitor many tasks and events, it is useful to know how to filter your view so that you focus on what is most important to you.

Note that the title of this section relates to viewing tasks and events in vCenter. This is the best practice method because, when your vSphere Client is connected directly to an ESXi host, the Tasks and Events option will not be offered. In fact, it is replaced by an Events tab. You can still view the Recent Tasks pane at the bottom of your vSphere Client, as shown in Figure 23-1.

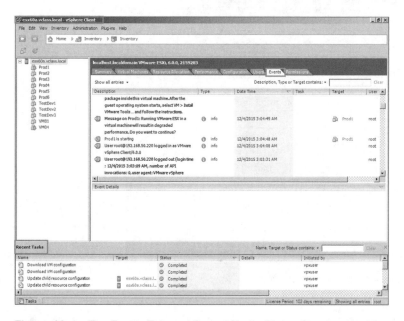

**Figure 23-1**   The Events Tab and Recent Tasks Status Bar on a Host Login

In contrast, when you view your vCenter through your vSphere Web Client, you will see two tabs under the Monitor tab: one for Tasks and another for Events. You can use these to gather information about either or both types of occurrences. In addition, you can filter the information in three ways. I will briefly discuss each of the ways by which you can filter the information shown in your vCenter Tasks and Events tabs.

### Viewing by Object Selected in the Navigator

The first choice that you make with regard to tasks and events is which object to select in the console pane (on the left, also called the Navigator) in the vSphere Web Client. By default, the Tasks list for an object includes that object and all its child objects in your inventory. This can give you a good overall view at any level of the inventory hierarchy that you desire. As Figure 23-2 shows, I selected **Lab Cluster** in the Navigator, but I can also view information about child objects, such as hosts and VMs, in my output.

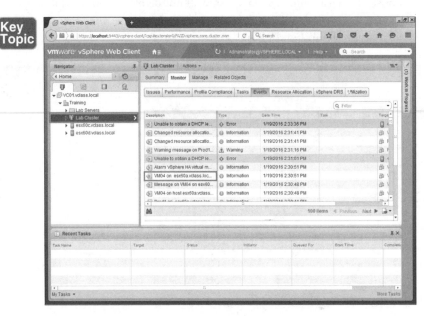

**Figure 23-2**   Viewing All Entries Within an Object

## Filtering the Output

You can also filter the information that you want to see regarding tasks or events. Filtering the output is easy to do and then easy to change again if needed. To filter the output for your Events, right-click the column headings and select the output that you want to see, as shown in Figure 23-3.

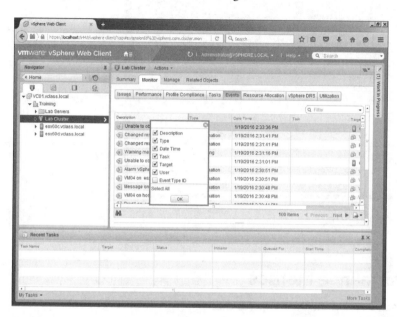

**Figure 23-3**    Filtering the Output

## Filtering by Keyword

In addition, you can filter tasks and events based on any attribute, including name, target, status, initiator, change history, and time. These can be associated to any keyword of your choice. In essence, you are asking vCenter, "What tasks or events do you know about that have 'this' in them?" You can choose one of these attributes or multiples of them, as shown in Figure 23-4. This can be an effective tool to quickly drill down to the information that you need to obtain.

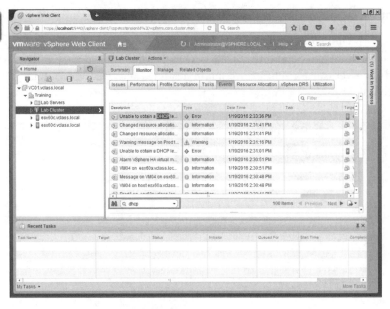

**Figure 23-4**    Filtering by Keyword

## Critical Performance Metrics

To reiterate what I said at the beginning of this chapter, you have four core resources to monitor and manage: memory, CPU, network, and storage. A weakness in any of these core four will most certainly be felt by your VMs and therefore by your end users. I will first briefly touch on the most common suspects in each of your core four, and then I will explain more about how you can monitor each one and what you should expect to see:

- **Memory:** Keep your attention on whether you are seeing any "ballooning," which indicates use of virtual machine memory control (vmmemctl). Ballooning indicates that memory is becoming scarce and therefore the VMkernel has instructed the VM to create a shared memory area from which each VM will draw a portion of its memory. As I will explain later in this section, a little ballooning is not bad, but a lot of ballooning is not good.

- **CPU:** Pay close attention to the CPU ready values on your VMs. A higher-than-normal CPU ready value is an indicator that the VM is starved for CPU resources. I know that sounds backward, but I will discuss it in detail later in this section.

- **Network:** You can do a number of things to improve network performance, such as installing the latest VMware Tools, using traffic shaping, using faster physical network interface cards (NICs), load balancing, and so on. You should also consider placing VMs that frequently communicate with each other on the same host, same switch, and same subnet, so they can communicate internally without using your LAN and free up that bandwidth on your LAN. To monitor network traffic, you are really measuring the effective bandwidth between the VM and its peer and looking for dropped transmit packets and dropped receive packets. This is discussed later in this section.

- **Storage:** The main factors here are with regard to the datastores that you've chosen and the speed of the logical unit numbers (LUNs) to which they are connected. You can enhance performance somewhat by using a multipathing method such as round-robin. You can also enhance availability using a multipathing method, such as fixed or most recently used (MRU). To measure the effectiveness of storage, you can compare your statistics to known standards, but it's much better to have your own baselines to use for comparison. That is also discussed later in this section.

## Common Memory Metrics

You should understand that many of the components in your vSphere are playing a "shell game" with regard to memory. As shown in Figure 23-5, the only true physical memory is the memory that is installed in your physical ESXi hosts. The guest operating system in each of your VMs "believes" that it has a specific amount of a physical memory available to it, expressed as its available memory. This is the memory that was assigned to the VM when it was created. In reality, the VMkernel could elect to supply that memory using a swap file, which would hamper the VM's performance. In addition, the guest operating system is telling the applications that are using its memory that it is physical as well, when it "knows" that some of the memory that it provides the applications is from its own virtual memory area on its connected disks. For example, pagefile.sys is used by Microsoft's client and server guest OSs.

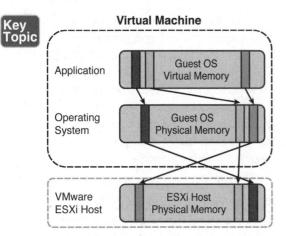

**Figure 23-5**   The Memory "Shell Game"

Because of this elaborate shell game with memory, it's possible to provide the VMs with the memory they need when they need it. However, because you don't want to hamper the VM's performance, you can use some cool patented technologies and processes that allow you to get the most out of the physical RAM provided by the host and use the swap file only as a last resort. To know what you are monitoring, you first need to understand these technologies and processes. In this section, you learn about each process and how the VMkernel uses them to enhance the memory usage of the VMs on your hosts:

- **Transparent page sharing (TPS):** The best way to describe this is that it's like memory dedupe. You may be familiar with data deduplication when running a backup so that redundant components have to be stored only once. This is like that, but with memory pages. As shown in Figure 23-6, if several VMs on a host are running the same guest OS and the same applications, this technology can be effective because it will require that only one copy of each page be stored in physical RAM on the host. This memory sharing ensures that the host uses far less physical memory than it otherwise would have and allows for significant overcommitment of memory resources without performance degradation. TPS is a built-in component of ESX/ESXi and is enabled by default. It is used whether or not there is contention for memory.

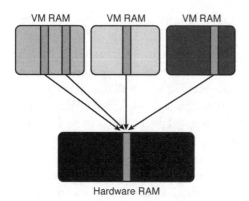

Key Topic

**Figure 23-6**   Transparent Page Sharing

- **Balloon driver mechanism (vmmemctl):** This system works along with the guest OS on the server to reclaim pages that are considered least valuable to the guest operating system. The balloon driver is installed when you install VMware Tools on a VM. It uses a proprietary technique that creates a shared memory area from the reclaimed pages and allows the VMs to use the shared (ballooned) memory without a significant performance hit. When the VMkernel has determined that memory is scarce and therefore in contention, this technique increases pressure on the guest OS and forces it to use more of its native swap file (pagefile.sys in Microsoft servers). The genius of this system is that the guest OS is the one that determines when pages are "old" and can come out of physical RAM (as it knows best), and the VMkernel takes advantage of the opportunity to reclaim the unused memory space for its own use. If you notice that a VM is using its swap file but has not used any ballooning, you should suspect that VMware Tools are not installed on the VM and verify their proper installation. Figure 23-7 illustrates the balloon driver mechanism.

Key Topic

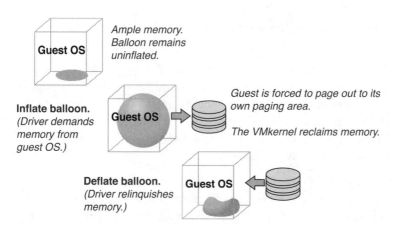

**Figure 23-7**   The Balloon Driver Mechanism

■ **Memory compression:** When there is contention for memory, large pages are broken down so that each memory page is 4 KB in size. With 100% memory compression, the VMkernel can compress each page to 2 KB, thereby allowing many more pages of memory to be stored in the same physical memory space. This patented memory compression technique is used only when the VMkernel has determined that memory is scarce. You might ask, "Why don't you just compress them all the time?" Compressed memory has to be decompressed before being used, causing a performance hit. However, the idea behind this technology is that the decompression performance hit is not as significant as the performance hit of running memory off a disk. Therefore, your ESXi host will attempt to compress the page first, if the memory compression cache allows and if it can compress the page to 2 KB, before sending it to disk. You can set the maximum size of the memory compression cache as a percentage of memory in the Advanced System Settings for each host, as shown in Figure 23-8. The default setting is 10% of VM memory.

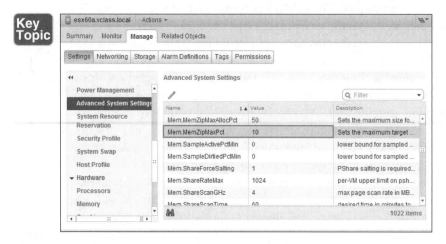

**Figure 23-8**    The Memory Compression Cache Setting

■ **Swap file:** A swap file named *VMname*.vwsp is created by the VMkernel whenever a VM is powered on and deleted when it is powered off. Its size is equal to the available memory of the VM (the amount the guest OS is told that it has) minus its reservation (a guarantee of physical RAM). Even though it is created when the VM is powered on, we don't really want to use it. Why, then, do we create it? Basically, just in case we need it.

If you were to push the system past its limits without a swap file, the VMs would each freeze up and the users, and ultimately you, would be negatively affected. With a swap file configured, you can determine by monitoring that it is being used and make the necessary changes, which might include adding more memory or maybe just redistributing VM loads. Any use of the swap file should be considered an issue to be resolved.

When you examine the Resource Allocation tab of a VM within the Monitor tab, as shown in Figure 23-9, you will notice many types of memory that bear mentioning here so that you have a better understanding of the big picture with regard to memory use.

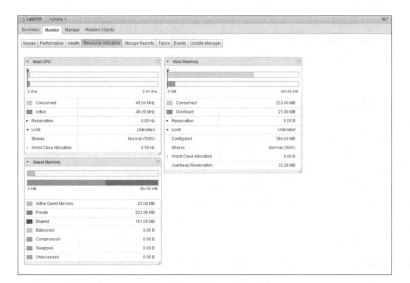

**Figure 23-9**  The Resource Allocation Tab of a VM

Be familiar with the following memory terms:

- **Host memory:** The amount of memory with which you provisioned your VM (in other words, the amount that you told the guest OS it could use).

- **Overhead:** The amount of memory that the VMkernel thinks it will use to run the virtualized workload.

- **Consumed:** The amount of physical memory (RAM) that has been allocated to the VM.

- **Private:** The amount of memory that is currently being provided from the physical memory (RAM) of the host.

- **Shared:** The total amount of memory that is currently being shared by Transparent Page Sharing (TPS).

- **Swapped:** The amount of memory that is currently being reclaimed by VMkernel swapping.

- **Compressed:** The amount of memory that is currently stored in the VM's compression cache.

- **Ballooned:** The amount of memory reclaimed by the balloon driver. It's best if this is a value of zero.

- **Unaccessed:** The amount of memory that has never been accessed by this guest.

- **Active Guest Memory:** The total amount of memory that is actively used, an estimate done by statistical sampling.

## Common CPU Metrics

First, you should understand that you can't necessarily believe everything that you see on the tools that are built in to the guest OS, because the guest OS is being fooled into "thinking" that it's on a physical machine. For example, Task Manager might report high usage of CPU for a VM because it doesn't "realize" that the CPU resource for that VM is dynamically expandable and it's "seeing" only part of the resource. Therefore, you can trust your performance charts on your vCenter, and you can trust VMware performance tools, such as Resxtop, which is discussed later.

What should you be looking for with regard to CPU metrics? As mentioned earlier, the most common CPU metric is called CPU Ready value. It's a crazy name for this metric because it seems backward—at least it does to me. What CPU Ready value really means is "wait time" for the vCPU. In other words, the vCPU is ready to perform and has been asked to perform by the guest OS, but it is waiting for a logical CPU to provide it the processing power that it needs. (A logical CPU is a physical core on a nonhyperthreaded system or half of a physical core on a hyperthreaded system.)

Typically, a CPU Ready value that is higher than 1 for a sustained period of time should be investigated. A CPU Ready value of 2 or higher is considered very bad. Where do these numbers originate? The performance charts are taking a sample of vCPU activity every 20 seconds. If during that 20 seconds, a vCPU spends greater than 2 seconds waiting on a physical core, that is a CPU Ready value of 2, which is certainly considered to be an issue that should be addressed. To further complicate this value, it is expressed on the performance charts as 2000 ms, but on esxtop/resxtop as 10% (2 seconds/20 seconds).

## Common Network Metrics

As discussed in the previous chapter, your network performance depends on your application workload and on your network configuration. Dropped network packets indicate a bottleneck in the network. Slow network performance can also be a sign of load-balancing issues.

Make sure you have installed VMware Tools on each machine and that the machine is using the proper vNIC driver. Whenever possible, use vmxnet3 vNIC drivers. You can then determine whether packets are being dropped by using Esxtop, Resxtop, or the advanced performance charts to examine droppedTx and droppedRx counter values.

## Common Storage Metrics

As mentioned earlier, it's important to have a baseline of your core four resources, when everything is performing well, to use as a comparison when things begin to slow down. This is most important in the area of storage metrics. One of the reasons for this fact is that there are many variables to consider with regard to storage.

First, there is the storage as the host sees it and uses it for its datastores. The performance of the datastores is based on the speed of the underlying LUNs and the speed and efficiency of your access method to the LUNs. Your access method could be through Fibre Channel connectors and switches, through your IP network, or even local to the host. In addition, you could be using Fibre Channel, Fibre Channel over Ethernet (FCoE), Internet Small Computer System Interface (iSCSI), or network-attached storage (NAS). Second, although the VM sees all its storage as "local SCSI," the underlying storage will still affect its performance.

You should be most concerned with two factors: the VMkernel command latency and the physical device command latency. If the average time spent in the VMkernel per SCSI command is higher than 2 ms to 3 ms, the array or the host may be overworked. Likewise, if the average time that the physical device takes to complete a SCSI command is greater than 15 ms to 20 ms, you have a slow and likely overworked or underdesigned array. As you can see, these standards have some flexibility in them, which is why it's important to know your own baseline.

## Comparing and Contrasting Overview and Advanced Charts

Your vCenter makes available a variety of tools to help you monitor and manage your vSphere. Included in these tools are performance charts for CPU, memory, storage, and networking. In this section, you learn about two forms of these charts: Overview and Advanced.

You can easily create a view that gives you a little information about each of the core four resources by using the Overview performance charts. Overview charts give you a lot of general information in one place, and therefore might be a good place to start if you know your own baselines and could quickly spot a metric that was significantly different from normal. In addition, you can filter the time range of the data that you are viewing so that you can spot a trend and even create a custom time range if needed. There are also tools for refreshing the data and for help if you need more information about a specific chart or metric, all shown in Figure 23-10.

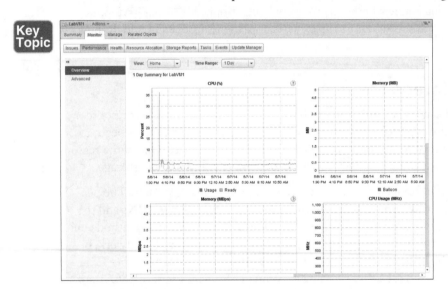

**Figure 23-10**   Overview Performance Charts

In contrast, the Advanced performance charts view allows you to drill down on a specific resource or metric and get more detailed information and even make comparisons to other objects. To begin making custom selections, first click **Advanced** and then the **Chart Options** link, as shown in Figure 23-11.

From there, you can easily choose the objects that you want to monitor and the counters for those objects. In addition to viewing all your selected objects, you can easily drill down on a specific counter to get the detailed information that you need. You can even specify the time period for the counters or examine them in real time. Then you can save your chart settings to use them over and over as the data changes, as shown in Figure 23-12.

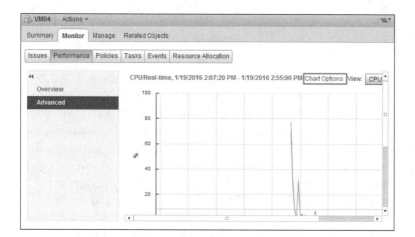

**Figure 23-11**   The Chart Options Link

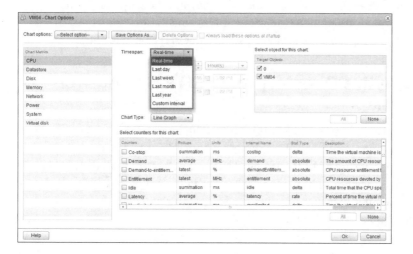

**Figure 23-12**   Choosing Options for Custom Advanced Charts

## Configuring SNMP for vCenter Server

Simple Network Management Protocol (SNMP) is a lightweight protocol that has been around for many years and allows administrators to collect information about the devices in their network. The network collection area is referred to as a community. Within a community are a Management Information Base (MIB) and usually many agents. The agents can initiate and send a trap to the MIB in their community. In addition, agents can receive GET requests that might contain a configuration command for the agent.

Each of your ESXi hosts includes an SNMP agent that is embedded into hostd. It can send traps and receive GET requests, but it is disabled by default. To enable it, you must configure it using the vSphere command-line interface (CLI) command **vicfg-snmp**. Through the CLI, you must first configure the SNMP community to match that of your MIB. You can then configure the vCenter as an agent that will send traps regarding the hosts and the VMs in your vSphere. You can also configure the hosts to receive hardware events from Intelligent Platform Management Interface (IPMI) or Common Information Model (CIM) indicators and send that information to the MIB, filtering the output for just what you need. After you have configured the hosts to send the traps, configure your vSphere Client to receive and interpret them. The precise configuration of each of these steps is command line-based; therefore, it is not on the exam and is beyond the scope of this text. You can find more information on the vSphere Documentation Center at https://www.vmware.com/support/pubs/vsphere-esxi-vcenter-server-6-pubs.html.

# Configuring Active Directory and SMTP Settings for vCenter Server

Configuring Active Directory and SMTP settings might seem at first like two topics that shouldn't go together. After all, configuring Active Directory settings is very different from configuring SMTP settings. The reason they are both discussed in this section is that they are right next to each other in the dialog box where the configuration is done, so it may make it all easier for you to remember. Even so, each of these settings is discussed individually.

## Configuring Active Directory Settings for vCenter

In this section, you learn about settings that affect the way that your vCenter interacts with Active Directory. In fact, this has actually been changed to User Directory because vSphere now accepts other centralized authentication sources, such as NIS. The defaults for the settings, shown in Figure 23-13, are usually sufficient, but you can change them if needed.

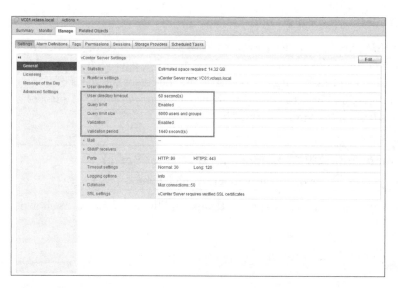

**Figure 23-13**   User Directory Settings for vCenter

The settings that you can configure and their general purpose are as follows:

- **User directory timeout:** This is the timeout interval in seconds for connecting to your Active Directory server. The default is 60 seconds, which is generally ample time to make the connection. You can increase or decrease as needed for your own Active Directory servers. You might need to increase this setting if authentication is slower than normal in your Active Directory.

- **Query limit:** Choices are Enabled or Disabled. Without a size limit selected, all users and groups appear in the Add Permissions dialog box. This prepopulation of the AD might take some time.

- **Query limit size:** To improve the speed at which you get the choices that you need, you can limit the number of users and groups that will be prepopulated. A setting of 0 here, after you select **Enable Query Limit**, will prepopulate all users and groups.

- **Validation:** This is the "master switch" to have the vCenter periodically check its known AD users against the AD server in your domain. The default is to enable the validation.

- **Validation period:** This is the number of minutes to wait before performing a synchronization and validation of vCenter known users and groups against your AD server. The default setting is 1440 minutes (24 hours). You should leave this setting enabled. In addition, you should leave it at the default setting except in extremely dynamic environments where many users are continually being added/deleted.

### Configuring SMTP Settings for a vCenter Server

You can use the Simple Mail Transfer Protocol (SMTP) agent included in vCenter to send email notifications when configured alarms are triggered. (Chapter 24, "Creating and Administering vCenter Server Alarms," discusses the types of alarms that you can configure and how to configure them.) To configure the SMTP setting, follow the steps outlined in Activity 23-1.

**Activity 23-1    Configuring SMTP Settings for a vCenter Server**

1. Log on to your vCenter with your vSphere Web Client.

2. Click the root object, then **Manage**, **Settings**, and finally **General**, as shown in Figure 23-14.

**Figure 23-14**    vCenter Settings

3. In the blue area next to General, select **Edit** and then select **Mail**.

4. On the **Mail Server** line, configure the address for your SMTP server in the form of an IP address or hostname, as shown in Figure 23-15.

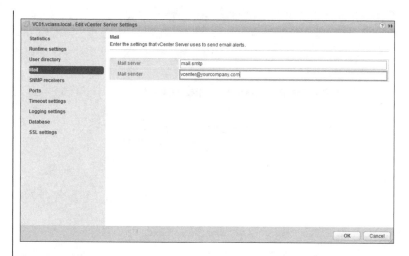

**Figure 23-15**    SMTP Server Settings

5. On the **Mail Sender** line, configure the sender account that the vCenter will use to send information. This should be a valid email address in your network, also shown in Figure 23-15.

6. Click **OK** to save the changes.

## Configuring vCenter Server Logging Options

In the General settings for your vCenter, you can easily configure the amount of detail that your vCenter collects in log files. You have six choices, as shown in Figure 23-16. Each selection from the top to the bottom of the list gets you more information on your log. The default is at midpoint and is called Information (Normal Logging). Because more logging is not always better and can cause performance degradation, you should leave the default selected unless you are specifically looking for information that would not appear in the Information logging, such as when you're troubleshooting.

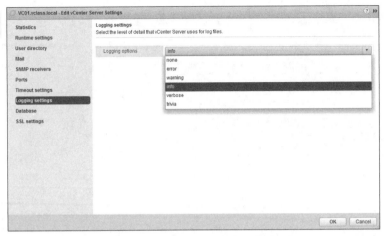

**Figure 23-16**    vCenter Server Logging Options

Your six choices, in order of increasing log information, are as follows:

- **None (disable logging):** This one speaks for itself. It is not a best practice to disable logging and is not recommended.

- **Error:** Displays only error log entries.

- **Warning (Errors and Warnings):** Displays information about errors and warnings. This setting might be useful as a filter, but the logs can be filtered when viewing as well.

- **Info (Normal Logging):** Displays information, error, and warning logs without verbose detail. This is the default and the recommended setting.

- **Verbose:** Displays information, error, and warning logs with verbose detail. It can be useful for obtaining additional information for troubleshooting purposes.

- **Trivia:** Displays information, error, warning, and trivia logs with verbose detail. Trivia logs give the most detailed information and should be enabled only for advanced troubleshooting scenarios.

## Creating a Log Bundle

As discussed in Chapter 20, "Performing Basic Troubleshooting of ESXi and vCenter Server," you can quickly create a log bundle, also called a diagnostic bundle, to send to VMware Support or for your own information. To create a log bundle, follow the steps outlined in Activity 23-2.

### Activity 23-2    Creating a Log Bundle

1. Log on to your vCenter with your vSphere Web Client.

2. Click your root object, and then select **Monitor**, **System Logs**, **Export System Logs**, as shown in Figure 23-17.

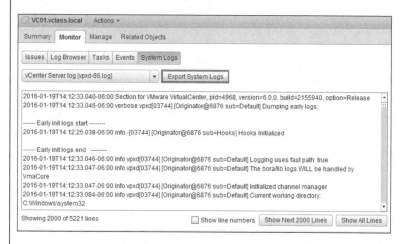

**Figure 23-17**    Preparing a Log Bundle

3. From Source, select hosts from which you want to collect data, and indicate whether you want to log for your vCenter Server Web Client, as shown in Figure 23-18, and then click **Next**.

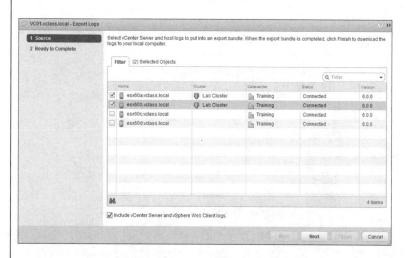

**Figure 23-18**    Choosing the vCenter Objects for Your Bundle

4. Select whether you want to record performance data as well. If you select to record performance data, configure the duration and interval of the logging information, and then click **Generate Log Bundle**, as shown in Figure 23-19. The default is to not record performance data. The default when selected is to record data for 5 minutes at 5-second intervals.

**Figure 23-19** Generating a Log Bundle

5. Click **Download Log Bundle** and browse for or type the location to which you will download your new bundle, as shown in Figure 23-20, and click **Next**.

**Figure 23-20** Choosing the Destination for Your Bundle

6. Review the Ready to Complete page to ensure that you have selected the proper logs and that your performance data selections are what you expect, and then click **Finish**. You should find your log files with the extension of .tgz at the storage location that you configured.

## Creating/Editing/Deleting a Scheduled Task

In general, a task is an action that is performed by the administrator. Most tasks are performed in real time by the administrator, but many tasks can also be configured to run at a later time or on a schedule set by the administrator. These scheduled tasks can be for actions on hosts, VMs, resource pools, and even cluster resources. Table 23-2 describes the tasks that you can schedule.

**Table 23-2**   Scheduled Tasks in vCenter

| Scheduled Task | Description |
|---|---|
| Add a host | Adds a host to a specified data center or cluster. |
| Change power state of a VM | Powers on, powers off, or resets the state of a VM. |
| Change cluster power settings | Enables or disables Distributed Power Management (DPM) for hosts in a cluster. |
| Change resource settings of a resource pool or VM | Changes any of the following resource settings: CPU (shares, reservation, and limit) Memory (shares, reservation, and limit) |
| Check compliance of a profile | Checks that a host's configuration matches the configuration specified in an attached profile. |
| Clone a VM | Makes a clone of a VM and places it on a specified host and datastore. |
| Create a VM | Creates a new VM and places it on a specified host and datastore. |
| Deploy a VM | Creates a new VM from a specified template and places it on a specified host and datastore. |
| Export a VM | Exports VMs that vCenter manages in a format that is specified by the administrator, such as OVF. Available only when vCenter Converter is installed. |
| Import a VM | Imports a physical machine, virtual machine, or system image into a new VM that vCenter manages. Available only when vCenter Converter is installed. |

Key
Topic

| Scheduled Task | Description |
| --- | --- |
| Migrate a VM | Moves a VM from one host to another or moves its files from one datastore to another. This can be done with cold migration or with vMotion/Storage vMotion if properly configured. |
| Make a snapshot of a VM | Captures the state of the VM at the specific point in time. |
| Scan for updates | Scans templates, VMs, and hosts for available updates. Available only when vSphere Update Manager (VUM) is installed. |
| Remediate | Downloads any new patches discovered during the scan operation and applies the newly configured settings. Available only when VUM is installed. |

You can create scheduled tasks using the Scheduled Task Wizard on the Windows-based vSphere Client. For some scheduled tasks, the wizard opens another wizard to help you complete the task. For example, if your task is to migrate a VM, the Scheduled Task Wizard will open the Migrate VM Wizard in which you can configure the details. However, because you are learning to rely on the vSphere Web Client, that's where my activity will be performed. On the Web Client, there is no wizard, but you won't need one.

Also, you should know that you cannot create a single task to run on multiple objects. For example, you cannot create a task that powers on a host and all the VMs on that host. You would need to create separate tasks for the host and each VM. As an example, to create a task that powers on a VM at a predetermined date and time, follow the steps outlined in Activity 23-3.

### Activity 23-3    Creating a Scheduled Task to Power On a VM

1. Log on to your vCenter with your vSphere Web Client.

2. Select the VM on which you want to schedule a task, click the **Manage** tab, and then **Scheduled Tasks**, as shown in Figure 23-21.

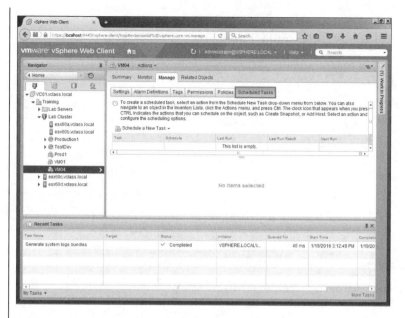

**Figure 23-21**   The Scheduled Tasks Tab

3. In the upper-left corner, click the drop-down next to the **Schedule a New Task** icon and select **Power On**, as shown in Figure 23-22.

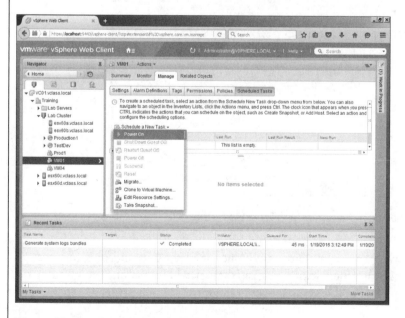

**Figure 23-22**   Creating a New Scheduled Task

4. On the General tab, verify whether you are creating the right task for the right VM, and select **Scheduling Options**, as shown in Figure 23-23.

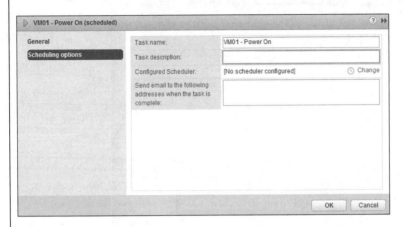

**Figure 23-23**   Verifying the Correct Task and Object

5. If desired, add a Task description and addresses of email recipients who will be notified when the task is complete, as shown in Figure 23-24, and then click **Change**.

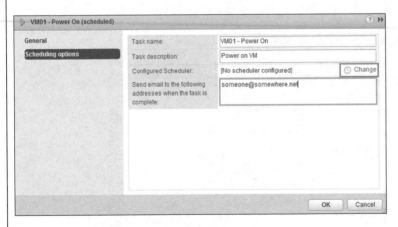

**Figure 23-24**   Adding a Description and Email Recipients

6. Select whether to run it now, run it once at a later time and/or date, or set up a recurring schedule. In this case, the task will be run once at 7:00 a.m. on 4/1/17, April Fool's day, as shown in Figure 23-25. Click **OK**.

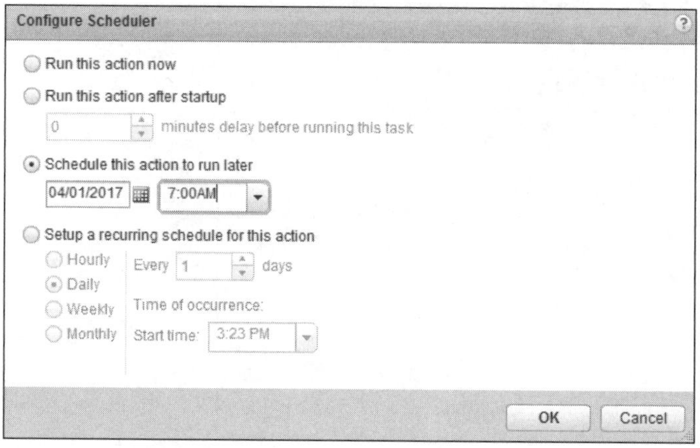

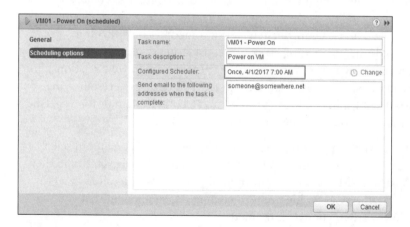

**Figure 23-25**   Specifying Scheduled Task Details

7. Verify your setting in Configured Scheduler, as shown in Figure 23-26, and click **OK**.

**Figure 23-26**   Verifying Your Settings

After you have configured your scheduled task, it will appear on the list of scheduled tasks. You can easily view the task, its description, the last time it was run, and the next time it is scheduled to run, as shown in Figure 23-27. To make changes to any of the properties of your scheduled task, click the **Edit the Configured Task** link that looks like a pencil and make the appropriate changes.

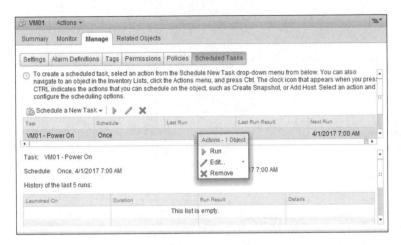

**Figure 23-27**    Viewing and Editing Scheduled Tasks

## Configuring/Viewing/Printing/Exporting Resource Maps

Your vSphere is a collection of components that work together to create a network of servers, switches, and other devices that can be used to provide applications and services to your end users. Unfortunately, it can sometimes be difficult to "get your head around" the big picture, especially considering that many of your components are invisible! Resource maps in vCenter enable you to view relationships among hosts, clusters, networks, VMs, and so on. You can view a resource map on the Windows-based vSphere Client for an entire vCenter System or for a specific object, based on how you configure your map.

Selecting what to view on your resource map is as easy as 1-2-3. You can select an object in the console in Hosts and Clusters view, open the Maps tab, and then choose the host and VM options, as shown in Figure 23-28. This allows you to create a map with the vCenter hierarchy, including the component that you suggested, and downward in your vCenter hierarchy.

**NOTE**    Strictly speaking, you should not be logging in directly to your vCenter with your vSphere Client unless you are performing an operation that is not available on your vSphere Web Client. Because, at the time of this writing, Resource Maps are not available on the vSphere Web Client, this is considered fair game.

You can also click **Home** and then click **Maps** under Management, as shown in Figure 23-29. This allows you to quickly select the portions of your inventory that you want to include in a custom map of your choice, as shown in Figure 23-30.

When you change the host and VM options and then select **Apply Relationships**, you will dramatically change your map. In this way, you can focus on the relationships that you want to examine and understand further.

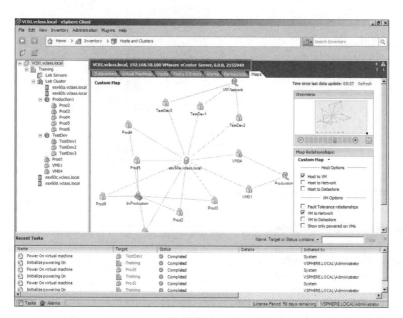

**Figure 23-28**    Creating a Resource Map from Hosts and Clusters View

**Figure 23-29**    The Maps Icon

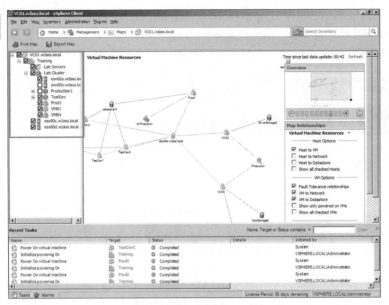

**Figure 23-30**    Creating a Custom Resource Map

One of the best times to have a copy of these maps is when something has gone wrong and there is an issue with your vSphere. As you might have guessed, this also might be a time at which obtaining a resource map would be impossible. To make sure that you have the maps that you need when you need them, you can print/export maps that you have created. To print a map that you are viewing, click **File** from the File menu at the top of vCenter, click **Print Maps**, and then **Print** (you will also be able to select **Print Preview**), as shown in Figure 23-31. To export a map, click **File** on the File menu and select **Export** and then **Export Maps**. Then enter or browse for the destination to which you will send the map, as shown in Figure 23-32.

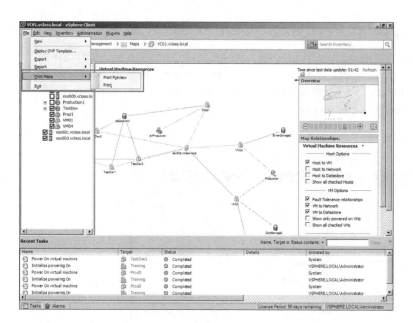

**Figure 23-31** Printing Resource Maps

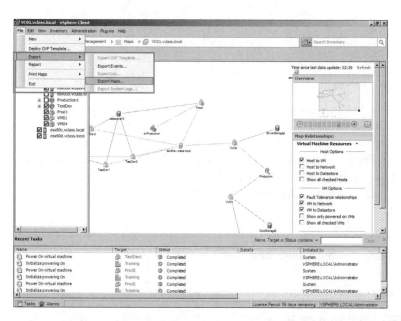

**Figure 23-32** Exporting Resource Maps

# Starting/Stopping/Verifying vCenter Service Status

When you install vCenter as a Windows machine, many services are started and run in the background. You can view these services by accessing Windows services and going "straight to the Vs." Just about everything VMware related starts with "V," so it's easy to verify all the services that are running, as shown in Figure 23-33.

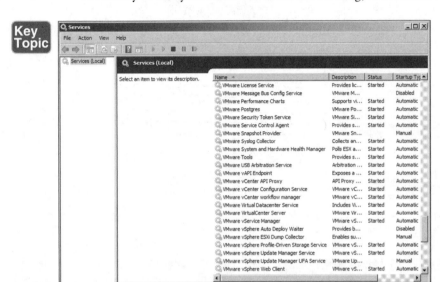

**Figure 23-33**    vCenter Services in Windows

One of the most important services is VMware VirtualCenter Server. If this service is not started, you will not be able to log in to the vCenter. From time to time, you might find it beneficial in troubleshooting to restart the VirtualCenter Server. For example, if a plug-in fails to enable, a restart of the services may very well fix the issue. To start, restart, and stop the VirtualCenter Server, follow the steps outlined in Activity 23-4.

**Activity 23-4    Starting, Restarting, and Stopping the vCenter Server Services**

1. Access your vCenter desktop. (Do not open a vSphere Client.)

2. Click **Start** and then **Run**. In the resulting window, shown in Figure 23-34, type **services.msc** to open the Services Microsoft Console.

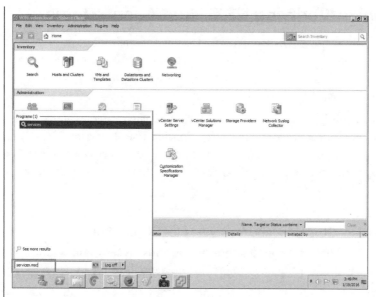

**Figure 23-34**   Accessing Windows Services

3. Scroll to the Vs or click any service and type **v** to get into the right area faster.

4. Locate the vCenter Service that you want to control. To start, restart, or stop the service, right-click the service and make the appropriate choice, as shown in Figure 23-35.

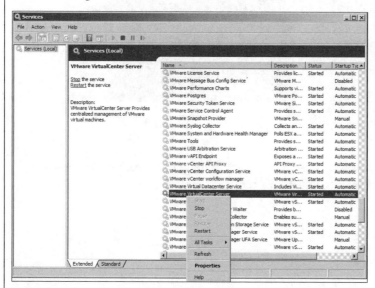

**Figure 23-35**   Starting, Restarting, or Stopping the vCenter Service

## Starting/Stopping/Verifying ESXi Host Agent Status

The host agents on your hosts synchronize with vCenter and allow you to access the ESXi hosts directly with the vSphere Client or to access them through a vSphere Client logged on to a vCenter Server. If remote access is interrupted, you might need to restart the host agents on your ESXi hosts.

The best way to control the host agent status is through management agents in the Troubleshooting Options section of your Direct Console User Interface (DCUI) on your host. This restarts the host agent (hostd) and all the other services involved. To restart host management agents and verify that you have done so, follow the steps outlined in Activity 23-5.

**Activity 23-5    Starting, Stopping, and Verifying Host Agent Status**

1. From your DCUI, select **Troubleshooting Options**, as shown in Figure 23-36. You will likely need to provide credentials to log on to your DCUI.

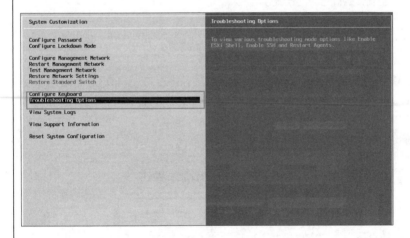

**Figure 23-36**  Troubleshooting Options in the DCUI

2. Using your arrow keys, select **Restart Management Agents**, as shown in Figure 23-37, and then press **Enter**.

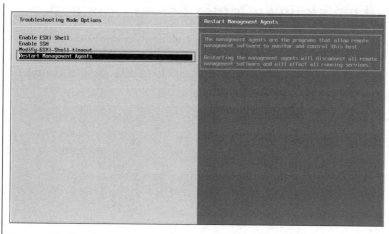

**Figure 23-37**   Restarting Management Agents

   **3.**  Press **F11** to confirm the restart.

## Configuring vCenter Server Timeout Settings

In most cases, the default setting for vCenter Server timeout will be sufficient. If you need to change these settings, you can find and edit them under the General tab within the **Manage**, **Settings** for your vCenter, as shown in Figure 23-38. The default settings are 30 seconds for normal operations and 120 seconds for long operations. These settings can be configured higher to allow an operation to complete. For example, if you experience an "operation timed out" error when trying to add a host to a vCenter, you can resolve the issue by changing the normal operations timeout from 30 seconds to 60 seconds. You should never set these to 0.

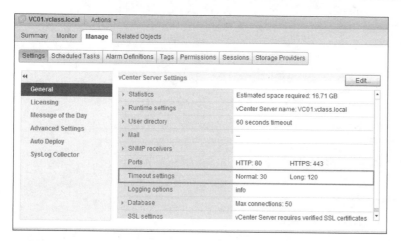

**Figure 23-38**   vCenter Server Timeout Settings

# Monitoring/Administering vCenter Server Connections

You can view the connections to your vCenter by clicking the **Sessions** tab within **Manage**, **Settings** for your vCenter, as shown in Figure 23-39. The Sessions tab shows the current number of Active and Idle sessions along with the username, full name, online time, and status of each session.

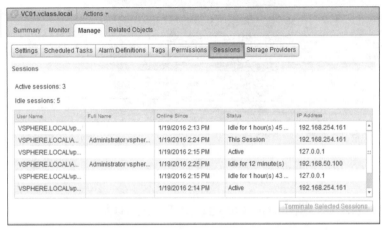

**Figure 23-39**   The vCenter Sessions Tab

You can terminate an active session other than yours by clicking it and selecting **Terminate Selected Sessions** on the lower-right corner, as shown in Figure 23-40. You cannot terminate the session that you are logged in to from here.

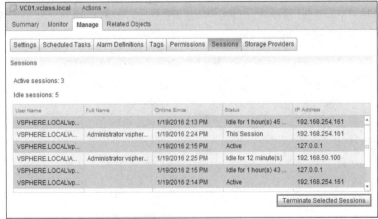

**Figure 23-40**   Terminating a vCenter Session

## Creating an Advanced Chart

Advanced performance charts were discussed earlier in this section, but it wasn't time to create one just yet. Now I am going to create an Advanced performance chart that will gather data about one of the most important counters for a VM: CPU Ready value. The VM that I will use is my LabVM1. Because you don't have time to wait, I'll just collect real-time data for it and report it back to you. I'll call my chart CPU Warning Sign.

To collect real-time data for CPU Ready value, I select **Chart Options** and then click **Real-Time** under CPU. For vCPUs, I will leave the default of 0 and LabVM1. (Because it has only one vCPU, the 0 instance is the one vCPU, so they are really the same, but there is a method to my madness.) Finally, under Counters, I click **None** and select only the **Ready** counter, as shown in Figure 23-41.

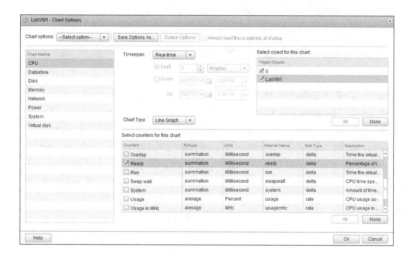

**Figure 23-41**   Choosing the Data to Gather on an Advanced Chart

When I click **OK**, the result is a real-time chart of CPU Ready value for LabVM1, as shown in Figure 23-42. As you can see, it is well within the acceptable range below 2000 ms. (If you create this same chart, you can click in the **Performance Chart Legend** on LabVM1 or instance 0 of the vCPU, and you will see that they are the same.)

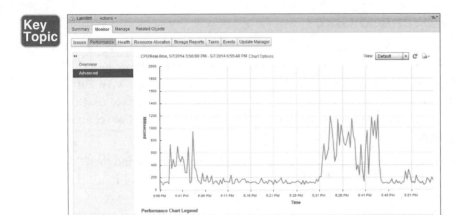

**Figure 23-42**  An Advanced Performance Chart for CPU Ready Value

To save these settings, I click **Chart Options** again and then click **Save Option As**, as shown in Figure 23-43. I enter the name **CPU Warning Sign** for these settings, and that will become a quickly available option for use on this VM only, as shown in Figure 23-44. As you can see, creating the charts is rather easy, and as you learn more about your own system, you'll know more of the counters that you want to see on your own charts.

**Figure 23-43**  Saving Performance Chart Settings

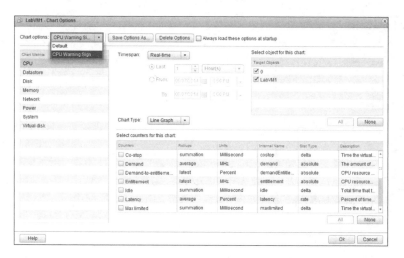

**Figure 23-44**   Referencing a Saved Performance Chart

# Determining Host Performance Using Guest Performance Monitor

In general, you should not implicitly trust all the data that you receive from performance tools that are built in to the OS, such as Perfmon and Task Manager. The reason is that resources, such as CPU and memory, are being dynamically allocated by the VMkernel, a process that is entirely hidden from the guest OS. In other words, the guest OS doesn't really understand the big picture of what is occurring with regard to resources.

To give you accurate information, VMware provides performance counters that attach to the Microsoft Windows Perfmon utility when you install VMware Tools on a VM with a Microsoft OS. You can view performance data specific to VM performance on these special counters. To use these special counters, select the objects that represent the counters in the Windows Perfmon utility, as shown in Figure 23-45.

By determining what is really occurring with regard to VM resources, you open a window into realizing what is happening with host resources as well. Then, by comparing this information to your performance charts in vCenter (and ultimately to your own baseline), you can make accurate decisions about your vSphere. This allows you to determine host performance and make the necessary corrections for improvement.

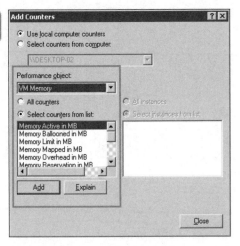

**Figure 23-45**  VM Performance Counters in Perfmon

## Given Performance Data, Identify the Affected vSphere Resource

There are many ways to collect performance data from your vSphere system and the VMs that it contains. You can choose from a variety of tools to obtain information. Equally important to the tools that you use is how you interpret the data that you gather. You should always take into account that a weakness in one resource may be affecting another resource. In other words, all the resources work together, not separate from each other. Knowing the standards, and especially your baseline, you should determine the weakest resource and make a change, and then "rinse and repeat." By making one change at a time and monitoring the results of that change, you will be able to continually strengthen your vSphere environment.

## Summary

This chapter covers the following main topics:

- How to view tasks and events in vCenter

- Critical performance metrics in general, followed by common metrics for each of the core four resources

- The types of charts that you can create, such as overview and advanced charts

- Configuring SMNP, Active Directory, and SMTP settings for your vCenter Server

- Logging options and even how to create a Log Bundle for VMware Support

- Creating, editing, and deleting scheduled tasks and creating resource maps for your hosts in the vSphere Client

- Starting, stopping, and verifying vCenter Server status and ESXi Host Agent status

- Configuring vCenter Server Timeout settings

- Monitoring and administering vCenter Server connections, creating advanced charts, and determining and improving host performance by identifying the affected resource.

## Exam Preparation Tasks

## Review All the Key Topics

Review the most important topics from the chapter, noted with the Key Topic icon in the outer margin of the page. Table 23-3 lists these key topics and the page numbers where each is found. Know the various tools that you can use to monitor your vSphere, and especially which ones you can trust.

**Table 23-3**   Key Topics for Chapter 23

| Key Topic Element | Description | Page Number |
|---|---|---|
| Figure 23-1 | The Events Tab and Recent Tasks Status Bar on a Host Login | 565 |
| Figure 23-2 | Viewing All Entries Within an Object | 566 |
| Figure 23-3 | Filtering the Output | 567 |
| Figure 23-4 | Filtering by Keyword | 568 |
| Bullet List | Critical Performance Metrics | 568 |
| Figure 23-5 | The Memory "Shell Game" | 570 |
| Figure 23-6 | Transparent Page Sharing | 571 |
| Figure 23-7 | The Balloon Driver Mechanism | 571 |
| Figure 23-8 | The Memory Compression Cache Setting | 572 |
| Figure 23-9 | The Resource Allocation Tab of a VM | 573 |
| Bullet List | Memory Terms | 573 |

| Key Topic Element | Description | Page Number |
|---|---|---|
| Figure 23-10 | Overview Performance Charts | 576 |
| Figure 23-11 | The Chart Options Link | 577 |
| Figure 23-12 | Choosing Options of Custom Advanced Charts | 577 |
| Figure 23-13 | User Directory Settings for vCenter | 579 |
| Bullet List | User Directory Settings for vCenter | 579 |
| Activity 23-1 | Configuring SMTP Settings for vCenter Server | 580 |
| Figure 23-16 | vCenter Server Logging Options | 582 |
| Bullet List | vCenter Server Logging Options | 582 |
| Activity 23-2 | Creating a Log Bundle | 583 |
| Figure 23-19 | Generating a Log Bundle | 584 |
| Table 23-2 | Scheduled Tasks in vCenter | 585 |
| Activity 23-3 | Creating a Scheduled Task to Power On a VM | 586 |
| Figure 23-28 | Creating a Resource Map from Hosts and Clusters View | 591 |
| Figure 23-29 | The Maps Icon | 591 |
| Figure 23-30 | Creating a Custom Resource Map | 592 |
| Figure 23-31 | Printing Resource Maps | 593 |
| Figure 23-32 | Exporting Resource Maps | 593 |
| Figure 23-33 | vCenter Services in Windows | 594 |
| Activity 23-4 | Starting, Restarting, and Stopping the vCenter Server Services | 594 |
| Activity 23-5 | Starting, Stopping, and Verifying Host Agent Status | 596 |
| Figure 23-38 | vCenter Server Timeout Settings | 597 |
| Figure 23-39 | The vCenter Sessions Tab | 598 |
| Figure 23-40 | Terminating a vCenter Session | 598 |
| Figure 23-41 | Choosing the Data to Gather on an Advanced Chart | 599 |
| Figure 23-42 | An Advanced Performance Chart for CPU Ready Value | 600 |
| Figure 23-43 | Saving Performance Chart Settings | 600 |
| Figure 23-44 | Refreshing a Saved Performance Chart | 601 |
| Figure 23-45 | VM Performance Counters in Perfmon | 602 |

## Review Questions

The answers to these review questions are in Appendix A.

1. Which of the following is *not* viewable on your vSphere Client when you are logged on directly to a host?

   a. The Events tab

   b. Recent Tasks

   c. Host and Clusters view

   d. The Performance tab

2. Which of the following memory technologies has a cache that determines the extent to which it is used?

   a. TPS

   b. vmmemctl

   c. Memory compression

   d. Swap

3. Which of the following is a memory conservation technique that uses vmmemctl?

   a. Ballooning

   b. Memory compression

   c. Swap file

   d. TPS

4. Which of the following are *not* true about CPU Ready value on VMs? (Choose two.)

   a. The lower the CPU Ready value, the better.

   b. A CPU Ready value of 5% is considered high.

   c. A CPU Ready value of 5% is considered acceptable.

   d. The higher the CPU Ready value, the better.

**5.** You are examining the Resource Allocation tab of one of your VMs. What does Host memory indicate?

    **a.** The amount of memory that the VMkernel thinks it will use to run the virtualized workload.

    **b.** The amount of RAM that has been allocated to the VM.

    **c.** The amount of RAM that is currently being provided to the VM.

    **d.** The total amount of the memory that is being shared by Transparent Page Sharing (TPS).

**6.** Which of the following would be considered storage issues that need to be addressed? (Choose two.)

    **a.** VMkernel command latency of 10 ms

    **b.** VMkernel command latency of 1 ms

    **c.** Physical device command latency of 5 ms

    **d.** Physical device command latency of 20 ms

**7.** You are the administrator of a vSphere 6 environment. You want to view Overview charts. Which of the following are true? (Choose two.)

    **a.** You can view Overview charts for the previous day, week, month, and even year.

    **b.** Overview charts are viewable only in real time.

    **c.** You can create a custom Time Range for Overview charts.

    **d.** You can only create custom Time Ranges for Advanced Charts.

**8.** What is generally the role of your vCenter server in regard to SNMP?

    **a.** It is the management information base (MIB) for your SNMP community.

    **b.** You cannot use vCenter with SNMP.

    **c.** SNMP requires an email address that the vCenter provides.

    **d.** It is an agent that can generate a trap.

9. You are the administrator of a vCenter that authenticates to Active Directory. You set the Query Limit Size to 0. Which of the following will be the result?

   a. The sever will not prepopulate any of the Active Directory users or groups.

   b. The server will prepopulate all the Active Directory users and groups.

   c. 30 sec

   d. This setting has no effect on the server.

10. Which of the following logging options is the default and recommended setting?

   a. Information

   b. None

   c. Warning

   d. Verbose

11. You are the administrator of a vSphere 6 environment. You want to create a log bundle to send to VMware Support. You have just selected the vCenter and clicked on Monitor/System. Which of the following will you click next?

   a. Create Log Bundle

   b. Export System Logs

   c. Source

   d. Add Files to Log

12. Which of the following cannot be a scheduled task?

   a. Add a host to the data center

   b. Delete a host

   c. Power off a VM

   d. Swap

**13.** You are the administrator of a vSphere 6 environment. You can ping the VM that is the vCenter Server at its hostname and IP address, but you cannot log on to the vCenter Server. Which of the following services should you check first?

   **a.** DNS client

   **b.** DNS server

   **c.** DHCP client

   **d.** VMware VirtualCenter Server

**14.** Which of the following are *not* valid reasons to restart vCenter Server? (Choose two.)

   **a.** A new plug-in, for example VUM, is not starting.

   **b.** You have just created a new VM.

   **c.** vCenter does not appear to be refreshing as normal.

   **d.** You cannot ping a host.

**15.** You are the administrator of a vSphere 6 environment. You want to restart the host agent of one of your ESXi hosts. Where is the best place to restart the host agent?

   **a.** There is no longer a host agent in vSphere 6.

   **b.** By logging on to your host with the vSphere Windows-based client and then going to Troubleshooting Options.

   **c.** In the DCUI under Troubleshooting Options.

   **d.** You will need to physically restart the host.

**16.** Which of the following is *not* a recommended setting for vCenter Server timeout?

   **a.** 30 sec

   **b.** 0 sec

   **c.** 45 sec

   **d.** 20 sec

**17.** As an administrator of your vSphere environment, you want to create an Advanced Performance Chart. Which of the following tabs will you need to select first?

  **a.** Advanced

  **b.** Options

  **c.** Monitor

  **d.** Charts

**18.** You are the administrator of a vSphere environment. You click on a host in Hosts and Clusters view, then on **Monitor**, and finally on **Performance**. You want to create an advanced chart. Which of the following will be the default Timespan of the chart?

  **a.** Last day

  **b.** Last week

  **c.** Last month

  **d.** Real-time

**19.** You are the administrator of your vSphere 6 environment. You want to use the performance objects of VM Memory and VM CPU on your Perfmon, but the performance objects are not available. Which of the following is the issue?

  **a.** You have not installed VMware Tools on the VM.

  **b.** These objects are no longer available on vSphere 6.

  **c.** You will need to use the Windows-based version of your client to see these objects.

  **d.** Another administrator has renamed the objects in Windows.

**20.** Which of the following are true regarding identifying the affected resource when troubleshooting vSphere?

  **a.** All resources are isolated from each other.

  **b.** You should change one thing at a time and then test again.

  **c.** To avoid confusion, you should only use one tool for each resource.

  **d.** The strength of a whole system will usually be determined by the strength of the weakest resource that it uses.

**This chapter covers the following subjects:**

- vCenter Server Default Utilization Alarms

- vCenter Server Default Connectivity Alarms

- Actions for Utilization and Connectivity Alarms

- Creating a vCenter Server Utilization Alarm

- Creating a vCenter Server Connectivity Alarm

- Configuring Alarm Triggers

- Configuring Alarm Actions

- For a Given Alarm, Identifying the Affected Resource in a vSphere Implementation

Alarms are an effective way to monitor your vSphere environment. The biggest advantage to using alarms as a monitoring tool is that an alarm is something you can "set and forget," and it will still alert you when a threshold is met. On your vSphere Web Client, the initial alert consists of a yellow Warning icon or a red Critical icon, depending on your settings and on the severity of the event. (What is now called Critical was previously called Alert on the vSphere Windows-based client.) This is referred to as going from *green status* (normal) to *yellow status* or *red status*. Creating the appropriate alarms and watching for these icons might allow you to stay ahead of the point at which the users will be affected.

## CHAPTER 24

# Creating and Administering vCenter Server Alarms

In fact, that's not even the whole story about alarms, because many alarms are already set for you on the default installation of vCenter Server. This section focuses on the default utilization and connectivity alarms in vCenter and the actions that are configured for these types of alarms. In addition, you learn how you can create your own utilization and connectivity alarms and how you can customize alarm triggers and alarm actions. Finally, you learn how to identify the source of an alarm in your vSphere implementation.

## "Do I Know This Already?" Quiz

The "Do I Know This Already?" quiz allows you to assess whether you should read this entire chapter or simply jump to the "Exam Preparation Tasks" section for review. If you are in doubt, read the entire chapter. Table 24-1 outlines the major headings in this chapter and the corresponding "Do I Know This Already?" quiz questions. You can find the answers in Appendix A, "Answers to the 'Do I Know This Already?' Quizzes and Chapter Review Questions."

**Table 24-1** "Do I Know This Already?" Section-to-Question Mapping

| Foundation Topics Section | Questions Covered in This Section |
|---|---|
| vCenter Server Default Utilization Alarms | 1, 2 |
| vCenter Server Default Connectivity Alarms | 3, 4 |
| Actions for Utilization and Connectivity Alarms | 5 |
| Creating a vCenter Server Utilization Alarm | 6 |
| Creating a vCenter Server Connectivity Alarm | 7 |
| Configuring Alarm Triggers | 8 |
| Configuring Alarm Actions | 9 |
| For a Given Alarm, Identifying the Affected Resource in a vSphere Implementation | 10 |

1. You want to see all the default alarms associated with your vCenter. You have selected the vCenter in the Navigator. Which tab should you select next?

    a. Monitor

    b. Alarms

    c. Manage

    d. Alarm Definitions

2. Which of the following is *not* a default utilization alarm in vCenter?

    a. Host CPU Usage

    b. Host Memory Usage

    c. Datastore Usage on Disk

    d. Available Bandwidth

3. Which of the following is *not* a default connectivity alarm?

    a. Cannot connect to storage

    b. Host connection failure

    c. Network connectivity lost

    d. VM out of disk space

4. Which of the following are default connectivity alarms? (Choose two.)

    a. Network uplink redundancy lost

    b. Virtual Machine Memory Usage

    c. Host connection failure

    d. Datastore Usage on disk

5. Which of the following are true regarding alarm actions? (Choose two.)

    a. A vCenter Server can be configured as an agent to generate a trap for SNMP.

    b. A vCenter Server cannot send an email to an administrator.

    c. A vCenter Server can send an email to an administrator.

    d. A vCenter Server cannot be configured to automatically run a script when an alarm is triggered.

6. Which of the following can your vCenter be configured as in your SNMP network?

   a. A Management Information Base (MIB)

   b. An agent

   c. A trap

   d. A community

7. You are the administrator of your vSphere environment. You want to create a new alarm. Which of the following is *not* true in regard to creating a new alarm?

   a. You choose what you want to monitor as part of creating the alarm.

   b. You need to check the **Enable This Alarm** box to enable the alarm.

   c. You have the choice between monitoring for events and monitoring for conditions.

   d. Triggers for events will be different from those for conditions.

8. Which of the following are types of alarm triggers? (Choose two.)

   a. Send a notification email

   b. Condition

   c. Migrate VM

   d. Event

9. Which of the following are possible alarm actions?

   a. Send a notification email

   b. Shut down a cluster

   c. Run a script

   d. Create a new vDS

10. Without the use of a script, which of the following can be an indication that an alarm has been triggered? (Choose two.)

   a. Additional icons on the object in the client

   b. An entire cluster of hosts suddenly powering off

   c. An email, containing the alarm information, sent to an administrator

   d. A switch suddenly shutting ports to a port group

## Foundation Topics

# vCenter Server Default Utilization Alarms

Properly configured utilization alarms can assist you in fixing a problem before it gets critical enough to have a negative effect on your users. In fact, it's so important to have at least some properly configured utilization alarms that VMware has decided to provide some right out of the box.

You can find all these alarms by selecting the root object of your vCenter, clicking the **Manage** tab, and then opening the **Alarm Definitions** tab, as shown in Figure 24-1. Because these alarms are set at root of the vCenter, they can be applied to all objects in the vCenter, based on the type of alarm that is set. In addition, alarm actions can include more than just alerting you; they can also run a script that could make your system somewhat "self-healing."

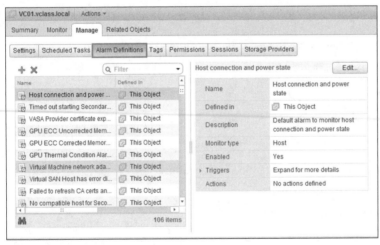

**Figure 24-1**    Default Alarm Definitions in vCenter

By understanding your own environment and keeping an eye out for your default utilization alarms, you can address developing problems and keep them from becoming more critical. Table 24-2 lists the default utilization alarms included with your vCenter as well as their general purpose and default threshold.

**Table 24-2**   Default Utilization Alarms in vCenter

| Alarm | Purpose | Default Threshold |
|-------|---------|-------------------|
| Host CPU usage | Monitors host CPU usage | 75% for 5 min—Warning |
|  |  | 90% for 5 min—Critical |
| Host Memory usage | Monitors host physical memory usage | 90% for 5 min—Warning |
|  |  | 95% for 5 min—Critical |
| Virtual Machine CPU usage | Monitors the use of the vCPU on each VM | 75% for 5 min—Warning |
|  |  | 90% for 5 min—Critical |
| Virtual Machine memory usage | Monitors the use of available memory on each VM | 85% for 10 min—Warning |
|  |  | 95% for 10 min—Critical |
| Datastore usage on disk | Monitors disk usage on all configured datastores on each host | 75%—Warning |
|  |  | 85%—Critical |

# vCenter Server Default Connectivity Alarms

Whereas utilization alarms can keep you ahead of potential issues, connectivity alarms generally give you the fastest start possible toward fixing an issue that has already developed. When a default connectivity alarm is triggered, there is a good chance that many users are affected. For this reason, you should be able to recognize the default connectivity alarms in vCenter. Table 24-3 lists the default connectivity alarms and their general purpose.

**Table 24-3**   Default Connectivity Alarms in vCenter

| Alarm | Purpose |
|-------|---------|
| Cannot connect to storage | Monitors host connectivity to the storage devices to which each host is configured |
| Host connection failure | Monitors connections to network to which each host is configured |
| Network connectivity lost | Monitors network connectivity of a virtual switch to the hosts to which it is configured |
| Network uplink redundancy lost | Monitors the network redundancy configured on a virtual switch |

## Actions for Utilization and Connectivity Alarms

If the only action that utilization and connectivity alarms could perform was to make "pretty colors" next to your vCenter objects, you might very well miss a critical alarm. Because of this, in addition to showing yellow Warnings and red Criticals, the alarms can also cause other actions to be performed when they are triggered. Table 24-4 lists possible actions for utilization and connectivity alarms on hosts, VMs, virtual switches, and datastores. Later in this section, you learn how you can configure alarm actions.

**Table 24-4**   Possible Actions for Utilization and Connectivity Alarms

| Alarm Type | Possible Actions |
| --- | --- |
| Host | Send a notification email |
| | Send a notification trap |
| | Run a command |
| | Enter Maintenance Mode |
| | Exit Maintenance Mode |
| | Enter standby |
| | Exit standby |
| | Reboot host |
| | Shut down host |
| Virtual Machine | Send a notification email |
| | Send a notification trap |
| | Run a command |
| | Power on VM |
| | Power off VM |
| | Suspend VM |
| | Reset VM |
| | Migrate VM |
| | Reboot guest on VM |
| | Shut down guest on VM |
| Virtual Switch | Send a notification email |
| | Send a notification trap |
| | Run a command |
| Datastore | Send a notification email |
| | Send a notification trap |
| | Run a command |

# Creating a vCenter Utilization Alarm

If you need a utilization alarm that is different from the default alarms, you should create a new utilization alarm rather than changing the default alarm. In other words, it is a best practice to leave the default alarms in place and add your own custom alarms to them. That way, if your alarms do not function properly or are removed or disabled at some point in the future, the default alarms will still be there backing you up, regardless of any other configuration. For example, if you want to create a new utilization alarm that monitors for VM CPU Ready Time for all the VMs on all the hosts in Cluster1, follow the steps outlined in Activity 24-1.

**Activity 24-1    Creating a vCenter Utilization Alarm**

1. Log on to your vCenter using your vSphere Web Client.

2. Right-click an object in your inventory that includes the hosts and VMs on which you want to set the alarm (in this case, I right-clicked my cluster named **Lab Cluster**), and select **Alarms** and then **New Alarm Definition**, as shown in Figure 24-2.

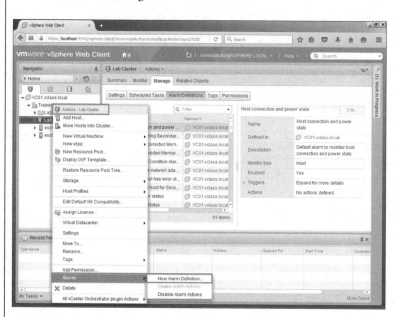

**Figure 24-2**    Adding a Custom Alarm to a Cluster

3. Type a name for your new alarm (in this case, **CPU Ready Time**, the same as CPU Ready value). You can also type a description to help you remember what the alarm is monitoring. Set the alarm type (in this case, **Virtual Machines**). Choose whether to monitor specific conditions or state or to monitor specific events. (Later in this section, you learn how this affects your trigger options.) In this case, I am monitoring specific conditions. Finally, leave the **Enable this alarm** check box checked, all shown in Figure 24-3. Click **Next**.

**Figure 24-3**   Creating a VM CPU Ready Time Alarm

4. On **Triggers** click the **Add +** icon, and then choose your trigger from the drop-down box, as shown in Figure 24-4. In this case, I'm choosing **VM CPU Ready Time** because I discussed this important counter earlier in this chapter.

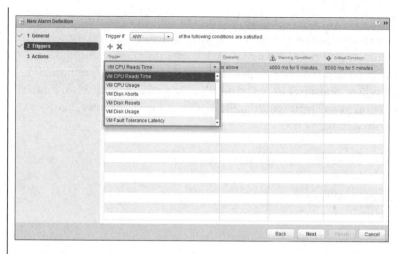

**Figure 24-4**   Configuring the Alarm Trigger

5. I will set the **Operator** to **is above** and the **Warning Condition** to **1000 ms for 5 minutes** as well as the **Critical Condition** to **2000 ms for 5 minutes**. I will leave the **Trigger if** setting at **ANY,** as shown in Figure 24-5.

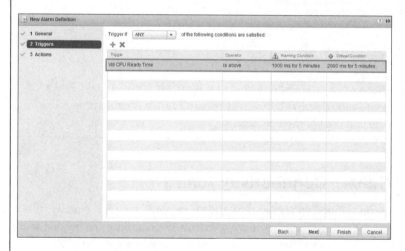

**Figure 24-5**   Setting a Conditional Trigger

6. Finally, I click **Next** to move to the Actions tab and click the **Add "+"** icon. I'm going to add an action that sends me (me@me.com) an email once when the status goes from green (normal) to yellow (warning). In addition, I am setting an action that will repeatedly send me an email every 15 minutes if it goes from yellow (warning) to red (critical), as shown in Figure 24-6. I don't need the action of an email sent to indicate that it's getting better, because I will be involved in fixing it.

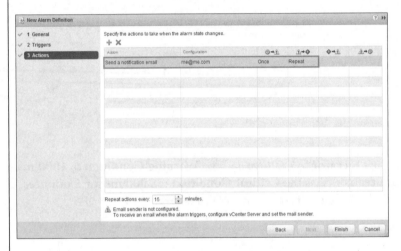

**Figure 24-6**   Configuring Alarm Action to Send Email

7. You can review your tabs and ensure that you have what you need, add additional triggers, and so on. When you are satisfied with your settings, click **OK** to create and enable the new alarm.

## Creating a vCenter Connectivity Alarm

The best practice mentioned with regard to utilization alarms applies equally to connectivity alarms. You will find that there are many connectivity alarms that you can configure in addition to the defaults, but leave the default alarms in place and intact. Now, to create a new alarm that monitors a specific VM's connection to its current port group, follow the steps outlined in Activity 24-2.

**Activity 24-2   Creating a vCenter Connectivity Alarm**

1. Log on to your vCenter using your vSphere Web Client.

2. Locate and right-click the specific VM that you want to monitor, and select **Alarms** and then **New Alarm Definition**, as shown in Figure 24-7. (You could also specify a higher inventory object, such as a host or cluster, and monitor the same connectivity for all VMs associated.)

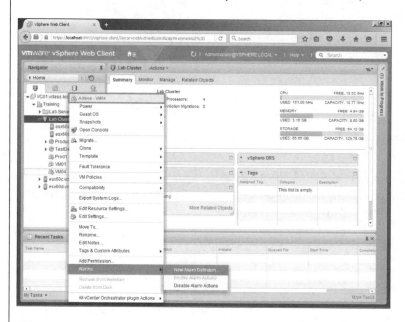

**Figure 24-7**   Adding an Alarm to a Specific VM

3. Type a name for your new alarm; in this case, I'm naming mine **Disconnect Warning**. You can also type a description if you choose. Leave the alarm type set to **Virtual Machine**. Change the setting below Alarm Type to **Monitor for Specific Events**, and leave the **Enable This Alarm** check box checked, as shown in Figure 24-8. Click **Next**.

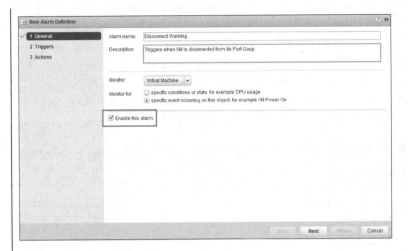

**Figure 24-8**   Monitoring for Specific Events

4. On the Triggers page, click the **Add "+"** icon, and then choose **VM Disconnected** from the drop-down box, as shown in Figure 24-9. Leave the status at **Alert** and do not set any advanced conditions.

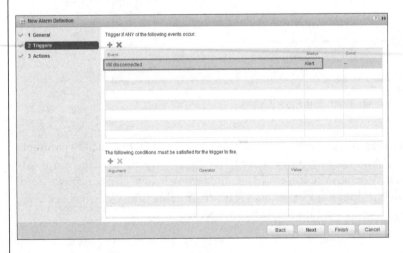

**Figure 24-9**   Choosing Your Alarm Trigger

5. Click **Next** to move to the Actions tab and click **Add**. Configure that an email will be sent to me@me.com when the alarm is triggered, as shown in Figure 24-10.

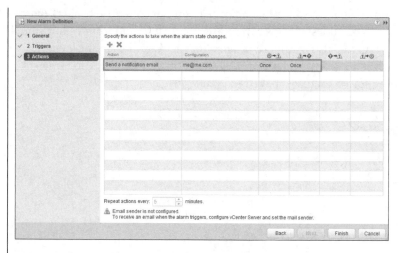

**Figure 24-10**   Configuring an Action for Email

6. Finally, review your settings, and when satisfied, click **Finish** to create and enable your new alarm.

## Configuring Alarm Triggers

As you can see from my examples, a trigger is a threshold that, once reached, activates the alarm. As mentioned earlier, when you choose the alarm type, you are also choosing the types of triggers from the Triggers tab. There are two main types of alarm triggers: Condition or State and Event. At first, the lines might seem a little blurry, to say the least. For example, why is "Cannot connect host" considered an event and not a condition?

Upon closer inspection, you will find that the Condition alarms can have a timer or another additional condition that may or must also be met, as in my first sample alarm. On the other hand, State and Event triggers do not have timers or any other conditions. State and Event triggers are more like "trip wires" that will go off if they are touched. Your only choice is where you put the "wire."

If you can accomplish the same result with a Condition alarm and have a time condition, or some other condition, that reduces false positives, that is the way to go. However, you will also find that there are many more Event triggers than there are Condition triggers, so you may have more flexibility with Event triggers as long as you don't need timers or other conditions.

Finally, as shown in Figure 24-11, remember that you can configure triggers that activate the alarm when the status goes from green to yellow and from yellow to red, as it gets worse. You can also configure triggers that activate the alarm when the status goes from red to yellow and yellow to green, as it gets better. Also notice that there is no setting for green to red or red to green.

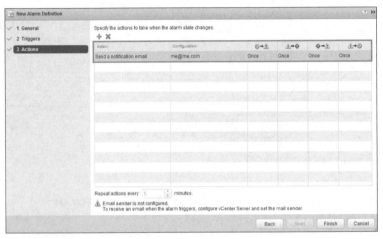

**Figure 24-11**   Trigger Options

## Configuring Alarm Actions

As I mentioned before, alarm actions can go much further than just making "pretty colors" on your vCenter inventory. As you observed from my examples, you can also have the alarms send an email to you or to another email address that you designate. In addition, you can have the alarm send a trap to your SNMP MIB. Even that is just scratching the surface as to what the alarm actions can do.

As you saw previously from Table 24-4, you have great flexibility with regard to alarm actions, and certain actions are available for only certain types of objects. Configuring the actions is simple, and you can configure whether you want them done just once or repeated, as you observed in my first sample alarm. As you get to know your vCenter and its components better, you should familiarize yourself with all your alarm options and see if there are some obvious combinations that might make life easier for you, such as my CPU Ready Time alarm with the send email action.

### For a Given Alarm, Identifying the Affected Resource in a vSphere Implementation

Unlike monitoring tools, such as Resxtop and Perfmon, on which you have to consider a number of factors to identify the affected resource, alarms announce much about the affected resource as soon as they are triggered. Based on the name and description of the alarm triggered, the trigger type and trigger specifics, and the object in your inventory that is suddenly boasting a new yellow "yield sign" or a red "diamond," you should be able to sleuth this one out!

After you have determined which alarm was triggered, you should be well on your way to knowing why, especially if you set the alarm yourself. If you did not set the alarm, you may need to speak to the administrator who set it. You might also determine that it was one of your default alarms, which is another reason that you should know your default alarms.

## Summary

This chapter covers the following main topics:

- The general concept of alarms and the default utilization and connectivity alarms that are built in to your vSphere installation.

- The possible actions that you can configure for these alarms, such as notifying the administrator or shutting down the VM. You learned that you can choose from many options in regard to alarm actions, according to your own needs.

- How you can create your own utilization and connectivity alarms.

- The two different types of triggers from which you can choose, condition and event; and the differences between these triggers and when to use each type.

- How to identify the affected resource for a given alarm.

## Exam Preparation Tasks

## Review All the Key Topics

Review the most important topics from the chapter, noted with the Key Topic icon in the outer margin of the page. Table 24-5 lists these key topics and the page numbers where each is found. Know the various tools that you can use to monitor your vSphere, and especially which ones you can trust. Understand how to use your default utilization and connectivity alarms and how to create custom alarms when needed.

**Table 24-5**    Key Topics for Chapter 24

| Key Topic Element | Description | Page Number |
|---|---|---|
| Figure 24-1 | Default Alarm Definitions in vCenter | 614 |
| Table 24-2 | Default Utilization Alarms in vCenter | 615 |
| Table 24-3 | Default Connectivity Alarms in vCenter | 615 |
| Table 24-4 | Possible Actions for Utilization and Connectivity Alarms | 616 |
| Activity 24-1 | Creating a vCenter Utilization Alarm | 617 |
| Activity 24-2 | Creating a vCenter Connectivity Alarm | 621 |
| Figure 24-11 | Trigger Options | 624 |

## Review Questions

The answers to these review questions are in Appendix A.

1. You want to see all the default alarms associated with your vCenter. Which of the following should you first select in the Navigator of your vSphere Web Client?

   a. Alarms

   b. Monitor

   c. The vCenter object

   d. Defaults

2. Which of the following is not a default utilization alarm in vCenter?

   a. Host CPU usage

   b. Maximum ports exceeded on a switch

   c. Datastore Usage on Disk

   d. Virtual Machine CPU Usage

3. Which of the following is not a default connectivity alarm?

   a. Host CPU Usage

   b. Host connection failure

   c. Network connectivity lost

   d. Network uplink redundancy lost

4. Which of following are *not* default connectivity alarms? (Choose two.)

    a. Network uplink redundancy lost

    b. Virtual Machine Memory Usage

    c. Host connection failure

    d. Datastore Usage on disk

5. Which of the following are true regarding alarm actions? (Choose two.)

    a. A vCenter Server cannot be configured as an agent to generate a trap for SNMP.

    b. A vCenter Server sends an email to an administrator.

    c. A vCenter Server cannot send an email to an administrator.

    d. A vCenter Server can be configured to automatically run a script when an alarm is triggered.

6. Which of the following are possible alarm actions for a VM? (Choose two.)

    a. Power off

    b. Reset

    c. Add a vnic

    d. Remove guest OS

7. You are the administrator of your vSphere environment. You want to create a new alarm. Which of the following are true in regard to creating a new alarm?

    a. You choose what you want to monitor as part of creating the alarm.

    b. You need to check the **Enable This Alarm** box to enable the alarm.

    c. You have the choice between monitoring for events and monitoring for conditions.

    d. Triggers for events will be the same as those for conditions.

8. Which of the following types of alarm triggers can reduce "false positives"? (Choose two.)

    a. No alarm trigger can reduce "false positives."

    b. Condition

    c. All alarm triggers prevent "false positives."

    d. Event

9. Which of the following are not possible alarm actions?

   a. Send a notification email

   b. Shut down a cluster

   c. Run a script

   d. Create a new vDS

10. Which of the following are configurable connectivity alarms on your vSphere Web Client? (Choose two.)

    a. Cannot connect to storage

    b. Power off this cluster

    c. Network connectivity lost

    d. Shut all ports on this port group

**This chapter covers the following subjects:**

- Differentiating Between Major/Minor vROPs Badges

- vROPs Architecture

- Deploying and Configuring a vROP Appliance

- Configure vCenter Adapter in vROP

- Upgrading vROPs

- Understanding Metrics Used by Minor/Major vROPs Badges

- Monitoring Your vSphere Environment

When I was discussing the need for recording a baseline of your environment when it's healthy, you might have said to yourself, "Can't the computers do that for me?" Doesn't it make sense, because you have all the computer resources anyway, that you should put the computers to work to calculate, track, understand, and communicate what "healthy" and "normal" look like in your environment? That way, the system could let you know when you are at risk before the risk is critical. Also, the system could inform you as to the efficiency of your resources based on the decisions that you have made and might even make some "suggestions" of its own. Wouldn't it be better to let the computers do that work because they can crunch the numbers much better and faster than you can?

## CHAPTER 25

# Installing and Administering vRealize Operations Manager

This, in essence, is what vRealize Operations Manager (vROPs) does for you. It's a tool that is now included in all editions of vSphere, from Essentials Plus on up through Enterprise Plus, although more features are added for each higher version of vSphere. vROPs collects performance data from each object at every level of your virtual environment. It stores the data, analyzes it, and uses the results to provide real-time information about problems and opportunities anywhere in your virtual environment.

To communicate with you, vROPs combines the many *metrics* that it collects into single *scores* indicating your environmental health, efficiency, and risk. It calculates a normal range of behavior over time and then can spot abnormalities for you. It presents these in a graphical representation made up of *badges* that are just…well, gorgeous!

In this section, I introduce you to vROPs and explain how you can install, configure, and administer it to monitor your environment. Specifically, you learn about vROPs architecture and differentiate between major and minor badges. In addition, this section covers the basics of deploying and configuring the vROPs appliance. Also, you learn how you can upgrade vROPs if you need to take advantage of even more features. Finally, you learn how you can use vROPs as an effective tool to monitor your vSphere environment.

There is so much to discuss about vROPs that I can't possibly cover it all in one chapter. It could fill an entire book; in fact, a few have been written about it. For our purposes, I'm going to cover the blueprint objectives in some detail so that you will have an overall understanding of vROPs that is beneficial for real life as well as for the test.

## "Do I Know This Already?" Quiz

The "Do I Know This Already?" quiz allows you to assess whether you should read this entire chapter or simply jump to the "Exam Preparation Tasks" section for review. If you are in doubt, read the entire chapter. Table 25-1 outlines the major headings in this chapter and the corresponding "Do I Know This Already?" quiz questions. You can find the answers in Appendix A, "Answers to the 'Do I Know This Already?' Quizzes and Chapter Review Questions."

**Table 25-1**  "Do I Know This Already?" Section-to-Question Mapping

| Foundation Topics Section | Questions Covered in This Section |
|---|---|
| Differentiating Between Major/Minor vROPs Badges | 1–3 |
| vROPs Architecture | 4 |
| Deploying and Configuring a vROP Appliance | 5, 6 |
| Upgrading vROPs | 7 |
| Understanding Metrics Used by Major/Minor vROPs Badges | 8, 9 |
| Monitoring Your vSphere Environment | 10 |

**1.** Which of the following is *not* a major badge of vCenter Operations Manager?

    **a.** Health

    **b.** Security

    **c.** Risk

    **d.** Efficiency

**2.** Which of the following is *not* a minor badge within Health?

    **a.** Workload

    **b.** Anomalies

    **c.** Time Remaining

    **d.** Faults

**3.** Which of the following is a minor badge within Efficiency?

   **a.** Capacity Remaining

   **b.** Density

   **c.** Time Remaining

   **d.** Stress

**4.** Which of the following are true about vROPs architecture? (Choose two.)

   **a.** It is installed as a vApp that contains two VMs.

   **b.** It is installed as a virtual appliance.

   **c.** Each instance of vROPs can be connected to only one vCenter.

   **d.** One instance of vROPs can be connected to multiple vCenters.

**5.** Which of the following are true regarding deploying and configuring a vROPs appliance? (Choose two.)

   **a.** The appliance can be deployed from an OVF.

   **b.** You should always use thin provisioning for storage.

   **c.** You should use Thick Provision Eager Zeroed for storage.

   **d.** You will not need to configure the size; one size fits all.

**6.** Which of the following are true regarding the deployment of vROPs? (Choose two.)

   **a.** You can select the folder in which to install it.

   **b.** It will always be installed in the vROPs folder.

   **c.** You can assign a static IP address.

   **d.** You can only assign an IP address using DHCP.

**7.** Which type of file is used to upgrade/update vROPs?

   **a.** .iso

   **b.** .vmx

   **c.** .pak

   **d.** .vmdk

**8.** Which of the following is *not* a minor badge within Health?

   **a.** Risk

   **b.** Workload

   **c.** Anomalies

   **d.** Faults

**9.** Which of the following is *not* a major badge of vCenter Operations Manager?

   **a.** Health

   **b.** Security

   **c.** Risk

   **d.** Efficiency

**10.** Which of the following best describes vROPs?

   **a.** A tool that automates the installation and configuration of vSphere components

   **b.** A tool that monitors a vSphere environment and makes changes without administrator intervention

   **c.** A tool that gives you information about your environment that you can use to decide when to make changes

   **d.** A tool that eliminates all faults in a vSphere environment

## Foundation Topics

# Differentiating Between Major/Minor vROPs Badges

To use vROPs to monitor your virtual environment, you must first understand the badges that vROPs uses to communicate information to you. vROPs uses two primary types of badges that are referred to as major and minor badges. All badges are color coded to represent a range from healthy (green) to potentially problematic yellow, orange, and (worst) red. The major badges are associated to scores that indicate a specific level for that metric. The meaning of these scores is relative to what is being scored. For example, high scores in Health are good, but high scores in Risk are not good.

Each major badge contains the results of minor badges that are related to it. As mentioned previously, the computer is very good at crunching all the numbers, and the rest is just communicating back to you what it has learned. The badges, and in fact all components of vROPs, are arranged in order of urgency and specificity from left to right on the Dashboard. For example, the major Health badge serves as the first high-level (30,000 ft.) indicator of the overall state of your virtual environment. It contains the metrics of multiple minor badges, which include Workload, Anomalies, and Faults. The major badge communicates a problem with its color and score, if even one of the minor badges is critical. In other words, it's not so much an "average" as it is a "weakest link in the chain" report. That way, you can quickly know where to dig deeper to eventually find the root source of a problem. Figure 25-1 shows the relationship between major and minor Health badges in vROPs.

**Figure 25-1**   Minor Badges Within the Major Badges

## vROPs Architecture

Hopefully, now I've got you sold, and you are wondering how you can start taking advantage of this gorgeous and intelligent tool! Well, vROPs is distributed as a virtual appliance that you can import and deploy with your vCenter Server system. It is managed using the Administration Portal, which is a Web console for configuration and management tasks. Prior to version 6, previous vROPs were deployed as vApp, as shown in Figure 25-2.

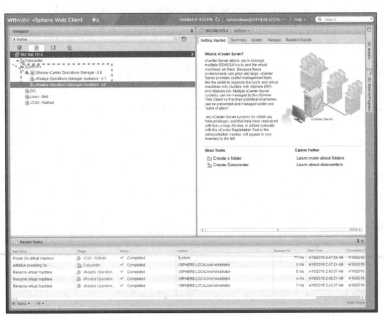

**Figure 25-2**  Previous vROPs Compared to Current Version

A single vROPs can connect to one or multiple vCenter Server instances. All communications take place over an SSL connection that can be authenticated by public key certificates or stored certificates. When vROPs is connected to multiple vCenters, it provides a common view across all vCenter instances for all reporting features. Figure 25-3 shows the installed vROPs appliance.

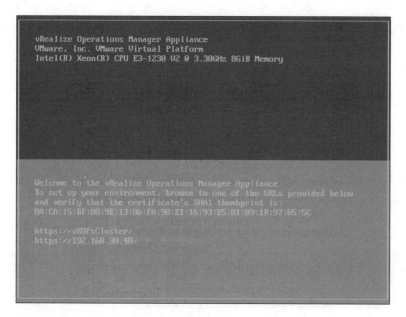

**Figure 25-3**   The vROPs Virtual Appliance

## Deploying and Configuring a vROPs Appliance

Deploying the appliance is done in a manner similar to deploying any other OVA. You first deploy the OVF template, and then you follow the prompts to configure its installation.

To deploy the vROPs appliance, follow the steps outlined in Activity 25-1.

---

**Activity 25-1   Deploying the vROPs Virtual Appliance**

1. From Home, click **vCenter Operations Manager** under Monitoring, as shown in Figure 25-4.

---

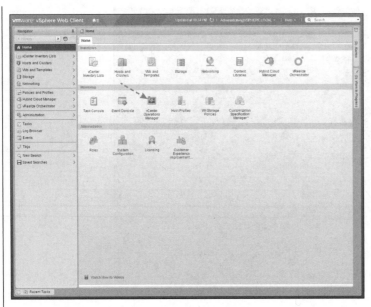

**Figure 25-4**   Accessing vCenter Operations Manager Tools

    **2.** From the Getting Started tab, click **Deploy vCenter Operations Manager**, as shown in Figure 25-5. If the Getting Started tab is not visible, click **Related Objects** and then the **Deploy vCenter Operations Manager** link, as shown in Figure 25-5.

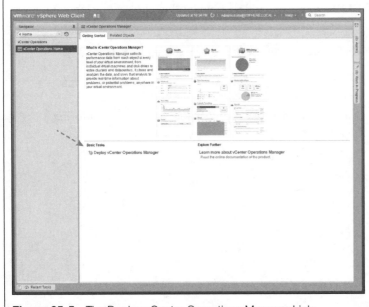

**Figure 25-5**   The Deploy vCenter Operations Manager Link

3. Type the URL and credentials to access the file from your partner site, or browse to the local file where you have stored the OVF and load the file. As you can see in Figure 25-6, I opted for the latter. Click **Next**.

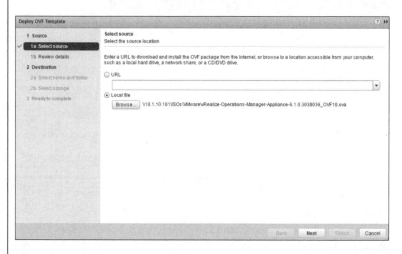

**Figure 25-6**   Loading the OVF File from the Source

4. Review the details to ensure that you are installing the right OVF and that you have the required space, as shown in Figure 25-7.

**Figure 25-7**   Reviewing the Details and Required Space

5. Read thoroughly (just kidding) and then click **Accept** at the bottom of the end user license agreement (EULA), as shown in Figure 25-8. Click **Next**.

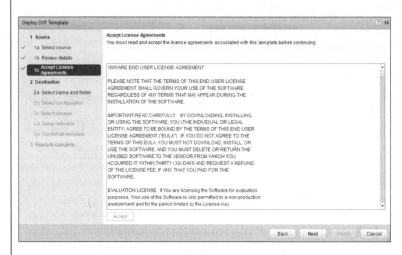

**Figure 25-8**    Accepting the EULA

6. Select the folder where vROPs will be located, as shown in Figure 25-9. Click **Next**.

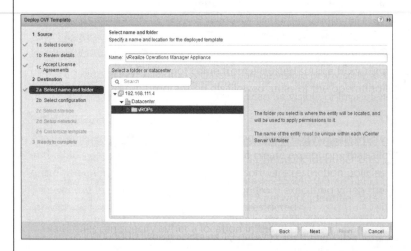

**Figure 25-9**    Selecting the Folder for vROP

7. Choose the appropriate configuration (small, medium, large, remote collector (standard), remote collector (large), and extra small) based on your need, as shown in Figure 25-10. Click **Next**.

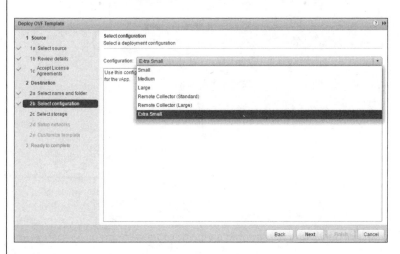

**Figure 25-10**   Choosing Configuration Size

8. Choose the storage location and disk format for the VM files. For best performance, choose **Thick Provision Eager Zeroed**, as shown in Figure 25-11. Click **Next**.

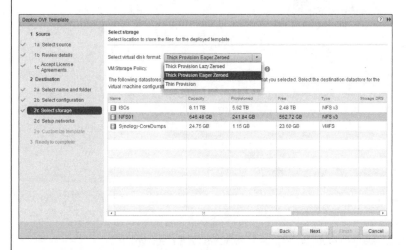

**Figure 25-11**   Choosing a Storage Location

9. On the Setup Networks page, configure the network on which vROPs will run, as shown in Figure 25-12. Click **Next**.

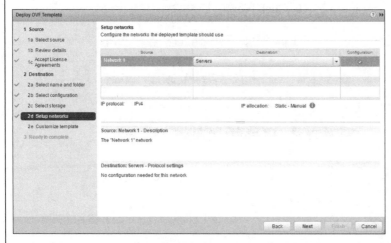

**Figure 25-12**    Setting Up the Network

10. On the Customize Template page, set the time zone for the appliance, as well as the IP settings. Click **Next**.

11. Review your settings, click the check box by **Power On After Deployment**, as shown in Figure 25-13, and click **Finish**.

**Figure 25-13**    The Ready to Complete Page for vROPs OVF Deployment

12. Monitor the progress of the deployment on Recent Tasks, as shown in Figure 25-14.

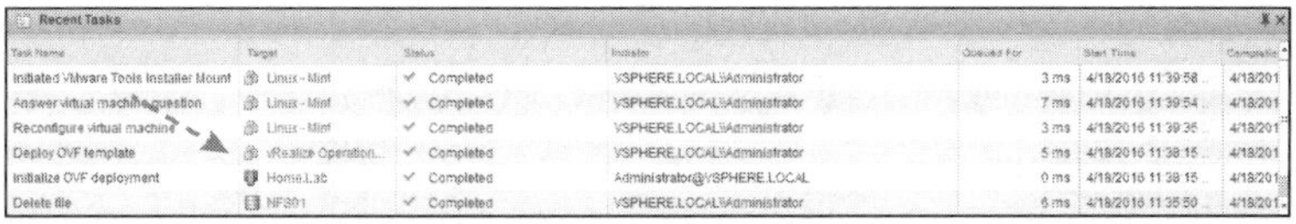

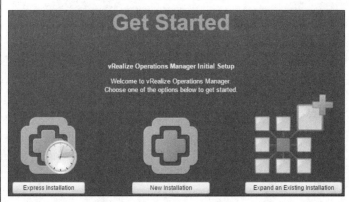

**Figure 25-14** Monitoring the Recent Tasks Tab

13. After you have deployed the appliance, you are ready to register your vCenter Server. Enter the FQDN or IP address of the appliance into a web browser. You will see the three installation options (Express, New, and Expand) shown in Figure 25-15. Select the appropriate option for your situation. Note that Figures 25-16 (Express), 25-17 (New), and 25-18 (Expand) include the Getting Started tab for each option, providing an easy-to-read flow diagram.

**Figure 25-15** Operations Manager Administration Information

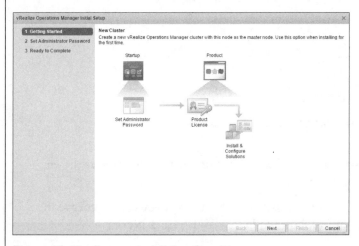

**Figure 25-16** Express Installation Flow Diagram

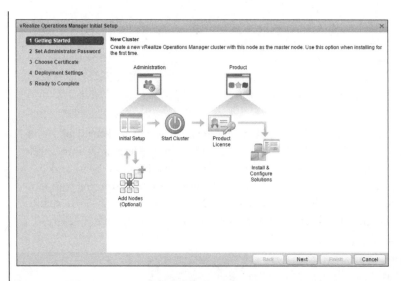

**Figure 25-17**   New Installation Flow Diagram

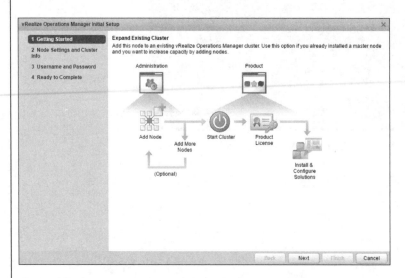

**Figure 25-18**   Expand an Existing Installation Flow Diagram

**14.** Select **New Installation** and click **Next** on the flow diagram, as shown previously in Figure 25-17.

**15.** Provide a password for the appliance. Notice that you cannot change the user name "admin," as shown in Figure 25-19. Click **Next**.

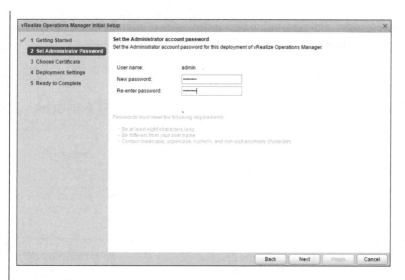

**Figure 25-19**   Provide Admin Password for the Appliance

16. On the next screen, you have the opportunity to deploy a signed certificate; for purposes here, the default certificates will be used, as shown in Figure 25-20. Click **Next**.

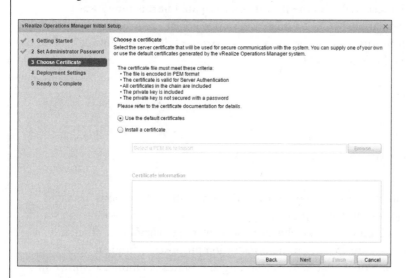

**Figure 25-20**   Choose a Certificate

**17.** In the Deployment Settings, you provide the name of the cluster and an NTP Server, as shown in Figure 25-21. Click **Next**.

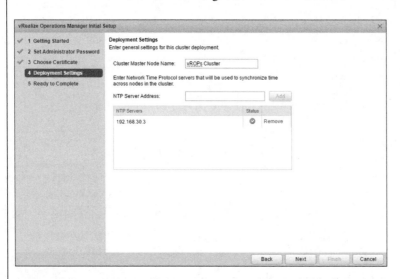

**Figure 25-21**    Deployment Settings

**18.** You are presented with the flow diagram again, but this time it says "Congratulations!" Click **Finish** and notice you are redirected to the **System Status** page, where it says "Preparing node for first use...", as shown in Figure 25-22.

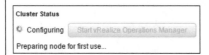

**Figure 25-22**    Preparing Node for First Use

**19.** To complete the setup, you must start the vRealize Operations Manager from the System Status page. You see a dialog box that mentions you should have enough nodes in the cluster to support the environment efficiently, as shown in Figure 25-23. For demonstration purposes, a single node is fine. Click **Yes**. Notice that State is Running and Status is Online, as shown in Figure 25-24.

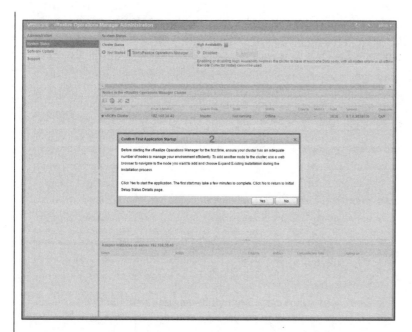

**Figure 25-23**   Starting vRealize Operations Manager

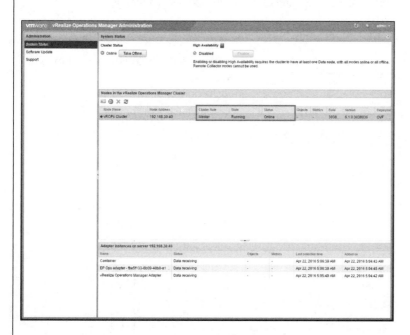

**Figure 25-24**   vRealize Operations Manager Started

**20.** After starting the Operations Manager, type in the FQDN or IP address again and log in. This time you are greeted with a different flow diagram that provides an overview of the remaining steps, as shown in Figure 25-25. Click **Next**.

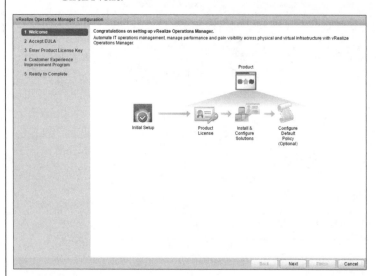

**Figure 25-25** Congratulations on Setting Up vRealize Operations Manager

**21.** Accept the EULA and click **Next**.

**22.** You can enter in a product key or continue with the Evaluation, as shown in Figure 25-26. Click **Next**.

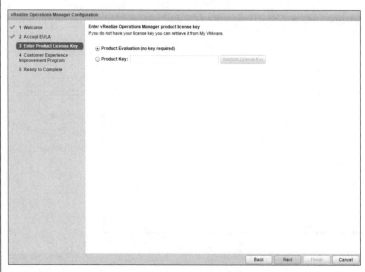

**Figure 25-26** vRealize Operation Manager Product License Key

**23.** Accept or Decline if you want to participate in the Customer Experience Improvement Program, and click **Next**.

**24.** You see the Ready to Complete page. Click **Finish**, as shown in Figure 25-27, and you are redirected to the web UI interface of vRealize Operations, as shown in Figure 25-28. This is where most of the daily operations and tasks occur.

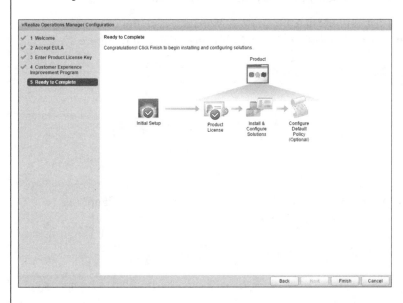

**Figure 25-27**   Ready to Complete

**Figure 25-28**   vRealize UI Interface

**NOTE**   vRealize Operations Manager has two different URLs: the User Interface side, https://FQDN/ui, and the Administration side, https://FQDN/admin. The admin page was where you started the Operations Manager service, but it's also where you can perform updates and upgrades. Learn more about upgrades in the next section.

### Configure vCenter Adapter in vROPs

vRealize Operations Manager is installed. Now you need to configure it to communicate with vCenter. Activity 25-2 outlines the process.

**Activity 25-2    Configure vCenter Adapter in vROPs**

1. Log in to vRealize Operations UI (https://FQDN/ui).

2. In the left pane of vRealize Operations Manager, click the **Home** icon, then the **Administration** icon, and click **Solutions**, as shown in Figure 25-29.

**Figure 25-29**    Navigate to Solutions Section

3. Select VMware vSphere and click the gear cogs icon to configure the vCenter Adapter, as shown in Figure 25-30.

**Figure 25-30**    Navigate to vCenter Adapter

4. The Manage Solution—VMware vSphere dialog box opens where you configure the adapters. Input your vCenter information, as shown in Figure 25-31. Click **Test Connection** to confirm that settings are correct. You will get a prompt to accept the self-signed SSL certificate, as shown in Figure 25-32 and Figure 25-33. Click **OK**. Click **Save Settings** and then **Next**, as shown in Figure 25-34.

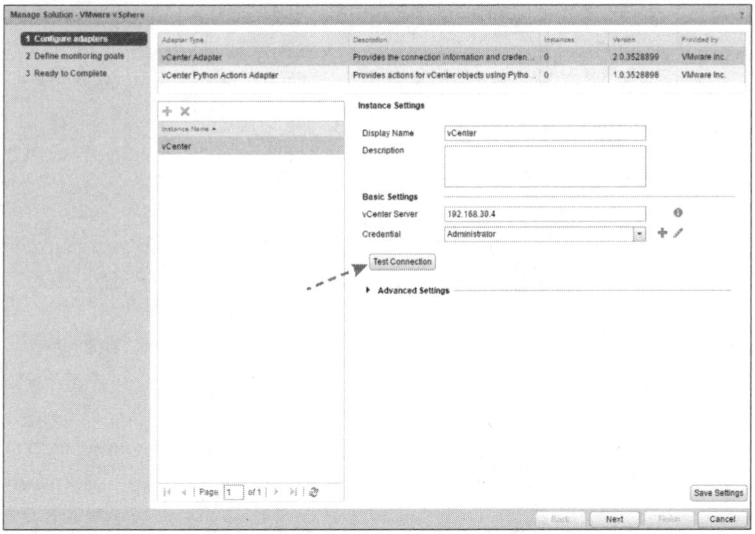
Manage Solution - VMware vSphere
1 Configure adapters
2 Define monitoring goals
3 Ready to Complete
vCenter Adapter
Provides the connection information and creden...
0
2.0.3528899
VMware Inc.
vCenter Python Actions Adapter
Provides actions for vCenter objects using Pytho...
0
1.0.3528898
VMware Inc.
vCenter
Instance Settings
Display Name
vCenter
Description
Basic Settings
vCenter Server
192.168.30.4
Credential
Administrator
Test Connection
Advanced Settings
Page 1 of 1
Save Settings
Back
Next
Finish
Cancel

**Figure 25-31** Configure vCenter Adapter

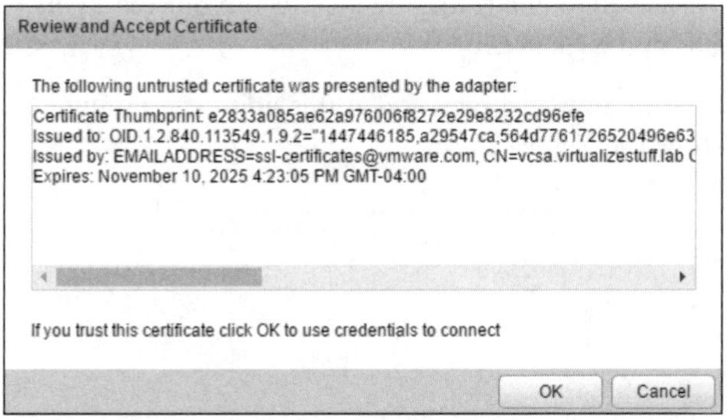
Review and Accept Certificate
The following untrusted certificate was presented by the adapter:
Certificate Thumbprint: e2833a085ae62a976006f8272e29e8232cd96efe
Issued to: OID.1.2.840.113549.1.9.2="1447446185,a29547ca,564d7761726520496e63
Issued by: EMAILADDRESS=ssl-certificates@vmware.com, CN=vcsa.virtualizestuff.lab C
Expires: November 10, 2025 4:23:05 PM GMT-04:00
If you trust this certificate click OK to use credentials to connect
OK
Cancel

**Figure 25-32** Self-signed SSL Warning

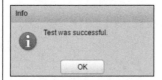

Info
Test was successful.
OK

**Figure 25-33** Successful Test Performed

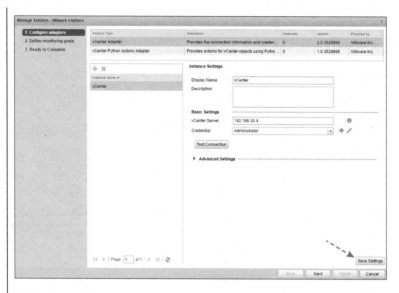

**Figure 25-34**   Save vCenter Adapter Settings

5. Define Monitoring Goals is where you configure a policy. In our case, you should accept the defaults and click **Next**.

6. Ready to Complete shows the flow diagram, and at this point everything should be checked, as shown in Figure 25-35.

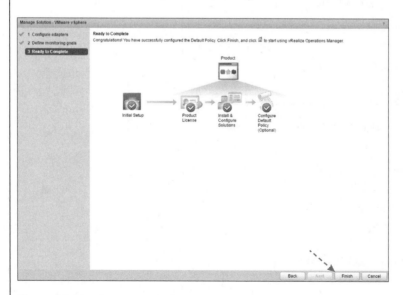

**Figure 25-35**   Complete vCenter Adapter Configuration

## Upgrading vROPs

As with anything else, the newer versions are generally better. If you're planning to upgrade from vCenter Operations Manager 5.8.x to the latest version of vRealize Operations Manager 6.2, you will need to perform a two-step process per VMware's release notes for vRealize Operations Manager 6.2:

> You cannot migrate vCenter Operations Manager directly to this version of vRealize Operations Manager. Instead, you follow a two-step process to migrate and import vCenter Operations Manager 5.8.x into vRealize Operations Manager 6.0.x, then use the vRealize Operations Manager Software Update option to upgrade vRealize Operations Manager 6.0.x to this version.

Before you begin the upgrade process, you should read the vROPs Sizing Guidelines KB article at http://kb.vmware.com/kb/2093783. VMware also recommends that you take a snapshot of the virtual appliance before you upgrade and, of course, delete the snapshots after the upgrade is successful. If you're already on version 6.0.x+ the procedure to upgrade/update is rather straightforward.

To upgrade vRealize Operations Manager from 6.1 to 6.2, follow the steps outlined in Activity 25-3.

---

### Activity 25-3   Updating vROPs

   **1.** Take a snapshot of the appliance, as shown in Figure 25-36.

**Figure 25-36**   Take a Snapshot

2. Download both OS and vROPs and update PAK.

3. Save the OS and vROPs PAK files of the latest vCenter Operations Manager build to your local storage.

4. Log in to the Administration portal using the admin user credentials.

5. On the right tab, click **Software Update**, and then click **Install a Software Update**. You must first upload the OS PAK file, as shown in Figure 25-37 per VMware's release notes.

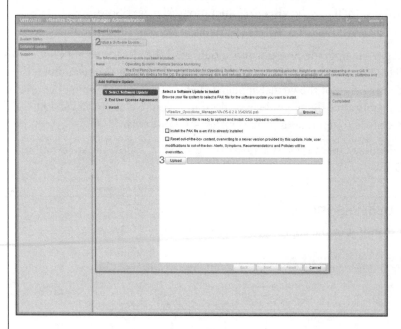

**Figure 25-37**    Select OS PAK Upgrade File

6. Review the PAK file details ensuring the OS PAK was selected and click **Next**, as shown in Figure 25-38. Accept the EULA and click **Next**; the upgrade will begin, as shown in Figure 25-39. You can confirm the OS PAK was installed successfully by returning to the Software Update section in the Administration portal, as shown in Figure 25-40.

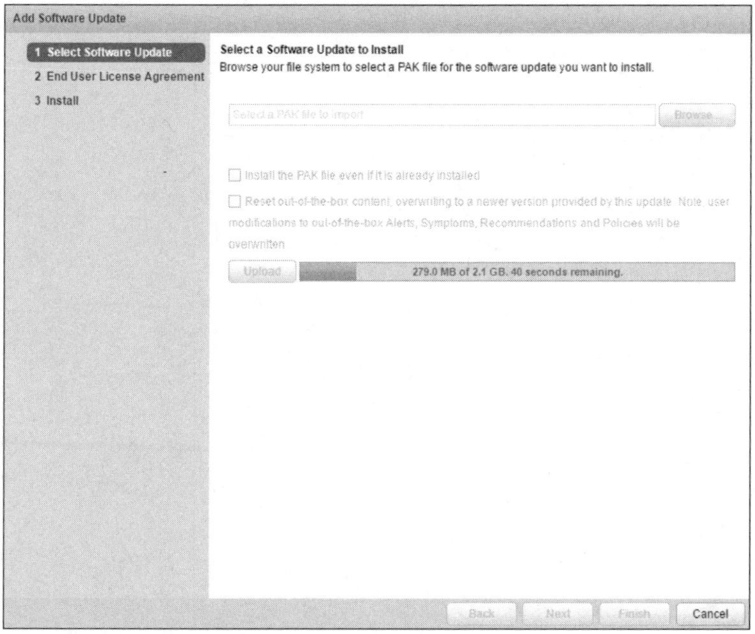

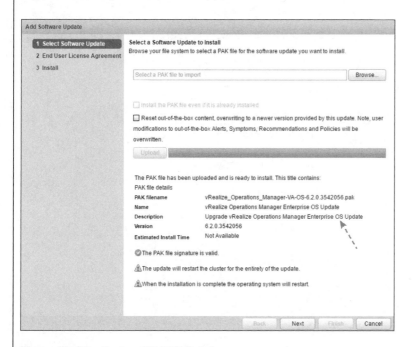

**Figure 25-38**   Upload OS PAK to Appliance

**Figure 25-39**   Review OS PAK Details

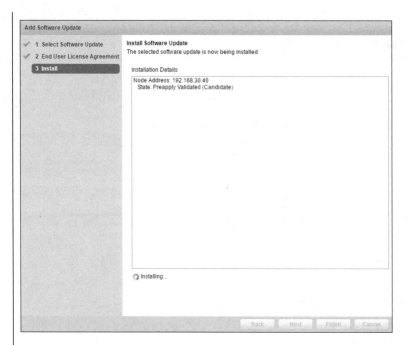

**Figure 25-40**   Installing OS PAK

7. Upload the vROPs PAK update, as shown in Figure 25-41 and Figure 25-42.

**Figure 25-41**   Confirm the OS PAK Was Installed Successfully

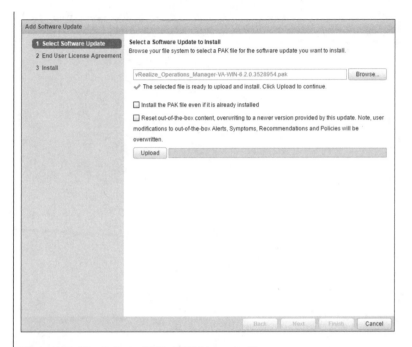

**Figure 25-42** Select vROPs PAK Upgrade File

8. Review the PAK file details again, ensuring the correct PAK file was selected, and click **Next**, as shown in Figure 25-43. Accept the EULA and click **Next** to begin the upgrade, as shown previously in Figure 25-37. You can confirm the vROPs PAK was installed successfully by returning to the Software Update section in the Administration portal, as shown in Figure 25-44.

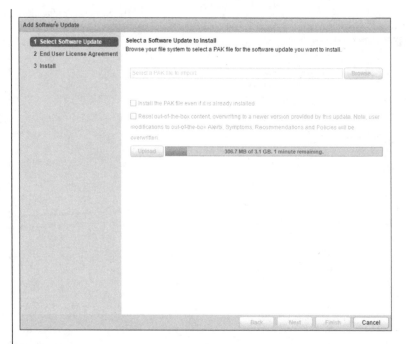

**Figure 25-43** Upload vROPs PAK to Appliance

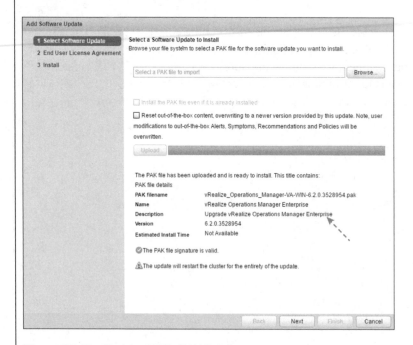

**Figure 25-44** Review vROPs PAK Details

9. Apply the new license for vRealize Operations Manager using the admin page, as shown in Figure 25-45.

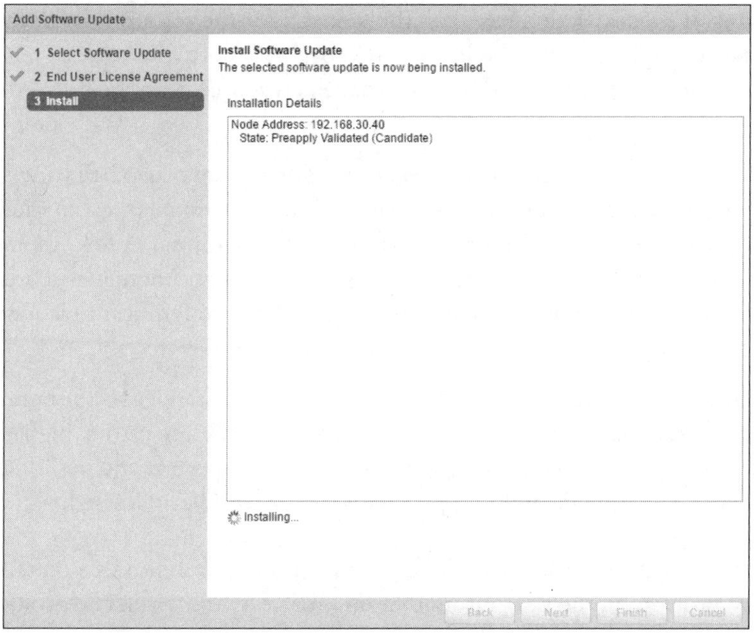

**Add Software Update**

✓ 1  Select Software Update
✓ 2  End User License Agreement
   3  Install

**Install Software Update**
The selected software update is now being installed.

Installation Details

Node Address: 192.168.30.40
   State: Preapply Validated (Candidate)

⚙ Installing...

Back    Next    Finish    Cancel

**Figure 25-45**   Installing vROPs PAK

10. In the Administration portal, navigate to the Status tab and restart all services.

11. Finally, log back in to your vSphere Web Client to verify that the interface is displayed properly.

## Understanding Metrics Used by Major/Minor vROPs Badges

Now that you have the latest software for vROPs, we'll take a look at a few more of those badges. I will focus on the three major badges that you will find in all versions of vROPs and the minor badges that are just inside them. As mentioned earlier, this description is still just scratching the surface of vROPs, but you'll get the general idea.

The first major badge to discuss is the Health badge. This badge indicates immediate issues that will likely require your prompt attention. vROPs calculates the

Health score by using scores of the minor badges that it contains. The three minor badges within Health are as follows:

- **Workload:** This badge is a measurement of how hard an object must work for its resources. It's a calculation based on the demand for the resource divided by the capacity of the object. The lower the Workload score, the better, although a score close to 0 would indicate that the resource is not being used at all.

- **Anomalies:** These badges are, in essence, indications of abnormal behavior. After vROPs has a record of what is normal for your environment, it can then spot metrics that seem to be out of bounds from what is normal. A low Anomalies score is good and indicates business as usual, but a high Anomalies score might indicate a potential issue, especially if you've had no significant planned changes or reconfigurations.

- **Faults:** These badges are generated when the unexpected happens—for example, a loss of redundancy in NICs or HBAs, memory checksum errors, high availability failover, and so on. A score of 0 is considered perfect and desirable, whereas a higher score may indicate problems that should be addressed.

The second major badge to discuss is the Risk badge. This badge indicates a potential performance problem in the near future that might affect your virtual environment. The three minor badges under the Risk badge are as follows:

- **Time Remaining:** This badge is a measurement of the amount of time before a resource associated with an object reaches its capacity. The default provisioning buffer is 30 days. That means that every resource for a given object should be able to last another 30 days based on its current amount and rate of growth. If any core resource of an object will last less than the provisioning buffer, the Time Remaining will be 0. Obviously, 0 is bad here, and 100 is perfect.

- **Capacity Remaining:** This badge is the number of additional virtual machines that an object can handle before reaching capacity. The objects that are measured for this metric include hosts, resource pools, and vApps (compute resources). Based on an average VM profile for the VMs in that object for the last *n* weeks, the system calculates the number of VMs that can be created considering the memory, disk I/O, network I/O, and disk space. The weakest of these will limit the number of VMs that can be created and will thereby determine the score. A score of 0 is very bad, and a score of 100 is very good and also rare.

- **Stress:** This badge is the long-term Workload that might involve undersized VMs or underprovisioned hosts. Although Workload is based on instantaneous value, Stress measures statistics over a longer period of time. The Stress badge helps you identify hosts and VMs that do not have enough resources allocated, and/or hosts that are running too many VMs. A Stress score of 0 is perfect, and 100 is very bad!

The third major badge to discuss is the Efficiency badge. This badge identifies potential opportunities to improve performance or reduce costs in your virtual environment. The two minor badges under the Efficiency badge are as follows:

- **Reclaimable Waste:** This badge accounts for resource types such as CPU, memory, or disk. It measures the extent of excessive overprovisioning for an object. A score of 0 is very good, whereas a score of 100 would be terrible!

- **Density:** This badge is a measure of your consolidation ratios against the ideal consolidation ratios in an environment similar to yours. In other words, it is a measure of how much you are really pushing the envelope to take advantage of everything that VMware has to offer. For example, "Could you really run more VMs with fewer resources and still not sacrifice performance or affect service level agreements?" In Density, a score of 0 is terrible, whereas a score of 100 would be awesome and very rare!

## Monitoring Your vSphere Environment

As you've seen, you can use many tools to monitor your vSphere environment. Some require more work on your part than others. Although vROPs can do a lot of the number crunching for you, effective monitoring of your environment requires that you understand what all the numbers mean. Also, vROPs make it easier to spot specific areas of concern, as long as you watch for them. So, to put it bluntly, the responsibility of monitoring your vSphere environment comes right back to you. However, you do have some pretty cool tools to assist you now!

## Summary

This chapter covered the following main topics:

- The major and minor badges in vRealize Operations Manager (vROPS) and how to differentiate between them

- The vROPs architecture, which basically consists of a single virtual appliance

- How to deploy the vROPs appliance in your organization and how you can upgrade the appliance as needed

- The metrics used to calculate the scores of the major and minor badges, and what they might mean to your organization

## Exam Preparation Tasks

## Review All the Key Topics

Review the most important topics from the chapter, noted with the Key Topic icon in the outer margin of the page. Table 25-2 lists these key topics and the page numbers where each is found. Know the various tools that you can use to monitor your vSphere, and especially which ones you can trust. Understand how to use your default utilization and connectivity alarms and how to create custom alarms when needed.

**Table 25-2**    Key Topics for Chapter 25

| Key Topic Element | Description | Page Number |
|---|---|---|
| Figure 25-1 | Minor Badges Within the Major Badges | 635 |
| Figure 25-2 | Previous vROPs Compared to Current Version | 636 |
| Figure 25-3 | The vROPs Virtual Appliance | 637 |
| Activity 25-1 | Deploying the vROPs Virtual Appliance | 637 |
| Activity 25-2 | Configuring vCenter Adapter in vROPs | 650 |
| Activity 25-3 | Updating vROPs | 653 |
| Bullet lists | Understanding Metrics Used by Major/Minor Badges | 659 |

## Review Questions

The answers to these review questions are in Appendix A.

1. Which of the following is a major badge of vCenter Operations Manager?

   a. Time Remaining

   b. Security

   c. Risk

   d. Capacity

**2.** Which of the following is a minor badge within Health?

   **a.** Workload

   **b.** Capacity Remaining

   **c.** Time Remaining

   **d.** Risk

**3.** Which of the following are *not* minor badges within Efficiency?

   **a.** Reclaimed Waste

   **b.** Density

   **c.** Time Remaining

   **d.** Stress

**4.** Which of the following are *not* true about vROPs architecture? (Choose two.)

   **a.** It is installed as a vApp that contains two VMs.

   **b.** It is installed as a virtual appliance.

   **c.** Each instance of vROPs can be connected to only one vCenter.

   **d.** One instance of vROPs can be connected to multiple vCenters.

**5.** Which of the following are *not* true regarding deploying and configuring a vROPs appliance? (Choose two.)

   **a.** The appliance can be deployed from an OVF.

   **b.** You should always use thin provisioning for storage.

   **c.** You should use thick provision lazy zeroed for storage.

   **d.** You will not need to configure the size; one size fits all.

**6.** Which of the following are *not* true regarding the deployment of vROPs?

   **a.** You can select the folder in which to install it.

   **b.** It will always be installed in the vROPs folder.

   **c.** You can assign a static IP address.

   **d.** You can only assign an IP address using DHCP.

7. Which of the following is *not* a major badge?

   a. Health

   b. Risk

   c. Environment

   d. Efficiency

8. Which of the following is a minor badge within Health?

   a. Efficiency

   b. Workload

   c. Risk

   d. Capacity Remaining

9. Which of the following is a major badge of vRealize Operations Manager?

   a. Health

   b. Workload

   c. Capacity Remaining

   d. Efficiency

10. Which of the following are minor badges within Efficiency?

    a. Reclaimable Waste

    b. Risk

    c. Density

    d. Stress

Congratulations on making it through all the technical chapters in this book! Now you are ready for your final preparation for taking the vSphere 6 Foundations exam (2V0-620), which you are required to pass before taking any of the following exams:

- VCP6-DCV (Datacenter Virtualization)

- VCP6-DTM (Desktop Mobility)

- VCP6-CMA (Cloud Management and Automation)

- VCP6-NV (Network Virtualization)

This chapter contains three sections: "Getting Ready," "Taking the Exam," and "Tools for Final Preparation."

## CHAPTER 26

# Final Preparation

## Getting Ready

Following is a list of actions and considerations that you should address prior to taking the exam:

- Gain hands-on experience with vSphere 6. If you have not done so already, you should access a vSphere 6 environment and use it to practice performing the procedures described in this book. If you do not have a suitable vSphere 6 environment, consider launching a hosted lab at https://my.vmware.com/web/vmware/evalcenter?p=vsphere-hol. If you are challenged with gaining hands-on access to vSphere environments with specific features, such as Virtual SAN, you should take a look at VMware Hands On Labs (http://labs.hol.vmware.com). Here you should be able to access virtual labs at no cost. For example, the labs HOL-SDC-1608 Virtual SAN 6 from A to Z and HOL-SDC-1627 VVol, Virtual SAN and Storage Policy-Based Management should be very useful to those of you who cannot readily implement Virtual SAN or Virtual Volumes in your own lab environment.

- Although the exam is multiple choice, one of its goals is to verify that you have hands-on expertise with software. Be prepared to answer questions that are aimed at determining if you know how to use a specific user interface to accomplish a specific task. For example, the correct choice for a question could depend on your knowledge of the exact text that appears on a link or button in the interface. I recommend that you at least practice performing the procedures that are described in this book.

- Because VMware may change the requirements for certifications and exams at any time, you should closely examine the requirements on the VMware Certification website at https://mylearn.vmware.com/mgrReg/plan.cfm?plan=64178&ui=www_cert just prior to registering for the exam. The following details are accurate at the time of this writing but are subject to change at VMware's discretion.

- Candidates who are preparing for any of these exams fall into one of two categories: those who currently hold a VMware Certified Professional (VCP) certification and those who are new to VMware certification (or hold only expired VCP certifications). New candidates are required to take a qualifying course as well as pass the vSphere 6 Foundation Exam.

- Candidates who are the holders of an earlier certification might be eligible for a delta exam. For example, a VCP5-DCV certification may take the VCP6-DCV *Delta* Exam rather than the standard VCP6-DCV Exam. The stated objectives of both exams are identical, but the following differences exist between the exams:

  - The delta exam is usually more condensed and does not include all the stated sub-objectives as the standard exam.

  - The delta exam is usually a bit shorter at 90 minutes and 65 questions versus 100 minutes and 85 questions.

  - Although it is not officially stated, you may expect to see that the questions in the delta exam focus more on new features in vSphere 6 and differences between vSphere 5.x and vSphere 6. I recommend that as you study for either exam, you pay extra attention to details on new features and changes in vSphere 6.

- On the VMware Certification website, select either the **New Candidate Requirements** tab or the **Existing Candidate Requirements** tab and navigate into the path description that best fits your current status. The path identifies all the requirements for the candidate, such as any qualifying courses and exams. For example, a candidate who holds a current VCP5-DT certification, but no other VCP certification, should select **Existing Candidate Requirements**, **Path 2**, which calls for the candidate to pass the standard VCP6-DCV Exam (not the delta exam).

- On the VMware Certification website, use the links that are provided to examine the details for your required exam. Select the **Exam Topics** tab, expand each section, expand each exam objective, and examine the knowledge items. For convenience, the outline of this book closely matches the exam objectives and knowledge items. Carefully compare the exam objectives and knowledge items in the Table of Contents in this book to identify any items that may have been recently added and are not covered in the book. To address any recently added items, begin by examining the online content for this book, which may include updates and bonus content for premium editions.

- In addition to the exam topics, objectives, and knowledge items, review other exam details. For example, the details for the VCP6 Foundations Exam are as follows:

  Exam number: 2V0-620

  Duration 90 minutes

  65 multiple choice questions

  Passing Score 300

  Recommended Training: vSphere: Install, Configure, Manage [V6]

  Languages: English

  Taken online—nonproctored

- Use the **How to Prepare** tab to examine the recommended training details. If you feel your knowledge and skillset is weak, consider some of the provided training courses.

- In the **Practice Exam** section on the **How to Prepare** tab, use the link to request access to a practice exam. The practice exam contains 20 questions. You may take the exam multiple times. At the end of each attempt, review your **Test Status** (Failed or Passed), your **Percent Correct**, and your **Missed Questions**. If you missed any questions, read the provided explanation and examine the related section in this book or the sources stated in the explanation. Continue taking the Practice Exam until you pass it, answering all the questions correctly at least once.

- Review the following items in each chapter in this book until you have them committed to memory.

  - "Do I Know This Already?" questions at the beginning of each chapter

  - "Review Questions" at the end of each chapter

- Prior to registering for the VCP6 Foundations Exam, you must request authorization. To do so, click the **Request Exam Authorization** link at https://mylearn.vmware.com/mgrReg/plan.cfm?plan=64180&ui=www_cert.

- After VMware provides the requested authorization, you can register for the exam at https://www1.pearsonvue.com/testtaker/signin/SignInPage/VMWAREINC. Sign in with your account (create a new account, if necessary), select the appropriated exam in the **Pre-approved Exams** section, and use the wizard to schedule the date, time, and location.

- Use the Pearson Cert Practice Test engine to practice. The Pearson Cert Practice Test engine can be used to study using a bank of unique exam-realistic questions available only with this book. The standard edition of this book includes two exams, and the Premium Edition includes two additional exams. If you miss any questions, read the provided explanation and the related section in this book. Continue taking the practice exam(s) until you feel you know and can explain each answer. Refer to the "Tools for Final Preparation" section for more information about the Pearson Cert Practice Test engine.

## Taking the Exam

Here is a list of considerations and actions for the day of the exam.

> **NOTE**  These first three bullet points do not apply to the VCP 6 Foundations Exam because you will take it online, but all of the rest of these points apply equally, online or in person. I've included the first three bullet points because I assume that you will soon be taking the VCP6-DCV, VCP6-NV, VCP6-DTM, or VCP6-CM exam, which you will take in person at a VUE testing center.

- Bring two forms of identification that include your photo and signature. You cannot bring personal items, such as laptops, tablets, phones, watches, pagers, wallets, or notes into the examination room. You may be able to place some of these items into a locker, but you should avoid bringing larger items into the training facility.

- Arrive at the exam center 30 minutes prior to the scheduled start time to provide ample time to complete the sign-in procedure and address personal needs. During the sign-in procedure, you should expect to place personal belongings in a locker, provide credentials, review the test regulations, and sign the agreement.

- Be sure to pay attention to the rules and regulations concerning the exam. For example, follow the venue's protocol for requesting help during the exam and for signaling your completion of the exam. Each venue's rules may be unique.

- The exam format is multiple choice, provided via a web-based user interface.

- Pay close attention to the wording of each question and each choice. Following are some examples of what to expect:

  - Some questions may ask you to select "which statement is correct," and some questions may ask you to select "which statement is incorrect."

- Most questions call for you to select a single choice from a list of multiple choices. Whenever a question calls for you to select more than one choice, it will do so explicitly, by including a phrase such as (Pick two).

- Read each question carefully enough to ensure that you successfully interpret feature names and terminology. For example, when a question contains the word *heartbeat*, you need to carefully determine if it is referring to an HA network heartbeat, HA datastore heartbeat, VMFS heartbeat, VMware Tools heartbeat, or some other heartbeat.

- Questions tend to be written in a concise manner, where at first glance you may think that insufficient details are provided. For example, the question could provide a symptom and ask you to select three actions that you should take to troubleshoot. Your first thought may be that you would take analytical steps or remediation steps that are not provided as choices for the question. You may even consider the provided choices to be unpractical or insufficient. Do not get frustrated. Just select the appropriate choices that fit the question.

- Questions that ask you to identify more than one choice to accomplish a specific configuration or troubleshooting task may not always clearly state if the steps in all the selected choices must be performed or if just the steps in any one of the choices must be performed. Although you may wish the question contained better clarity, you should see that only one solution actually fits the question and the specified number of choices that you must select.

- Strive for good time management during the exam. Don't allow yourself to get stuck on a question for too long. If a question is tricky, such as if more than one choice seems to fit on a question that calls for a single choice, ask yourself, "Which choice is most likely the choice that VMware wants?" You may find some questions easier to solve by focusing on which choices to eliminate.

- Whenever you are unsure of an answer or you are rushed with making a decision, use the web interface to mark the question for review.

- After answering all the questions, a **Review Page** is provided that identifies all questions that you marked for review and all questions that are incomplete. If sufficient time remains, use the provided links on the review page to return to any of those questions.

# Tools for Final Preparation

This section lists some information about the available tools and how to access them.

### Review Tools on the Companion Website

The companion website for this book includes all the electronic files and review tools. To access this site, follow these steps:

**Step 1.**    Go to http://www.pearsonitcertification.com/register.

**Step 2.**    Either log in to your account (if you have an existing account already) or create a new account.

**Step 3.**    Enter the ISBN of your book (9780789756497) and click **Submit**.

**Step 4.**    Answer the challenge questions to validate your purchase.

**Step 5.**    In your account page, click the **Registered Products** tab, and then click the **Access Bonus Content** link.

After you have registered your book, to access the companion website, all you need to do is go to www.pearsonitcertification.com and sign in to your account. From there, select the Registered Products tab and click the Access Bonus Content link.

### Pearson Cert Practice Test Engine and Questions

The companion website includes the Pearson Cert Practice Test engine (software that displays and grades a set of exam-realistic, multiple-choice questions). Using the Pearson Cert Practice Test, you can either study by going through the questions in Study mode or take a simulated (timed) VCP6 Foundations exam.

The installation process requires two major steps. The companion website has a recent copy of the Pearson Cert Practice Test engine. The practice exam—the database of VCP6 Foundations exam questions—can be downloaded after you redeem your access code found in the sleeve in the back of the book.

### Download and Install the Software

**NOTE**   If you have purchased another Pearson study guide, you may have already installed the PCPT software. If you already have the software installed, there is no need to install the software again. Skip ahead to the next section to activate your new practice exams.

The software installation process is routine compared with other software installation processes. To be complete, the following steps outline the download and installation process:

**Step 1.** Go to the book's companion website (instructions for access are included in the previous section).

**Step 2.** Locate the download link for the Pearson IT Certification Practice Test (PCPT) software, and download the latest version of the engine to your computer.

**Step 3.** When the download is complete, unzip the software and run the installer.

**Step 4.** Respond to window prompts as with any typical software installation process.

The installation process gives you the option to activate your exam with the activation code supplied on the paper in the sleeve in the back of the book. This process requires that you establish a Pearson website logon. You will need this logon to activate the exam, so please do register when prompted. If you already have a Pearson website logon, there is no need to register again. Just use your existing logon.

## Activate and Download the Practice Exam

After the exam engine is installed, you should then activate the exam associated with this book (if you did not do so during the installation process), as follows:

**Step 1.** Start the Pearson Cert Practice Test (PCPT) software from the Windows Start menu or from your desktop shortcut icon.

**Step 2.** To activate and download the exam associated with this book, from the My Products or Tools tab, click the **Activate** button.

**Step 3.** At the next screen, enter the activation key from the paper inside the cardboard sleeve at the back of the book. Then click the **Activate** button.

**Step 4.** The activation process downloads the practice exam. Click **Next**, and then click **Finish**.

When the activation process has completed, the My Products tab should list your new exam. If you do not see the exam, make sure you have selected the My Products tab on the menu. At this point, the software and practice exam are ready to use. Select the exam and click the **Use** button.

To update a particular exam you have already activated and downloaded, select the **Tools** tab and click the **Update Products** button. Updating your exams ensures you have the latest changes and updates to the exam data.

If you want to check for updates to the Pearson Cert Practice Test engine software, select the **Tools** tab and click the **Update Application** button. Doing so ensures that you are running the latest version of the software engine.

## Activating Other Exams

The exam software installation process and the registration process have to happen only once. Then, for each new exam, only a few steps are required. For instance, if you buy another new VMware Press Official Cert Guide or Pearson IT Certification Cert Guide, extract the activation code from the sleeve at the back of that book. From there, all you have to do is start the exam engine (if it is not still up and running), and perform steps 2 through 4 from the previous list.

## Premium Edition

In addition to the free practice exam provided with this book, you can purchase additional exams with expanded functionality directly from Pearson IT Certification. The Premium Edition of this title contains an additional two full practice exams and an eBook (in PDF, EPUB, and Kindle formats). In addition, the Premium Edition title has remediation for each question to the specific part of the eBook that relates to that question.

Because you have purchased the print version of this title, you can purchase the Premium Edition at a deep discount. There is a coupon code in the sleeve in the back of the book that contains a one-time-use code and instructions for where you can purchase the Premium Edition.

To view the premium edition product page, go to www.informit.com/title/9780789756497.

## Using the Exam Engine

The Pearson Cert Practice Test engine includes a database of questions created specifically for this book. The Pearson Cert Practice Test engine can be used either in Study mode or Practice Exam mode, as follows:

- **Study mode:** This mode is most useful when you want to use the questions for learning and practicing. In Study mode, you can select options like randomizing the order of the questions and answers, automatically viewing answers to the questions as you go, testing on specific topics, and many others.

- **Practice Exam mode:** This mode presents questions in a timed environment, providing you with a more exam-realistic experience. It also restricts your ability to see your score as you progress through the exam and view answers to questions as you are taking the exam. These timed exams not only allow you to study for the actual VCP6 Foundations exam, they help you simulate the time pressure that can occur on the actual exam.

When doing your final preparation, you can use Study mode, Practice Exam mode, or both. However, after you have seen each question a couple of times, you will likely start to remember the questions, and the usefulness of the exam database might diminish. So, consider the following options when using the exam engine:

- Use this question database for review. Use Study mode to study the questions by chapter, just as with the other final review steps listed in this chapter. Plan to get another exam (possibly from the Premium Edition) if you want to take additional simulated exams.

- Save the question database, not using it for review during your review of each book part. Save it until the end, so you will not have seen the questions before. Then, use Practice Exam mode to simulate the exam.

Picking the correct mode from the exam engine's user interface is pretty obvious. The following steps show how to move to the screen from which to select Study or Practice Exam mode:

**Step 1.**    Click the **My Products** tab if you are not already at that screen.

**Step 2.**    Select the exam you want to use from the list of available exams.

**Step 3.**    Click the **Use** button.

The engine should then display a window from which you can choose Study mode or Practice Exam mode. When in Study mode, you can further choose the book chapters, limiting the questions to those explained in the specified chapters of the book.

Best of luck on passing your exam! Please let me know when you pass, or if I can give any words of wisdom or encouragement. You can always reach me at billferguson@charter.net.

# Answers to the "Do I Know This Already"? Quizzes and Chapter Review Questions

## "Do I Know This Already?" Quizzes

**Chapter 1**
1. B, C
2. A, B
3. C
4. B
5. A, C
6. A, B
7. A
8. B
9. A
10. D

**Chapter 2**
1. B
2. C
3. D
4. A
5. B
6. D
7. A
8. B
9. A
10. A

**Chapter 3**
1. B
2. B, D
3. D
4. C
5. A, C
6. A
7. C
8. A
9. D
10. C

**Chapter 4**
1. C, D
2. B
3. D
4. A, D
5. B
6. A, C
7. B
8. A, B
9. A, B
10. A

**Chapter 5**
1. B
2. D
3. A
4. B
5. C
6. B
7. D
8. B
9. A, B
10. A, C

**Chapter 6**
1. C
2. B
3. D
4. C
5. C
6. D
7. A, D
8. B
9. C
10. B, D

| Chapter 7 | Chapter 10 | Chapter 13 |
|---|---|---|
| 1. C | 1. D | 1. A |
| 2. D | 2. A, B | 2. D |
| 3. D | 3. A, D | 3. B |
| 4. C | 4. C | 4. A |
| 5. C | 5. A, C | 5. B, C |
| 6. A | 6. B, D | 6. A, B |
| 7. A, C | 7. C | 7. B, D |
| 8. D | 8. A, C | 8. A |
| 9. B, D | 9. A, D | 9. C |
| 10. C | 10. A | 10. A, D |

| Chapter 8 | Chapter 11 | Chapter 14 |
|---|---|---|
| 1. C | 1. B, D | 1. C, D |
| 2. A, D | 2. A, B | 2. B, C |
| 3. C | 3. A, C | 3. C |
| 4. A | 4. A | 4. D |
| 5. C | 5. B | 5. B |
| 6. A | 6. B | 6. A, D |
| 7. A, C | 7. A, C | 7. B, C |
| 8. C, D | 8. A, B | 8. C, D |
| 9. B | 9. A | 9. B, C |
| 10. C | 10. C | 10. B, C |

| Chapter 9 | Chapter 12 | Chapter 15 |
|---|---|---|
| 1. B | 1. B, C | 1. C |
| 2. A, B | 2. A, C | 2. B |
| 3. B | 3. D | 3. D |
| 4. A | 4. A, B | 4. A, D |
| 5. B | 5. C | 5. B, D |
| 6. A, C | 6. B, D | 6. A, D |
| 7. A, C | 7. A, B | 7. A, D |
| 8. A, C | 8. B, C | 8. C |
| 9. B, D | 9. B, C | 9. B, C |
| 10. A, C | 10. B, C | 10. A, B |

**Chapter 16**

1. A, C
2. D
3. A, B
4. D
5. C
6. B, D
7. B
8. B
9. B, D
10. B, D

**Chapter 17**

1. B, C
2. B
3. C
4. B
5. B, C
6. D
7. A, D
8. D
9. A, D
10. A, D

**Chapter 18**

1. B, C
2. C, D
3. C, D
4. B, D
5. D
6. B, D
7. B, D
8. B, D
9. B, D

10. B, C
11. B, C
12. A, B

**Chapter 19**

1. B, D
2. A, B
3. A, D
4. B, D
5. B, D
6. A, D
7. B, D
8. B
9. B, D
10. B, C

**Chapter 20**

1. C
2. B
3. A
4. A, C
5. C
6. B
7. C
8. A
9. D
10. B

**Chapter 21**

1. C
2. B, D
3. A, D
4. C
5. A, C

6. A, C
7. A, C
8. B, D
9. A, D
10. A, B

**Chapter 22**

1. A, C
2. A, B
3. A
4. A
5. A, C
6. A, C
7. B, C
8. B, D
9. A, D
10. A, D

**Chapter 23**

1. C
2. B
3. D
4. A, C
5. A
6. A, C
7. C
8. D
9. D
10. A
11. A
12. B
13. A, D
14. A, C
15. A

**16.** C

**17.** C

**18.** D

**19.** C, D

**20.** A

## Chapter 24

**1.** C

**2.** D

**3.** D

**4.** A, C

**5.** A, C

**6.** B

**7.** B

**8.** B, D

**9.** A, C

**10.** A, C

## Chapter 25

**1.** B

**2.** C

**3.** B

**4.** B, D

**5.** A, C

**6.** A, C

**7.** C

**8.** A

**9.** D

**10.** C

## Chapter Review Questions

**Chapter 1**
1. B, C
2. A, B
3. D
4. B
5. B, D
6. C, D
7. A
8. C, D
9. C
10. D

**Chapter 2**
1. C
2. C
3. D
4. B
5. B
6. D
7. A
8. B
9. B
10. C

**Chapter 3**
1. A
2. A, C
3. C
4. C
5. A, C
6. A
7. C

8. A
9. D
10. C

**Chapter 4**
1. D
2. B, D
3. D
4. A, D
5. B
6. B, D
7. A
8. A, B
9. C, D
10. D

**Chapter 5**
1. D
2. C
3. A
4. B
5. C
6. C
7. D
8. A, C
9. B
10. A

**Chapter 6**
1. A
2. D
3. B

4. B, C
5. A
6. B
7. B, D
8. C
9. B, C
10. A, C

**Chapter 7**
1. D
2. B, D
3. B
4. C
5. C
6. A
7. B
8. A
9. A
10. A

**Chapter 8**
1. A, B
2. B, C
3. C
4. C
5. A, D
6. B, D
7. B, D
8. A, B
9. C
10. C

## Chapter 9

1. A, D
2. C, D
3. C, D
4. B
5. C
6. B, D
7. B, D
8. B, D
9. A, C
10. B, D

## Chapter 10

1. D
2. C, D
3. B, C
4. B
5. B, D
6. B, D
7. B
8. B, D
9. B, C
10. B

## Chapter 11

1. A, C
2. A, B
3. B, D
4. A, C
5. B, C, D
6. B
7. A, C
8. C, D
9. D
10. C

## Chapter 12

1. A, D
2. B, D
3. D
4. A, B
5. B
6. A, C
7. C, D
8. A, D
9. A, D
10. A, D

## Chapter 13

1. B
2. C
3. B
4. C
5. A, D
6. A, B
7. A, C
8. B
9. B
10. B, C

## Chapter 14

1. A, D
2. B, D
3. B
4. B, D
5. B, C
6. D
7. B
8. B
9. A
10. B

## Chapter 15

1. A
2. A, C
3. D
4. B, C
5. A, D
6. B, C
7. B, C
8. C, D
9. A, D
10. C, D

## Chapter 16

1. A, B
2. D
3. C, D
4. D
5. B
6. B, D
7. B
8. B
9. A, C
10. B, D

## Chapter 17

1. A, D
2. B
3. A, D
4. A, C
5. C, D
6. D
7. B, C
8. D
9. A, C
10. B, C

## Chapter 18

1. A, D
2. C, D
3. C, D
4. B, D
5. A
6. B, D
7. B, D
8. B, D
9. B, D
10. B, C
11. B, C
12. C, D

## Chapter 19

1. B, D
2. A, B
3. A, D
4. A, C
5. A, C
6. B, C
7. C, D
8. D
9. A, C
10. A, D

## Chapter 20

1. C
2. A, B
3. A
4. A, C
5. A
6. A
7. B
8. C

9. A
10. B

## Chapter 21

1. C
2. A, C
3. A
4. B
5. A, B
6. B, C
7. A, B
8. B, D
9. A, D
10. A, B

## Chapter 22

1. A, D
2. C, D
3. A, B
4. C, D
5. A
6. B, D
7. A
8. B, D
9. A, D
10. A, D

## Chapter 23

1. C
2. C
3. A
4. B, D
5. B
6. A, D
7. A, C
8. D

9. B
10. A
11. B
12. B
13. D
14. B, D
15. C
16. B
17. C
18. D
19. A
20. B, D

## Chapter 24

1. C
2. B
3. A
4. B, D
5. B, D
6. A, B
7. A, C
8. B
9. B, D
10. A, C

## Chapter 25

1. C
2. A
3. C, D
4. A, C
5. B, C
6. B, D
7. C
8. B
9. A
10. A, C

# Index

## Symbols

**3D graphics, 9**

## A

**accessing**
ESXi host logs, 497-498
runtime names, 167-168
Syslogs, 498
vCenter server logs, 499-500
VM console, 239

**accounts**
Single Sign-On, 26
Windows Local System, 28

**actions (alarms)**
configuring, 624
connectivity, 616
utilization, 616, 620

**activating Pearson Cert Practice Test engine, 673-674**

**Active Directory, vCenter settings, 578-579**

**active guest memory, 574**

**active uplinks, 119**

**adapters**
host bus (HBAs), 170
physical network, troubleshooting, 531
storage
*DAS, 164*
*FCoE, 164*
*Fibre Channel, 164*
*iSCSI, 165*
*NAS, 165*
*VSAN, 165*

uplink
*adding to dvUplink groups, 96-98*
*deleting from dvUplink groups, 99-100*
vCenter vROPs, 650-652
vDSs, 88
virtual
*configuring, 104-105*
*creating, 100-103*
*deleting, 105-106*
*dvPort groups, selecting, 101*
*IP addresses, 103*
*migrating from vSSs to vDSs, 107-109*
*port properties, 102*
vSSs, adding, 58-59

**add a host scheduled task, 585**

**addresses**
IP
*datastores, 206*
*vApps, 269*
*virtual adapters, 103*
*VSAN supported, 192*
*vSSs, assigning, 60*
MAC, notifying switches of changes, 139
multiple, multipathing, 189

**administration**
content libraries
*creating, 323-326*
*defined, 323*
*subscribing, 327*
*types, 323*
VMs
*files, 314-318*
*IP pools, 320-322*
*security, 319-320*